The
Black Abolitionist
Papers

Board of Editorial Advisors

The
Black Abolitionist
Papers

VOLUME V
The United States, 1859–1865

C. Peter Ripley, *Editor*

Roy E. Finkenbine, *Associate Editor*

Michael F. Hembree, *Assistant Editor*

Donald Yacovone, *Assistant Editor*

The University of North Carolina Press
Chapel Hill and London

The paper used in this book meets the guidelines for
permanence and durability of the Committee on Production Guidelines for Book Longevity of the Council on
Library Resources.

Manufactured in the United States of America

96 95 94 93 92   5 4 3 2 1

Library of Congress Cataloging-in-Publication Data
(Revised for vol. 5)

The Black abolitionist papers.

Includes bibliographical references and indexes.
Contents: v. 1. The British Isles, 1830–1865—
v. 2. Canada, 1830–1865—v. 3. The United States,
1830–1846—v. 5. The United States, 1859–1865.
    1. Slavery—United States—Anti-slavery movements—
Sources. 2. Abolitionists—United States—History—19th
century—Sources. 3. Abolitionists—History—19th cen-
tury—Sources. 4. Afro-Americans—History—To 1863—
Sources. I. Ripley, C. Peter, 1941–   .
E449.B624   1985   973'.0496   84-13131
ISBN 0-8078-1625-6 (v. 1)
ISBN 0-8078-1698-1 (v. 2)
ISBN 0-8078-1926-3 (v. 3)
ISBN 0-8078-1974-3 (v. 4)
ISBN 0-8078-2007-5 (v. 5)

The preparation and publication of this volume were made possible in part by grants from the Program for Editions and the Division of Research Programs of the National Endowment for the Humanities, an independent federal agency, and by grants from the National Historical Publications and Records Commission, The Florida State University, the Skaggs Foundation, and the H. W. Wilson Foundation.

For Benjamin Quarles

Contents

Illustrations xv

Maps xvi

Acknowledgments xvii

Abbreviations xix

Editorial Statement xxiii

Documents

Illustrations

Maps

Acknowledgments

The support of a large number of individuals and institutions made it possible for the Black Abolitionist Papers Project to complete its work in a timely fashion.

Editors Roy E. Finkenbine, Michael F. Hembree, and Donald Yacovone spent nearly twenty-five years between them preparing the volumes of the Black Abolitionist Papers. The editors brought to the task at hand persistent hard work and good cheer under pressing deadlines, despite their uncertain professional future once they completed the volumes. With proper regard for the historical heritage entrusted to the project, they sought to give a fair hearing to the men and women whose documents appear in the published volumes. The Afro-American struggle for freedom and equality filled our thoughts for many years and conferred to us a shared sense of mission, which made the work rich and rewarding.

We wish to thank the countless scholars who over the years evaluated grant applications for funding agencies, sat on awards panels, read our manuscripts for the University of North Carolina Press, and in one manner or another endorsed or improved our work. Many of them lent their considerable professional cache to the project during the difficult early stages, when we had little more than a good idea and faith that a largely anonymous Afro-American community had indeed left an extraordinary documentary record of antebellum life and culture.

Support from The Florida State University, the National Endowment for the Humanities, the National Historical Publications and Records Commission, the H. W. Wilson Foundation, and the L. J. and Mary C. Skaggs Foundation made possible the preparation of this volume. Academic Affairs Vice-President Augustus Turnbull and Black Studies Program Director William R. Jones at Florida State; Kathy Fuller and Richard Ekman at NEH; Roger Bruns, Mary Giunta, Sarah Jackson, and Richard Sheldon at NHPRC; L. M. Weems of the Wilson Foundation; and the board of the Skaggs Foundation made a special effort to see the project through this fifth and final volume. And I would like to acknowledge once again the Ford Foundation, the Rockefeller Foundation, and the Exxon Education Fund for their support for earlier volumes.

We wish to recognize the manuscript curators, repository directors, and librarians who responded to our inquiries for elusive information and allowed us to publish documents from their collections: Howard Dodson of the Schomburg Center for Research in Black Culture; the staff of the Moorland-Spingarn Research Center; the staff of the Boston Public Library; Clifton Johnson of the Amistad Research Center; Karl Kabelac of the Department of Rare Books and Special Collections at the University of Rochester; Theresa Vann of New York City; the Special Collections staff at the George Arents Research Library of Syracuse University; Linda Bailey of the Cincinnati Historical Society; Peggy Halle and Cynthia Seay of the Norfolk Public Library; the Special Collections and Archives staff of Kent State University; and Michael Meier of the National Archives. The interlibrary loan staff of The Florida State University Library was enormously helpful through the years.

Pamela Upton, Johanna Grimes, Paula Wald, Lewis Bateman, Iris Tillman Hill, and Kate Douglas Torrey of the University of North Carolina Press shared our enthusiasm for the Black Abolitionist Papers in a five-volume collaboration that spanned seven years.

At Florida State, I am particularly grateful to Gus Turnbull, Tom McCaleb, Bill Jones, Charles Cnudde, Sherry Phillips, Kay Sauers, and Shamuna Malik.

Jeffery Rossbach's thoughtful application of the historian's craft influenced our work long after he departed the project.

John L. Parker, Jr., kept us current in the world of word processing technology, and Christopher Meyer once again updated our style sheet, deciphered documents, and prepared the manuscript for electronic publication with a watchful eye and a devotion to precision.

For fifteen years—through an international search for documents, a seventeen-reel microfilm compendium, and a five-volume printed edition—the Editorial Board provided sound advice, scholarly insight, and steady encouragement. Special thanks to local board members Jerry Stern and Joe Richardson, whose good judgment helped shape the volumes and guided the project.

Martha, John, Mary Ann, Jerry, Joe, Phil, Jim, and Hal—you are here too.

Tallahassee, Florida   C. P. R.
April, 1991

Abbreviations

Newspapers, Journals, Directories, and Reference Works

ACAB	James Grant Wilson and John Fiske, eds., *Appletons' Cyclopaedia of American Biography*, 6 vols. (New York, New York, 1888–89).
AJE	*American Journal of Education.*
AlexM	*Alexander's Magazine* (Boston, Massachusetts).
AM	*American Missionary* (New York, New York).
ASA	*Anti-Slavery Advocate* (London, England).
ASB	*Anti-Slavery Bugle* (Salem, Ohio; New Lisbon, Ohio).
BACA	*Baltimore American and Commercial Advertiser* (Baltimore, Maryland).
BDAC	*Biographical Directory of the American Congress, 1774–1971* (Washington, D.C., 1971).
BelSt	*Belvidere Standard* (Belvidere, Illinois).
BHM	*Bulletin of the History of Medicine.*
CA	*Colored American* (New York, New York).
CBD	J. O. Thorne and T. C. Collocott, eds., *Chambers Biographical Dictionary*, rev. ed. (Edinburgh, Scotland, 1984).
CC	*Connecticut Courant* (Hartford, Connecticut).
CHSB	*Cincinnati Historical Society Bulletin.*
CJH	*Canadian Journal of History.*
CL	*Cleveland Leader* (Cleveland, Ohio).
Comm	*Commonwealth* (Boston, Massachusetts).
CR	*Christian Recorder* (Philadelphia, Pennsylvania).
CT	*Chicago Tribune* (Chicago, Illinois).
CWD	Mark Mayo Boatner, ed., *Civil War Dictionary* (New York, New York, 1959).
CWH	*Civil War History.*
DAAS	Randall M. Miller and John David Smith, eds., *Dictionary of Afro-American Slavery* (Westport, Connecticut, 1988).
DAB	Allen Johnson and Dumas Malone, eds., *Dictionary of American Biography*, 20 vols. (New York, New York, 1928–36).
DANB	Rayford W. Logan and Michael R. Winston, eds., *Dictionary of American Negro Biography* (New York, New York, 1982).
DM	*Douglass' Monthly* (Rochester, New York).

DNB	Sir Leslie Stephen and Sir Sidney Lee, eds., *Dictionary of National Biography*, 22 vols. (London, England, 1885–1901; reprint, 1921–22).
ESF	*Elevator* (San Francisco, California).
FDP	*Frederick Douglass' Paper* (Rochester, New York).
FHQ	*Florida Historical Quarterly.*
FI	*Friends' Intelligencer* (Philadelphia, Pennsylvania).
G	*Gazette* (Cleveland, Ohio).
HTECW	Patricia L. Faust, ed., *Historical Times Illustrated Encyclopedia of the Civil War* (New York, New York, 1986).
IC	*Impartial Citizen* (Syracuse, New York; Boston, Massachusetts).
IHJ	*Illinois Historical Journal.*
JBS	*Journal of Black Studies.*
JDC	*Daily Clarion* (Jackson, Mississippi).
JNH	*Journal of Negro History.*
JSH	*Journal of Southern History.*
LCEU	*Le Courrier des Etats-Unis* (New York, New York).
Lib	*Liberator* (Boston, Massachusetts).
Louis	*Louisianan* (New Orleans, Louisiana).
MDC	*Daily Clarion* (Meridian, Mississippi).
MH	*Michigan History.*
NASS	*National Anti-Slavery Standard* (New York, New York).
NAW	Edward T. James, ed., *Notable American Women, 6207–1950: A Biographical Dictionary*, 3 vols. (Cambridge, Massachusetts, 1971).
NCAB	*National Cyclopaedia of American Biography*, 61 vols. to date (New York, New York, 1898–).
NECAUL	*National Enquirer and Constitutional Advocate of Universal Liberty* (Philadelphia, Pennsylvania).
NEW	*National Era* (Washington, D.C.).
NHB	*Negro History Bulletin.*
NSFA	*Northern Star and Freeman's Advocate* (Albany, New York).
NSt	*North Star* (Rochester, New York).
NV	*Norfolk Virginian* (Norfolk, Virginia).
NYCJ	*New York Colonization Journal* (New York, New York).
NYEP	*New York Evening Post* (New York, New York).
NYT	*New York Tribune* (New York, New York).
NYTi	*New York Times* (New York, New York).
OE	*Oberlin Evangelist.*
PA	*Pacific Appeal* (San Francisco, California).
PEB	*Evening Bulletin* (Philadelphia, Pennsylvania).

PF   *Pennsylvania Freeman* (Philadelphia, Pennsylvania).

PFW   *Provincial Freeman* (Windsor, Ontario, Canada; Toronto, Ontario, Canada; Chatham, Ontario, Canada).

PH   *Pennsylvania History.*

PHR   *Pacific Historical Review.*

Phy   *Phylon.*

PP   *Pine and Palm* (Boston, Massachusetts; New York, New
York).

RCHS   *Records of the Columbia Historical Society*, 53 vols. to
date (Washington, D.C., 1897–).

RG   *Raleigh Gazette* (Raleigh, North Carolina).

RP   *Richmond Planet* (Richmond, Virginia).

SCHM   *South Carolina Historical Magazine.*

TG   *Globe* (Toronto, Ontario, Canada).

TL   *Times* (London, England).

VF   *Voice of the Fugitive* (Sandwich, Ontario, Canada;
Windsor, Ontario, Canada).

VMHB   *Virginia Magazine of History and Biography.*

WAA   *Weekly Anglo-African* (New York, New York).

WPHM   *Western Pennsylvania Historical Magazine.*

WWWCW   Stewart Sifakis, *Who Was Who in the Civil War* (New
York, New York, 1988).

Manuscript Repositories

AMA-ARC   American Missionary Association Archives, Amistad
Research Center, Tulane University, New Orleans,
Louisiana.

CaOLU   University of Western Ontario, London, Ontario,
Canada.

CaOTAr   Ontario Provincial Archives, Toronto, Ontario, Canada.

CaOTP   Metropolitan Toronto Central Library, Toronto,
Ontario, Canada.

DHU   Moorland-Spingarn Research Center, Howard
University, Washington, D.C.

DLC   Library of Congress, Washington, D.C.

DNA   National Archives, Washington, D.C.

MB   Boston Public Library and Eastern Massachusetts
Regional Public Library System, Boston,
Massachusetts.

MH   Houghton Library, Harvard University, Cambridge,
Massachusetts.

NN-Sc	Schomburg Center for Research in Black Culture, New York Public Library, New York, New York.
NRU	Rush-Rhees Library, University of Rochester, Rochester, New York.
NSyU	George Arents Research Library, Syracuse University, Syracuse, New York.
OO	Seeley G. Mudd Center, Oberlin College, Oberlin, Ohio.
PHi	Historical Society of Pennsylvania, Philadelphia, Pennsylvania.
PPP	Presbyterian Historical Society, Philadelphia, Pennsylvania.
RHi	Rhode Island Historical Society, Providence, Rhode Island.
UKOxU-Rh	Rhodes House Library, Oxford University, Oxford, England.
VNP	Norfolk Public Library, Norfolk, Virginia.

Editorial Statement

The Black Abolitionist Papers Project began in 1976 with the mission to collect and publish the documentary record of black Americans involved in the movement to end slavery in the United States from 1830 to 1865. The project was conceived from an understanding that broad spans of Afro-American history have eluded scholarly attention because the necessary research materials are not readily available. Many personal papers, business records, newspapers, and other documentary sources simply have not survived. Materials that have endured are often inaccessible because they have not been systematically identified and collected. Except for several small manuscript collections of better-known black figures (usually those that continued to be public figures after emancipation),[1] the letters, speeches, essays, writings, and personal papers of black abolitionists have escaped professional attention. The same is true of antebellum black newspapers.

But the publications of individual historians demonstrated that black abolitionist documents could be unearthed.[2] The black documents that

---

1. See Mary Ann Shadd Cary Papers, Public Archives of Canada (Ottawa, Ontario), DHU, and CaOTAr; Shadd Family Papers, CaOLU; Rapier Family Papers, DHU; Daniel A. Payne Papers, Wilberforce University (Wilberforce, Ohio); Anderson R. Abbott Papers, CaOTP; John M. Langston Papers, Fisk University (Nashville, Tennessee); Ruffin Family Papers, DHU; Amos G. Beman Papers, Yale University (New Haven, Connecticut); Charles Lenox Remond Papers, Essex Institute (Salem, Massachusetts) and MB; William Still Papers, Rutgers University (New Brunswick, New Jersey); Jacob C. White, Jr., Papers, PHi; Frederick Douglass Papers, DLC, NN-Sc, and DHU; Alexander Crummell Papers, NN-Sc; James T. Holly Papers, General Theological Seminary (New York, New York); J. W. Loguen File, NSyU; Paul Cuffe Papers, New Bedford Free Public Library (New Bedford, Massachusetts). Of these, only the Cary, Cuffe, Remond, Douglass, and Beman collections have significant antebellum documents.

2. A number of black abolitionist documents were reprinted before this project began its work in 1976: Carter G. Woodson, ed., *Negro Orators and Their Orations* (Washington, D.C., 1925), and *The Mind of the Negro as Reflected in Letters Written during the Crisis, 1800–1860* (Washington, D.C., 1926); Dorothy B. Porter, ed., "Early Manuscript Letters Written by Negroes," *JNH* 24:199–210 (April 1939); Benjamin Quarles, ed., "Letters from Negro Leaders to Gerrit Smith," *JNH* 27:432–53 (October 1942); Philip S. Foner, ed., *The Life and Writings of Frederick Douglass*, 5 vols. (New York, N.Y., 1950–75); Howard H. Bell, ed., *Minutes of the Proceedings of the National Negro Conventions, 1830–1864* (New York, N.Y., 1969); Dorothy Sterling, ed., *Speak Out in Thunder Tones: Letters and Other Writings by Black Northerners, 1787–1865* (New York, N.Y., 1973). Pioneer scholarship on the subject that further suggested the availability of documents includes a number of articles on antebellum black Canadian fugitive communities by Fred Landon that appeared in the *Journal of Negro History* and *Ontario History* during the 1920s and 1930s; Dorothy B. Porter, "Sarah Parker Remond, Abolitionist and Physician," *JNH* 20:287–93 (July 1935), and "David M. Ruggles, an Apostle of Human Rights," *JNH*

enriched those books and articles were not located in a single collection, repository, or newspaper in any quantity. They were found scattered in the manuscript collections of others (usually whites involved in nineteenth-century reform movements) and in newspapers of the day (usually reform papers but also in the traditional press). Clearly, a significant body of black abolitionist documents survived, but it seemed equally certain that locating the documents would require a thorough search of large numbers of newspapers and a systematic review of a wide range of historical materials, particularly the papers of white individuals and institutions involved in the antislavery movement.

An international search for documents was the first phase of the Black Abolitionist Papers Project. A four-year collection process took the project to thousands of manuscript collections and countless newspapers in England, Scotland, Ireland, and Canada as well as in the United States. This work netted nearly 14,000 letters, speeches, essays, pamphlets, and newspaper editorials from over 200 libraries and 110 newspapers. What resulted is the documentary record of some 300 black men and women and their efforts to end American slavery.[3]

The Black Abolitionist Papers were microfilmed during the second phase of the project. The microfilmed edition contains all the primary documents gathered during the collection phase. The seventeen reels of film are a pristine presentation of the black abolitionist record.[4] The microfilmed edition offers materials that previously were uncollected, unidentified, and frequently unavailable to scholars.

28:23–50 (January 1943); Herbert Aptheker, *The Negro in the Abolitionist Movement* (New York, N.Y., 1941); Benjamin Quarles, *Frederick Douglass* (Washington, D.C., 1948); Philip S. Foner, *Frederick Douglass* (New York, N.Y., 1950); Benjamin Quarles, "Ministers without Portfolio," *JNH* 39:27–43 (January 1954); Leon F. Litwack, *North of Slavery: The Negro in the Free States, 1790–1860* (Chicago, Ill., 1961); William H. Pease and Jane H. Pease, *Black Utopia: Negro Communal Experiments in America* (Madison, Wis., 1963); Benjamin Quarles, *Black Abolitionists* (London, 1969); William Edward Farrison, *William Wells Brown: Author and Reformer* (Chicago, Ill., 1969); Robin W. Winks, *The Blacks in Canada: A History* (New Haven, Conn., 1971); Jane H. Pease and William H. Pease, *They Who Would Be Free: Blacks' Search for Freedom, 1830–1861* (New York, N.Y., 1974); Floyd J. Miller, *The Search for a Black Nationality: Black Emigration and Colonization, 1787–1863* (Urbana, Ill., 1975); Richard Blackett, "In Search of International Support for African Colonization: Martin R. Delany's Visit to England, 1860," *CJH* 10:307–24 (December 1975). Several examples of early research on black abolitionists were reprinted in John H. Bracey, Jr., August Meier, and Elliott Rudwick, eds., *Blacks in the Abolitionist Movement* (Belmont, Calif., 1971).

3. This project has not collected or published documents by Frederick Douglass. Douglass's papers are being edited and published by John W. Blassingame and the staff of the Frederick Douglass Papers Project at Yale University.

4. The Black Abolitionist Papers are on seventeen reels of film with a published guide and index (New York, N.Y.: Microfilming Corporation of America, 1981–83; Ann Arbor, Mich.: University Microfilms International, 1984–). The guide contains a description of the collection procedures.

Now in its third phase, the project is publishing a five-volume series of edited and annotated representative documents. Black abolitionist activities in the British Isles and in Canada are treated in separate volumes; three volumes are devoted to black abolitionists in the United States. The volume organization was suggested by a systematic review of the documents. The documents made clear that black abolitionists had a set of broadly defined goals and objectives wherever they were. But the documents also demonstrated that black abolitionists had a set of specific goals and actions in England, another set in Canada, and a third in the United States.

The U.S. volumes are treated as a series. A single introduction, which appears in volume III, introduces the series. Notes to the documents are not repeated within the U.S. volumes.

The microfilmed and published editions are two discrete historical instruments. The 14,000 microfilmed documents are a rich Afro-American expression of black life in the nineteenth century. Those black voices stand free of intrusion by either editor or historian. The microfilmed edition presents the collected documents. The published volumes are documentary history. Substantial differences separate the two.

The five volumes will accommodate less than 10 percent of the total collection, yet the volumes must tell the ambitious history of a generation of black Americans and their involvement in an international reform movement that spanned thirty-five years in the United States, the British Isles, and Canada. We reconstructed that story by combining documents with written history. A thorough reading of the documents led us to the major themes and elements of black abolitionist activity—the events, ideas, individuals, concepts, and organizations that made up the movement. Then we sought documents that best represented those elements. But given their limited number, the documents alone could only hint at the full dimensions of this complex story. The written history—the volume introduction, the headnotes that precede each document, and the document notes—helps provide a more complete rendition by highlighting the documents' key elements and themes.

The documents led us to yet another principle that governs the volumes. Antislavery was a critical and persistent aspect of antebellum black life, but it cannot correctly be separated from the remainder of black life and culture. Antislavery was part of a broad matrix of black concerns that at times seemed indistinguishable from race relations in the free states, black churches and schools in northern cities, black family life, West Indian immigration, African missionary work, fugitive slave settlements in Canada, and a host of other personal, public, and national matters. Ending slavery was but the most urgent item on the crowded agenda of the black Americans represented in these volumes.

A number of considerations influenced the selection of specific documents published in the volumes. The most important was the responsibility to publish documents that fairly represent the antislavery goals, attitudes, and actions of black abolitionists and, to a lesser extent, that reveal their more personal concerns. There were other considerations as well. We wanted to present documents by as many black abolitionists as possible. We avoided the temptation to rely on the eloquent statements of just a few polished professionals. We sought to document immediate antislavery objectives (often dictated by local needs and issues) as well as broad goals. A mix of document types—letters (both public and private), essays, scientific pieces, short autobiographical narratives, impromptu remarks, formal speeches, circulars, resolutions, and debates—was selected for publication.

We resisted selecting documents that had been reprinted before our work began. But occasionally when a previously published document surfaced as a resonant black expression on an issue, topic, or incident, it was selected for publication. And, with the release of the Black Abolitionist Papers on microfilm, all the documents are more available than in the past. We often found different versions of the same document (usually a speech that appeared in several newspapers). When that happened, we selected the earliest published version of the most complete text. The cluster of documents around particular time periods and topics mirrors black abolitionist activities and concerns. The documents are arranged chronologically within each volume. A headnote introduces each document. The headnote provides a historical context for the document and offers information designed to enhance the reader's understanding of the document and black abolitionist activities.

Notes identify a variety of items that appear within the documents, such as people, places, events, organizations, institutions, laws, and legal decisions. The notes enrich and clarify the documents. People and events that are covered in standard biographical directories, reference books, or textbooks are treated in brief notes. We have given more space to subjects on which there is little or no readily available information, particularly black individuals and significant events and institutions in the black community. A full note on each item is presented at the first appropriate point in the volume. Notes are not repeated within the volume. Information that appears in a headnote is not repeated in an endnote. The index includes references to all notes.

We have listed sources at the end of notes and headnotes. When appropriate, source citations contain references to materials in the microfilmed edition; they appear in brackets as reel and frame numbers (3:0070 reads reel 3, frame 70). The titles of some sources are abbreviated (particularly newspapers, journals, and manuscript repositories); a list of abbreviations appears at the front of the volume.

The axiom that "less is better" governed the project's transcription of documents. Our goal was to publish the documents in a form as close to the original as possible while presenting them in a fashion that enabled the reader to use them easily.

In the letters, the following items are uniformly and silently located regardless of where they appear in the original: place and date, recipient's name and address, salutation, closing, signature, marginal notes, and postscripts. In manuscript documents, idiosyncratic spelling, underlining, and quotation marks are retained. Words that were crossed through in the original are also retained.

The project adopted the following principles for documents found in published sources (newspapers, pamphlets, annual reports, and other nineteenth-century printed material): redundant punctuation is eliminated; quotation marks are converted to modern usage; obvious misspellings and printer's errors are corrected; printer's brackets are converted to parentheses; audience reaction within a speech is treated as a separate sentence with parentheses, for example, (Hear, hear.). We have let stand certain nineteenth-century printing conventions such as setting names or addresses in capital or italic letters in order to maintain the visual character of the document. A line of asterisks signals that material is deleted from a printed document. In no instance is black abolitionist material edited or deleted; but if, for example, a speech was interrupted with material extraneous to the document, the irrelevant material is not published.

The intrusive *sic* is rarely used. Brackets are used in their traditional fashion: to enclose information that we added and to indicate our inability to transcribe words or phrases with certainty. Some examples: we bracketed information added to the salutation and return address of letters; we bracketed material that we believe will aid the reader to comprehend the document, such as [illegible], [rest of page missing]; and we bracketed words and phrases that we believe appeared in the original but are uncertain about because of the quality of the surviving text. We have used brackets in the body of documents sparingly and only when necessary to avoid confusing the reader. We have not completed words, added words, corrected spelling, or otherwise provided material in the text of manuscript documents except as noted above.

Our transcription guidelines for manuscript documents differ slightly from those we used for printed sources. We took greater editorial liberties with documents from printed sources because they seldom came to us directly from a black abolitionist's hand. Speeches in particular often had a long editorial trail. Usually reporters wrote them down as they listened from the audience; in some cases this appeared to be done with precision. For example, William Farmer, a British abolitionist and newspaper reporter, was an accomplished stenographer who traveled with William Wells Brown and took down his speeches verbatim, then made them available to the local press. More often, a local reporter recorded speeches in a less thorough fashion. Speeches and letters that black abolitionists sent to newspapers were apt to pass through the hands of an editor, a publisher, and a typesetter, all of whom might make errors in transcription. Because documents that were reprinted in newspapers often had sections changed or deleted, we have attempted to find the original publication of printed documents.

Our transcription guidelines were influenced by the availability of all the documents in the microfilmed edition. Microfilmed copies of the original documents give the reader ready access to unedited versions of the documents that appear in the published volumes.

The
Black Abolitionist
Papers

1.
The Emigration Alternative

Circular by the African Civilization Society
16 February 1859

Essay by James Theodore Holly
[May 1859]

Federal government policies of the 1850s—from the Fugitive Slave Law
to the Dred Scott decision—shattered black hopes for racial progress in
the United States. As conditions deteriorated, proposals for black settlement beyond the North American continent grew more attractive. Endorsement of the emigration alternative by several prominent black abolitionists enhanced the credibility of the movement. By the end of the
decade, a variety of emigration programs competed for attention in the
black community. Henry Highland Garnet launched the African Civilization Society in the fall of 1858 to promote black settlement in West
Africa. An AfCS circular, reprinted below, outlined Garnet's vision of
black Americans working in Yoruba to eradicate the slave trade, promote the growth of free labor cotton, and establish Christian missions.
James Theodore Holly framed his emigration appeal in the context of a
strong black nationality. He looked to Haiti, with its imposing legacy of
revolution and black nation building, as the best site for settlement. His
most comprehensive statement on the emigration question, a six-part
series entitled "Thoughts on Hayti," was published between June and
November 1859 in the *Anglo-African Magazine*. In the opening essay, which appears below, Holly hailed Haiti's achievements and declared that the young nation would play a pivotal role in the destiny of
black Americans. Floyd J. Miller, *The Search for a Black Nationality:
Black Emigration and Colonization, 1787–1863* (Urbana, Ill., 1975),
170–263.

Office of African Civilization
Society[1]
23 BIBLE HOUSE
New York, [New York]
———, 1859

The Board of Directors of the African Civilization Society[2] would respectfully call your attention to the objects and prospects of the cause
they represent. The objects are, as set forth in the second article of the
Constitution, "The Evangelization and Civilization of Africa, and the
descendants of African ancestors wherever dispersed. The destruction of

the African Slave-trade by the introduction of lawful commerce into Africa; the promotion of the growth of cotton, and other products there, whereby the natives may become industrious producers as well as consumers of articles of commerce; and generally, the elevation of the condition of the colored population of our own country and of other lands." The third article provides that missionaries may be sent out by this Society, "without regard to sect," provided they hold the doctrines usually termed evangelic.

We invite your attention to the magnitude of the interests involved in these objects, and their paramount claims upon us all as lovers of humanity, as well as Christians. Hitherto the colored people of the United States have felt less interest in the welfare of Africa than their white brethren, but now a deep and widespread solicitude is manifested for the conversion and elevation of the nations of sunny Africa. The time has arrived when they perceive their duty as well as privilege in regard to that long-neglected region. They feel that they may be the agents, in God's providence, to introduce the Gospel and a true Christian civilization into Africa. The remarkable discoveries of Livingstone, Bowen, and Barth, and the interesting accounts by Wilson and Thompson, have opened a new field of Christian enterprise, as well as commercial activity; and the millions of Central Africa are now awaiting those movements of Christians in America and Great Britain which contemplate their temporal as well as spiritual welfare. Through the accounts furnished us in Bowen's *Central Africa*, and by the letters of Mr. Clark, and other missionaries in Yoruba, the colored churches in the United States are awaking to the consciousness that they have a work to perform for Africa, and that they possess those elements of power, mental and moral, which fit them to share in the glorious work of Africa's redemption.[3] The idea that they can aid in destroying the inhuman Slave-trade, as well as introduce pure Christianity to their "fatherland," besides directly elevating all branches of the great African family of nations, has deeply moved the hearts of multitudes of noble-minded Christians of African descent, and they desire to be made instrumental in accomplishing the great work.

They desire to establish Christian industrial settlements in Yoruba, west of the Niger, and near its banks, in a fertile, healthy, and attractive region, which at present is uninhabited, owing to causes described in the work referred to. This region is admirably situated in the highway of trade for Central Africa, and can produce cotton, indigo, rice, sugar, and other articles of constant demand, thus affording a supply of free-labor groceries and cotton to those who prefer them. That region might soon be transformed into a flourishing Christian nationality, from whence the blessings of the gospel of peace would flow to the myriads of teeming Ethiopia. Thus the preaching of the Gospel would be accompanied with the powerful ocular demonstration of Christian communities, springing into active existence, and presenting models for the imitation of the inquisitive tribes of Africa. The cotton plant is indigenous there, and a trade has already commenced which bids fair to supply all the demands which are made through the rapidly increasing use of the article. It is already a serious obstacle to the Slave-trade, as the natives find it more profitable to engage in the cotton culture than in the inhuman traffic in men. It may prove in time to be the solution of the problem, "How to remedy the curse of American Slavery?" The laws of trade may unite with the efforts of philanthropists to secure the peaceful extinction of that evil system.

Another point is, that a lawful commerce of exceeding magnitude will result from these efforts, and manufactures to the extent of millions will be imported to supply the wants of the people as they become civilized; and legitimate trade will supplant the agonizing desolations produced by the inroads of pirate slavers.

Thus the preaching of Christ, and the introduction of Christian civilization and lawful commerce, will elevate the nations of Africa, and also afford a sphere for the development of Christian zeal and commercial activity among the educated men of color in the United States, thus aiding in the work of elevation HERE, which is so imperatively necessary. These objects may all be accomplished, with the Divine blessing, if the means are furnished to send forth those who are anxious to go. Many educated colored ministers are now waiting to be sent forth to preach the gospel of Christ in their beloved fatherland. In addition, a large number of agriculturists, and mechanics of all kinds, stand ready to undertake the work of founding a Christian nationality in Central Africa, but most of them lack the necessary means. Owing to cruel prejudice still existing at the North, their avocations are such as to preclude them generally from amassing wealth, and they therefore look to the Christian love and generosity of their more privileged white brethren to aid them.

The American churches and people owe to their fellow countrymen of African descent a very heavy debt. Generation after generation have toiled in anguish and poverty here, and have materially aided in building up our present commercial greatness; we should not refuse to aid them then, now that *they* have responded to the Macedonian cry,[4] from the palmy plains and sunny fountains of Africa. The preaching of the Gospel must be in the spirit of unity, love, and truth, and it is therefore hoped that this design will meet with the favor and support of all classes and denominations who desire the spread of the Gospel, and the redemption of Africa.

The colored churches of America wish to engage in this glorious work, and the African Civilization Society affords an opportunity for all to combine under the banner of Immanuel, forgetting their minor differences in the ennobling work of preaching Christ to the benighted nations.

With the divine blessing, "Ethiopia will soon stretch out her hands unto God,"[5] and by a blessed providence, through the instrumentality of her own children, whose hearts are now burning within them for an opportunity to preach the Gospel in the land of their ancestral greatness. The natives of Central Africa earnestly implore our aid; they are loudly calling for missionaries and teachers, and we can not neglect them.

The Board of Directors of the African Civilization Society earnestly appeal to the liberal-hearted for the necessary means to secure these important results. They feel certain that when it is known that colored brethren of the faith, the children of our common Father, now await their aid, it will be cheerfully and affectionately granted them.

Donations and subscriptions may be forwarded to the Treasurer or Corresponding Secretary, by whom they will be acknowledged.

Annual subscription, One Dollar, or more; Life Membership, Twenty-five Dollars.

> HENRY HIGHLAND
> GARNET, President
> ELLIS A. POTTER, *Recording*
> *Secretary*[6]
> ISAAC T. SMITH, *Treasurer,*
> *Mariners' Savings Institution,*
> *No. 1 Third Avenue*[7]
> T. BOURNE, *Corresponding*
> *Secretary, 23 Bible House*[8]

Gerrit Smith Papers, George Arents Research Library, Syracuse University, Syracuse, New York. Published by permission.

Thoughts on Hayti
BY J. THEODORE HOLLY[9]

The Important position that this Nationality holds in relation to the Future Destiny of the Negro Race.

The recent bloodless revolution through which Hayti has passed and which has resulted in the dethronement of Faustin I and in the elevation of Geffrard to the chair of the Chief Magistracy, together with the revival of the subject of Haytian emigration among colored Americans, have contributed to bring the claims of this negro nationality prominently before the public mind.[10]

I, therefore, propose to profit by the attention which is now being bestowed upon the affairs of that country, to furnish some food for the public mind, by exposing some of my own thoughts derived from a somewhat careful and extended study of the history of the Haytian people. These thoughts, I will give in a short series of articles on various topics, such as may be of the most important consideration, and shall begin in this one to speak of *the important relation that this sovereign people hold to the future destiny of the negro race.*

In the first place, then, let me say, that *the successful establishment of this negro nationality, the means by which its establishment was sought and accomplished, and the masterly vigilance by which the same has been maintained for upwards of a half-century*, present us with the strongest evidence and the most irrefragable proof of the equality of the negro race that can be found anywhere, whether in ancient or modern times. Among all the nationalities of the world, Hayti stands without any question the solitary prodigy of history. Never before in all the annals of humanity has a race of men, chattelized and almost dehumanized, sprung by their own efforts and inherent energies from their brutalized condition into the manly status of independent, self-respecting freemen at one gigantic bound; and thus took their place at once, side by side with nations whose sovereignty had been the mature growth of ages of human progress. The ancient glory of Ethiopia, Egypt, and Greece grows pale in comparison with the splendor of this Haytian achievement. Because civilization having grown to gradual maturity under the most favorable circumstances on the banks of the Ganges, rolled its slow length along until it penetrated into Ethiopia, and from thence following the course of the Nile passed into Egypt, coursed onward into Greece, and finally has rolled its restless tide over Modern Europe and the Western world. But the people of Hayti, without the elevating influence of civilization among them, without a favorable position for development, without assistance from any quarter, and in spite of the most powerful combination of opposing circumstances—in which they found themselves at times contending against the armies of France, England, and Spain—these people, I say, in the face of all these obstacles, aroused themselves to the consciousness of their own inherent dignity, and shook off from their limbs the shackles and badges of their degradation, and successfully claimed a place among the most enlightened and heroic sovereignties of the world.[11] Such, in short, is the important position that Hayti holds when compared with the nations of all ages, past and present, that have figured in the world's history.

But this importance does not diminish in the least if we take a more circumscribed view of her relations. Let us confine ourselves to this continent alone and compare her with the nationalities of the New World. She is second on the list of independent sovereignties in the Western hemisphere that have successfully thrown off European domination during the last 80 years. And if the United States can claim to have preceded her in this respect, Hayti can claim the honor of having contributed to the success of American independence by the effusion of the blood of her sable sons, who led by the gallant Rigaud, a man of color, fought side by side with the American heroes in the Battle of Savannah.[12] And, if since her

independence, her government cannot claim the same stability of administration as that of the United States and Brazil, yet she can claim to have
been far superior in this respect to all the Hispano-American nationalities
that surround her.[13]

Hence, then, with this living, breathing nationality rearing its sovereign
head aloft over the Caribbean Sea, and presiding as the Queen of the
Antilles, we need not resort to any long-drawn arguments to defend negro ethnography against the Notts and Gliddons of our day.[14] Let them
prove, if they can, to the full satisfaction of their narrow souls and gan-
grened hearts, that the black-faced, woolly-haired, thick lipped, and flat-
nosed Egyptians of Ancient times did not belong to the same branch of
the human family that those negroes do who have been the victims of the
African Slave-trade for the past four centuries. Let them prove by the
subtlest refinement of reasoning that those ancient darkies were pure
white men; and without stopping to expose the fallacies of their argument, we may grant their conclusions, and adduce the people of Hayti as
the most unexceptionable specimen of the degraded negro race, and
prove their equality, nay, may I not say, their absolute superiority to any
other nation of men that have ever sprung into existence.

From these thoughts, it will be seen that whatsoever is to be the future
destiny of the descendants of Africa, Hayti certainly holds the most important relation to that destiny. And if we were to be reduced to the dread
alternative of having her historic fame blotted out of existence, or that
celebrity which may have been acquired elsewhere by all the rest of our
race combined, we should say preserve the name, the fame, and the sovereign existence of Hayti though everything else shall perish. Yes, let Britain and France undermine, if they will, the enfranchisement which they
gave to their West Indian slaves by their present apprenticeship system;[15]
let the lone star of Liberia,[16] placed in the firmament of nationalities by a
questionable system of American philanthrophy, go out in darkness; let
the opening resources of Central Africa be again shut up in their wonted
seclusion; let the names and deeds of our Nat Turners, Denmark Veseys,
Penningtons, Delanys, Douglasses, and Smiths[17] be forgotten forever, but
never let the self-emancipating deeds of the Haytian people be effaced;
never let her heroically achieved nationality be brought low; no, never let
the names of her Toussaint, her Dessalines, her Rigaud, her Christophe,
and her Petion be forgotten, or blotted out from the historic pages of the
world's history.[18]

The vantage ground given us in the former cases can be dispensed with,
rather than in the latter, because the white race can claim credit for having aided us to attain thereto; and thus they have ground to say that
without them we could not have made this advancement; they might still
continue to argue that when left to ourselves, we retrograde into barbarism. But in the case of Hayti, the question of negro capacity stands out

a naked fact, as vindication of itself—not only without any aid whatever from the white man, but in spite of his combined opposition to keep down in brutal degradation these self-emancipated freemen. From this view of the matter, it may be seen that if Haytian independence shall cease to exist, the sky of negro destiny shall be hung in impenetrable blackness; the hope of princes coming out of Egypt and Ethiopia soon stretching forth her hands unto God will die out; and everlasting degradation become the settled doom of this downtrodden, long-afflicted, and then God-forsaken race.

Therefore to despise the claims of Hayti is to despise the cause of God, by which he promises to bring deliverance to the captives and to those who are bound; to be indifferent to these claims is to neglect the holiest duties that Providence imposes upon us; and to refuse to make any and every sacrifice to advance the interest and prosperity of that nation is to be a traitor both to God and humanity. Hence, then, let that tongue cleave to the roof of its mouth that could dare speak against her; and let that arm wither that would not be upraised to defend her cause against a sacrilegious desecration by the filibustering tyrants of mankind, and the sworn enemies of God. And to this solemn prayer let every manly heart that beats within a sable bosom respond, Amen.

Anglo-African Magazine (New York, N.Y.), June 1859.

1. The African Civilization Society was founded in New York City in September 1858. Its offices were located at the Bible House, a building shared with the New York State Colonization Society. The AfCS constitution pledged to promote "the civilization and evangelization of Africa, and the descendants of African ancestors in any portion of the earth, wherever dispersed." But under the leadership of Henry Highland Garnet and local colonizationists, the organization concentrated on establishing a settlement in Yoruba. Members believed that from this base, commerce, civilization, and Christian missions could be spread throughout the African continent. They also hoped to make slavery and the slave trade less profitable by teaching indigenous Africans to grow free labor cotton. Despite frequent criticism from antiemigrationists such as James McCune Smith, J. W. C. Pennington, and George T. Downing, the AfCS built a substantial following among local blacks.

The AfCS found it easier to gain endorsements than to achieve its financial goal. In early 1860, the AfCS sent Theodore Bourne to England to raise funds and promote the planned colony. An English AfCS auxiliary, the African Aid Society, was formed to assist his mission. But the simultaneous presence of Martin R. Delany in Britain, and Bourne's unwillingness to distinguish between their two competing programs, diminished his effectiveness; his agency was rescinded before the year was out. In late 1860, Rev. Elymus P. Rogers led an exploring party sent to investigate sites and complete the arrangements for a settlement, but his death soon forced the mission to be aborted. Garnet continued to agitate for the Yoruban scheme. He sailed to Britain in August 1861 in another unsuccessful attempt to raise funds. In the fall of 1863, he lobbied the federal commissioner of emigration for the same purpose. But by that time, the association was already shifting its focus from Africa to freedmen's education. From 1863 through 1867, the organization sponsored several black schools in Washington, D.C., and other parts of the South. Miller, *Search for a Black Nationality*, 192–93, 195, 197, 217–31, 258–63; *WAA*, 12 November 1864, 25 March 1865; *NYCJ*, January 1859; Joel Schor, *Henry Highland Garnet: A Voice of Black Radicalism in the Nineteenth Century* (Westport, Conn., 1977), 153–68, 181–85.

2. In early 1859, the interracial board of directors of the African Civilization Society consisted of eighteen members, primarily from New York City, Brooklyn, and Newark. Four prominent black clergymen—Henry Highland Garnet, Henry M. Wilson, Elymus P. Rogers, and Benjamin W. Wilkins—were on the board. Other blacks included Tunis G. Campbell, Abraham W. Larkin, Robert Hamilton, Peter S. Porter, Stephen V. Douglass, and J. B. Wilson. Three white directors—Theodore Bourne, Francis Bourne, and Isaac T. Smith—were leading figures in the New York State Colonization Society. Other white members of the board included Robert Sears, Stephen Wood, James O. Pond, A. S. Ball, and Robert Lindley Murray. Circular by the African Civilization Society, 16 February 1859, Gerrit Smith Papers, NSyU [11:0588]; Miller, *Search for a Black Nationality*, 184–86, 191, 229; *WAA*, 16 November 1861, 3 January 1863.

3. European and American missionaries and explorers produced a substantial body of literature about Africa during the 1850s, which intensified popular interest in the "Dark Continent." David Livingstone (1813–1873), the celebrated Scottish missionary-explorer, described his adventures in the widely read *Missionary Travels and Researches in South Africa* (1857). German explorer Heinrich Barth (1821–1865) recorded his five-year, ten thousand–mile expedition in *Travels and Discoveries in North and Central Africa* (1857). John Leighton Wilson (1809–1886), an American Presbyterian missionary, wrote *Western Africa: Its History, Conditions, and Prospects* (1856). George Thompson (1817–1893), who headed the American Missionary Association's Mendi Mission in Sierra Leone from 1847 to 1856, provided accounts of missionary work in West Africa in *Thompson in Africa* (1852) and *The Palm Land* (1858). In *Central Africa: Adventures and Missionary Labors* (1857), Thomas J. Bowen (1814–1875) recalled his experiences as a missionary for the Southern Baptist Convention in Yoruba. The correspondence of William H. Clark, who also worked for the Southern Baptists in Yoruba, was widely reprinted in American religious periodicals. This body of literature, particularly the writings of Livingstone and Bowen, influenced emigration advocates such as Martin R. Delany and Henry Highland Garnet and stimulated the interest of the black denominations in African missionary work. Christopher Hibbert, *Africa Explored: Europeans in the Dark Continent, 1769–1889* (London, 1982), 178–89; Miller, *Search for a Black Nationality*, 173, 183; *DAB*, 20:337–38; Clifton H. Johnson, "The American Missionary Association, 1846–1861: A Study in Christian Abolitionism" (Ph.D. diss., University of North Carolina, 1959), 150–53.

4. The circular compares the response of black denominations concerning a perceived need for African missionary work to the "Macedonian cry" described in Acts 16:9–10. When a Macedonian appeared to Paul in a dream and implored him to "come over into Macedonia, and help us," he began a missionary journey through that region of northern Greece.

5. The circular quotes from Psalms 68:31.

6. Ellis A. Potter (1825–1874), a clerk and activist, was born and reared in New York City and participated in a variety of movements in the local black community during the 1850s. He served on the board of trustees of the Society for the Promotion of Education among Colored Children and helped supervise the operation of the association's School No. 2. He also belonged to the Committee of Thirteen, a group of local black leaders who regularly criticized the colonization movement and the Fugitive Slave Law of 1850. Attracted to African immigration proposals by the end of the decade, Potter became the first recording secretary of the African Civilization Society. He resettled in Liberia in July 1859, accompanying Martin R. Delany and Robert Campbell on the first leg of their Niger valley exploration venture. Having seen New York City's white merchants enriched by the African trade, he determined "to share a part in the productions of his father-land" and remained in Liberia until his death. *ESF*, 27 June 1874; *NASS*, 10 October 1850, 22 May 1851 [6:0606, 0944]; *VF*, 1 June 1851 [6:0951]; *WAA*, 1 October 1859 [12:0098].

7. Isaac T. Smith (1813–1906), a New York City shipping merchant, made a fortune through the Africa, China, and East Indies trades before turning to banking. In 1853 he founded the Mariners' Savings Institution, later the Metropolitan Savings Bank; he served as its president for several decades. Smith also acted as commissioner of emigration for the state of New York and sat on the board of managers of the New York State Colonization Society. For fifty years, he worked closely with the government of Siam and functioned as its local consul general. *ACAB*, 5:568; *NYTi*, 31 March 1906; Alan L. Olmstead, *New York City Mutual Savings Banks, 1819–1861* (Chapel Hill, N.C., 1976), 16, 45–46; Miller, *Search for a Black Nationality*, 197.

8. Theodore Bourne (1821–1910), a Presbyterian clergyman and the son of early antislavery leader George Bourne, was a professor of languages at the Huguenot Institute on Staten Island, New York. A man of eclectic reform interests, he became an agent of the New York State Colonization Society and corresponding secretary of the African Civilization Society in 1858. He visited England in the summer of 1859 as the AfCS's foreign secretary and used his father's reputation among British abolitionists to solicit funds for the organization. After returning to the United States in March 1861, he advocated Liberian and Jamaican immigration schemes. Bourne founded the Society for the Prevention of Crime in New York following the Civil War. Walter M. Merrill and Louis Ruchames, eds., *The Letters of William Lloyd Garrison*, 6 vols. (Cambridge, Mass., 1971–82), 4:598; Miller, *Search for a Black Nationality*, 183–87, 192, 217–22, 226.

9. James Theodore Holly (1829–1911), the younger brother of antislavery lecturer Joseph C. Holly, championed black nationalism and Haitian immigration during the Civil War years. Born to free black parents in Washington, D.C., he grew up in the city and attended a segregated school there. After his parents moved to Brooklyn in 1844, he worked as a clerk in the offices of the American Missionary Association. In 1850 Holly and his brother moved to Burlington, Vermont, and established a boot-making business with financial assistance from Lewis Tappan. For a time they lectured together but soon developed diametrically opposed views on the emigration question. Although Joseph Holly attacked the colonization movement, James concluded that blacks would never achieve free-

dom in the United States and endorsed the American Colonization Society. But repulsed by the racism he found in the organization, he turned to Canadian immigration. In Canada, he believed, blacks could build a "secure asylum" and a foundation for "the destiny of the whole Afro American race." He settled in Windsor, Canada West, in 1852 and became associate editor and coproprietor of Henry Bibb's *Voice of the Fugitive.* Holly worked with Bibb to orchestrate the North American Convention (1851) and helped establish the short-lived North American League, an organization intended to forge unity among blacks throughout the continent.

Bibb's death and the demise of the *Voice* frustrated Holly's hopes for Canada West and turned his attention to Haiti. Holly attended the 1854 National Emigration Convention in Cleveland and was selected to negotiate an immigration treaty with the Haitian government. After completing studies for the priesthood, he used his pulpit at St. Luke's Episcopal Church in New Haven, Connecticut, to promote Haitian settlement. Linking Haitian immigration to Episcopal missionary work, he argued that racial progress and the war against slavery could only succeed if blacks erected an independent Christian nation. He viewed Haiti's successful revolution as "one of the strongest proofs that can be adduced to substantiate the capabilities of the Negro race for self-government." Between 1859 and 1861, during the peak of black enthusiasm for emigration, Holly joined forces with James Redpath's Haytian Emigration Bureau. In early 1861, he organized the New Haven Pioneer Company of Haytian Emigration and founded a colony with 111 blacks from New England, New York, Pennsylvania, and Canada West. By November 1862, the settlement had collapsed and four members of Holly's family had died of disease.

Holly never abandoned Haiti. He moved the remnants of his settlement to Port-au-Prince, where he labored against considerable obstacles to build an Episcopal mission. Consecrated bishop of Haiti in 1874, he spent the next thirty-seven years founding and supervising schools and medical clinics on the island. Near the end of the century, he became an ardent anti-imperialist and advocated the theories of French communitarian Charles Fourier. Holly joined the Pan-Africanist movement in 1900, returning to his ideas of black nationalism and to his dream of establishing a model black nation in the Caribbean. David M. Dean, *Defender of the Race: James Theodore Holly, Black Nationalist Bishop* (Boston, Mass., 1979); C. Peter Ripley et al., eds., *Black Abolitionist Papers,* 4 vols. to date (Chapel Hill, N.C., 1985–), 2:110; Miller, *Search for a Black Nationality,* 109–14, 157, 161, 168–69, 235, 239–44, 246; James Theodore Holly, *Vindication of the Capacity of the Negro Race for Self-Government* (New Haven, Conn., 1857), [10:0444–68].

10. In January 1859, Fabre Nicholas Geffrard (1806–1878), a popular Haitian general, became president after deposing dictator Faustin Soulouque. He immediately encouraged black Americans to settle and farm Haiti's fertile Artibonite valley and to augment the indigenous labor force. Geffrard offered a series of inducements to immigrants and sponsored the Boston-based Haytian Emigration Bureau, with its well-organized network of agents throughout the northern United States, to recruit blacks and arrange for their transport. He continued to rule Haiti until 1867, when the threat of insurrection forced him to resign and

retire to Jamaica. Roland I. Perusse, *Historical Dictionary of Haiti* (Metuchen, N.J., 1977), 41, 97; Miller, *Search for a Black Nationality*, 235–38.

11. Haiti achieved political independence in 1804 as the result of a successful revolution against French rule.

12. André Rigaud (1761–1811) fought with a black Haitian brigade called the Volunteer Chasseurs as part of a Franco-American effort (1779) to evict British forces from Savannah, Georgia, during the American Revolution. He later returned to Haiti, led rebel troops against the French and British invaders in the 1790s, then turned against his former ally, Toussaint L'Ouverture, in an unsuccessful bid for political dominance. Perusse, *Historical Dictionary of Haiti*, 87–88, 104; Sidney Kaplan and Emma N. Kaplan, *The Black Presence in the Era of the American Revolution*, rev. ed. (Amherst, Mass., 1989), 68–69.

13. Holly exaggerates Haiti's political stability. Between 1806 and 1859, six Haitian heads of state were overthrown in coups or civil wars. Despite widespread political turmoil in other areas of Latin America, the governments of some emerging nations—Venezuela, Paraguay, and Chile—were considerably more stable.

14. Josiah C. Nott (1804–1873) and George R. Gliddon (1809–1857) were pioneering ethnographers who lent scientific authority to social theories of black inferiority. They collaborated on two treatises, *Types of Mankind* (1854) and *Indigenous Races of the Earth* (1857), which employed scientific method to allege separate human origins for blacks and whites. Nott, a Mobile, Alabama, physician, condemned miscegenation and argued that mulattoes were "a degenerate, unnatural offspring, doomed by nature to work out its own destruction." He rejected black freedom as a scientific absurdity. Gliddon, a leading Egyptologist, popular lecturer, and U.S. vice-consul at Cairo, examined mummified skulls to prove that ancient Egyptians were white and that blacks, because of smaller brain size, were incapable of social progress. William Stanton, *The Leopard's Spots: Scientific Attitudes toward Race in America, 1815–1859* (Chicago, Ill., 1960), 45–53, 65–70, 158–59, 162–63, 169, 175–79.

15. No formal apprenticeship system existed in the British or French colonies in the Caribbean at this time. The Emancipation Act of 1833, which abolished slavery in the British Empire, had established an apprenticeship arrangement for former slaves over six years of age, which kept them in slavelike conditions. But pressure by British abolitionists and the freedmen prompted most of the colonies to abandon the system by 1838. In the French West Indies, decrees on punishment, work, and living conditions ameliorated the situation of slaves and created a system approximating apprenticeship there in the mid-1840s. France abolished bondage outright in 1848. But in the following decade, British and French authorities allowed planters to institute informal restrictions on black workers, again placing them in the middle ground between slavery and freedom. William A. Green, *British Slave Emancipation: The Sugar Colonies and the Great Experiment* (Oxford, England, 1976), 84–175; Shelby T. McCloy, *The Negro in the French West Indies* (Lexington, Ky., 1966), 141–69.

16. The Liberian flag consisted of a single white star placed against a blue background in the upper left quadrant of a field of alternating red and white stripes.

17. Holly refers to J. W. C. Pennington, Martin R. Delany, Frederick Douglass, and James McCune Smith.

18. Holly refers to five heroes of the Haitian Revolution—Toussaint L'Ouverture, Jean-Jacques Dessalines, André Rigaud, Henri Christophe, and Alexandre Pétion. Dessalines (1758–1806), a former slave, was commander-in-chief of the Haitian forces that resisted French attempts to reoccupy the island. He proclaimed Haiti a republic in 1804 but soon established a dictatorship and ruled as Emperor Jacques I until his assassination in 1806. Christophe (1767–1820), the Grenada-born slave of a French naval officer, reportedly fought against the British in Georgia during the American Revolution. After purchasing his freedom, he gained political prominence during the struggle for Haitian independence. When Dessalines died, he was chosen president of Haiti, but military opposition led by Pétion limited his control to the northern region. He reigned as King Henri I from 1811 until 1820, when a military mutiny led him to commit suicide. Pétion (1770–1818), a Haitian-born mulatto, was educated in Paris but returned to his homeland to join in the liberation struggle. From 1806 to 1818, he ruled the southern part of Haiti as president. Pétion was known as the "Panamericanist" for providing military aid to Simon Bolívar to advance political independence and the antislavery cause throughout Latin America. Perusse, *Historical Dictionary of Haiti*, 17–19, 27–28, 79–80.

2.
William J. Whipper to Benjamin S. Jones
15 April 1859

In the wake of the Dred Scott decision, blacks faced new threats to their limited civil and political rights. In early 1859, the Ohio Supreme Court struck down an act that gave the vote to mulattoes of more than one-half white ancestry. The state legislature compounded the crisis by requiring election judges to reject any voter with "a distinct and visible admixture of African blood." Ohio blacks fought the new law. John Mercer Langston and the Ohio State Anti-Slavery Society organized a statewide campaign for equal suffrage; Cleveland and Cincinnati blacks took local election judges to court; blacks throughout northeastern Ohio tested the law at the polls. On 4 April, light-skinned William J. Whipper cast a ballot in Charlestown's township elections. Whipper discussed his defiant act and the resulting controversy in a 15 April letter to Benjamin S. Jones, the editor of the *Anti-Slavery Bugle*. The year-long struggle ended when the Ohio Supreme Court reversed itself and overturned the "visible admixture" law that December. The black vote proved critical to Abraham Lincoln's narrow victory in Ohio during the 1860 presidential election. Frank Quillin, *The Color Line in Ohio* (Ann Arbor, Mich., 1913), 97; *CL*, 31 March, 15 July 1859; William Cheek and Aimee Lee Cheek, *John Mercer Langston and the Fight for Black Freedom, 1829–1865* (Urbana, Ill., 1989), 322–23, 333, 344n, 365, 372.

Charlestown, [Ohio]
April 15th, 1859

Mr. Editor: [1]

The fourth of April being the day for the election of township officers in Charlestown, and feeling that I had a right to vote notwithstanding my dark complexion, I went to the polls and offered my vote, which was rejected. I insisted on my right to vote, but in vain. One of the judges being absent, I waited until he returned; then I went back and offered my vote again, which occasioned considerable discussion, in which the bystanders generally took part, most of whom were opposed to my voting. Some two or three were in favor of it, among whom was Frederick Loomis. I claimed that I was a citizen of the United States, and had been a resident of Charlestown over one year, and that there was nothing in the statute to prohibit me from voting, which says that all white male citizens over the age of twenty-one *may* vote, but does not say that colored ones shall not. It also says that minors, and persons that had been convicted of a heinous crime, should not vote. I told them that I was not among these minors, nor these criminals, and insisted on my right to vote, until I obtained it.

Democracy, which had vigorously opposed it in the discussion, then walked off cursing and swearing as though it was greatly insulted. It afterwards concentrated itself in the person of one Dr. Heath, a man who stands indicted by the Grand Jury for selling liquor by the dram and thus spreading misery and crime broadcast through community. This Dr. Heath entered a criminal prosecution against Frederick Loomis, claiming in his affidavit that Mr. Loomis had aided, assisted, and abetted in procuring an illegal vote, knowing it to be such. The affidavit was filed before Justice Selby. It is due to the justices of Charlestown, Ravenna, and Freedom to say that none of them would so lower their dignity as to issue a warrant, consequently the matter was tried before Mr. Selby of Paris. The parties met on the 13th. John L. Ranney, of Ravenna, appeared for the State, and O. P. Brown, of the same place, for the defendant. Mr. Ranney rose and made a statement, to which Mr. Brown replied that he thought that the Union would survive, although a negro had voted in Ohio.

The witnesses on the part of the State were examined (ten in number), four of whom knew nothing about it, and the other six swore that they heard Mr. Loomis say that he believed that I had as good a right to vote as he had, and that there was nothing in the State to prevent it; such he expressed as his candid opinion. This was all that the State proved. Mr. Brown said as the State had failed to prove his client guilty of the charges set forth in the affidavit, he should present his evidence, and make a motion that his client be discharged. He made the opening plea with much earnestness and ability. He said that this case had no precedent on record, and that it was one of great importance. When Mr. Brown took his seat, Mr. Ranney rose and made a lengthy plea. He took off his coat, gesticulated furiously, and cried at the top of his voice, "nigger, dark, black nigger," and "black, dark nigger; black as the ace of spades," &c., &c., also abusing defendant and defendant's counsel. Much of his argument was more indicative of a street loafer, than a member of the bar.

He finally took his seat, when Mr. Brown rose and made a lengthy and able plea. Mr. Loomis was, however, bound over to court in the sum of three hundred dollars, for his appearance to answer to a criminal charge, because he simply expressed his opinion.[2] This is freedom of speech in Ohio! Hurrah for Charlestown Democracy!

They next quietly informed me that I would have to keep quiet, or I would be the next victim. I am thankful for the information, but must inform them that their threats are not sufficiently alarming to induce me to obey, although they have Squire Selby, and the State of Ohio—a patriotic firm—with the army and navy, with bristling bayonets, great openmouthed cannons, thousands of armed men, captains, majors, and generals. I guess they will conquer, but conquer who? not the Mexicans, nor the Brighamite Mormons.[3] Well, then, who is it? A colored man in Charlestown, Portage County, Ohio, who stands armed with the statute of Ohio, and a determination to insist upon his rights, notwithstanding the established custom of past years. So come on with your forces, for being quiet is no part of my mission.

The excitement rages high in Charlestown, and we feel like singing, "There is a good time coming, boys,"[4] for the present gapings and contortions of Democracy is certainly indicative of its death. While we regret that Mr. Loomis is thus arraigned, we are glad that there has been something done that will bring the mean men to the surface, where they will be visible to the naked eye, for they only need to be seen to be despised, and to be heard to draw upon themselves the just contempt of a Christian people. Yours, respectfully,

W. J. WHIPPER[5]

Anti-Slavery Bugle (Salem, Ohio), 23 April 1859.

1. Benjamin Smith Jones (1812–1862), a Philadelphia-born Quaker, became a Garrisonian abolitionist in the mid-1830s. Settling in Ohio in the early 1840s, he cooperated with black leaders, lectured for the Western Anti-Slavery Society, and participated in the underground railroad. Jones edited the *Anti-Slavery Bugle* with his wife, Jane E. Hitchcock Jones, from 1845 to 1849; he returned as editor in January 1859 and remained in that position until the paper's 1861 demise. *Lib*, 24 October 1862; Merrill and Ruchames, *Letters of William Lloyd Garrison*, 3:517, 4:564; *NECAUL*, 29 October 1836 [1:0724]; *NASS*, 7 April 1855 [9:0526]; *ASB*, 20 August 1859 [11:0939]; Douglas A. Gamble, "Moral Suasion in the West: Garrisonian Abolitionism, 1831–1861" (Ph.D. diss., Ohio State University, 1973), 308–56, 451–65.

2. Several local whites encouraged Whipper to cast his ballot. One of them, a farmer named Frederick F. Loomis (1825–?) expressed his opinion to the election judges that Whipper should be allowed to vote. Because of this action, Dr. Theodore F. Heath (1828–?), a prominent physician in nearby Cuyahoga Falls, who had recently been indicted for violating Ohio's liquor law, charged Loomis with abetting an infraction of state election statutes prohibiting black suffrage. After officials in Charlestown, Ravenna, and Freedom townships refused to hear the case, Loomis was tried on 13 April 1859 before Justice of the Peace Thomas B. Selby (1800–?), in nearby Paris Township. John L. Ranney (1815–1866) of Ravenna, a Democratic candidate for Congress the year before, argued the state's case. Attorney Oliver P. Brown (1817–1864) appeared in Loomis's defense. A leading Republican, he had recently served as mayor of Ravenna (1853–55) and in the Ohio state senate (1856–58). Brown was "highly gifted as a popular speaker" and publicly championed the antislavery and temperance movements. After hearing testimony and the arguments of the attorneys, Selby bound Loomis over on $300 bond to appear before the county court of common pleas later in the month, where he was acquitted. U.S. Census, 1850; *ASB*, 14 May 1859; William Cumming Johnson, *List of Voters in Portage County, Ohio* (n.p., 1985), 31, 43; *A Portrait and Biographical Record of Portage and Summit Counties,*

Ohio (Logansport, Ind., 1898), 311–12; *Combination Atlas Map of Portage County, Ohio* (Chicago, Ill., 1974), 23, 142; *History of Portage County, Ohio* (Chicago, Ill., 1885), 340–42, 541, 845.

3. Whipper refers to those members of the Church of Jesus Christ of Latter-day Saints (commonly referred to as Mormons) who trekked westward during 1846–48 under the leadership of Brigham Young. Settling near the Great Salt Lake in present-day Utah, they attempted to establish their own semi-independent state named Deseret. This Mormon desire for political autonomy, combined with official aversion to their polygamist practices, nearly led to armed conflict with occupying federal troops during 1857–58. Leonard J. Arrington and Davis Bitton, *The Mormon Experience: A History of the Latter-day Saints* (New York, N.Y., 1979), 83–169.

4. Whipper quotes from the poem "The Good Time Coming" by Scottish poet and journalist Charles Mackay. It first appeared in Mackay's *The Lump of Gold, and Other Poems* (1856).

5. William James Whipper (1834–?) was the son of black abolitionist William Whipper. Born and reared in Pennsylvania, he settled near Charlestown, Ohio, as a young man and became active in the antislavery movement. Whipper chaired local meetings, organized protests against the Ohio black laws, and served as an agent of the Ohio State Anti-Slavery Society. In January 1861, he participated in the attempted rescue of Sara Lucy Bagby, one of the last runaway slaves returned from the North under the Fugitive Slave Law. Shortly thereafter, he moved to Detroit, where he clerked and read law in an attorney's office. Whipper was a leading figure in the 1863 state convention of Michigan blacks and helped coordinate its campaign to have the word "white" struck from the state constitution. He enlisted in the Thirty-first U.S. Colored Troops in March 1864 and saw action in Texas during the latter months of the Civil War.

Whipper settled in South Carolina at the end of the war. One of the first three blacks admitted to the bar in the state, he established a thriving law practice—first in Charleston, then in Columbia—and gained a reputation for his talented legal mind. He was the only black named to a commission to revise the state's legal code during the early years of Reconstruction. In 1868 Whipper bought a rice plantation near Beaufort. From this base, he became one of the leading figures in the statewide Republican party organization. He was a delegate to the 1868 state constitutional convention, served three terms in the state legislature, and edited several Republican journals, including the *Beaufort Times*. Whipper advocated a variety of humanitarian reforms, fought for the regulation of labor contracts to better protect black workers, and encouraged the development of black businesses.

Both friends and opponents respected Whipper's talent. Even Ben Tillman, a virulent racist, called him the "ablest colored man" he had ever known. But his penchant for drinking, gambling, and extravagant spending hampered his career and destroyed his family life. In 1875 his profligate behavior cost him an appointment to the Charleston circuit court. It eventually led to his estrangement from his second wife, Frances A. Rollin, and their four children—who included social reformer Ionia Rollin Whipper and distinguished actor Leigh Whipper. After serving as the probate judge of Beaufort County from 1882 to 1888, Whipper was defeated in a controversial election and jailed for refusing to leave office.

Despite the vicissitudes of his career, he remained politically powerful and chaired the Republican state executive committee through the 1880s. One of six black delegates to the 1895 state constitutional convention, Whipper watched in horror as the gathering stripped his race of the very political rights he had fought for during Reconstruction. Richard P. McCormick, "William Whipper: Moral Reformer," *PH* 43:45n (January 1976); Gerri Major, *Black Society* (Chicago, Ill., 1976), 105–6, 177–78, 195; *ASB*, 20 November 1858, 14 May, 20 August 1859, 2 February 1861; Cheek and Cheek, *John Mercer Langston*, 373–74; *WAA*, 7 March 1863; Certificate of Military Enlistment for William J. Whipper, 2 May 1890, RG 94, Adjutant General's office, U.S. Colored Troops, DNA; Joel Williamson, *After Slavery: The Negro in South Carolina during Reconstruction, 1861–1877* (Chapel Hill, N.C., 1965), 330–31, 333; Robert H. Woody, *Republican Newspapers in South Carolina* (Charlottesville, Va., 1936), 22; Thomas Holt, *Black over White: Negro Political Leadership in South Carolina during Reconstruction* (Urbana, Ill., 1977), 161, 165, 221, 241; Arthur L. Gelston, "Radical versus Straight-Out in Post-Reconstruction Beaufort County," *SCHM* 75:229, 234–35 (July 1974).

3.
Samuel Ringgold Ward to G. W. Reynolds
7 May 1859

Proslavery and antislavery advocates looked to Jamaica as an experiment in emancipation, each seeking evidence to support their assumptions about black readiness for freedom. The proslavery press cited the declining profitability of the plantation economy and the poverty among former slaves as proof that emancipation was a failure—that slaves were incapable of making a successful transition to free labor. Black abolitionists offered another explanation. Samuel R. Ward presented his assessment in a 7 May 1859 letter to G. W. Reynolds, the editor of the Franklin (N.Y.) *Visitor*. Ward, a former slave from Maryland who had settled in Jamaica in 1855, wrote that the island's economic problems resulted from poor judgment and mismanagement by the sugar planters; their difficulties, he observed, derived more from the lingering influence of slavery than from the changes wrought by emancipation. In an ironic twist, Ward concluded that it was the white planters, not the slaves, who were "utterly disqualified to endure the shock of freedom." Ripley et al., *Black Abolitionist Papers*, 1:407–11n; Green, *British Slave Emancipation*, 99–161.

Kingston, Jamaica
May 7, 1859

My Dear Sir:

You can scarcely conceive how delighted I was to receive two copies of your *Visitor*.[1] You are the first and only American editor who has thus exhibited a kind remembrance of me since I came to this island in November 1855.

Having resided here now three years and a half, I can say something about my adopted country. If you will, I shall say it through your columns, hoping that I may, at least, interest a few of your juvenile readers. If you think otherwise, why, there is your wastepaper basket, and yonder is the kitchen fire!

While our laws make no distinction as to the color of Her Majesty's subjects, still, for reasons which existed anterior to emancipation, it is common to speak of our different classes as white, colored, and black. The first are Anglo-Saxons, of course (or rather that amalgamation of English, Welsh, Irish, Scotch, Dutch, Dane, Norman, Saxon, and what not, which is called Anglo-Saxon); the second is made up of the several shades betwixt white and black; and the last are, like myself, unmistakable negroes.[2]

From the time of Cromwell's conquest of the island[3] to the era of emancipation, all power was in the hands of the whites, but the colored class received more or less education—some, indeed, were thoroughly educated, and, inheriting more or less the property of their white fathers, they were qualified, at the time of emancipation, to enter into the full enjoyment of equal rights, privileges, and powers with the whites.

The blacks were denied all education, and almost all means of moral and intellectual enlightenment. Such are always the demands of slavery. As a consequence, emancipation found the negroes, as a whole—there were a few in the towns in better circumstances—as ignorant, and almost as much heathens, as when they were first stolen from Africa. Since emancipation, something has been done for the education of the negroes, and more for their evangelization, but when I tell that out of a revenue of 200,000, our sapient Legislature doles out but 3,000 a year for the education of the entire population—400,000—you will not be surprised to learn that the education of the masses goes on but slowly.

But as I wish to speak more in detail of the different classes of our population, I will begin with

THE WHITE CLASS

The number of whites now in the island, it is said, does not exceed 5,000. I believe the estimate to be pretty correct, though no census has been taken for several years. When the slaves were freed, the great majority of the planters were vexed and dissatisfied. But few of them can forgive the British Government for "taking away their property," albeit they received 20,000,000 by way of compensation. Indeed, within a few days, I have seen two articles in the *Planter's Organ*,[4] the "standard" newspaper, finding fault with the abolition of the slave trade and the shortening of the apprenticeship. From 1838 until this day, they have done their utmost to prove themselves "ruined" by the Emancipation Act.[5] Having told this untruth until they themselves believe it, they have conformed their actions to it. Hence, among other things, they have abandoned their estates and gone to reside in England, or those who have remained a few years, and acquired fortunes, have sold out and retired from the island, taking every farthing of their money, leaving the island, of course, poorer by so much as they abstracted from it. None are louder than they in crying out about the poverty and "ruin" of Jamaica, *since* and *because of* emancipation. It were just the same as if your farmers of Delaware county should abandon their farms, allowing them to grow up with thorns and briars, and, selling everything they owned, should move *en masse* to Albany, because laborers in Delaware were free. Search the world over and you will find no set of farmers who have so verily played the fool as our Jamaica planters of the old regime.

But are they "ruined"? Farms here produce from 5 to 20 net profits. No matter what be the cost of cultivation, such are the net profits. But labor can be had *in any abundance* at what is the minimum rate in En-

gland, nine shillings per week—in England, where farms net but from 1
to 3 the acre—yet these men are "ruined" for the want of labor because
of emancipation! Suppose Delaware county farmers were suddenly, by
some legislative enactment, placed in such circumstances that it would
cost them, with proper implements of husbandry, $15, without them $30
the acre to raise crops, which would bring from $140 to $150 the acre,
who among them would be "ruined" except such as, from their laziness
deserved to be "ruined"?

But did emancipation "ruin" our planters? From the reign of the second Charles to this of the first Victoria,[6] Jamaica planters have been "ruined" about as often as your "fire-eaters"[7] have dissolved the Union and
your "doughfaces" saved it. Every alteration in the tariff, down to that of
1846, has "ruined" them.[8] Emancipation is only one of a hundred causes
of their "ruin," themselves being witnesses. They are "ruined" now for
the want of heathen semi-slaves, from India, to work at sixpence per day.[9]
Their devil is named Legion. Yet they hold onto their estates. While I
write, I am looking at two thousand acres of wilderness within two miles
of town, belonging to a "ruined" planter in England, who will not sell
"for love nor money." When I was in England, an old planter, who takes
snuff, said to me:

"Mr. Ward, I have an estate, the coffee from which would bring the
highest price in this market, if I merely mentioned that it was from such
a place. Now I do not get the value of" (helping himself and offering me
his snuffbox) "a pinch of snuff from it."

"What will you take for that estate?" said I.

"O!" he replied, "I would not part with it at any price."

A friend invited me to dine with him at the west end of London, and
meet a young Jamaica proprietor who had been "ruined" by emancipation. I went. We met. As I was just about to sail for this island, the con-
versation easily turned to the subject of the West Indies.

"My uncle," said my young acquaintance, "has three estates in Jamaica, which are a dead loss to him, and his expenses upon them are far
greater than what he receives from them."

"Then why does he not sell them?"

"Because he does not wish to."

Bear in mind that these planters, "ruined" as they are, live just five
thousand miles from their plantations. Could Delaware county farmers
make their acres profitable at such a distance?

Besides, a Jamaica planter, unlike a Delaware county farmer, cannot
work; a hoe-handle, a plow-handle, must never enter his precious hands.
No, no! Like Dives, he must dress in purple and fine linen, and fare sumptuously every day;[10] and the negro, or somebody else, must work cheap
enough to give him such profits as will afford living like a lord, and not
like a farmer—otherwise he is "ruined."

Now, the plain truth is, our Jamaica planters were utterly disqualified to endure the shock of freedom. They had unfitted themselves to live and thrive among a free peasantry, and to this day they have not adapted themselves to the circumstances into which they were brought one-and-twenty years ago. They are not men of improvement, of progress, of enterprise, of freedom, of sterling, sturdy Anglo-Saxon manhood.

At the same time, if such farmers and farming as abound, happily, in Otsego and Delaware, were introduced here, our wilderness would literally blossom as the rose—Jamaica would be what God made it to be—a paradise.

The white people of this island are, as you may judge from what I have already said, exceedingly like the Southern whites of your continent, and therefore very unlike those of the North. Slaveholders everywhere, as a rule, being in a false, unmanly, dependent position, acquire habits of effeminacy. Hence, whether they descended from, or were connected with, the most robust, the most vigorous, the most enterprising of the human race, or not, they are sure to present, in body, and mind, and morals, the saddest specimens of weakness and degeneracy. Not even the natural depravity of our fallen nature is so fruitful a source of untold and universal mischief, when left free, as the most refined, the best regulated age, and the most religious state of society wherein despotism is an admitted and a recognized element. If no other reason could be given, the following would be abundantly conclusive—viz.: Slavery cramps, cripples, obscures, enervates, and, in the end, destroys the religious principle, just as it blasts, withers, scorches every other thing of "lively report"—every other thing upon which the welfare of society depends.

Hence it is, that slaveholding communities, left to themselves, present none of the features—much less of the achievements—of such enterprise as digs canals, constructs railroads, builds colleges, sends forth missionaries, and evangelizes unenlightened districts. Slavery never overspread Lancaster with spindles, nor Lowell with looms.[11] No, no; the cotton of Carolina has to be carried by *freemen* thousands of miles to be converted by *freemen* into decent fabrics. Your Southern post-roads must be kept in repair by Northern money. And but for the incessant flow of Northern mind and Northern capital to the South, your Southern States, because slave States, would never have a decent college, nor even an academy like yours of Franklin.[12] Enervation, imbecility, and an absence of all enterprise—indeed, an unfitness to breathe the very air of freedom—is the result of slavery upon the dominant class. Just this will you see in every part of this island. We have, growing spontaneously all around us, in the greatest abundance, some half-dozen different fibrous plants. We could make from them paper enough to supply half the world. We import *wrapping paper* for our shops.

Yonder lies a mountain seven miles in length; it is a mass of limestone within, while its surface abounds in wood, fit to burn the stone into lime. Yet, except at the penitentiary, we have not a decent limekiln within thirty miles of us. We are farmers. But we import pork, lard, butter, hams, cheese and—save the mark!—Indian corn!! So it was in the days of slavery—so it is now.

Here is the city of Kingston, with 36,000 inhabitants. We have forty miles of streets in this city. There is not a quarter of a mile of sidewalk or any other decent footpath in the whole city. You must go to Aleppo or Bagdad[13] before you shall see such barbarous streets and lanes as ours for driving. We have a natural descent, from north to south, from the mountain to the bay; yet no other gutters or channels for the drainage of our town, than such as the water finds for itself. Our mails are carried on mules' backs; ninety-nine one-hundredths of our population never saw a stagecoach, for the very good reason that there never was one on the island. We have a railway running sixteen miles into a bush, and a telegraph line, recently established, betwixt Kingston, the metropolis, and Spanishtown, the capitol. One hour's travel in the first-class carriages would fatigue you as much as a drive of five miles over a corduroy road, in a lumber wagon. The trade around the island is committed entirely to sailing vessels of the smallest size, rudest construction, and slowest movement. We depend upon the United States for almost everything.[14] We need, therefore, the advantage of steam communication with you. The matter has been before two sessions of Parliament. In the first, the proposition was negotiated; in the second, it was carried, and that was all. Nothing whatever was done—nothing will be done.

These are the people whom emancipation "ruined." * * * *[15]

[Samuel R. Ward]

Weekly Anglo-African (New York, N.Y.), 20, 27 August 1859.

1. G. W. Reynolds, an abolitionist, established the Franklin (N.Y.) *Visitor* in May 1855 and continued to edit and publish the paper through the end of the decade. The weekly journal was "devoted to the advocacy of Moral Reform." *FDP*, 11, 18 May 1855 [9:0633, 0651].

2. According to the census of 1861, some 3.1 percent of the Jamaican population was white, 78.5 percent was black, and 18.4 percent belonged to the racially mixed group referred to as "Coloured." George W. Roberts, *The Population of Jamaica* (Cambridge, England, 1957), 65.

3. In May 1655, an English naval expedition under Admiral William Penn forced the outmanned Spanish garrison at Kingston, Jamaica, to surrender control of the island. This was part of a larger design by Oliver Cromwell, the lord protector of England, to seize Spanish colonies in the Caribbean. Clinton V. Black, *The History of Jamaica*, 3d ed. (London, 1983), 34–36.

4. Ward refers to the *Colonial Standard and Jamaica Despatch*, a daily paper published from 1849 to 1895 in Kingston, which functioned as the voice of the planter class. Frank Cundall, ed., *Bibliographia Jamaicensis* (New York, N.Y.,

1902), 62–63; Philip D. Curtin, *Two Jamaicas: The Role of Ideas in a Tropical Colony, 1830–1865* (New York, N.Y., 1970), 57–58, 263–64n.

5. Ward refers to the Emancipation Act of 1833, which abolished slavery in the British Empire.

6. Charles II was king of England from 1660 to 1685. Queen Victoria was the constitutional monarch of Britain and the British Empire from 1837 until 1901.

7. "Fire-eaters" was a popular term used to describe radical southern politicians who agitated for secession during the 1850s.

8. Prior to 1826, Jamaican sugar imported into Britain enjoyed a sizable price advantage because of the high tariffs placed on sugar grown elsewhere. But changes in the sugar duties in 1826 and 1836 lessened Jamaica's advantage by extending protections to sugar growers throughout the British Empire. The Sugar Duties Act of 1846 ended all protections. Douglas Hall, *Free Jamaica, 1838–1865: An Economic History* (New Haven, Conn., 1959), 37, 40, 82–85.

9. Between 1845 and 1847, Jamaican colonial authorities imported more than forty-five hundred contract laborers from India to alleviate a shortage of cheap labor on the sugar plantations. The government abandoned the experiment in 1847 because of the expense involved. Despite political pressure from the planters, no more Indian workers arrived on the island until 1860. Hall, *Free Jamaica*, 53, 89–90, 272.

10. "Dives" is the name usually ascribed to a rich man mentioned in a New Testament parable. According to Luke 16:19, he "was clothed in purple and fine linen, and fared sumptuously every day."

11. Lancaster, England, and Lowell, Massachusetts, were leading centers for the manufacture of raw cotton into finished cloth. Nearly half of the cotton factory spindleage in the world was located in Lancaster and surrounding Lancashire. The mechanized looms in the mills at Lowell produced more cotton goods than any other city in the United States. D. A. Farnie, *The English Cotton Industry and the World, 1815–1896* (Oxford, England, 1979), 180; Anthony Howe, *The Cotton Masters, 1830–1860* (Oxford, England, 1984), 1–2.

12. Ward refers to the Delaware Literary Institute in Franklin, New York, which was founded in 1839 and continued to operate into the twentieth century. George F. Miller, *The Academy System in the State of New York* (Albany, N.Y., 1922; reprint, New York, N.Y., 1969), 88.

13. Aleppo and Baghdad were major cities in the Ottoman Empire during the nineteenth century.

14. The Jamaican economy was based primarily on sugar and coffee production during the nineteenth century. As a result, most food staples and manufactured goods used on the island were imported from Britain and the United States. Hall, *Free Jamaica*, 164, 179.

15. These asterisks appear in the original document.

4.
Thomas Hamilton to John Jay
27 May 1859

The black press struggled under adverse conditions throughout the antebellum years. Limited numbers of subscribers, meager advertising revenues, and competition with white antislavery papers kept black journals on the brink of ruin. What successes the black press achieved resulted in large part from the initiative, skill, and sacrifice of its editors. Thomas Hamilton's efforts to sustain the *Anglo-African Magazine* followed in the tradition of such black journalists as Philip A. Bell, Mary Ann Shadd Cary, Samuel E. Cornish, and Frederick Douglass. An experienced editor, Hamilton launched the monthly literary journal in January 1859 as a forum for black intellect and talent. To keep it afloat, he appealed to wealthy white abolitionists John Jay and Gerrit Smith for a loan, offering his life insurance policy as collateral. Hamilton's attempt to generate funds for this ambitious project underscored the tenuous nature of the black press and the tenacious spirit of its editors. Despite his appeals, financial problems forced Hamilton to cease publication of the magazine in March 1860. Ripley et al., *Black Abolitionist Papers*, 3:32–34; Penelope L. Bullock, *The Afro-American Periodical Press, 1838–1909* (Baton Rouge, La., 1981), 59–60.

Off[ice] of Anglo African
Magazine[1]
New York, [New York]
May 27, [18]59

Dear Sir:

Permit me to make as briefly as possible a statement in regard to my operations, and to submit for your consideration a proposition. On the 18th of Nov. last I obtained from the Mass. Life Ins. co.[2] a life policy for $2000 with the view of getting a loan on it to commence the publishing business (making negro literature the main feature), and on the 15th Dec. with less than $10 capital I issued the prospectus of the Anglo African Magazine, the first no. of which appeared on the 3rd of Jan. and it has been published regularly ever since. Finding that our Agents needed some publication to sell with the Mag. I got out a fresh edition of Dr. Cheever's famous production "Dea. Giles's Distillery[,]" a copy of which I herewith send you. Being desirous of publishing two or three other works, the productions of colored authors, and purchasing a quantity of the Life of Touissant L'Ouverture and other saleable publications that can now be had on good terms,[3] I find it necessary to resort to my original plan for raising the means, and thinking of no one more likely to aid me in my earnest efforts to accomplish an object from which great good to my people will result than yourself, would therefore ask of you a loan of $500 for two years, taking my Life Policy as security.

Hoping that you will pardon the liberty I have taken in asking this great favor, and will give the matter your careful consideration, I am Yours respectfully,

Tho. Hamilton[4]

Jay Family Papers, Rare Book and Manuscript Library, Columbia University, New York, New York. Published by permission.

1. The *Anglo-African Magazine*, which first appeared in January 1859, was a monthly journal of black literature and social criticism. Thomas Hamilton, its publisher, hoped the magazine would demonstrate black ability, survey the history and contemporary condition of blacks in the United States, expose racism and its effects, and serve as a forum for black talent. He assembled an impressive list of contributors—including J. W. C. Pennington, James McCune Smith, Mary Ann Shadd Cary, Frances Ellen Watkins Harper, James T. Holly, and Frederick Douglass—whose essays on a wide range of social, scientific, and literary topics expressed the vitality of northern black culture. He also reviewed recent works by black authors and published excerpts of Martin R. Delany's novel, *Blake: or, The Huts of America*. Despite Hamilton's efforts to keep the *Anglo-African Magazine* afloat, it never achieved financial viability, failed to pay its contributors, and ceased publication in March 1860. Bullock, *Afro-American Periodical Press*, 57–63.

2. Hamilton obtained a policy from the Massachusetts Mutual Life Insurance Company, which was founded in 1851 in Springfield, Massachusetts. In 1855 the company opened a New York City office. Richard Hooker, *A Century of Service: The Massachusetts Mutual Story* (Springfield, Mass., 1951), 1–35.

3. Hamilton sold reform books and tracts through the agents of the *Anglo-African Magazine* and at his 48 Beekman Street office in New York City. Among these works was his own reprint of George B. Cheever's *The Dream, or the True History of Deacon Giles's Distillery and Deacon Jones's Brewery* (1859), an 1835 temperance tract that had prompted rioting and a successful libel suit in Salem, Massachusetts, at the time of its original publication. Although the full extent of Hamilton's reprint venture remains unclear, he distributed other books by black authors, including Solomon Northrup's *Twelve Years a Slave* (1853), Frederick Douglass's *My Bondage and My Freedom* (1855), and William C. Nell's *The Colored Patriots of the American Revolution* (1855). Hamilton also hoped to sell copies of *The Life of Toussaint L'Ouverture, the Negro Patriot of Hayti* (1853), a strident and largely accurate depiction of the Haitian revolutionary by English Unitarian clergyman John Reilly Beard. *WAA*, 23 July 1859; *DAB*, 4:48–49; C. L. R. James, *The Black Jacobins: Toussaint L'Ouverture and the San Domingo Revolution*, 2d ed. (New York, N.Y., 1963), 389.

4. Thomas Hamilton (1823–1865) and his brother, Robert Hamilton (1819–?), were leading black journalists of the Civil War era. The sons of William Hamilton, an early black abolitionist of local and national repute, they spent their lives in the New York City area. Growing up in the Hamilton household,

they were attracted to the antislavery movement and the reform press at an early age. Thomas Hamilton's newspaper career began in 1837 as a carrier for the *Colored American*; he later worked as a bookkeeper and mailing clerk for the *New York Evangelist*, the *National Anti-Slavery Standard*, and the *Independent*. In October 1841, he began the *People's Press*, a weekly antislavery journal known for its militant sentiments. Under his editorship—and with the later assistance of Robert Hamilton, Samuel I. Wood, and John Dias—the paper consistently called for independent black antislavery efforts and questioned black allegiance to the United States. Following the *Press*'s 1843 demise, he became a bookseller and distributed black, antislavery, and temperance literature. Robert Hamilton, a talented musician, taught for several decades in the local black public schools. He also served as chorister of the Zion Baptist Church and often performed at local reform meetings and First of August celebrations.

While Thomas Hamilton preferred to work behind the scenes, Robert earned renown during the 1840s and 1850s as an articulate spokesman for black concerns. An outspoken critic of the African colonization movement, he fought efforts by the New York State Colonization Society to obtain state funding for its Liberian settlement program. He participated in the statewide campaign for equal suffrage, attending strategy sessions, circulating petitions, and representing local interests at black state conventions. He also organized and led Brooklyn's black division of the Sons of Temperance. His reputation grew after he helped to mobilize local resistance to the Fugitive Slave Law of 1850. He served on the Committee of Thirteen, a watchdog organization formed to represent the interests of blacks in New York City and Brooklyn. In 1853 he was elected to the New State Council of the Colored People. Three years later, he sat on the executive committee of the American League of Colored Laborers, which was established to encourage and assist black businesses and vocational education throughout the North.

The Hamilton brothers are best remembered as the founders and editors of the *Weekly Anglo-African* and the *Anglo-African Magazine*. Thomas published the *Magazine*, a monthly journal of black literature and social criticism, from January 1859 to March 1860. He founded the *Weekly Anglo-African* in July 1859 and made it into the foremost black newspaper of the Civil War era. Robert assisted him with this enterprise. In March 1861, Thomas sold the paper to the Haytian Emigration Bureau and relinquished the editorship to George Lawrence, Jr., the bureau's local agent. It soon became the *Pine and Palm*. Five months later, Robert established another *Weekly Anglo-African* with the financial support of James McCune Smith. He forged it into a strident opponent of emigration and a defender of black rights. He continued to edit the paper until after the war, expanding its role and circulation and making it the official organ of the National Equal Rights League and an unflinching advocate of Radical Reconstruction. Both brothers recruited for black regiments, and Robert made several tours of Union-occupied areas of the South during the latter years of the war. On these occasions, Thomas again performed many of the editorial chores. He died of typhoid fever in November 1865. Robert suspended publication of the *Weekly Anglo-African* the following month, and after attempts to revive it failed, he disappeared from public life. Although he died during the early years of Reconstruction, his sons, Robert H. Hamilton and William G. Hamilton, continued the family's journalistic tradition, working with the *Anglo-African, Elevator* and several general New York City papers. Bullock, *Afro-American Periodical Press,* 55–63; U.S. Census, 1850; *ESF,* 14 July 1865, 8 June 1872 [15:1038]; *CA,* 21 November 1840, 27 June, 30 October, 20 November 1841 [3:0711, 0748, 4:0064, 0078, 0273, 0278, 0308–9]; *New York City Directory,* 1842; Benjamin Quarles, *Black Abolitionists* (London, 1969), 225; *Lib,* 1 April, 13 May 1842, 24 May 1844 [4:0812]; *NSFA,* 8 December 1842 [4:0494]; I. Garland Penn, *The Afro-American Press and Its Editors* (Springfield, Mass., 1891), 55, 83–88, 364–66; *NASS,* 16 July 1846 [5:0249]; Carleton Mabee, *Black Education in New York State: From Colonial to Modern Times* (Syracuse, N.Y., 1979), 121–23; *WAA,* 19 November 1859, 28 March, 5 December 1863, 5 March, 16 July 1864, 26 August 1865 [16:0125]; *PP,* 25 May, 10 August 1861, 6 February 1862; *PF,* 10 October 1850; *FDP,* 26 February 1852, 9 December 1853 [7:0440]; *ASB,* 27 July 1856 [10:0258]; George Walker, "The Afro-American in New York City, 1826–1860" (Ph.D. diss., Columbia University, 1975), 219, 221; Dean, *Defender of the Race,* 35–36, 117–18n; *Brooklyn City Directory,* 1858–66; *G,* 2 January 1886.

5.
Essay by William J. Watkins
5 September 1859

Black abolitionists viewed politics through issues, not political parties. The opportunity to advance abolitionism mattered more to them than party principles or platforms. By the late 1850s, most black leaders recognized the Republican party as their best hope of assailing slavery through the political process. Although attracted by the Republicans' pledge to halt the spread of slavery in the territories, blacks openly criticized the party's limited antislavery commitment and its unwillingness to challenge the constitutional rights of slaveholders. Blacks worked to insure the party's electoral success, while chastising it for its shortcomings. William J. Watkins, a journalist, lecturer, and suffrage activist, was hired by the party in 1858 to rally blacks behind the ticket in New York state. But his duties did not prevent him from censuring the party for equivocating on the issue of slavery. Watkins's 5 September 1859 essay in the *Weekly Anglo-African* called on blacks to work within Republican ranks to promote a stronger antislavery position, arguing the view commonly held by black abolitionists that there were only two political parties in the United States—those "who are *opposed* to slavery; and . . . those who are *in favor* of this accursed evil." *NASS*, 9 October 1858 [11:0385]; Philip S. Foner and George E. Walker, eds., *Proceedings of the Black State Conventions, 1840–1865*, 2 vols. (Philadelphia, Pa., 1979–80), 1:99–100; Walker, "Afro-American in New York City," 207–9.

Rochester, [New York]
Sept[ember] 5th, 1859
THE ISSUE PLAINLY STATED

When Senator Seward, in his celebrated Rochester speech, alluded in distinct and emphatic terms to the irrepressible conflict between freedom and slavery, a wolfish howl leaped from the brazen throats of menstealers and their confederates all over the land.[1] This illustrious statesman was denounced and vilified from one end of the Union to the other. Republicans began to inquire whether or not the prospective President of these United States had not, by his rather too bold utterances, placed himself in a dilemma from which he could not be extricated in time for election. Some of the weak-kneed brethren declared that Mr. Seward did not mean what he said, and in some *"respectable"* quarters an evisceration of the speech was attempted.

Now, this was a very foolish course for white men, with all their boasted Anglo-Saxon wisdom, to pursue. Negroes—Timbuctoo negroes[2]—

could have done no worse. Senator Seward said nothing in that speech that had not been said a thousand times before by Gerrit Smith, Wm. Lloyd Garrison, and a host of others; nothing that was not known to be true; nothing that would have been clutched at in an ordinary speech, and at an ordinary time. Everyone knows that the virulent denunciation of which the Senator was the victim was manifested for political effect. The gentleman, however, survived, and will, in all probability, astonish the "natives" on the 4th of March, 1861, by a few more "irrepressible" assertions of a similar character in his inaugural.[3] Ye who have tears to shed—honest tears, tears which are orthodox, tears which are constitutional—prepare to shed them now.

We live in perilous times. No dodging *now* among the Delphic oracles[4] of bygone years—no mental reservations—no equivocations. When Cromwell was about to sit for his portrait,[5] the artist suggested to him that an omission of the scars which disfigured him would enhance the comeliness of the picture. "*Paint me as I am!*" he indignantly replied. The artist did so, and a faithful picture—one that represented Cromwell as he was—was the result. So should the issue of the hour, the true principle involved in the present conflict, be portrayed before the people. What is it? Let it be plainly stated.

Politically speaking, there are but two parties in this Republic. These are composed, on the one hand, of all those at the North or at the South, at the East or at the West, who are *opposed* to slavery; and on the other of all those who are *in favor* of this accursed evil.

Those who view the present aspect of affairs with a philosophic eye, and whose range of vision enables them to descry, as in the strong, clear light of eternity, the resistless undercurrent which is upheaving the foundation of our already diseased and tottering body politic, will find no difficulty in discerning and assenting to the correctness of this plain and positive declaration. These are aware of the fact that the question of the life or the death of liberty in these United States is the all-absorbing, aye, the test question in American politics.

On the part of a majority of those composing the Democratic party there is manifestly a disposition to ignore *the real* issue and substitute some other in its stead. A few bold and determined Southern politicians do not hesitate to avow their intention and determination to make slavery the "God over all and blessed forevermore"[6] of this Republic, and to compel men and women everywhere in the land to fall down and worship this incarnation of crime and corruption—this embodiment of death and damnation. But a majority of the slavocratic party, both at the North and at the South, hesitate, for certain reasons, to make this candid avowal.

The Republican party is likewise fearful, but for a different reason, of a presentation of the only true, living, real issue. With a few exceptions, its leaders are not disposed to take the broad, consistent, and righteous ground of opposition to the *existence* of slavery. They prefer to harp upon the popular and palatable doctrine of its non-extension to the Territories of the Republic, and appear exceedingly afraid of the imputation of Abolitionism. They talk of the slaveholders' rights "*under the Constitution*" about as flippantly as the slaveholders do themselves. But if they were to interpret the Constitution in accordance with the well-established rules of legal hermeneutics, they would discover that the slaveholder, *as such*, has no more rights under the Constitution than he has under the shadow of the protecting wing of Heaven—has no more right, *as a slaveholder*, a human flesh-jobber, to live in the Republic, under a Constitution ordained to "*establish justice*" and "*secure liberty*," than a wolf has in the cradle of a newborn babe.

Now, the Republican party is the only political party in the land in a position, numerically speaking, to strike a deathblow to American slavery—such a blow as will send it staggering to hell. It is important, then, that it assumes a defensible and right position in the present conflict. It does not deserve success, it ought not expect success, while in the occupancy of any other position. I believe it will take such a position. It *must* do so in order to preserve its distinctiveness, its vitality. If it is not right, let Abolitionists strive to make it right. More can be accomplished on the part of those who are right, by going into the party and renovating and revolutionizing it, than by standing outside harping upon a beautiful theory, but without the requisite machinery to crystalize it into practical life. If slavery is to be voted down in this Republic, it becomes a question of arithmetic. We must look at this question from the standpoint of common sense, and the single rule of three.

It is my opinion, founded upon actual observation, that the masses of the people of the free States are prepared to act in the right direction. I have just returned from a lecturing tour of four weeks through the Western part of this State and Vermont. What do I find to be the fact? That the most radical utterances which escaped my lips were the most cordially received and the most loudly applauded. Now, to those who reason from premise to conclusion, this is a fact truly significant—a fact which means something.

Let us, then, I repeat it, state the issue boldly. Let the people thoroughly understand it, and they will *lead their leaders*, and lead them on to victory. We all know that such are the dissimilarity and consequent antagonism existing between liberty and slavery, that there never can be a reconciliation between them. While slavery is allowed to exist anywhere in the land, it *will* develop itself; it *will* breathe its pestilential breath into the nation's lungs; it *will* cast its murky shadow across the path of liberty. Such is its nature. Just so with the spirit of liberty. It is jealous of its honor. The envenomed hatred of its antagonist cannot fail to be most cordially reciprocated. The two must be in perpetual conflict, in conformity with their respective instincts, in accordance with the changeless laws of their being.

If these premises be correct, the irresistible deduction is that the present bitter conflict must result in the extinction of the one or the other; and the fallacy of any theory based upon the assumption of the possibility of harmonizing their belligerent instincts is as clearly demonstrated as the plainest mathematical problem. Either the two become one—one in nature, one in sympathy, one to all intents and purposes—or one or the other must cease to exist.

Then how absurd it is to attempt to ignore the issue! And how inconsistent the endeavor to oppose the further spread of slavery, while refusing to assume the position of hostility to its continuance in a certain locality! One might as well expect to thaw an iceberg by the cold, pale beams of a winter moon, as to expect to promote the peace and happiness of the nation by such a course of procedure.

The dividing line is already drawn. It may not be perceptible to the contracted and darkened vision of the mere politician; but no great truth ever evolved in the world of matter or of mind stands out in more bold relief than this: *He who is not for slavery is against it, and must take his station accordingly.* Under which king, Benzonio—which king?[7]

WM. JAMES WATKINS

Weekly Anglo-African (New York, N.Y.), 24 September 1859.

1. On 25 October 1858, while politicking for Republican candidates in Rochester, New York, Senator William H. Seward made one of the most controversial speeches of his political career. He branded the struggle between northern free labor and southern slavery as an "irrepressible conflict," declaring that the United States would one day become entirely slaveholding or entirely free. Seward urged voters to defeat Democratic politicians, whom he cast as tools of the slaveholders, and to confound the "betrayers of the constitution and freedom." The speech was praised by Republican papers and the reform press, but conservatives throughout the country denounced it as a call for the federal government to end slavery by force. Glyndon G. Van Deusen, *William Henry Seward* (New York, N.Y., 1967), 193–94.

2. Watkins refers to blacks in the city of Timbuktu, an early center of Islamic learning and commerce on the northern Niger River in West Africa.

3. Although William H. Seward's "irrepressible conflict" speech reduced his popularity, many Republicans in New York state expected him to win the Republican presidential nomination in 1860. Van Deusen, *William Henry Seward*, 215–16.

4. Delphi, the site of a venerated shrine in ancient Greece, was believed to be the source of a powerful oracle.

5. Watkins recounts an incident involving Oliver Cromwell, the lord protector of England from 1651 to 1658, that is recorded in Horace Walpole's massive *Anecdotes of Painting in England* (1762).

6. Watkins paraphrases Romans 9:5.

7. Watkins borrows from part 2, act 5, scene 3 of *Henry IV* (1600) by William Shakespeare. When country justice Robert Shallow informs another character that he is acting under the authority of the king, he is asked, "Under which king, Bensonian? Speak or die." "Bensonian" was a term used in Elizabethan England to refer to someone lacking in skill or knowledge. Watkins recounts the scene to note that the time had come for antebellum Americans to indicate whether their allegiance was to slavery or freedom.

6.
Henry Highland Garnet to Simeon S. Jocelyn
14 September 1859

Destroying slavery was but one element of a black agenda devoted to
the social, political, economic, moral, and religious elevation of all
Afro-Americans. Over three decades, missionary work, moral reform,
and racial uplift remained central features of black abolitionism. During
the 1840s, the Union Missionary Society, the black predecessor to the
American Missionary Association, promoted outreach to the black poor
in New York City and to fugitive slaves in Canada West. In 1856 Henry
Highland Garnet persuaded the AMA to finance similar efforts among
New York City blacks. Three years later, he again requested AMA support "for the especial purpose of improving the moral, and intellectual
condition of the people of color." Garnet's 14 September 1859 letter to
AMA official Simeon S. Jocelyn demonstrates the extent to which black
clergymen viewed their missionary labors as part of their abolitionism.
Garnet requested funds to expand his religious and educational mission
to the local black community, confident that such efforts would "show
[our] love to the slave at the South, by doing good to the free black man
at the North." In November he made a second plea to Jocelyn for support, arguing that his labor was "within the legitimate work of the association—and a most promising use of its funds." The AMA granted
his request. Clara Merritt De Boer, "The Role of Afro-Americans
in the Origin and Work of the American Missionary Association,
1839–1877" (Ph.D. diss., Rutgers University, 1973), 41–44, 196–98.

> 52 Laurens St[reet]
> New York, [New York]
> Sept[ember] 14, [18]59

Dear Brother: [1]
　It was my intention to have been present at the monthly meeting of the
Home Department of the Ex. Com. of the Association,[2] but I unfortunately supposed it was to take place today the (14th) and I was not ap-
prised of my mistake until I received your notice, and that, as is often the
case came two hours after the hour of meeting. It will not be in my power
to be present today as I have a funeral of one my congregation to attend—who leaves behind him a family of seven, all of whom are decided
Roman Catholics.
　For years my mind has been turned upon the great importance, and
necessity, of doing more in our Anti Slavery organizations for the free
people of Color in in the non slaveholding States. Especially does there
seem to be need of labour among our people in large towns, and cities.

New York, and the towns along the banks of the Hudson offer a field that is already ~~white~~ ripe for the harvest. We need, earnest, Godly, men, to go forth <u>among the people</u>—to sympathise with them, and teach them in divine things and to encourage them in everything that belongs to well ordered living. I am confident that such agencies would do much to inspire the confidence of our friends and to stop the mouths of our enemies, who say with no small degree of truth, and consistency "Show your love to the slave at the South, by doing good to the free black man at the North." This, so far as I know is the unniversal opinion of the intelligent, and working men among the colored people, and very many white men are of the same way of thinking. Mr Garrison expressed this opinion in my hearing last Spring. And the New York Col Soc[3] would to day employ such an agency in this city if any competent colored man would accept it. It is only extreems that can meet, and here we have it.

When three years ago I returned from Jamaica I was promised your assistence in undertaking such a work, but in one brief year I was sumarily, and with a very little ceremony sent adrift,[4] and my plans, and hopes were dashed to pieces, and the stroke was felt by others, even as much as it was by myself. But forgetting past mistakes to which we are all liable, let us act wisely for the future. While we tell the Colored people to do their duty, and strong efforts are made to bring us up to it, let it not be forgotten that wherever we live, <u>there</u> is missionary ground, and will be such till slavery and its many evil effects are done away. I am yours truly in the cause of our Labour,

Henry Highland Garnet

American Missionary Association Archives, Amistad Research Center, Tulane University, New Orleans, Louisiana. Published by permission.

1. Simeon S. Jocelyn (1799–1879), an engraver and the pastor of a black Congregational church in New Haven, Connecticut, fought for black rights and the abolition of slavery. He helped found the American Missionary Association in 1846 and, with Lewis Tappan and George Whipple, gave energy and purpose to the organization. As corresponding secretary of the AMA after 1853, he traveled extensively and helped raise operating funds. In 1864 he resigned his post because of ill health. Merrill and Ruchames, *Letters of William Lloyd Garrison,* 1:120–21, 2:536; Joe M. Richardson, *Christian Reconstruction: The American Missionary Association and Southern Blacks, 1861–1890* (Athens, Ga., 1986), 6, 8, 87–88, 90, 95–96.

2. Garnet sat on the executive committee of the American Missionary Association during 1847–48 and again from 1856 to 1860. The nonsectarian AMA was founded in 1846 to promote Christian abolitionism, and membership was open to all nonslaveholding Christians. Under the leadership of treasurer Lewis Tappan and secretaries Simeon S. Jocelyn and George Whipple, the association supported mission work and Christian education among nonwhite peoples in the Americas and abroad during the antebellum period. By 1855 it had missions in

Egypt, Siam, Haiti, Jamaica, and West Africa, in addition to more than one hundred domestic or home missions in North America. After the Civil War, the AMA became the largest supporter of freedmen's education in the South, founding and funding over five hundred black schools and colleges. Johnson, "American Missionary Association"; Richardson, *Christian Reconstruction*.

3. Garnet refers to the New York State Colonization Society.

4. After serving as a missionary in Jamaica for three and a half years, Garnet returned to the United States for health reasons by February 1856. That September he was called to the pulpit of the First Colored Presbyterian Church in New York City. Both the American Home Missionary Society and the American Missionary Association appointed him a missionary at that time and provided $250 stipends to sustain his ministry, but neither renewed this support after the first year. Schor, *Henry Highland Garnet*, 125–30, 144, 148n; De Boer, "Afro-Americans in American Missionary Association," 197–98.

7.
Editorial by Thomas Hamilton
5 November 1859

On 16 October 1859, John Brown and a force of twenty-one men seized
the federal arsenal at Harpers Ferry, Virginia, and attempted to incite a
slave revolt. Although the raid failed, it riveted national attention on
slavery and revealed a deep chasm between North and South. Since the
early 1830s, abolitionists had warned that a violent fate awaited southerners if they continued to perpetuate bondage; southerners responded
by burning antislavery literature and denouncing antislavery advocates
as incendiaries. Writing in the *Weekly Anglo-African* three weeks after
the raid, Thomas Hamilton corrected those southerners who blamed
abolitionists for provoking John Brown's attempted rebellion. Hamilton
argued that antislavery advocates posed no threat to the peace and security of the South, but rather had prevented insurrections by fostering the
hope among slaves that they would eventually be freed, thereby acting as a "great safety valve; the escape pipe through which the dangerous element incident to slavery found vent." The real threat, claimed
Hamilton, came from the South's own stubbornness. Stephen B. Oates,
To Purge This Land with Blood: A Biography of John Brown (New
York, N.Y., 1970), 320–24.

MISTAKES OF THE SOUTH
Passions often blind men to such an extent that they not unfrequently
fail to attend to their real interest; often to the neglect of an examination
even into the cause of the hindrances that lie in their way. This is true as
often of communities as of individuals, and the South in this respect have
made a gross mistake.

Let us instance at this time but two points. First: that within the last
quarter of a century a change has been coming over the Northern mind
in relation to the subject of slavery, and of this change the South has
persistently refused to make herself acquainted. She has persistently refused to study, read, or even look into what is termed Abolition publications and Abolition journals. She has persistently shut out all true knowledge and all proper light on the subject, and is today almost utterly
ignorant of both the nature and extent of this great change—of the great
advance made in the North on the subject of man's rights. Her servile
press and paid menials among us here in the North, for the sake of their
tenure of office, have not been true to the South in that matter. So far
from stating the real facts as they have transpired, and keeping the South
posted, they have deceived her by continually stultifying the truth, and
when the Harpers Ferry affair occurred, it was like a shock of thunder.

The South was not prepared for such a result, nor has she even yet opened her eyes to the depth or extent of sympathy felt in the North for the poor oppressed bondmen in their midst, notwithstanding the hard endeavors of the political and otherwise interested journals to gloss it over.

These journals may talk as they will, laws for the punishment of offenders and those who dare to meddle with the peculiar institution may be summarily executed, severe codes for the government of the poor slave may be enacted and rigorously enforced, demagogues may plot and politicians may plan, notwithstanding all, the feeling that justifies American slavery is daily growing less and less, and rests today on an incalculably feebler foundation than ever before.

But to our second point: the Abolitionism of the North, so far from making war on, or being inimical to, the institution of slavery, has been for the last twenty years its great safety valve; the escape pipe through which the dangerous element incident to slavery found vent. Prior to the existence of Abolitionism, outbreaks and fearful mutterings and threatenings among slaves were frequent, and to the holders alarming. We can all trace back to the Nat Turners and the Denmark Veseys and others. The slave then had no hope of deliverance except by his own right arm, however feeble. He saw no farther, and believing that it was appointed to man but once to die, felt willing to do so or gain his liberty. But when Wm. Lloyd Garrison and his coadjutors enunciated the doctrines of Abolitionism and non-resistance, the slave received a new and far different lesson. He was taught to hope for deliverance—to feel that he was not forsaken nor forgotten—that some day, however distant, he would be enabled to lay aside his chains and be acknowledged a man. With these hopes the fierceness of his passions subsided, he agreed to submit to his hard task, and thenceforth up till recently but little comparative discontent has been manifested, and yet the South to this important fact has also been blind. Let them henceforth read Abolition journals and Abolition literature—let her read our paper,[1] if she wishes to study and know the signs, and interpret the meaning thereof, as they appear in the moral horizon of the North, be wise.

We shall recur to this subject again.

Weekly Anglo-African (New York, N.Y.), 5 November 1859.

1. The *Weekly Anglo-African*, the leading black newspaper of the Civil War era, began publication in July 1859 under the direction of owner-editor Thomas Hamilton. The New York City–based weekly aggressively championed black cultural independence and a strong racial identity. It conveyed the vitality of local black society, while at the same time dozens of correspondents from Boston to San Francisco regularly reported on black life and culture in their communities, giving the journal a truly national appeal. Hamilton's vigorous editorials ex-

plored a variety of black concerns, ranging from slavery and secession to the racial implications of Darwinian thought. By late 1860, the paper displayed an increased interest in emigration movements, opening its columns to news and arguments favoring Haitian and African settlement. In March 1861, Hamilton sold the *Anglo-African* to the Haytian Emigration Bureau and relinquished the editorship to George Lawrence, Jr., the bureau's local agent. Under the latter's guidance, the paper became the bureau's official organ and was soon rechristened the *Pine and Palm*.

In August 1861, another *Weekly Anglo-African* filled the void created by the loss of its namesake to the Haitian movement. Edited by Robert Hamilton—the former editor's brother—and financed in large part by James McCune Smith, the new journal was outspoken in its criticism of emigration and its defense of black rights. As the Civil War progressed, the *Anglo-African* assumed an expanded set of responsibilities. Its offices doubled as a recruiting station for black soldiers; its columns served as a communications link for displaced fugitive slaves, families separated by slavery and the war, and the lonely black soldier. Hamilton reprinted letters from blacks involved in every aspect of the war effort. Black correspondents provided firsthand accounts of Union military campaigns. In mid-1865 Henry Highland Garnet became editor of the *Anglo-African*'s southern department and supplied news from the war-torn region. Through the diligent work of subscription agents and local soldiers' aid societies, the paper circulated widely among black troops in the field and southern blacks in Union-occupied territory. Despite the threat of financial insolvency in 1862 and damages sustained in the 1863 draft riots, Hamilton continued to issue the paper through December 1865, when publication was suspended. In its final year, the *Anglo-African* became the official organ of the National Equal Rights League and an aggressive advocate of Radical Reconstruction. Penn, *Afro-American Press and Its Editors*, 83–88; Martin E. Dann, ed., *The Black Press, 1827–1890: The Quest for National Identity* (New York, N.Y., 1971), 26, 55, 57, 78, 83–84, 261, 265; *WAA*, 23 July, 29 October 1859, 17 March, 29 December 1860, 16 March, 27 April, 17, 24 August, 21 December 1861, 6 April 1862, 9 January 1864, 12 August, 3 September, 7 October 1865 [11:0877, 12:0163–64, 0579, 13:0486–87]; *PP*, 25 March 1861; Miller, *Search for a Black Nationality*, 170, 242–43, 279; Dean, *Defender of the Race*, 35–36, 117–18n.

8.
Editorial by Thomas Hamilton
19 November 1859

Black abolitionists defended John Brown's actions. They spoke openly and approvingly of slave rebellion as the legitimate act of an oppressed people—"I believe in insurrections," John S. Rock declared. Convinced that only armed resistance could topple the institution of slavery, black leaders increasingly discussed the efficacy and morality of violence. Addressing the new mood in the black community, black leaders announced that since "tyrants and slaveholders have no right to live," their deaths would be acts of "purest benevolence." In a 19 November 1859 editorial, Thomas Hamilton defended the violent action of Brown and his men as a righteous effort to "restore stolen chattels to their proper owners—to restore the slave to himself." *WAA*, 21 January, 16 March 1860, 6 April 1861 [12:0494, 0562–63, 13:0440].

BREAKING INTO A STATE

Burglary is common, but State-breaking is a new species of crime; and in the case to which we shall make reference, some have been bold enough to term it a virtue. Men generally build, bolt, and bar their houses so strongly that access is had with great difficulty; and it is only in extreme cases, or by the most expert operators, that it is at all accomplished. But the business of State-breaking, it seems, is less difficult, though we fear far more hazardous.

John Brown, with twenty-one other men, a few days ago threw himself against the State of Virginia, and in less time than it has taken to record the fact, the partition gave way, and he had and held possession of the Ancient Dominion and the terror-stricken chivalry, chattels, and all, and might have continued possession but for the interference of Uncle Sam's troops.

But the idea of State-breaking for the purpose of winning what might be won, is, considering the hazard, novel indeed. The burglar breaks into your house that he may despoil you of your goods; but if we were asked why John Brown broke into Virginia, we would answer that it was to bring stolen goods out of the State—goods and chattels that had been stolen and pent up there for past centuries. Surprising as it may seem, it is, nevertheless, true.

Here in the North we spend annually thousands of dollars in catching and punishing thieves and robbers and preventing theft and robbery, but John Brown and his few surviving followers, on the other hand, are to forfeit their lives[1] for simply endeavoring to obtain and restore stolen chattels to their proper owners—to restore the slave to himself.

What right has Virginia to protect theft and punish with death him, who from honest conviction, attempts to do just what every law of right, humanity, and true religion prompted him to do? What is done with every other species of interest? But it may be claimed that the law stands in the way of all such attempts. What right has Virginia to legalize theft in the bodies and souls of men?

It was a mercy to the property holders that the stolen goods—the chattels—did not tumble out of the State through the breach made by Brown; and as one step makes way for another, it may occur to the chattel some day to make a breach for itself. With an eye to this possibility, and to the future John Browns who may take it into their heads to again break into the State of Presidents, or some other of her sister States, it is now proposed that the whole South wheel out of the Union, and build a strong barrier against future inroads, and set up for itself. Out of what materials this barrier is to be erected, does not appear.

Whatever may have been the mistakes of the South on the subject of Slavery, and the sentiments of the North upon it, we scarcely think it will be guilty and blind enough to add the fatal error of disunion to the already fearful list,[2] or accept from their Northern toadies advice leading to that end.

For a State like Virginia, whose partition gives way at the slightest touch of the arm of an aged man, whose inhabitants become frantic before the face of twenty-two men, whose military finds it impossible to collect their scattered senses sufficiently to make even a semblance of resistance, whose authorities lose all dignity, and the sleep of whose inhabitants has been murdered—to talk of wheeling out of the Union is one of the thinnest and meanest scarecrows ever set up before the eyes of sensible men.

Weekly Anglo-African (New York, N.Y.), 19 November 1859.

1. During 2–9 November 1859, the county circuit court at Charlestown, Virginia, sentenced John Brown, Edwin Coppoc, Shields Green, John A. Copeland, Jr., and John E. Cook to death for their role in the Harpers Ferry raid. All five were executed by hanging the following month. Two other conspirators—Aaron Stevens and Albert Hazlett—were convicted in February 1860 and hung the following month. Oates, *Purge This Land with Blood*, 308–9, 326–29.

2. Despite Hamilton's suggestion to the contrary, the Harpers Ferry raid strengthened secessionist sentiment in the South. Many in the region viewed John Brown's action as a conspiracy between abolitionists and Republicans and feared that it would be the first of a wave of slave revolts. Considering this anxious state, continued compromise between North and South seemed impossible. During the months that followed, a growing number of southern editors and politicians called for secession from the United States. Oates, *Purge This Land with Blood*, 320–24.

9.
John A. Copeland, Jr., and the Harpers Ferry Raid

John A. Copeland, Jr., to John A. Copeland, Sr., and Delilah Copeland
26 November 1859

John A. Copeland, Jr., to Addison M. Halbert
10 December 1859

Five blacks fought beside John Brown at Harpers Ferry. Dangerfield Newby and Lewis S. Leary were killed in the raid; Osborne P. Anderson escaped to Canada West; Shields Green and John Copeland, Jr., were captured, tried, and sentenced to die—they watched the construction of their own gallows from the cell that they shared with white conspirator Albert Hazlett. For northern blacks, the actions and fate of these five men represented the ultimate antislavery sacrifice. Copeland, a nephew of Leary's from Oberlin, Ohio, informed abolitionists that he and the others had joined Brown to "liberate a few of my poor & oppressed people." The following two letters, to his parents and to a white friend at Oberlin, were among the last Copeland wrote prior to his 16 December 1859 execution. They discuss the raid and reveal the private thoughts of a man prepared to give his life for his antislavery convictions. *WAA*, 19 November 1859, 6, 13, 27 April 1861 [12:0230, 13:0440, 0465]; Benjamin Quarles, *Allies for Freedom: Blacks and John Brown* (New York, N.Y., 1974), 87–88, 96–97, 109–10, 120, 133–42.

Charlesto[w]n, V[irgini]a
Nov[ember] 26, [18]59

Dear father & mother:[1]

I now take my pen to address you for the first time since I have been in the situation that I am now in. My silence has not been occasioned by my want of love for you but because I wished to wait & find what my doom would be. I am well at this time & as happy as it is possible to be under the circumstances. I received your kind and affectionate letter, which brought much consolation to me, & the advice that you have therein given me. I thank God I can say I have accepted, & I have found that consolation which can only be found by accepting & obeying such advice.

Dear father & mother, happy am I that I can now truthfully say that I have sought the Holy Bible & have found that everlasting Life in its holy advice, which man can from no other source obtain. Yes, I have now in

1. John A. Copeland, Jr.
Courtesy of Library of Congress

the eleventh hour sought for & obtained that forgiveness from my God, whose kindness I have outraged nearly all my life.

Dear Parents, my fate so far as man can seal it, is sealed, but let not this fact occasion you any misery; for remember the <u>cause</u> in which I was engaged; <u>remember it was a holy cause,</u> one in which men in every way better than I am, have suffered & died. Remember that if I must die, I die in trying to liberate a few of my poor & oppressed people from a condition of servitude against which God in his word has hurled his most bitter denunciations, a cause in which men, who though removed from its direct injurious effects by the color of their faces have already lost their lives, & more yet must meet the fate which man has decided I must meet. If die I must, I shall try to meet my fate as a man who can suffer in the glorious cause in which I have been engaged, without a groan, & meet my Maker in heaven as a christian man who through the saving grace of God has made his peace with Him.

Dear Parents, dear bros & sisters; miserable indeed would I be if I were confined in this jail awaiting the execution of the law for committing a foul crime; but this not being the case, I must say (though I know you all will feel deeply the fate I am to meet), that I feel more deeply on acc't of the necessity of myself or any other man having to suffer by the existence of slavery, than from the mere fact of having to die. It is true I should like to see you all once more on the earth, but God wills otherwise. Therefore I am content, for most certainly do I believe that God wills everything for the best good, not only of those who have to suffer directly, but of all, & this being the case I beg of you not to grieve about me. Now dear Parents I beg your forgiveness for every wrong I have done you, for I know that I have not at all times treated you as I ought to have done. Remember me while I shall live & forget me not when I am no longer in this world. Give my love to all friends. There are some little matters that I would give most anything to have settled & made right. There have been misrepresentations of things which I have said; & if I can I shall correct them.

Oh brothers, I pray you may never have to suffer as I shall have to do: stay at home contentedly, make your home happy not only to yourselves but to all with whom you may be connected.

Dear Brothers & sisters, love one another, make each other happy, love, serve & obey your God, & meet me in heaven. Now, dear father & mother, I will close this last—or at present I think last letter—I shall have the pleasure of writing to you.

Good-bye Mother & Father, Goodbye brothers & sisters, & by the assistance of God, meet me in heaven. I remain your most affectionate son,

John A. Copeland[2]

2. Shields Green, John A. Copeland, Jr., and Albert Hazlett in the Charlestown jail

From Frank Leslie's Illustrated Newspaper, 10 December 1859

Charl[e]sto[w]n, [Virginia]
Dec[ember] 10, 1859

Friend Halbert:

I take my pen in hand to pen you a few lines in answer to you kind and affectionate letter of 5 Inst. Well dear friend I am happy that I can say to you that I am well both in body and mind. It is true that placed in the position that I am that it seams almost impossibleposable to me to pen such a letter as I should. But although this is the case I will try to pen a few words of perhaps som interest to you.

Your kind letter came to me brining such pleasure as a traverler across som drery deasert fells when for many long day he has been traverling with out water to quench his thirst and to cool his parched lips. I was happy to hear that you was well and that though I am confined within the walls of a prison and that under sentence of death,[3] you have not forgoten me. Ah friend it is true that I am now under sentence of death and to die on the 16 of this month (perhaps before you get this) and that upon the gallows and for doing what. For what crime or crimes am I to die[;] is it for som black-hearted crime[;] is becaus I have dipt my hand in my brothers blood that I am to be hung[,] not at all for what is it this. It is for obeying the commandment of my God in doing to others as I would have them so to me.[4] It is because I have attemp[ted] to assist in giving that freedom to at least a few of my poor and enslaved bretherin who has been m[o]st foully and unjustly deprived of theire liberty, by cruel and unjust men[;] but you are too well acquainted with all of the circumsances for me to add more on this point.

You ask me to tell you about poor Leary.[5] Well when we came to the Ferry we were put under the command of Cap. Kagi,[6] and [went] about half a mile from the bridg where Capt. Brown and men were station, to Halls Rifle Factory this was about 10:00 at night. We remain there untill Monday about 2:00 P. M. waiting for orders from Cap Brown without receiving any. At this we discovered that we were being surrounded by men when Capt Kagi give orders to leave the building and make our escape which we accordingly did, but upon getting in the road at the back of the building we had occupied we discoverd that our only means of escape if any was to cross the Shanadore river, which we tride to cross. On entering the river we turned and fired one round at those who had by this time opened a hot fire on us from all sides. Cap Kaga succeeded in getting about two thirds across the river when he was shot through the head and sank beneath the river. The who[le] fire of at leas fifty men was then turned upon poor Leary and myself, when he being next to Kaga and in advace of me about ten or twelve feet saw that thier their was no posable chance of escape. Left us[,] got up on a ston that was near him and turned his back upon those on the side of the river to which we were tring escape and was shot through the body but did not die untill about ten hours afterward as I have been informed since I have been in Jail. At the time Leary was shot I had succeeded in getting above som stones that were just above me in the river and floated down behind them and remain so untill through (o. c.) thot we were all killed[,] when som of them coming out to wher Leary was discovred me and I was puled upt out of the water with the ~~inten~~ intetion of being shot, but som of those that were present not being such cowards as to want to kill a man when disarmed and a prisener prevented it.[7] When I was taken to Charstown Jail wher I have been ever sence as you full well know. And now dear frie[n]d I will write but a few words more and I must close my correspondence with you forever on this earth[,] which I hope may resume in heaven where it will never be again interrupted. Give my love to you Mother and brothers and my Mother father and to all my friends So Goodby dear friend, serve you God and meet me in heaven. I remain yours now and forever,

John A Copeland.

Oswald Garrison Villard Collection, Rare Book and Manuscript Library, Columbia University, New York, New York. Published by permission.

1. John Anthony Copeland, Sr. (1808–1894), and Delilah Evans Copeland (1809–1888) were born and reared near Raleigh, North Carolina. Although initially a slave, John was freed at age seven by the will of his deceased master; Delilah was born to free black parents. They married in 1830 and settled in Raleigh, where John followed the carpentry trade. In 1843 they left North Carolina for Oberlin, Ohio. John again found work there as a carpenter and joiner, preached to local Methodist congregations, and enlisted in local efforts to aid and protect fugitive slaves. During the Civil War, he served as cook for the chaplain of the Fifty-fifth Ohio Regiment. The Copelands reared six children of their own—Henry, John, Jr., William, Frederick, Sarah, and Mary— and adopted two orphans, Catharine Ann Smith and Reuben Turner. Two followed their father's example and joined the Union army during the Civil War. Henry became a lieutenant in the black First Kansas Volunteers. Turner enlisted in the Third U.S. Colored Heavy Artillery. Another son, William, was active in Arkansas politics during Reconstruction. William E. Bigglestone, *They Stopped in Oberlin: Black Residents and Visitors of the Nineteenth Century* (Scottsdale, Ariz., 1981), 50–52, 202–3; Cheek and Cheek, *John Mercer Langston*, 351, 356, 378n; OE, 21 December 1859, 4 January 1860 [12: 30307, 0410].

2. John Anthony Copeland, Jr. (1834–1859), one of five black participants in John Brown's Harpers Ferry raid, was born in Raleigh, North Carolina. In 1843 his free black parents—John and Delilah Copeland—moved the family to Oberlin, Ohio. The younger Copeland acquired a thorough primary education in the public schools of Oberlin. From 1851 to 1855, he studied each winter and spring in the preparatory department at Oberlin College, while working the remaining

months with his father as a carpenter and joiner. He then taught at a black school in Logan County, Ohio, over the next two winters.

Living in Oberlin, an abolitionist stronghold, Copeland soon found himself attracted to the antislavery movement. After attending several meetings and being deeply moved by the tales told by visiting fugitive slaves, he became an enthusiastic and outspoken member of the Oberlin Anti-Slavery Society. Skilled with weapons, he increasingly advocated the use of violence to protect runaway blacks. On 13 September 1858, Copeland used force to help free escaped slave John Price in the famous Oberlin-Wellington rescue. Indicted for his involvement in the action, he may have accompanied Price to Canada West. Although technically a fugitive from justice, Copeland soon returned home. The following year, he was recruited by his uncle, Lewis S. Leary, for the Harpers Ferry raid. Wounded and captured in the raid, he was quickly indicted for treason, murder, and inciting slaves to revolt. He was executed on 16 December 1859 in Charlestown, Virginia. Although Brown's effort failed, Copeland viewed it as a necessary "prelude" to emancipation. He died convinced that he had fought in a "noble cause." *PP*, 20 July 1861; Bigglestone, *They Stopped in Oberlin*, 50−52; Cheek and Cheek, *John Mercer Langston*, 329, 352, 355−59; Nat Brandt, *The Town That Started the Civil War* (Syracuse, N.Y., 1990), 94, 103−4, 118, 129, 242−45; *OE*, 21 December 1859 [12:0307].

3. Fearing that the presence of John A. Copeland, Jr., John Brown, and the other captured raiders might provoke mob violence in Harpers Ferry, officials quickly hurried them by train eight miles southwest to Charlestown, Virginia, where they were incarcerated in the county jail under heavy guard. Copeland and his cellmate, Shields Green, were found guilty of murder and conspiring with slaves to foment insurrection. On 9 November 1859, despite the able defense provided by a young Boston attorney named George Sennott, they were sentenced to hang on 16 December. Oates, *Purge This Land with Blood*, 307; Quarles, *Allies for Freedom*, 109−10, 133−37.

4. Copeland alludes to an admonition of Jesus that "whatsoever ye would that men should do to you, do ye even so to them." It is popularly known as the Golden Rule. Matt. 7:12; Luke 6:31.

5. Lewis Sheridan Leary (1836−1859) was born in Fayetteville, North Carolina, to free black parents Matthew and Juliette Leary. After settling in Oberlin, Ohio, in 1856, he found work as a harnessmaker and briefly attended Oberlin College. Involved in local antislavery activities, Leary spoke at meetings of the Oberlin Anti-Slavery Society and probably participated in the 1858 rescue of fugitive slave John Price at Wellington, Ohio. He married Mary S. Patterson, the daughter of a prominent Cleveland black. Convinced that "men must suffer in a good cause," he was among the first recruits for John Brown's planned invasion of Harpers Ferry and persuaded his nephew, John Copeland, Jr., to join the scheme. Leary died in the raid. *DANB*, 388; "The Leary Family," *NHB* 10: 27−29 (November 1946); Cheek and Cheek, *John Mercer Langston*, 355−59; Brandt, *Town That Started the Civil War*, 79, 149, 242.

6. John Henry Kagi (1835−1859), an articulate Ohio schoolteacher, met John Brown in 1857, while serving as a western correspondent for the *New York Tribune* and several other journals. Over the next two years, the "intensely moral and idealistic" Kagi was Brown's most trusted ally, fighting with free-state forces in

Kansas and helping to plan the Harpers Ferry raid. Kagi, who claimed his death would be "worth the sacrifice," was killed during the attack. Oates, *Purge This Land with Blood*, 219–23, 243–44, 246, 267, 296; Richard J. Hinton, *John Brown and His Men* (New York, N.Y., 1894), 451–66.

7. Capturing the federal armory at Harpers Ferry, Virginia, was a primary objective of John Brown's raid. The armory, which was located near the confluence of the Potomac and Shenandoah rivers, consisted of an arsenal, the U.S. Musket Factory, and Hall's Rifle Works. Late on the evening of 16 October, after securing the arsenal and the engine house at the entrance to the musket factory (near the Potomac toll bridge), Brown led several raiders half a mile westward and seized the rifle works. He left John H. Kagi and John A. Copeland, Jr., to guard the complex; they were later joined by Lewis S. Leary. The three men remained there until militiamen and armed local citizens stormed the rifle works the next afternoon. Kagi was killed, and Leary was mortally wounded while attempting to escape across the Shenandoah and died the following morning. Copeland's rifle failed to fire and he was easily captured. Although his captors threatened to lynch him, they were dissuaded by a local physician. Oates, *Purge This Land with Blood*, 288–96; Merritt Roe Smith, *Harpers Ferry Armory and the New Technology: The Challenge of Change* (Ithaca, N.Y., 1977), 156–57, 338–39; Quarles, *Allies for Freedom*, 97.

10.
Resolutions by William Lambert
Presented at the Second Baptist Church
Detroit, Michigan
2 December 1859

Militancy peaked in northern black communities in the weeks following the Harpers Ferry raid. John Brown and his men were hailed as martyrs to the antislavery cause. The date of Brown's execution was proclaimed a day of mourning, calls went out for fasting and prayer, businesses closed their doors, and the *Weekly Anglo-African* framed its pages in black. Meetings were held in every black community across the North to commemorate the man and his motives. An interracial throng of three thousand jammed Boston's Tremont Temple to honor Brown. In Hartford, Connecticut, three men scaled the state capitol dome and shrouded a statue of liberty in black. On the evening of 2 December 1859, blacks in Detroit crowded into the city's Second Baptist Church to pay homage to Brown. In the course of the meeting, William Lambert—a local leader who had helped raise men and money for Brown's venture—read the following "declaration of sentiment and resolves," which reflected the new militant mood among northern blacks. After he finished, the gathering sang the "Marseillaise Hymn," then adjourned amid shouts of "On, on to battle—we fear no foe!" *WAA*, 3, 10 December 1859; *Lib*, 9 December 1859, 24 February 1860 [12:0508]; Philip S. Foner, *History of Black Americans*, 3 vols. to date (Westport, Conn., 1975–), 3:260; Quarles, *Allies for Freedom*, 125–31.

Whereas, We, the oppressed portion of this community, many of whom have worn the galling chain and felt the smarting lash of slavery, and know by sad experience its brutalizing effects upon both the body and the mind, and its damning influence upon the soul of its victim; and

Whereas, We, by the help of Almighty God and the secret abolition movements that are now beginning to develop themselves in the southern part of this country, have been enabled to escape from the prison house of slavery, and partially to obtain our liberty; and having become personally acquainted with the life and character of our much beloved and highly esteemed friend, Old Capt. John Brown, and his band of valiant men, who, at Harpers Ferry, on the 16th day of October, 1859, demonstrated to the world his sympathy and fidelity to the cause of the suffering slaves of this country by bearding the hydra-headed monster, Tyranny, in his den, and by his bold, effective, timely blow is now causing the whole South to tremble with a moral earthquake, as he boldly and freely deliv-

3. Mobbing of a John Brown meeting in Boston, 1860
From *Harper's Weekly*, 15 December 1860

ered up his life today as a ransom for our enslaved race; and thereby, "solitary and alone," he has put a liberty ball in motion which shall continue to roll and gather strength until the last vestige of human slavery within this nation shall have been crushed beneath its ponderous weight. Therefore,

Resolved, That we hold the name of Old Capt. John Brown in the most sacred remembrance as the first disinterested martyr for our liberty, who, upon the true Christian principle of his Divine Lord and Master, has freely delivered up his life for the liberty of our race in this country. Therefore will we ever vindicate his character throughout all coming time as our temporal redeemer, whose name shall never die.

Resolved, That, as the long lost rights and liberties of an oppressed people are only gained in proportion as they act in their own cause, therefore are we now loudly called upon to arouse to our own interest, and to concentrate our efforts in keeping the Old Brown liberty ball in motion and thereby continue to kindle the fires of liberty upon the altar of every determined heart among us, and continue to fan the same until the proper time, when a revolutionary blast from liberty's trump shall summon them simultaneously to unite for victorious and triumphant battle.

Resolved, That we tender our deepest and most heartfelt sympathy to the family of Capt. John Brown[1] in their sad bereavement, and pledge to them that they shall ever be held by us as our special friends, in whose welfare we hope ever to manifest a special interest.

Weekly Anglo-African (New York, N.Y.), 17 December 1859.

1. John Brown's second wife, Mary Ann Day Brown, and seven of his children—John, Jr. (b. 1821), Jason (b. 1823), Owen (b. 1824), Ruth (b. 1829), Salmon, Annie (b. 1844), and Ellen (b. 1855)—were living at this time. Two sons, Watson and Oliver, had been killed in the Harpers Ferry raid. Oates, *Purge This Land with Blood*, 16–17, 23, 47, 88, 241, 272, 299, 302, 316–17, 340.

11.
Circular by Frances Ellen Watkins Harper for Arkansas
Free Blacks
January 1860

Southern whites recoiled in terror at John Brown's raid. Fearing widespread insurrection, they called for the exile or enslavement of all free
blacks. Arkansas was the first state to act. In November 1859, the legislature ordered free blacks to leave the state by the start of the new year.
As word of the decree spread, Arkansas free blacks packed their belong-
ings and bid good-bye to family and friends in slavery. Some left for the
North, others headed to Memphis or New Orleans, and a few settled in
the West. One group of twelve exiles from Little Rock and the Mississippi River ports of Napoleon and Redfork arrived in Cincinnati on 4
January 1860. Homeless and impoverished, they appealed for compassion and aid. Their "Appeal to Christians Throughout the World,"
which was written by black abolitionist Frances Ellen Watkins Harper,
asked clergymen, politicians, and the press to unite in protest against
this forced winter exodus, which had made them "homeless strangers in
the regions of the icy North." The "Appeal" was initially published in
the Cincinnati *Daily Gazette* and was widely reprinted in the antislavery press, including the *Weekly Anglo-African*. The crisis of the Arkansas exiles reminded northern blacks of the tenuous position of free
blacks in the South. Ira Berlin, *Slaves without Masters: The Free Negro
in the Antebellum South* (New York, N.Y., 1974), 373–77; *ASB*, 4 February 1860; *WAA*, 4, 11 February 1860.

AN APPEAL
TO CHRISTIANS THROUGHOUT THE WORLD
In consequence of a law passed by the Legislature of Arkansas, compelling the free colored people either to leave the State or be enslaved,[1]
we, a number of exiles driven out by this inhuman statute, who reached
Ohio on the 4th of January, 1860, feeling a deep sense of the wrong done
us, make this Appeal to the Christian world.

We appeal to you, as children of a common Father, and believers in a
crucified Redeemer. Today we are exiles, driven from the homes of our
childhood, the scenes of our youth, and the burial places of our friends.
We are exiles, not that our hands have been stained with guilt, or our
lives accused of crime. Our fault, in a land of Bibles and Churches, of
baptisms and prayers, is that in our veins flows the blood of an outcast
race; a race oppressed by power and proscribed by prejudice; a race
cradled in wrong and nurtured in oppression.

In the very depth of the winter, we have left a genial climate of sunny skies to be homeless strangers in the regions of the icy North. Some of the exiles have left children, who were very dear but to stay with them was to involve ourselves in a lifetime of slavery. Some left dear companions; they were enslaved, and we had no other alternative than slavery or exile. We were weak, our oppressors were strong. We were a feeble, scattered people; they, being powerful, placed before us slavery or banishment. We chose the latter. Poverty, trials, and all the cares incident to a life of freedom are better, far better, than slavery.

From this terrible injustice, we appeal to the moral sentiment of the world. We turn to the free North, but even here oppression tracks our steps. Indiana shuts her doors upon us. Illinois denies us admission to her prairie homes. Oregon refuses us an abiding place for the soles of our weary feet. And even Minnesota has our exclusion under consideration.[2] In Ohio we found kind hearts; hospitality opened her doors; generous hands reached out a warm and hearty welcome. For this, may the God of the fatherless ever defend and bless them.

And now, Christians, we appeal to you, as heirs of the same heritage, and children of the same Father, to protest against this gross and inhuman outrage, which has been committed beneath the wing of the American Eagle, and in the shadow of the American Church. We ask you by the love, the pity, and the mercy, in the religion of Jesus Christ, that you will raise your voices and protest against this sin.

Editors of newspapers, formers of public opinion, conductors of intelligence and thought, we entreat you to insert this appeal in your papers and unite your voices against this outrage which disgraces our land and holds it up to shame before the nations of the earth. We entreat you to move a wave of influence, which will widen and spread through all the earth, and roll back and wash away this stain.

Christian mothers, by our plundered cradles and child bereft hearts, we appeal to you and ask your protest.

Christian fathers, by all the sacred associations that cluster around the name father, we appeal to you to swell the tide of indignation against our shameful wrongs.

We appeal to the Church of Christ among all nations, kindreds, tongues, and peoples to *protest* against the inhumanity that has driven us from our homes and our kindred.

Members of all political parties, we ask *your* protest, in the name of a common humanity, against this cruel act of despotism.

Christian Ministers, we appeal to you, in the name of Him who came "to preach good tidings to the meek, to bind up the brokenhearted, to proclaim liberty to the captive, and the opening of the prison to them that are bound,"[3] to lay before your congregations the injustice done us, and the wickedness of a system that tramples on the feeble and crushes out the rights of the helpless.

And we appeal to the God of the fatherless, and the Judge of the widow, that He will remember His word, "Inasmuch as ye have done it unto one of the least of these, ye have done it unto me"; [4] that He will move the hearts of His children everywhere to unite their testimony against this unequalled iniquity that writes "property" on man, that chattelizes the immortal mind, and makes merchandise of the deathless soul. We appeal to Him who does not permit a sparrow to fall to the ground unnoticed to plead the cause of the poor and needy, [5] and set him at rest from him that puffeth at him. [6]

E. A. West,	Redfork,	Desha Co.,	Ark.
A. E. West,	"	"	
Elizabeth T. West,		"	"
Agnes West,		"	"
Landy Waggoner,		"	"
Rachel Love,	Napoleon,		"
Wm. H. Newcomb,	"		"
Henry McGrath,	"		"
Polly Taylor,	Little Rock,		"
Caroline Parker,	"		"
Jane Thomson,	"		"
Nelly Grinton,	"		"

Anti-Slavery Bugle (Salem, Ohio), 4 February 1860.

1. In response to growing political pressure, the Arkansas legislature approved an 1859 act requiring all free blacks to leave the state by 1 January 1860 or face enslavement. Whites in the state had become increasingly alarmed that the continued presence of free blacks would provoke slave insurrection. The expulsion measure proved reasonably effective. Although an 1858 sheriff's census counted 682 free blacks in the state, U.S. Census enumerators found only 144 in 1860. In early 1861, the Arkansas legislature suspended enforcement of the law. Harry S. Ashmore, *Arkansas: A Bicentennial History* (New York, N.Y., 1978), 72; James M. Woods, *Rebellion and Realignment: Arkansas's Road to Secession* (Fayetteville, Ark., 1987), 29.

2. Several northern states passed laws prohibiting further black settlement within their borders during the antebellum period. Three of them—Illinois (1848), Indiana (1851), and Oregon (1857)—incorporated black exclusion provisions into their constitutions. In 1860 the Minnesota legislature considered but defeated a measure that would have barred blacks from coming into the state and required the registration of those already in residence. Leon F. Litwack, *North of Slavery: The Negro in the Free States, 1790–1860* (Chicago, Ill., 1961), 66–72; David V. Taylor, "The Blacks," in *They Chose Minnesota: A Survey of the State's Ethnic Groups*, ed. June Drenning Holmquist (St. Paul, Minn., 1981), 74.

3. The circular quotes from Isaiah 61:1.

4. The circular quotes from Matthew 25:40, the closing verse of a divine admonition to care for the less fortunate in society.

5. The circular alludes to Matthew 10:29. In this verse, Jesus assures his listeners of divine omniscience, noting that since not even a sparrow falls to the ground unnoticed, God is fully aware of the human condition.

6. The circular quotes from Psalms 12:5.

12.
Speech by John S. Rock
Delivered at the Meionaon
Boston, Massachusetts
5 March 1860

Following the Dred Scott decision, William C. Nell organized annual celebrations to memorialize Crispus Attucks and affirm black claims to American citizenship. For many blacks, Attucks's death in the "Boston Massacre" of 5 March 1770 marked the start of the American Revolution and symbolized Afro-American contributions to the nation's history. But after the Harpers Ferry raid, black abolitionists looked for new heroes to represent their changing attitudes toward the antislavery movement and violence. On 5 March 1860, Boston blacks commemorated the ninetieth anniversary of Attucks's death. That evening, amid relics of the Revolution, William Lloyd Garrison, William C. Nell, J. Sella Martin, and John S. Rock spoke to a large gathering at the Meionaon. Rock, a lawyer and antislavery lecturer, noted in the following address that both Attucks and John Brown represented "that potent power, the sword, which proposes to settle at once the relation between master and slave." But he hesitated to "idolize" Attucks, who had given his life in a cause that perpetuated the enslavement of his race. Rock argued that Nat Turner and Brown, with their commitment to freeing the slaves, were far more potent symbols for the "new American Revolution"—the antislavery crusade. James Oliver Horton and Lois E. Horton, *Black Bostonians: Family Life and Community Struggle in the Antebellum North* (New York, N.Y., 1979), 119–20; *Lib*, 16 March 1860.

LADIES AND GENTLEMEN:

I[1] have been invited by my friend, Mr. Nell, to say something to you on the occasion of this, the ninetieth anniversary of the birth of the American Revolution, and that, too, in the face of my recorded opinion that that event was ushered in by the rashness of one of our "noble, but misguided ancestors." If, under the circumstances, I should give you a little plain talk, differing somewhat from that which you have been accustomed to hear, on occasions like this, you need not be surprised. The times require us to speak out. I am free to confess that the remembrance of the details of the event which we are assembled here to celebrate are, by no means, dear to me. I am not yet ready to idolize the actions of Crispus Attucks,[2] who was a leader among those who resorted to forcible measures to create a new government which has used every means in its power to outrage and degrade his race and posterity, in order to oppress them more easily, and to render their condition more hopeless in this country.

I am free to confess that I have strong attachments here, in this my native country, and desire to see it prosperous and happy; yet, situated and outraged as I am, in common with a race whose lives have been one of toil to make this country what it is, I would deny the manly promptings of my own soul if I should not say that American liberty is a word which has no charms for me. It is a name without meaning—a shadow without substance, which retains not even so much as the ghost of the original.

The only events in the history of this country which I think deserve to be commemorated are the organization of the Anti-Slavery Society[3] and the insurrections of Nat Turner and John Brown. (Applause.)

I believe in insurrections (applause)—and especially those of the pen and of the sword. Wm. Lloyd Garrison is, I think, a perfect embodiment of the moral insurrection of thought, which is continually teaching the people of this country that unjust laws and compacts made by fathers are not binding upon their sons, and that the "higher law" of God, which we are bound to execute, teaches us to do unto others as we would have them do unto us. William H. Seward (the most prominent Republican candidate for the Presidency), who has been a "Helper" in speeding on the "irrepressible conflict" between freedom and slavery,[4] has suddenly lowered his moral standard, and dwindled from a great statesman to a cunning politician. I agree with *Le Courrier des Etats-Unis* that "his recent speech has disappointed both his friends and his foes: the former he has deceived, and the latter are authorized to look upon it as a snare." Chicago and the Presidency have done this.[5] But when the crisis is passed, I think you will agree with me, that while he has sinned, he has not wholly fallen from grace.

John Brown was, and is, the representative of that potent power, the sword, which proposes to settle at once the relation between master and slave—peaceably if it can, forcibly if it must. This is, no doubt, the method by which the freedom of the blacks will be brought about in this country. It is a severe method; but to severe ills it is necessary to apply severe remedies. Slavery has taken up the sword, and it is but just that it should perish by it. (Applause.) The John Brown of the second Revolution is but the Crispus Attucks of the first. A few years hence, and this assertion will be a matter of history.

Crispus Attucks was a brave man, and he fought with our fathers in a good cause; but they were not victorious. They fought for liberty, but they got slavery. The white man was benefitted, but the black man was injured. I do not envy the white Americans the little liberty which they enjoy. It is their right, and they ought to have it. I wish them success, though I do not think they deserve it. I desire to see all men enjoy freedom and prosperity. (Applause.) But by this I do not mean to imply, that, should our country be again situated as it was then, we would be willing to recommit the errors of our Revolutionary fathers. The Scotch have a

4. John S. Rock
From *Harper's Weekly,* 25 February 1865

saying, "When a man deceives me once, shame on *him*; but when he deceives me twice, shame on *me*."

I see one thing in celebrating this day, which it would be well not to overlook, and that is, Crispus Attucks has demonstrated to us that insurrections, when properly planned, may lead to successful revolutions.

If the present aspect of things is an index to the future, then, indeed, our prospects are gloomy. Of the two great political parties in this country, one is openly hostile to us, and seeks to reduce us to the position of beasts of burden; and the other has evidently but little sympathy for us, only as we may serve to advance its interests. The only class who avow themselves openly as the friends of the black man are the Abolitionists; and it would be well for the colored people to remember this fact. (Applause.) I do not wish to be understood as saying that we have no friends in the Republican party, for I know that we have. But the most of those who sacrifice for our cause are among the Abolitionists. Next to them I place the Republicans, many of whom I have found more practically interested in our welfare than the rank and file of the Abolitionists. But I place no one before the leading Abolitionists in this country—they who have spoken for the dumb, and who have braved the storms in their fury. In this connection, I must not omit Gerrit Smith (applause), the leader of the Liberty party, who is one of the most liberal and disinterested of nature's noblemen. He has done more for our race, pecuniarily, than any other man in this country. May a kind Providence preserve him! (Applause.)

It is the Anti-Slavery men and women who have made our cause a holy thing. I always feel proud of my humanity after an interview with any one of them. In the language of Moore, I can say:

> Oh, there are looks and tones that dart
> An instant sunshine through the heart;
> As if the soul that minute caught
> Some treasure it through life had sought.[6]

The position of the colored man today is a trying one; trying, because the whole country has entered into a conspiracy to crush him; and it is against this mighty power that he is forced to contend. Some persons think we are oppressed only in the South: this is a mistake. We are oppressed everywhere on this slavery-cursed land. To be sure, we are seldom insulted here by the vulgar passersby. We have the right of suffrage. The free schools are open to our children, and from them have come forth young men who have finished their studies elsewhere, who speak two or three languages, and are capable of filling any post of profit and honor. But there is no field for these men. Their education only makes them suffer the more keenly. The educated colored man meets, on the one hand, the embittered prejudices of the whites, and on the other the jealousies of his own race. Perhaps you may think that there are exceptions. This is true; but there are not enough of them in the whole United States to sustain, properly, a half dozen educated colored men. The colored man who educates his son, educates him to suffer. When Lamartine said to an Arminian chief at Damascus, "You should send your son to Europe, and give him that education you regret the want of yourself," the Arminian answered, "Alas! what service should I render to my son, if I were to raise him above the age and the country in which he is destined to live? What would he do at Damascus, on returning thither with the information, the manners, and the taste for liberty he has acquired in Europe? If one must be a slave, it is better never to have known anything but slavery. Woe to the men who precede their times: their times crush them."[7] And woe to the black man who is educated: there is no field for him.

The other day, when a man who makes loud anti-slavery pretensions, and who has the reputation of being the friend of the blacks, had it in his power to advance the interests of a colored man, and was asked to do so, he said, "Colored men have no business to aspire—the time has not come!" This gentleman no doubt regrets that he did not originate the ideas that "black men have no rights that white men are bound to respect," and that "a white skin is the only legitimate object of ambition." He has now only to sigh for "a plantation well stocked with healthy negroes," and his cup of pleasure will be full. Some men are ruined by success. I remember very well that about five years ago he was an active laborer with us, and I am certain he did not say, "the time has not come," when he asked us to elect him to the Legislature. (Applause.)

Nowhere in the United States is the colored man of talent appreciated. Even here in Boston, which has a great reputation for being anti-slavery, he is by no means treated like other talented men. Some persons think that because we have the right to vote, and enjoy the privilege of being squeezed up in an omnibus, and stared out of a seat in a horsecar, that there is less prejudice here than there is farther South. In some respects this is true, and in others it is not true. For instance, it is five times as hard to get a house in a good location in Boston as it is in Philadelphia, and it is ten times as difficult for a colored mechanic to get work here as it is in Charleston, where the prejudice is supposed to be very bitter against the free colored man. Colored men in business here receive more respect and less patronage than in any other place that I know of. In this city, we are proscribed in some of the eating houses, many of the hotels, and all the theatres but one. Boston, though anti-slavery and progressive, supports, in addition to these places, two places of amusement, the sole object of which is to caricature us, and to perpetuate the existing prejudices against us! I now ask you, is Boston anti-slavery? Are not the very places that proscribe us sustained by anti-slavery patronage? Do not our liberal anti-slavery politicians dine at the Revere House, sup at the Parker

House, and take their creams and jellies at Copeland's? We have several friends (whose tested anti-slavery is like gold tried in the fire which comes out purer every time it is tried), who speak occasionally upon platforms that are claimed to be anti-slavery, and which are dependent upon their eloquence for support, which have, up to this time, refused to give any colored man a hearing. The Boston Theatre, an institution which has been fighting death ever since it came into existence, could not survive a single year without anti-slavery patronage![8]

The friends of slavery are everywhere withdrawing their patronage from us, and trying to starve us out by refusing us employment even as menials. Fifteen or twenty years ago, colored men had more than an equal chance in menial employments; today, we are crowded out of almost everything, and we do not even get the patronage of our professed friends. The colored stevedores, who could once be found all along the wharves of Boston, may now be found only about Central wharf, where they meet with just encouragement enough to keep soul and body together.[9] Such is the progress of the public sentiment and of humanity in Boston!

Last summer, a colored servant who was stopping at the Revere House, with a gentleman from New York, was maltreated by the Irish servants. He told his employer, who made complaint to Mr. Stevens.[10] Mr. Stevens replied that he would not interfere in anything that his servants should do to any colored man—that if gentlemen travel with colored servants, they must expect to be insulted, and he would rather that such gentlemen would stop somewhere else. That is the idea—colored men have no right to earn an honest living—they must be starved out.

Fifteen or twenty years ago, a Catholic priest in Philadelphia said to the Irish people in that city, "You are all poor, and chiefly laborers; the blacks are poor laborers, many of the native whites are laborers; now, if you wish to succeed, you must do everything that they do, no matter how degrading, and do it for less than they can afford to do it for." The Irish adopted this plan; they lived on less than the Americans could live upon, and worked for less, and the result is that nearly all the menial employments are monopolized by the Irish, who now get as good prices as anybody. There were other avenues open to American white men, and though they have suffered much, the chief support of the Irish has come from the places from which we have been crowded.

Now, while we are denied the humblest positions, is there anything higher opened to us? Who is taking our boys into their stores at a low salary, and giving them a chance to rise? Who is admitting them into their workshops or their counting rooms? Who is encouraging those who have trades? With the exception of a handful of Abolitionists and a few black Republicans, there are none. If a few more of those who claim to be our friends would patronize us when they can, and in this manner stimulate us to be industrious, they would render us infinitely more service than all of their "bunkum" speeches.

You can have but a faint idea of the charm their friendship would carry with it, if they would spend a dollar or two with us occasionally. It will not do to judge men by what they say. Many speak kindly of us when their hearts are far from us. Or, as Shakespeare has it,

> Words are easy like the wind,
> Faithful friends are hard to find.[11]

This is our experience, and we have learned to appreciate the Spanish proverb, "He is my friend who grinds at my mill."[12] In New England, we have many good mechanics who get very little patronage. Indeed, a trade appears to be of but little service to any of us, unless we can, like the tailor of Campillo, afford to work for nothing, and find thread.

I hope that our friends will look at these things, and receive my remarks in the spirit in which they have been given. I do not mean to underrate the efforts of our friends, or to speak disparagingly of their labors; but I would discriminate between our real and our pretended friends. I differ, however, from many of our true friends, as to the means to be used to elevate our race. While I believe that anti-slavery speeches, whether political or otherwise, will do much to correct a cruel and wicked public sentiment, I am confident that such means alone can never elevate us. My opinion is that the only way by which we the free colored people can be elevated is through our own exertions, encouraged by our friends. Every colored man who succeeds is so much added to the cause. We have nothing to stimulate our young men. They see many of us struggling hard, and not appreciated, and they become discouraged. The success of such a man as Mr. Martin[13] is worth more to us than a pile of resolutions and speeches as high as Tremont Temple. (Applause.) All honor to Mr. Kalloch, who had the courage and the *will* to give him a hearing in his pulpit,[14] where he could and did do credit to himself and his race. (Applause.) I thank Mr. Kalloch and the immense congregation that assembles at his church every Sunday for the interest they have manifested in his welfare. I do this in behalf of a struggling people who seldom meet with such friends. Mr. Kalloch has done for Mr. Martin what the abolitionists have long been doing for others, and the enchanted audiences who have listened to the lively and witty speeches of Wm. Wells Brown, the inimitable mimicry and pungent sarcasm of Frederick Douglass, and the burning eloquence of Charles Lenox Remond, must agree with us that the abolition idea of human rights is the correct one. (Applause.)

It is in this manner that we ask our friends to help us open those thoroughfares through which all others are encouraged to pass, and in this manner keep continually breathing into the Anti-Slavery movement the breath of life. Then will we become educated and wealthy, and then the roughest looking colored man that you ever saw or ever will see will be pleasanter than the harmonies of Orpheus,[15] and black will be a very pretty color. (Laughter.) It will make our jargon, wit; our words, oracles; flattery will then take the place of slander, and you will find no prejudice in the Yankee whatever. (Applause.)

The question whether freedom or slavery shall triumph in this country will no doubt be settled ere long, and settled in accordance with the eternal principles of justice. Whether the result is to be brought about by the gradual diffusion of an anti-slavery gospel, or the method introduced by Crispus Attucks, and seconded by John Brown, no one can tell. I hope it may be done peaceably; but if, as appears to be the case, there is no use in crying peace, then let us not shrink from the responsibility. My motto has always been, "Better die freemen than live to be slaves."[16] In case of a contest with our enemies, fifty negroes would take the State of Virginia without the loss of a man. Gov. Wise, as a matter of course, would be the first to surrender. (Applause.) One thousand negroes would sweep the slave States from the Potomac to the Rio Grande, and the time and places that know the slaveholders now would shortly know them no more forever. It has been said that "Virginia was frightened by seventeen men and a cow"; but if I remember aright, Virginia, even when under arms, was frightened by a *cow*. (Laughter.) Verily, verily, I say unto you, the slaveholders are a base race of *cow*ards. (Laughter and Applause.)

The slaveholders affect to despise the leaders of the Anti-Slavery cause, as you have a fair illustration in Gov. Wise's bombastic speech to the half-civilized southern medical students, who left Philadelphia for Philadelphia's good.[17] But we too well know that it is common for men to affect disdain, when in reality their only sentiment is fear. Metellus ridiculed Sertorius, and called him "fugitive" and "outlaw"; and yet he offered for the head of this "fugitive" and "outlaw" no less than one hundred talents of silver, and twenty thousand acres of land![18] The barbarous offers of large sums of money by the slaveholders for the heads of prominent Anti-Slavery men prove that the latter are a power that is not disdained. All efforts, thus far, to crush the pioneers in our cause have proved the most miserable failures. Our cause is of God, and cannot be overthrown. (Applause.) Governor Wise, the distinguished Virginia knight-errant, after his imaginary victory of driving Wendell Phillips into Canada,[19] might have quoted these lines from Homer:

> I saw my shaft with aim unerring go,
> And deemed it sent him to the shades below;
> But still he lives; some angry god withstands,
> Whose malice thwarts these unavailing hands.

And when he commences his raid upon the North, he will find it exceedingly difficult to drive a windmill with a pair of bellows. (Laughter.)

Our cause is moving onward. The driving of the free colored people from the slave States, and the laws preventing their ingress into the free States, is only the tightening of the already stranded cord that binds the slave; and I am daily looking for some additional force to sever it, and thereby annihilate forever the relation existing between master and slave. (Applause.)

Liberator (Boston, Mass.), 16 March 1860.

1. John Swett Rock (1825–1866), a leading black intellectual and abolitionist, was born and reared in Salem, New Jersey. As a young man, he taught at black schools in Salem and nearby Philadelphia, while studying medicine under the tutelage of two local physicians. After being repeatedly rejected for admission to medical schools because of his race, he enrolled in the city's American Medical College, which awarded Rock the doctor of medicine degree in 1852. One year later, he moved to Boston and opened a medical and dental office, attracted by the city's reputation as a center of antislavery agitation.

Devoted to antislavery, civil rights, women's rights, temperance, and other reform movements, and celebrated as a forceful and eloquent speaker, Rock committed much of his adult life to reform work. The white press credited him with "rare talents" and observed that his lectures displayed "a fine education, superior scholarship and much careful research." Rock informed white audiences of the "character, capacity, and attainments of the African and his descendants," pointing proudly to the African cultural heritage, boasting of black intellectual attainments, and celebrating the beauty of black physical appearance. A skilled teacher, physician, dentist, lawyer, lecturer, and linguist—he spoke German, French, and Spanish fluently—he was himself an outstanding example of black ability and achievement.

Rock was a leader of the Boston black community. He joined the Twelfth Baptist Church, led several fraternal and benevolent organizations, attended ill and injured fugitives for the Boston Vigilance Committee, and represented local interests at the 1855 black national convention. Writing under the pseudonyms "S." and "Rock," he reported on Boston events for *Frederick Douglass' Paper*. Rock's health, never good, further deteriorated in 1857, forcing him to give up his medical practice; the following year, he traveled to Paris to seek advanced surgical treatment. Back in Boston in early 1859, he returned to the lecture circuit, criticizing the Dred Scott decision and contrasting his treatment in France to that at home. Disillusioned by the failure of other antislavery means, he praised slave resistance and endorsed John Brown's tactics in the late 1850s.

Rock began to study law in 1859, was admitted to the Massachusetts bar in September 1861, and established a record as an outstanding trial lawyer for his erudition and legal innovation. Although he continued to lecture and practice law during the Civil War, he devoted more and more energy to the war effort. From the beginning of the conflict, Rock had urged black allegiance to the Union cause. When blacks were finally permitted to enlist in 1863, he recruited for the Fifty-fourth Massachusetts Regiment, the Fifth Massachusetts Cavalry, and other black units, declaring that "the colored soldier has the destiny of the colored race in his hands." In February 1865, he was admitted to practice before the U.S. Supreme Court, which symbolically reversed the Dred Scott decision. Rock's health deteriorated rapidly after that, and he died of tuberculosis in December 1866. George E. Levesque, "Boston's Black Brahmin: Dr. John S. Rock," *CWH* 26:326–46 (December 1980); *PF*, 31 May 1849 [6:0003]; *NASS*, 25 October 1849, 12 May 1855; *IC*, 7 September 1850; Horton and Horton, *Black Bostonians*, 59, 101, 119–24; *FDP*, 9 February, 2 March, 12 October 1855 [9:0871]; *CR*, 15 December 1866; *WAA*, 24 December 1859, 26 May 1860, 16 November 1861; *Lib*, 16 March 1860, 26 April 1861 [12:0562, 13:0479]; John S. Rock to N. C. Russell, 4 April 1864, John S. Rock to Soldiers of the Fifth U.S. Colored Heavy Artillery Regiment, 30 May 1864, Ruffin Papers, DHU [15:0299, 0379].

2. Beginning in 1858, Boston blacks organized annual Crispus Attucks Day celebrations to commemorate the "first martyr of the Boston Massacre." Attucks (ca. 1723–1770), an escaped slave from Framingham, Massachusetts, had been killed while leading a protest against the presence of British troops in the city. Boston blacks kept Attucks's memory alive for decades. William C. Nell organized the annual 5 March observances to affirm black claims to American citizenship in the wake of the Dred Scott decision. The gatherings, which honored Attucks with parades, speeches, songs, and displays of artifacts from the American Revolution, continued through the Civil War years. Nell also memorialized the black hero in his *Colored Patriots of the American Revolution* (1855) and led local blacks in petitioning the Massachusetts legislature for an Attucks monument in Boston. It was finally erected in 1888. *Lib*, 26 February 1858; *DANB*, 18–19; Horton and Horton, *Black Bostonians*, 118–19.

3. Rock refers to the formation of the American Anti-Slavery Society in 1833.

4. Rock compares Seward to Hinton Rowan Helper (1829–1909), the author of a controversial free labor critique of slavery called *The Impending Crisis* (1857). Helper, who had been reared in an area of North Carolina populated by nonslaveholding German immigrants and Quakers, attacked slavery for impoverishing the South and maintaining planter dominance over the poor whites. The volume aroused controversy in the South. After serving as American consul to Buenos Aires, Argentina, during the Civil War, Helper returned home and wrote three works ridiculing Reconstruction and calling for black expulsion or extinction. Hinton Rowan Helper, *The Impending Crisis of the South: How to Meet It*, ed. George Fredrickson (Cambridge, Mass., 1968), ix–lxiii.

5. Rock refers to a 29 February 1860 speech given by William H. Seward on the floor of the U.S. Senate and designed to strengthen his chances of being named the Republican presidential candidate at the party's upcoming 16–18 May national convention in Chicago. Seward defended the party and called for union. He denied that Republicans intended to overthrow slavery in the South and dismissed the likelihood of southern secession, calling white Americans one in "race, language, liberty, and faith." Although criticized by southerners, the speech drew widespread praise in the North. But abolitionists took exception to Seward's remarks about those involved in John Brown's raid. Labeling it "an act of sedition and treason" carried out by misguided and desperate men acting on "earnest though fatally erroneous convictions," he had called their execution "necessary and just." *Le Courrier des Etats-Unis* probably commented on Seward's remarks in its 1 March issue, which is no longer extant. *Le Courrier*, an independent French-language daily published in New York City, was edited and published by Charles Lasalle during the 1860s. It served as the "organ of the Franco-

American population" and carried news from France and other information of general interest. Van Deusen, *William Henry Seward*, 217–20; *LCEU*, 2 March 1860; Winifred Gregory, *American Newspapers, 1821–1936* (New York, N.Y., 1937), 464.

6. Rock quotes from *Lalla Rookh: An Oriental Romance* (1817) by Irish romantic poet Thomas Moore (1780–1852).

7. Alphonse Marie Louis de Lamartine (1790–1869), a French poet, historian, and politician, traveled throughout the Ottoman Empire during 1832–33 and recounted this tour in *Voyage en orient* (1835). It proved popular and was widely reprinted in English as *Travels in the East*. Rock quotes loosely from Lamartine's description of a 2 April 1833 meeting with one of the leading Armenians in Damascus. Charles M. Lombard, *Lamartine* (New York, N.Y., 1973); Alphonse de Lamartine, *Travels in the East*, 2 vols. (Edinburgh, 1850), 41–44.

8. Despite Boston's image as a center of antislavery and racial toleration, blacks were excluded from or segregated in many local hotels, restaurants, and places of amusement. The Revere House and the Parker House, two of the city's most fashionable hotels, denied them equal treatment. So did Copeland's, a stylish eatery. Blacks were required to sit in crowded upper tiers at most theaters, including the Boston Theatre, the National Theatre, Howard Athenaeum, and Ordway Hall. Morris Brothers and Pell and Huntley's Opera House closed their doors to them. The city also supported six white minstrel troupes, most notably Ordway's Aeolians, which regularly performed in blackface. Boston blacks began testing such discriminatory treatment in the local courts during the 1850s and continued these efforts through the Civil War years. Horton and Horton, *Black Bostonians*, 68; Mary Caroline Crawford, *Romantic Days in Old Boston* (Boston, Mass., 1910), 279, 349–50; *Lib*, 22 January 1858; Russel Nye, *The Unembarrassed Muse: The Popular Arts in America* (New York, N.Y., 1970), 166; William C. Nell to Wendell Phillips, 20 August 1866, Crawford Blagden Collection of the Papers of Wendell Phillips, MH.

9. Blacks had traditionally found ready employment in Boston's maritime trades. But in the decade after 1850, opportunities declined dramatically for black sailors and stevedores on the city's wharves. Blacks were often replaced by Irish immigrants. Horton and Horton, *Black Bostonians*, 77.

10. Rock is apparently mistaken about where this incident occurred. Paran Stevens, a noted Boston hotelier, managed the Tremont House from 1852 to 1863. He had earlier managed the Revere House and helped establish its reputation. Crawford, *Romantic Days in Old Boston*, 349–50.

11. Rock incorrectly attributes these lines to William Shakespeare. They appear in "To His Friend, Mr. R. L." by English poet Richard Barnfield and were first published in his *Poems: In Divers Humours* (1598).

12. Rock quotes a proverb, here attributed to Spanish origins, but also found in traditional English folklore.

13. John Sella Martin (1832–1876), one of the foremost black orators in the abolitionist crusade, was the son of a mulatto slave. Between 1838 and 1856, he was sold eight times to a variety of owners throughout the South. Although in bondage, Martin taught himself to read and write and attained an unusual measure of independence. In 1856, while working as a boatman on the Mississippi River, he escaped at Cairo, Illinois. He settled in Chicago, where he met H. Ford

Douglas and Mary Ann Shadd Cary, served as an agent for the *Provincial Freeman*, and started lecturing against slavery. Within a year, he moved to Detroit and began preparing for the Baptist ministry. After briefly filling a Buffalo pulpit, he moved in 1859 to Boston and soon became pastor of the all-black First Independent Baptist Church (often called the Joy Street Church), one of the city's most active antislavery congregations. Martin quickly earned a national reputation as a militant antislavery speaker; he endorsed slave insurrections and defended the African Civilization Society's emigration program as a legitimate response to America's intractable racism.

The coming of the Civil War persuaded Martin to abandon his emigrationist views. In late 1861, he made the first of four trips to Britain. He became a pivotal figure in building British support for the Union war effort, especially among the working class. Martin returned to the United States in early 1862, resigned his Joy Street pastorate, and accepted a call to a comeouter congregation near London. After assuming this new position in the spring of 1863, he renewed his efforts to counter Confederate propaganda, lecturing frequently throughout Britain. In poor health, Martin returned home again in the spring of 1864 to become pastor of the First Colored Presbyterian Church in New York City. But increasingly dissatisfied with his ministerial duties, he went back to Britain as an agent of the American Missionary Association. In two separate visits between 1864 and 1868, he raised thousands of dollars for freedmen's aid efforts in the South. In 1866 he was put in charge of AMA solicitations for the whole of Europe.

Martin remained abroad until 1868, when he was offered the pulpit of the Fifteenth Street Presbyterian Church in Washington, D.C. He became active in the city's black labor movement and served as editor of the *New Era*, the official organ of the Colored National Labor Union. Over the next eight years, Martin held a variety of public positions in Washington, Alabama, and Louisiana, struggling to secure permanent employment and fighting persistent illness. From 1870 to 1872, he worked with black Republicans in New Orleans, becoming embroiled in the state's chaotic politics of Reconstruction. After flirting with Horace Greeley's Liberal Republican movement, he rejoined Republican stalwarts and was named coeditor of the *New National Era*. Left without employment by the paper's 1873 merger with the *New Citizen*, Martin returned to New Orleans and his work for the Republican party. Although he quickly reestablished himself as a leading political figure in the city, his final years were marked by financial insecurity, estrangement from his family, and drug addiction. His eventual suicide was a profound loss to black Americans, denying them one of their most eloquent and persuasive speakers. R. J. M. Blackett, *Beating against the Barriers: Biographical Essays in Nineteenth-Century Afro-American History* (Baton Rouge, La., 1986), 185–285.

14. Isaac Smith Kalloch (1832–1890), a popular preacher from Maine, was pastor of Boston's Tremont Temple from 1856 to 1860. The interracial Baptist congregation, which frequently hosted antislavery gatherings, had been founded in 1836 in response to discriminatory seating practices in many of the city's white churches. Already controversial because of his abolitionism and involvement in a sensational adultery scandal, Kalloch invited black clergyman J. Sella Martin in 1859 to temporarily fill his pulpit. Kalloch settled in the West during the Civil War, served in the Kansas legislature, and later became mayor of San Francisco.

M. M. Marberry, *The Golden Voice: A Biography of Isaac Kalloch* (New York, N.Y., 1947); Horton and Horton, *Black Bostonians*, 43, 48, 108, 124–25; William Wells Brown, *The Rising Son* (Boston, Mass., 1874; reprint, New York, N.Y., 1970), 536.

15. In Greek mythology, Orpheus, a son of Apollo, played the lyre with such skill that no one, not even the gods, could resist the allure of his music.

16. Rock borrows an oft-repeated phrase from Henry Highland Garnet's "Address to the Slaves of the United States of America," which was delivered before the 1843 black national convention. Ripley et al., *Black Abolitionist Papers*, 3 : 408–10.

17. Shortly before Christmas in 1859, Governor Henry A. Wise of Virginia addressed a group of students at the Medical College of Richmond who had recently withdrawn from two Philadelphia schools—the University of Pennsylvania Medical School and Jefferson Medical College—as a protest against John Brown's raid. In his remarks, Wise blamed abolitionists for jeopardizing the Union and suggested that war with Britain might be one way to reforge national unity. Although he pledged allegiance to the Union, he also proclaimed, "I am a Virginian." Craig M. Simpson, *A Good Southerner: The Life of Henry A. Wise* (Chapel Hill, N.C., 1985), 226–27; John Hope Franklin, *A Southern Odyssey: Travelers in the Antebellum North* (Baton Rouge, La., 1976), 78–79.

18. In 80 B.C., a popular military leader named Quintus Sertorius challenged the authority of Rome by attempting to create an independent state in Spain. Quintus Caecilius Metellus, a Roman general, led his army to Spain to crush this threat. Unable to defeat Sertorius in battle, Metellus offered one hundred talents of silver and several thousand acres of land to anyone who would assassinate his rival. Sertorius was murdered in 72 B.C. Philip O. Spann, *Quintus Sertorius and the Legacy of Sulla* (Fayetteville, Ark., 1987), 73–75.

19. Fearing arrest for conspiring to aid John Brown, three Massachusetts abolitionists—Franklin B. Sanborn, George L. Stearns, and Samuel Gridley Howe—fled to Quebec and Canada West following the Harpers Ferry raid. Wendell Phillips, another conspirator, remained in the United States and praised Brown's actions in lectures throughout the North. Jeffery Rossbach, *Ambivalent Conspirators: John Brown, the Secret Six, and a Theory of Slave Violence* (Philadelphia, Pa., 1982), 220–30; James Brewer Stewart, *Wendell Phillips: Liberty's Hero* (Baton Rouge, La., 1986), 204–8.

13.
Editorial by Thomas Hamilton
17 March 1860

H. Ford Douglas's assertion that the major political parties were "barren and unfruitful" reflected the hard experience of black leaders. The Democrats were the party of slaveholders. The Republican party offered blacks little beyond the hope that northern politicians might halt the advance of slavery. Yet blacks worked to push the Republicans toward an antislavery platform. For the most skeptical black abolitionists, voting Republican merely guaranteed the existence of slavery "where it is, and endorse[d] a policy which looks to the expulsion of the free black American from his native land." Few black leaders were enthused by Abraham Lincoln's presidential candidacy in 1860. They bemoaned his rejection of racial equality, his failure to condemn America's vexing black laws, and his pledge to enforce the Fugitive Slave Law. To one black abolitionist, Lincoln represented "the fag end of a series of proslavery administrations." In this 17 March 1860 editorial in the *Weekly Anglo-African*, Thomas Hamilton conveys the political discouragement that pervaded the black community during Lincoln's campaign. Hamilton instructed readers that Republican antislavery rhetoric was based on a thinly veiled racism and a belief in colonization, rendering the party's opposition to slavery "opposition to the black man—nothing else." *WAA*, 27 August 1859, 22 December 1860, 16 March 1861; *Lib*, 13 July 1860.

THE TWO GREAT POLITICAL PARTIES

The two great political parties separate at an angle of two roads, that they may meet eventually at the same goal. They both entertain the same ideas, and both carry the same burdens. They differ only in regard to the way they shall go, and the method of procedure. We, the colored people of this country, free and enslaved, who constitute the burthen that so heavily bears down both of these parties—we, who constitute their chief concern, their chief thought—we, who cause all their discord, and all their dissentions, and all their hates, and all their bitter prejudices—we, say both of these religious political parties, we, the blacks, must, in some form or other, be sacrificed to save themselves and the country—to save the country intact for the white race.

The Democratic party would make the white man the master and the black man the slave, and have them thus together occupy every foot of the American soil. Believing in the potency of what they term the superior race, they hold that no detriment can come to the Republic by the spread of the blacks in a state of servitude on this continent; that with proper treatment and shackles upon him, proper terrors over him, and vigorous operations for the obliteration of his mind, if he have any—that with these, and whatever else will brutify him, he can be kept in sufficient subjection to be wholly out of the pale of danger to the Republic; that he can never be so much as a consideration in any calculation of imminence to the government. On the contrary, it is held by this party that his presence, under these restrictions, is of incalculable benefit to the nation—the chief instrument in the development of her resources, and the cornerstone of her liberties. What the Democratic party complains of is that the Republican party—not for the negro's, but for their own political advancement—advocate the necessity for a check upon the spread of the blacks— not as free, but in chain, not as men, but as slaves; for in this—that the blacks, as free men, shall have neither rights, footing, nor anything else, in common with the whites, in the land—both parties are agreed; and in looking at matters as they present themselves to us at this moment, we are not sure that if any of the many withheld rights were to be secured to us, they would not come from the Democratic side after all, notwithstanding the great excesses their leaders frequently carry them into. We mean the great body, acting, as it will some day, independent from the party leaders. The great masses, if left to themselves to act up to their true instincts, would always do much better in matters involving right and wrong than they do when operated upon by what are generally supposed to be intelligent leaders. These are generally great demagogues or great conservatives, neither of which have done the world any positive good. Whatever of worth it receives from them is the result of their negative position.

The Republican party today, though we believe in the minority, being the most intelligent, contains by far the greatest number of these two classes of men, and hence, though with larger professions for humanity, is by far its more dangerous enemy. Under the guise of humanity, they do and say many things—as, for example, they oppose the reopening of the slave trade. They would fain make the world believe it to be a movement of humanity; and yet the world too plainly sees that it is but a stroke of policy to check the spread, growth, and strength of the black masses on this continent. They oppose the progress of slavery in the territories, and would cry humanity to the world; but the world has already seen that it is but the same black masses looming up, huge, grim, and threatening, before this Republican party, and hence their opposition. Their opposition to slavery means opposition to the black man—nothing else. Where it is clearly in their power to do anything for the oppressed colored man, why then they are too nice, too conservative, to do it. They find, too often, a way to slip round it—find a method how not to do it. If too hard pressed or fairly cornered by the opposite party, then it is they go beyond said opposite party in their manifestations of hatred and contempt for the black man and his rights.

Such is the position of the two parties today, and it is yet to be seen whither they will drive in the political storm they are creating, and which is now raging round them. In their desire to "hem in" and crush out the black man, they form a perfect equation. They differ only in the method. We have no hope from either as political parties. We must rely on ourselves, the righteousness of our cause, and the advance of just sentiments among the great masses of the Republican people, be they Republicans or Democrats. These masses we must teach that it will not do for them to believe nor yet act upon the declaration of their party leaders that we are a naturally low and degraded race, and unfit to have or enjoy liberty and the rights of men and citizens, and hence must be crushed out of the land. We must teach these masses that all this is a fabrication, a great political lie, an abominable injustice to an outraged but honest and determined people, who cannot be crushed out—a people outraged by overpowering brute force, and then declared unfit to come within the pale of civilization. All this is our work, and rising by all the forces within our grasp high above the chicanery and vulgar policies of the day, we must perform fully and well our duty in these respects.

Weekly Anglo-African (New York, N.Y.), 17 March 1860.

14.
William Anderson to William C. Nell
April 1860

Most black abolitionists viewed white Republicans as reluctant allies
in 1860. Although blacks applauded Republican opposition to the extension of slavery, they looked with dismay at their frequent summons
to popular prejudice. Republican candidates and the party press often
appealed to the racist sentiment of white voters by employing racial
epithets, advocating colonization, or supporting black laws and segre-
gationist practices. In an April 1860 letter to William C. Nell, black
activist William Anderson of New London, Connecticut, challenged
Horace Greeley's racist campaign rhetoric during a recent Republican
campaign swing through his state. Anderson dismissed Greeley's call for
colonization and defended Afro-American ability. Blacks, he argued,
had contributed to the building of the nation—their toil had created the
agricultural economy of the South; their music had enriched American
culture; and above all, their military service in America's wars had given
them an undeniable right to citizenship. Anderson praised such Republican spokesmen as John P. Hale who avoided racist appeals and took
"broad ground for all men." Richard H. Sewell, *Ballots for Freedom:
Antislavery Politics in the United States, 1837–1860* (New York, N.Y.,
1976), 318–19, 321–42; William C. Nell, *The Colored Patriots of the
American Revolution* (Boston, Mass., 1855; reprint, Salem, N.H.,
1986), 137–41.

                                       New London, C[onnecticu]t
                                       April 1860

Dear Friend Nell:

   The late political strife in this State, so far as regards myself (being an
outsider), has awakened some old thoughts, and produced some new
ones on the subject of Slavery.[1] It is of no use for the Republican Party to
smother the uprising of liberty by declaring that they want free territory
for white men, and have the Hon. Horace Greeley travelling over the
country stating as he did here, that he did not like the black man, and for
his part he wished that the black man was out of the Country apart by
himself. I stood and heard him utter such logic and—wondered if he
knew where he was standing, right in sight of Groton Monument, where
one colored man fell pierced with <u>thirty three</u> bayonet wounds.[2] Yes fell
fighting for the freedom of this Country that Horace Greeley can enjoy,
but is unwilling that the descendants of that noble patriot and hero
should even slightly partake of; and now to the point. I would ask Mr.
Greeley what has given his paper the Tribune its present fame? Has he

forgotten that several years ago he slightly espoused the colored mans cause, in common with those of other men,[3] then his paper came into notice and has flourished since like a green bay tree; perhaps he thinks that he has gone too far. Now Mr. Greeley well knows there is no middle ground between Slavery and Freedom, that time has gone by, he must either be the friend of the black man—or his enemy. It is a hard task for some to swallow the Antislavery pill, but it has got to be taken for their own safety. Here is one fact that perhaps has escaped the notice of Mr. Greeley and which I wish for every so called white man to ponder over; setting aside the superiority or inferiority of either race, one thing is undeniably certain, and that can be said in plain words, "That the whiter slavery grows, the more money it will bring,["] suppose we take a look at the slave marts of New Orleans, Mobile, Savannah, Charleston, St. Louis, Baltimore or any other slave market, what do we see? Why all the different hues of complexion from the pure unadulterated stock of the black man, down through every grade to the (as the white man will have it) degenerate race that can pass for white, and yet so eagerly sought after (the female part particularly) at any price.[4] Will the children follow the destinies of the Mother, and already they begin to grow restless under restraint, what are they going to do with them, send them to Africa? I guess not, that color dont flourish well in that country, for if so, that Land long ere this would have been covered with white men, for there is gold there. Well what is to be done with them? My friends these great national characteristics have got to stay here, they are a part of you. African Colonization, Civilization, nor Canada in the end is to be their home, but these United States. The great questions of the day are, for Freedom? or for Slavery? Color cannot come into the account, for Slavery steals every thing from us, even our color, and to day the insult that has been added to the injured ~~colored~~ black man, shews itself in seven tenths of the so called slave population of the United States, and according to the statements of slaveholders themselves, the mixing of the races has been the cause of weakening the black race, which if a fact, does not shew such superior stock of the white race. Certainly not bodily, and I am inclined to think not mentally. I would ask Mr. Greeley, if it could so happen that the black men should all be taken out of the Country immediately, what would be the prospects of the United States for the next six months? Who is to raise the Cotton, Rice, Hemp, Tobacco, Sugar, Corn &c that ~~tend to~~ enrich, and tend to the life and strength of the United States? I imagine that I have got to wait a long time for an answer, therefore I will go on further and enquire, if those great staples are produced by the labor mainly of ignorant slaves, what would be the increase if produced by intelligent freemen? I think Mr. Greeley will be more able to solve this last problem, by refering to his oft repeated "Home among the rugged hills of New England."[5] I hope that when Mr. Greeley comes here again

to talk in meeting that he will be converted, and not be "like sounding
brass and a tinkling cymbal,"[6] as he certainly was in my ears. John P.
Hale was here and spoke to the purpose as I heard, taking broad ground
for all men.[7] I honor him for it. The so called Democrats had their <u>Mum-
mies</u> here. Fernandy and others tried hard to catch voters, but could not
do it, although they baited their hooks with six thousand big black men
that would certainly be here and work for ten cents a day if the Republicans carried the Election, for they carried the idea that the slaves would
all be free and of course come North.[8] ~~when~~ When in Boston last August
I laughed to hear a colored woman say that she was one of the onions in
the wheat of the country; that could not be seperated, rather significant!
But permit me to say that the black man, free or enslaved, pure or
mix[ed,] is the great National Character of the United States. I have mentioned that he is the producer of all the great staples. Another feature of
his character is prominently National, I allude to the Music of the United
States. The World is familiar with it, the plaintive cadence of "Oh Susannah!," the mournful song of "Way down in Tennessee" or the lively
strains of "Jim along a Josey," "Dandy Jim of Carolina," with hundreds
of others of the same tenor, constitute the National Music of the United
States.[9] It is marched [after] by the Soldiers, danced after by the aristo-
cratic pleasure seekers of the Ball Room, and sung as a lulaby by the
Mothers of Young America. In view of the above facts, do you think that
we can be spared, Why what would become of the remainder? No work!
No Music! Petrifaction would take place, and before many years some
traveller, perhaps some Ethiopian tourist, would find the white man in
th[is] Country a fossil. Now in view of what we have done for the Country, we say give us a chance to get education, trades, professions, a thorough understanding of the arts & sciences, instead of pulling us back by
bad laws, enact laws to assist us, and we shall certainly add to the
honor—wellfare and stability of ~~your~~ this our Country. In case of War
under the present state of affairs could Judge Taney[10] say to the black
man as Gen Jackson did on the banks of the Mobile, "<u>my fellow citi-
zens</u>," or could any Naval Commander say as did Com Perry on Lake
Erie "<u>my brave boys</u>," the black man is not ungrateful, a very small word
of encouragement will prompt him to mighty deeds. Bunker Hill, Monmouth, Yorktown, Trenton, Rhode Island, Groton Heights, New Orleans, on the Lakes on the Ocean or on the Land, all testify to the unflinching bravery of the black man,[11] and at this hour of the day deserves
better treatment than what he is receiving. We want to hear those Men
that were born among the rugged green hills of New England speak and
act out that Bible knowledge that was instilled into them by their Parents
and Ministers, those words of truth, that the black man believes, "That
God has made of one blood all nations that dwell upon the face of all the
earth," and "He who says that he loves God, and hates his brother, has

not the truth in him." [12] When the Hon Tom Corwin spoke here a few weeks ago, [13] he made use of some remarks that were rather conflicting with the present political [p]arties of either side, yet they were true, one was this, "that as Shem, Ham and Japheth were brothers, consequently their children must have been cousins." [14] So we must acknowledge the relationship and be ready to call Mr. Greeley, Mr. Corwin and Mr. Bennet [15] cousins if they wish it. Now this is the hard pill to swallow on our side; but are willing to forgive & forget all injuries that have been sustained by us from our near relatives. The colored people of this Country love their homes and their friends, and if need be will fight for them, it will not be any thing new, they are not cowards I [declare] it, from the Martyrdom of Attucks [16] in the beginning of the Revolution (whose blood be it remembered was the first shed for the Freedom and liberty of this country) down to the last man that immortalized himself at Harpers Ferry, but we do not wish to fight, all we want is a fair chance to live and progress; we do not wish for any odds in our favor, only give us a fair unrestricted chance with the rest of mankind, and we will try to improve it, and I hope that every colored person male or female will embrace every opportunity for improvement. We are yet in our infancy so far as regards the culture of our minds, or the attainment of trades and professions, but great effects may yet be seen resulting from our own humble efforts. Never go down the ladder of respectability and honorable position, but hold on untill you catch another round to assist your upward progress to that station where you will command the approbation of your fellow men and the blessings of the Creator. So Friend Nell if you can find anything in the foregoing that will be of any service, you are wellcome to make use of it. I wish that my abilities were such that I could contribute something that was really worthy of your attention, but what little education I have got was obtained in a similar manner that a pigeon gets his food, a little here and a little there. If any thing new transpires, please let me know, remember me to all friends, and accept from your friend,

Wm. Anderson [17]

1. Anderson refers to spirited political campaigning during early 1860 for candidates in the April state election in Connecticut. Several leading Republicans, including Horace Greeley, made speaking tours of the state. Anderson notes that he and other blacks viewed the campaign as "outsiders" because they were not allowed to vote in Connecticut. *CC*, 31 March, 7, 14 April 1860; Litwack, *North of Slavery*, 75, 79.

2. Across the Thames River from New London, Connecticut, stands a monument erected in 1830 "in memory of the brave patriots who fell" on 6 September

1781 at the battle of Groton Heights. During the fighting, British forces captured Fort Griswold. Among the fort's defenders were two blacks—Jordan Freeman and Anderson's great uncle, Lambert Latham. Following the seizure of the fort, Latham bayoneted a British officer who had summarily executed the commander of the colonial forces. Several British soldiers retaliated, using their bayonets to kill Latham, who received thirty-three wounds. Kaplan and Kaplan, *Black Presence in the Era of the American Revolution,* 55–56.

3. Horace Greeley's attitude toward blacks was marked by ambivalence and apparent contradiction. The editor of the *New York Tribune* opposed the Fugitive Slave Law and advocated emancipation, black suffrage, and an end to racial discrimination. He worked with black abolitionists in Albany and New York City and contributed funds to aid the black press and the underground railroad. But Greeley often criticized blacks for their conduct and lack of self-improvement. His support for colonization and compensated emancipation also made his abolitionism suspect, although by the summer of 1861, he had concluded that the destruction of slavery was an essential part of the struggle to save the Union. Glyndon G. Van Deusen, *Horace Greeley: Nineteenth-Century Crusader* (New York, N.Y., 1953), 283–84; Litwack, *North of Slavery,* 90; Ripley et al., *Black Abolitionist Papers,* 4:409–10.

4. Anderson refers to the trade in attractive mulatto females (called "fancy girls") carried on in the slave markets of Richmond, Charleston, New Orleans, and other southern cities during the antebellum period. Because these slave women were often sought after as concubines by white slaveholders, they commanded unusually high prices. Michael Tadman, *Speculators and Slaves: Masters, Traders, and Slaves in the Old South* (Madison, Wis., 1989), 126–27.

5. Anderson suggests that Horace Greeley could ascertain the value of free labor by recalling his own experiences growing up in rural New England. After living his first ten years on a farm near Amherst, New Hampshire, Greeley moved with his family to Westhaven, Vermont, an area of rocky soil and limestone ledges. As an adult, Greeley sought whenever possible to be "home among the rugged hills of New England"—a reference to his frequent visits to Vermont. Van Deusen, *Horace Greeley,* 5, 8, 10.

6. Anderson quotes from 1 Corinthians 13:1.

7. John Parker Hale toured Connecticut on behalf of Republican candidates for two months prior to the April 1860 state election. A lawyer, diplomat, and maverick antislavery politician from New Hampshire, Hale (1806–1873) was the first avowed abolitionist named to the U.S. Senate (1847–53, 1855–65). He won the respect of antislavery leaders for his legal defense of fugitive slaves, especially Anthony Burns. Hale ran for the presidency as the candidate of the Free Soil party in 1852, but later joined the Republican party and became one of its foremost spokesmen. *CC,* 10 March 1860; *DAB,* 8:105–6.

8. "Mummies" is an archaic term of disparagement. Anderson uses it here to ridicule Fernando Wood and other leading Democrats who campaigned in Connecticut prior to the April 1860 state election. Wood (1812–1881), the controversial mayor of New York City, toured the state during March and attempted to arouse the white electorate's racial fears. A skilled political boss, he had risen to national prominence by controlling local patronage and party discipline. He became a leading spokesman for the Peace Democrats during the Civil War. Wood

later served in the U.S. Congress (1863–65, 1867–81), where he regularly denounced Republican Reconstruction measures. Lester Berry and Melvin Van Den Bark, *The American Thesaurus of Slang*, 2d ed. (New York, N.Y., 1948), 396, 433; Samuel A. Pleasants, *Fernando Wood of New York* (New York, N.Y., 1948), 103; *DAB*, 20:456–57.

9. Despite Anderson's suggestion that these songs reflected black musical styles, they had been composed by whites with little understanding of Afro-American musical forms. All four were identified as "Ethiopian" melodies and were originally written for the blackface minstrel stage. "Oh Susannah!" (1847) was one of Stephen Foster's first popular minstrel tunes. "Jim Along Josey" (ca. 1830s), "Dandy Jim, From Caroline" (1844), and "Way Down in Tennessee" were composed in an affected black dialect by lesser-known songwriters. Nye, *Unembarrassed Muse*, 165, 311; Robert C. Toll, *Blacking Up: The Minstrel Show in Nineteenth-Century America* (London, 1974), 33, 36–37, 69, 98.

10. Roger B. Taney.

11. Several thousand slaves and free blacks fought with the colonial forces in the American Revolution, exhibiting bravery at the battles of Bunker Hill, Monmouth, Trenton, Rhode Island, Groton Heights, and Yorktown. A smaller number participated in the War of 1812, yet they contributed to important American victories on Lake Erie and at New Orleans. On 10 September 1813, Oliver Hazard Perry (1785–1819) commanded the American fleet on Lake Erie to victory over the British at Put-in-Bay, winning control of the strategically important lake. Nearly a quarter of his crew was black. Although an avowed racist, Perry acknowledged the crucial role that black sailors played in the victory. On 21 September 1814, fearing a British invasion of New Orleans, Andrew Jackson issued a plea for black volunteers from his headquarters at Mobile, Alabama. He honored them as "brave fellow citizens" and promised the same pay, bounties, supplies, and 160-acre land grant given to white soldiers. More than six hundred free blacks fought with Jackson at the 8 January 1815 battle of New Orleans. Black leaders often cited these engagements as evidence of black valor, contributions to American independence, and claims to American citizenship. Kaplan and Kaplan, *Black Presence in the Era of the American Revolution*, 20–23, 34, 54–56, 64–66; *DAB*, 14:490–92; Foner, *History of Black Americans*, 1:486–91; *NSt*, 8 February 1850 [6:0393]; *WAA*, 19 October 1861 [13:0845]; *DM*, October 1862 [14:0520].

12. Anderson quotes from Acts 17:26 and 1 John 4:20.

13. Thomas Corwin, a prominent Ohio politician, campaigned in Connecticut during March 1860 on behalf of Republican candidates in the upcoming state election. This included stops at New London, New Haven, Hartford, and Middletown. Corwin (1794–1865), a former Whig, had served in the U.S. House of Representatives (1831–40), as governor of Ohio (1840–42), in the U.S. Senate (1845–50), and as secretary of the treasury in the administration of Millard Fillmore (1850–53). Reelected to Congress in 1859, he vocally opposed the expansion of slavery, although committed to enforcement of the Fugitive Slave Law. Compared to the statewide Republican campaign, Corwin's racial views probably appeared temperate to Anderson. Connecticut Republicans demanded that the territories be reserved for the "sons of white men" and advised that a vote for the Democrats was "a vote for MORE NEGROES." *CC*,

10, 24, 31 March 1860; *BDAC*, 7887; Josiah Morrow, ed., *Life and Speeches of Thomas Corwin: Orator, Lawyer, and Statesman* (Cincinnati, Ohio, 1896), 87–88, 385–407, 449.

14. Shem, Ham, and Japheth are the names given in Genesis 10:1 to the three sons of Noah. According to tradition, Shem was the father of the Semitic peoples, Ham's descendants became blacks, and Japheth was the progenitor of the white race.

15. Anderson refers to James Gordon Bennett (1795–1872), the publisher of the *New York Herald*. After founding the paper in 1835, he employed sensationalism and innovative use of technological advances to build it into an enormous success. Abolitionists were outraged by Bennett's racist journalism, prosouthern leanings, and partisan Democratic politics. *DAB*, 2:195–99.

16. Crispus Attucks.

17. William Anderson (1805–ca. 1870) was a lifelong resident of New London, Connecticut, where his free black parents, Scipio and Jane Anderson, operated a local chimney sweeping business. The younger Anderson, a barber, served as an agent for the *Liberator* from 1831 to 1834. He later became a spokesman for equal suffrage, signed the call for the 1849 state convention of Connecticut blacks, and served as a vice-president of the 1859 New England Colored Citizens Convention. Delegates to the latter gathering selected him to an ongoing central committee to "devise ways and means" to attain black rights. A participant in local and regional efforts to aid southern freedmen during the Civil War, he hosted New London's 2 January 1863 celebration of the Emancipation Proclamation at his home. Anderson, whose great uncle Lambert Latham had fought and died in the American Revolution, worked throughout his life to gain recognition for black veterans of that conflict. On at least three occasions between 1830 and 1860, he spoke at local ceremonies honoring the memory of those who fought in the battle of Groton Heights (1781). U.S. Census, 1860; Barbara Brown and James M. Rose, *Black Roots in Southeastern Connecticut, 1650–1900* (Detroit, Mich., 1980), 8–9; *Lib*, 1 October 1831–20 December 1834; *Proceedings of the Connecticut State Convention of Colored Men, Held at New Haven, on the September 12th and 13th, 1849* (New Haven, Conn., 1849), 4 [6:0143]; Foner and Walker, *Proceedings of the Black State Conventions*, 2:208, 224; *WAA*, 17 January 1863, 2 January 1864; *NASS*, 4 April 1863; Nell, *Colored Patriots*, 136–40.

15.
Frances Ellen Watkins Harper to
Jane E. Hitchcock Jones
21 September 1860

Racial progress through moral reform, a dominant theme in the early development of black abolitionism, never completely lost its appeal. Some black leaders stubbornly maintained their faith in mutual aid, hard work, thrift, learning, piety, and sobriety, despite a growing consensus among blacks that the antislavery struggle required more aggressive tactics. Frances Ellen Watkins Harper reaffirmed her belief in moral reform in a 21 September 1860 letter to Jane E. Hitchcock Jones, a Quaker abolitionist in Ohio. Announcing her plans to lecture on "character" among the black settlements in the West, Harper carried the broader message of black abolitionism—a concern for breaking the bonds of racial prejudice as well as those of the slave. Encouraging the moral elevation of free blacks, she concluded, was "some of the best anti-slavery work that can be done." Dorothy Sterling, ed., *We Are Your Sisters: Black Women in the Nineteenth Century* (New York, N.Y., 1984), 159–64.

GREEN PLAIN, O[hio]
Sept[ember] 21, 1860

RESPECTED FRIEND:

I hardly think that I shall be at your meeting after all. The distance is far, and the road most accessible that I know of, is proscriptive to colored persons. I was interrupted and insulted on it one day this week—the Cincinnati and Zanesville road—but I could consent to ride on it again if I knew it was necessary that I should be at your meeting. You expect Mr. Pillsbury and Mrs. Foster, early champions of the cause, who espoused it in an hour when to be anti-slavery meant something else than walking on the smoothest paths, and drinking in the plaudits of admiring crowds; to be among them might prove to me a moral feast, and an intellectual banquet, a replenishment of ideas, and the acquisition of fresh hopes and increased strength; and then it might be very pleasant to meet with Mr. Douglass, who may come to you with his lips freighted with eloquence and utterance clothed with power.[1] But in the presence of all those who will visit you, my words might seem like feeble and purposeless utterances.

I am going to spend part of this fall visiting and lecturing among the colored people. We need some earnest and elevating influence among ourselves, and possibly some of the very best anti-slavery work I can do is to labor earnestly and faithfully among those with whom I am identified by complexion, race and blood. Upon our alleged inferiority is based our social ostracism and political proscription, and so long as they are down, I belong to a downtrodden race. To teach our people how to build up a character for themselves—a character that will challenge respect in spite of opposition and prejudice; to develop their own souls, intellect and genius, and thus verify their credentials, is some of the best anti-slavery work that can be done in this country. I do not say that this is the whole work, but it should be an important department of reform effort. Will you suggest to Mrs. Foster and Mr. Pillsbury that there are a number of colored settlements in the West,[2] where a few words of advice and encouragement among our people might act as a stimulant and charm; and if they would change the public opinion of the country, they should not find it, I hope, a useless work to strive to elevate the character of the colored people, not merely by influencing the public *around* them but *among* them; for after all, this prejudice of which such complaint has been made, if I understand it aright, is simply a great protest of human minds rising up against slavery, and so hating it for themselves that they learn not only to despise it, but the people that submit to it, and those identified with them by race. It is the same feeling that the Norman had against his Saxon Slave[3]—it is the protest of strength against weakness, of power against feebleness, an unconscious recognition that slavery is not the normal condition of man.

Well, if I am not present, may God speed every loving word, heroic utterance or earnest expression that may be heard in your midst. Yours,

FRANCES ELLEN WATKINS

Anti-Slavery Bugle (Salem, Ohio), 29 September 1860.

1. Parker Pillsbury, Abby Kelley Foster, and H. Ford Douglas attended the annual meeting of the Western Anti-Slavery Society at the Town Hall in Salem, Ohio, on 22–24 September 1860. Pillsbury served on the business committee and Foster on the finance committee for this gathering of western Garrisonians. Pillsbury (1809–1898), an ardent New Hampshire abolitionist and women's rights advocate, left the Congregational clergy in 1840 to pursue a reform career. He served as general agent for several antislavery organizations, including the American Anti-Slavery Society, and temporarily edited the *Herald of Freedom* and the *National Anti-Slavery Standard*. Pillsbury is best remembered as the author of *Acts of the Anti-Slavery Apostles* (1883), a memoir of the movement. *ASB*, 29 September 1860; Merrill and Ruchames, *Letters of William Lloyd Garrison*, 4:28.

2. Dozens of flourishing black farming settlements were founded in Ohio and Indiana between 1808 and the Civil War, many of them by emancipated slaves from Virginia and North Carolina. These often became key stops on the underground railroad. Moved by their success, the 1843 black national convention recommended the formation of similar communities in Michigan, Illinois, Iowa, and Wisconsin. Sizable black farming settlements were established in southern

Illinois and Cass County, Michigan, by 1860. Carter G. Woodson, *A Century of Negro Migration* (Washington, D.C., 1918), 21–30; David A. Gerber, *Black Ohio and the Color Line, 1860–1915* (Urbana, Ill., 1976), 16–19; *Minutes of the National Convention of Colored Citizens: Held at Buffalo, on the 15th, 16th, 17th, 18th and 19th of August 1843* (New York, N.Y., 1843), 32–35 [4:0647–49].

3. Slavery existed in Anglo-Saxon England long before the Norman conquest in 1066, but after a century of Norman rule it had virtually disappeared. Harper probably refers to those Saxons reduced to slavelike conditions of serfdom by their French Norman rulers. Frank M. Stanton, *Anglo-Saxon England* (London, 1947), 310, 469, 472, 507.

16.
James McCune Smith and the Struggle for Equal Suffrage

James McCune Smith to Stephen A. Myers
21 September 1860

James McCune Smith to Gerrit Smith
20 October 1860

Blacks failed to win equal suffrage until 1870, but three decades of
persistent struggle kept the issue before politicians and the white
electorate. The battle for the vote reached new levels of sophistication on the eve of the Civil War, especially in New York state, where
black leaders succeeded in placing a referendum on equal suffrage on
the ballot in the fall election of 1860. New York's black leaders promoted an expanded franchise and repudiated the racist antisuffrage
campaign of the Democratic party. Based in black communities, they
organized local suffrage committees throughout the state—sixty-six
were formed in New York City and Brooklyn alone. On 10 May, representatives from eleven counties assembled in New York City to plot
strategy and to form a thirty-five-member central committee to orchestrate the statewide suffrage campaign. This committee worked
with local suffrage clubs to sponsor speakers, to publish and distribute thousands of tracts and sample ballots (many in the languages
of major immigrant groups), and to influence white opinion leaders.
Racism, limited resources, and the indifference of the Republican
party doomed their effort, yet black leaders dramatically enlarged
the prosuffrage vote and increased support for black rights in the
state. The following letters by James McCune Smith, written in the
midst of the fall suffrage campaign, provide an inside view of black
politics at work. Phyllis F. Field, *The Politics of Race in New York:
The Struggle for Black Suffrage in the Civil War Era* (Ithaca, N.Y.,
1982), 114–46.

New York, [New York]
Sept[ember] 21, 1860

My Dear Sir:
    Your letter in reply to Prof Reason,[1] and your call for a State Conven-
tion to be held in Albany on the 25th Inst were laid before the New York
and County Suffrage Committee last evening.[2]
    A motion to send five delegates to said Convention was almost unani-
mously voted down.
    A motion was adopted directing me as "chairman, and in behalf of

said comee, to request that you will withdraw the call and that you will not hold said Convention"; which I hereby do.

1. Because the notice is entirely too short to warrant such full attendance on the part of the people, as the occasion demands.

2. Because of the strong probability that such Convention may directly or indirectly identify the colored people with one of the leading political parties—which would be suicidal to the Suffrage cause.

3. All that need be done for the advancement of the Suffrage question, can be done by local committees,[3] which shall correspond with each other and pursue a uniform course of labor in behalf of the cause.

4. While a Convention by its publicity, its discussions, its strife, will not fail, very largely to attract the attention and hostility of the foreign vote and of the Democrats who would otherwise be busy enough with their own party quarrels.

5. As to money, none of any account ever has been raised at any of our state Conventions! while the cost of travel to and from the Convention might be put in the treasuries of the local committee and thus better help the cause.

Our City and County Suffrage Comee have been steadily at work the last three months; holds weekly meetings and have accomplished and purpose to do as follows

1. We have issued seven thousand copies of address enclosed marked no 1. and distributed them in New York and vicinity.

2. We have issued three or four thousand of tract enclosed marked no 2. and distributed them in the City and in many parts of the state, among citizens generally.[4]

3. In response to address no 1. there are formed in this city forty eight Suffrage Clubs, and in Brooklyn eighteen Suffrage Clubs—in all sixty-six—which send in their collections weekly to the City and County Committee. Receipts last night forty dollars.

We propose early next month

1. To appoint and distribute four hundred thousand copies of another tract which is a great improvement on the one enclosed. Each tract shall contain a ballot in favor of Suffrage extension.

2. We are about to issue a circular requesting co-operation in funds and labor from our leading men throughout the state.

I may say in conclusion that I earnestly hope that you will join us in this quiet but effective work, and that you will omit a noisy and bootless convention.

We are thankful for your suggestion about the ballots and will obtain them from the source you named.

Will you please inform me, privately, what your white friend and namesake[5] is going to do for us, Sincerely yours,

J. McCune Smith

New York, [New York]
Oct[ober] 20, 1860

Dear friend:

Your letter of 13th Inst did not reach me until 18th.

Your additional donation of fifty dollars came very opportunely, and was received with cheers by the Comee, inasmuch as we had been disappointed in the five hundred dollars expected from the Garrisonians.

The Executive Comee of the Am. Anti-Slavery society declined making any appropriation; but noble hearted Wendell Philips sent us the Hundred dollars from his own purse.[6]

I am glad to hear from you, as I have heard from several other sources, that his role against suffrage will be a diminished one.

We sent you per Express on the 16th Inst 6000 Tracts with ballots enclosed, in English, and about 300, without ballots in German.

We sent in like manner on the 15th twenty five thousand tracts to Frederick Douglass who is pledged to spread them thru' the state west of and including Rochester.

Please acknowledge receipt of your tracts. We have printed 8000 tracts in German and they have been received with enthusiasm and more demanded by one German friend in this City Brooklyn.

We would like to print Some in French could we afford it.

Whatever the result, the movement is getting up a fine tone of thought and action especially among our young men.

Mr. Schieffelin[7] is as active as ever and begs to be gratefully remembered. He preserves and cherishes your short note to him.

We are hard put to it for funds yet labor cheerfuly.

Wife & family join me in regards to you & yours. Sincerely and gratefuly yours,

James McCune Smith

1. Charles L. Reason.

2. Because the New York City and County Suffrage Committee failed to support Smith's call for a statewide black suffrage convention, such a gathering was never held. The New York City and County Suffrage Committee had been organized in June 1860 to coordinate the local campaign to extend black suffrage in New York state. It sought to persuade the electorate to vote for equal suffrage in a statewide referendum that November. Under the leadership of James McCune Smith, the NYCCSC sponsored weekly meetings in the local black community, established sixty-six neighborhood suffrage clubs, distributed thousands of tracts and sample ballots (including pamphlets in German for immigrant voters),

worked behind the scenes to influence white opinion leaders throughout the state, and collected donations for the cause—ranging from 10 cents to several hundred dollars. The NYCCSC showed the organizational sophistication of the New York City black community by 1860, but it disbanded after voters rejected equal suffrage in November. Rhoda G. Freeman, "The Free Negro in New York City before the Civil War" (Ph.D. diss., Columbia University, 1966), 146–52; *DM*, October 1860 [12:1022]; James McCune Smith et al., *The Suffrage Question in Relation to Colored Voters in the State of New York* (New York, N.Y., 1860), 4.

3. Smith refers to local auxiliaries of the New York State Suffrage Association.

4. Smith refers to two pamphlets distributed widely during the 1860 suffrage campaign in New York state. He coauthored one tract entitled *The Suffrage Question in Relation to Colored Voters in the State of New York* (1860), which was published by the New York City and County Suffrage Committee and reprinted in the popular and reform press. It claimed that whites feared blacks as voters because they were "strangers to our characters, ignorant of our capacity, [and] oblivious to our history and progress." A second tract, *Property Qualification or No Property Qualification* (1860) by William C. Nell of Boston, recounted the accomplishments of New York blacks in military service, in business, and in social organizations to demonstrate that they were "patriotic, industrious, provident, exemplary citizens deserving equal rights at the ballot box."

5. Smith probably refers to Austin Myers, a Syracuse Republican and stalwart supporter of William H. Seward, who served in the New York state assembly during the early 1860s. He backed the campaign to extend black suffrage in the state and undoubtedly made Stephen Myers's acquaintance as a result of the latter's legislative lobbying for the New York State Suffrage Association. Van Deusen, *Horace Greeley*, 251; *WAA*, 18 February 1860 [12:0500].

6. Smith estimated that the local suffrage campaign would cost nearly $2,000, and he hoped to obtain the necessary funds from black suffrage clubs, individual political abolitionists, and the American Anti-Slavery Society. Bradhurst Schieffelin, a large contributor to the AASS, urged the organization's executive committee to make a donation to Smith's cause. The twelve-member committee, which consisted of Wendell Phillips and other Boston Garrisonians, initially "yielded" to Schieffelin's request, with the caveat "that no public mention be made of it at present." The pledge was later revoked, but Phillips privately assisted the suffrage campaign. James McCune Smith to Gerrit Smith, 22 September 1860, Gerrit Smith Papers, NSyU [12:1016]; *Annual Report of the American Anti-Slavery Society, by the Executive Committee, for the Year Ending May 1, 1860* (New York, N.Y., 1861), 322.

7. Bradhurst Schieffelin (1824–1909), a member of an affluent New York City family, used his wealth to back a variety of reform and charitable causes. He contributed to the American Anti-Slavery Society, helped fund the 1860 campaign to extend black suffrage in New York state, and provided relief to victims of the financial panics that rocked the city in the early 1870s. Schieffelin organized a local citizens' committee to promote cooperation with the Lincoln administration during the Civil War. A populist, he advocated restrictive inheritance laws, but never succeeded in gaining election to the state legislature. *ACAB*, 5:419; *NYTi*, 11 March 1909; Freeman, "Free Negro in New York City," 150–51.

17.
Speech by H. Ford Douglas
Delivered at the Town Hall
Salem, Ohio
23 September 1860

Slavery's growing influence over the federal government during the 1850s nourished a persistent strain of Garrisonianism in black antislavery thought. When Chief Justice Roger B. Taney denied black claims to American citizenship in the Dred Scott decision, even black political abolitionists were hard-pressed to view the U.S. Constitution as an antislavery document or to hope for a political end to slavery. Garrisonian assertions that the Constitution and the political system served slaveholding interests and crushed black freedom resonated through northern black communities with each fugitive slave returned and each right denied. H. Ford Douglas, a leading black lecturer, echoed this theme in a speech before the annual meeting of the Western Anti-Slavery Society, a Garrisonian organization, on 23 September 1860. The gathering, which was chaired by Marius Robinson, convened in the Town Hall at Salem, Ohio. Douglas repudiated the Constitution and proclaimed his refusal to "stand connected with a government that steals away the black man's liberties." He rebuked the major political parties, explained how the influence of slavery poisoned the principles of supposed antislavery politicians (naming William H. Seward, Abraham Lincoln, and Lyman Trumbull), and chided his largely white audience for supporting such men. Claiming that "there is too much of this hypocritical abolitionism," he praised John Brown, but reminded the gathering that the best route to emancipation lay in changing men's minds, not in violence or the vote. *ASB*, 6 October 1860.

MR. CHAIRMAN:

The difference between my distinguished namesake,[1] to whom you have referred, and myself, is this. He is seeking his mother; I am not. I feel but little, just now, like making a speech. We have just been listening to the very able report of your Executive Committee,[2] and I fear I can add nothing to the interest of the occasion by any poor words that I may utter.

We have listened to a recital of the imminent dangers which threaten the liberties of the people; and I am sure none of us can go away from this meeting without feeling that we all have much to do—that our mission is not fulfilled till slavery shall cease to exist in every portion of our widely extended country.

Thirty-five years ago, when the abolitionists began their labor, they supposed all that was necessary was to let the people know the true character of slavery—to hold the hateful system up to the scorn and indignation of the world, and the work would be done. But we have lived to learn that slavery is no weak and impotent thing, but a giant power, so fortified by potent influences, social, political and religious, that it can be rooted out only by uncompromising and untiring effort. We have proved it true, as was said by Benjamin Franklin, that "a nation may lose its liberty in a day and be a century in finding it out." When the people of this country consented to a union with slaveholders—when they consented to strike out, at the bidding of South Carolina, from the original draft of the Declaration of Independence, the clause condemning the King of Great Britain for bringing Africans into this land, and dooming them to slavery[3]—at that moment they sold their own liberties. If there was ever any doubt of this, we can doubt it no longer, now that the rights of the white man, as well as the black, are so ruthlessly stricken down.

I do not mean to assert, at present, that the Constitution of the United States is not susceptible of an anti-slavery interpretation. I believe if I was a Supreme judge, and there was in the country a public sentiment that would sustain me in it, I would find no difficulty in construing that instrument in favor of the freedom of all men. But that is not now the question. You have decided upon the character of the Constitution, and I must accept your own interpretation; and with that rendering, I repudiate the instrument, and the government and the institutions which it is made to sustain. I will not stand connected with a government that steals away the black man's liberties, that has corrupted our best political leaders, by leading them to the support of the greatest crimes, the vilest of all institutions. Even William H. Seward has lately declared that this is to be the white man's government.[4] Ten years ago he would have been thought incapable of such a declaration; but such is the influence of slavery. Hence the necessity of attacking the system now, in a deadly warfare; otherwise, our people will be—if they are not now—wholly and hopelessly lost.

Yes! we must do as John Brown did, not necessarily in the *way* he did it, but we must labor with the sure determination to effect, in some way, the complete overthrow of slavery. I am not an advocate for insurrection; I believe the world must be educated into something better and higher than this before we can have perfect freedom, either for the black man or the white. In the present moral condition of the people, no true liberty can be established, either by fighting slavery down, or by voting it down. Hence our object is not to put anybody into office, as a means of abolishing slavery, or to keep anybody out. I care not for the success or defeat of any party, so far as the interests of freedom are concerned. The failure or success of any of the present political parties can neither injure nor aid us. Our business must be to educate the people to the highest sentiment that shall make them recognize the white man, the black man, the red man, *all* men, to all the rights of manhood. There is not to be, as your noblest statesman seems to imagine, a government for the *white* man alone. What merit is there in your boasted liberty or the christianity you profess to adopt, unless they recognize the brotherhood of all men, in all time? Till we have protected the rights of all, we have secured the liberties of none—that government is no government which fails to protect the freedom of its meanest subject. I will put the rights of the meanest slave against the greatest government of the world—for liberty is more than any institution, or any government.

But the idea that man is superior to institutions finds no favor in this country. The principles of justice are forgotten. The question is not what is right; but rather, "how shall we accomplish our selfish ends?" And all parties make success a foregone conclusion. Under no circumstances must the government be endangered, to give the black man his rights; yet, let me tell you, my liberty is more to me, and more in fact, than all the glory of your government. I have it from God, and you have no more right to compromise my freedom for the sake of the success of your party, than you have to take my life. For what is my life worth to me, when you take away all that makes it worth the living?

As I said I am no advocate for revolution. I would only resort to it after all other means have failed. I believe in the right of self-defence; it was given us at the creation. I believe it a duty, as well as a right, and no man has a *right* to become a slave for a single hour, if by defending himself he can prevent it. If you can take away the freedom of one man, you strike at the liberty of all. The same means required to prepare the white man for enslaving the black, prepares the black man to enslave the white; and the master and the slave are alike in chains. "Man never fastens a chain upon the limbs of a slave, but God, in his divine justice, fastens the other end around his own neck."[5]

So in this country we have four political parties,[6] all talking of liberty, yet all in chains! Stephen A. Douglas said, yesterday, at Cleveland, that he would stop this slavery agitation;[7] he would put the slave question outside of Congress. They had nothing to do with it, and he did not care whether slavery was voted up or voted down. He did not know, when he thus sneered at liberty, that he was himself a slave! So of W. H. Seward; when he talks of a government of white men, he may think he is free, but he is not, and cannot be. And when Abraham Lincoln opposes the rights of the free colored people, even in his own state[8]—when he shuts them out from the courts of justice, he does not know that he makes himself a slave. When you have made me a slave, no white man is free. Strike down my liberty, if you will, but when you do it, you can no longer enjoy your own.

Hence this struggle interests not one class alone, but all classes of the people. While the colored people are bowed down by slavery, they can accomplish nothing great or noble; nor can you, while you oppress them. They are men as you are, demoralized by slavery. Often they oppose anti-slavery lecturers, just as you do. I find many of them in New York and New England opposing anti-slavery. All classes are alike degraded, and if anything is done for freedom, we must make this question of slavery, not a colored question, but a white question as well. Thus you see where the Republican party stands when it calls itself the white man's party—it stands arrayed against the freedom of all, white or black. I have said sometimes, in view of the fact that the Republican party fell so far short of its professions, and was deceiving so many honest anti-slavery men, that I would rather hear of its defeat than of its success. I have said I would rather Douglas would be elected President of the United States than Lincoln. But I have changed my feelings on that matter; and now my choice would be to see Douglas and his party, with all their arrogance and impudence, overthrown, and Lincoln elected, rather than any other of the candidates. Not that I suppose there is any essential difference between the two men, or would be any in their action. But there is in the Republican party a strong anti-slavery element. And though the party will do nothing for freedom now, that element will increase; and before long—I trust—springing up from the ruins of the Republican party will come a great anti-slavery party that will be true to freedom, and recognize the rights of all men. But while I thus declare my desire to see the Republican party succeed, I must say that as a party, I regard it false to freedom and in no higher position than the Democratic party. And in its pres[ent] position it can do nothing for the salvation of the nation, notwithstanding the noble anti-slavery men who are in it. For God has made it certain that the truth cannot be advanced by the telling of lies. I believe that in giving the enemy the one half, you cannot save the other; for as somebody has said, every compromise with the devil weakens the man that makes it.

The Republicans say they are bringing the Government back to the policy of the fathers.[9] I do not desire to do this; the policy of the fathers was not uncompromising opposition to oppression; and nothing less than a position far higher than they occupied will ever make us worthy of the name of freemen. If we cannot succeed by the force of ideas, then I go for a policy far different from that of the fathers, if you refer to their policy in the management of the government; for in that case this blood-stained despotism must be overthrown. But all peaceful means must first be exhausted. And for one, though I cannot accomplish what many others can, I am disposed to do everything I can by moral and pacific means to educate the people into true ideas of their duty—to eradicate the mean spirit of selfishness that makes almost everyone in the country look upon himself, his color, his race, as alone worthy of consideration.

This is the most wicked and the meanest kind of infidelity; yet it is

in all your churches, even your professors of religion do not know the A
B C of the Bible, or of christianity, do not know that God is no respector
of persons, and has made of one blood all the nations of man, do not
know that colored men have the rights of humanity. They condemn John
Brown as the vilest of criminals, yet laud the Revolutionary fathers for
doing what John did. If Washington and his associates of the Revolution were right, so was John Brown. I know that Henry Ward Beecher
preached a sermon in which he argued that John Brown was in the
wrong, in doing as he did, because there was no prospect of success; [10]
thus making success the test of the matter. But if John Brown was wrong
in defeat, would he have been right in success? If our Revolutionary
fathers had failed, would they, therefore, have been the greatest of
criminals?

What the age wants is a confidence in justice and a determination to
do it. We are in fellowship with slaveholders, and so long as we remain
in this position we are no better than they. The receiver is as bad as the
thief. When you consent to carry out the fugitive slave law, you do as
badly as to hold slaves. What difference does it make to me whether you
hold me in bondage yourself, or deliver me up to the man who will.
Anthony Burns could feel as much respect—and far more—for his master, than for those Boston minions of slavery who gave him up to bondage. Yet Abraham Lincoln will carry out the fugitive slave law, and you
will carry him into office! He will be the bloodhound to catch the slave,
and send him back to his hard life of toil, and you by sustaining him, will
make yourselves as guilty as he. I want to see the day when no slaveholder
will dare to come here for his slave. But that day cannot come so long as
you are willing to exalt to the presidency men who endorse the Dred
Scott decision. And all your Presidential candidates do this. I know this
has been denied of the Republican candidate. But does anyone who hears
me deny that Abraham Lincoln endorses even the worst features of that
infamous decision, "that the black man has no rights which the white
man is bound to respect"? If anyone denies or doubts it, let him speak.
In the state of Illinois, I cannot testify against a white man in any court
of justice. Any villain may enter my house at Chicago and outrage my
family, and unless a white man stands by to see it done, I have no redress.
Now, I went to Abraham Lincoln, personally, with a petition for the repeal of this infamous law, and asked him to sign it, and he refused to do
it. I went also to Lyman Trumbull, with the same petition, and he also
refused; and he told me, if I did not like the laws of Illinois, I had better
leave the State! [11] This is the doctrine of the Dred Scott decision in its
most odious form. It is declaring, not only in words, but in action, the
infamous principle that colored people have no rights which you are
bound to respect. And yet, you tell me, you are anti-slavery men, while
you support such men as these for the highest offices of the nation! Surely,

you will not expect me to regard you as in favor of freedom, when you will not recognize me as a free man, or protect me on your own soil. Your anti-slavery should begin at home, or it is not to be trusted. There is too much of this hypocritical abolitionism. You profess to be in favor of freedom, and then allow the slaveholder to come among you and carry away your citizens. You allow it, and you agree to it, if you do not *approve* it, and you have no right thus to sacrifice principle and practice, to save any political party. To elevate men to office is not an object for which a man should barter away his manhood. Let us act nobly and justly—do right, and leave the consequences to God.

But, you may inquire, who shall we vote for? I answer, vote for an anti-slavery man, or do not vote at all. God put you here to do your duty and be true to your own souls. He never commanded you to tell a lie, and violate principle, even to break the fetters from the slave. And you cannot break the slave's fetters by thus trampling on every righteous principle. You gain no power for good by sacrificing principle to gain numbers. God and one true man, are in a majority over all the hosts of error and falsehood; and we never can, as anti-slavery men, do the work we have to do, till we make our own hands clean.

Garrisonians have been denounced as disorganizers, and the enemies of all Government.[12] But what is the object of Government? Is it to make money—the rich richer and the poor poorer? Is it merely to raise wheat and corn and rye? No; it is to make men; and if it fails in this—as your government has done—it fails in everything and is no government. Man, as I have said, is above and will survive all governments. Garrisonians desire to be true to humanity; and will respect no government that tramples upon it. But you are sacrificing *man* to the government, humanity to success. An ancient king decreed that all the male children born in his kingdom should die to save his government; and you are following his example—sacrificing a whole race to sustain an iniquitous tyranny. And this nation should go away to Judea and dig up the rotten bones of Herod, and should seek for the bones of Captain Kidd the pirate, collect them together and build monuments over them, instead of seeking for the remains of Sir John Franklin in the frozen regions. Why should you not meet together to glorify the bloody Herod and the pirate Kidd?[13] You have dethroned God, and enthroned the devil, and why not go to work and have a devilish good time.

Three hundred years ago, your English ancestors were opposed by the bloody Stuarts. You said the king had no right to violate your rights and trample on all law and justice. Charles the First replied that he would have his will, that the king could do no wrong. So you beheaded Charles the First and established the government of 1678.[14] Afterward your fathers came to New England, and again made battle against the despotism of these same despotic kings of England. And you rose up against the power of George III and established the government of 1776. Then you thought you had done something worthy of the friends of freedom. But what has been the result? You have today Freedom only in name. You are no better than the worst governments of the Old World. I would rather live in the most tyrannical government in Europe, so far as freedom is concerned, than in yours, which atheistically declares itself to be the white man's country, and has not risen above the lowest despotism. You have no true ideas of government or of law. No conception, with all your boasts, of the true ideas of liberty.

I do not come among you, as a colored man, to ask any special favor at the hands of the white people; I ask only that my manhood be recognized before the law—only that you shall repeal your unjust enactments against the colored race. I do not ask you to invite me into your parlors; I ask not to be recognized, socially, by any man in the world. We are not demanding social equality. All we ask is the same rights, legally, as yourselves, and to grant this is as necessary to your own well-being as to ours. When our rights are recognized, and let our merits decide the rest.

I see colored men before me; and I would say to them, that every colored man in the community is an anti-slavery speech. Let us try to do our duty, and so conduct ourselves as to convince the white man that we are capable of liberty. Let us, by improving the few opportunities we have, show ourselves worthy of the rights we demand, and so live and act as to leave the world better than we found it.

Anti-Slavery Bugle (Salem, Ohio), 6 October 1860.

1. Douglas refers to Senator Stephen A. Douglas of Illinois, the presidential candidate of the northern Democrats in 1860.

2. Shortly before Douglas spoke, Jane E. Hitchcock Jones read the "Eighteenth Annual Report of the Executive Committee of the Western Anti-Slavery Society," which she had coauthored with Marius Robinson and her husband, Benjamin S. Jones. It recounted the society's activities over the past year, denounced Ohio's black laws, criticized Wisconsin authorities for enforcing the Fugitive Slave Law, and praised John Brown's actions at Harpers Ferry. The *Anti-Slavery Bugle* reprinted the report in its 29 September 1860 issue. *ASB*, 1, 22, 29 September 1860.

3. A clause in Thomas Jefferson's initial draft of the Declaration of Independence held King George III of Britain responsible for sustaining the Atlantic slave trade, perpetuating slavery in the American colonies, and inciting slave insurrections. When southern delegates to the Continental Congress found this clause unacceptable, it was stricken from the document. John Chester Miller, *The Wolf by the Ears: Thomas Jefferson and Slavery* (New York, N.Y., 1977), 7–17.

4. On several occasions during a western campaign tour for Republican candidates in September 1860, William H. Seward suggested that blacks were racially inferior and not capable of participating in politics. In an 18 September speech in St. Paul, Minnesota, he referred to whites as "the great governing race."

George E. Baker, ed., *The Works of William H. Seward*, 5 vols. (Boston, Mass., 1887–90), 4:84–110, 317, 342.

5. Douglas paraphrases a line from "Compensation" in Ralph Waldo Emerson's *Essays* (1841): "If you put a chain around the neck of a slave, the other end fastens itself around your own."

6. Four major political factions nominated presidential candidates in the election of 1860. Abraham Lincoln was the standard-bearer for the Republican party. When the Democratic national convention selected Stephen A. Douglas of Illinois, southern Democrats reconvened and chose Vice-President John C. Breckinridge of Kentucky as their candidate. The Constitutional Union party, a sizable remnant of former Whigs, nominated John Bell of Tennessee. The election broke down into two separate contests—Lincoln against Douglas in the free states, Bell versus Breckinridge in the slave states. With the electorate so divided, Lincoln won with only 39.8 percent of the popular vote. David M. Potter, *The Impending Crisis, 1848–1861* (New York, N.Y., 1976), 405–47.

7. Stephen A. Douglas made these remarks in a 22 September 1860 speech in Cleveland, which came in the midst of his arduous presidential campaign. Robert W. Johannsen, *Stephen A. Douglas* (New York, N.Y., 1973), 795.

8. Abraham Lincoln (1809–1865), the presidential candidate of the Republican party in the election of 1860, believed that blacks were racially inferior and unqualified to vote, to serve as witnesses or jurors, or to hold office. Lincoln, a frontier lawyer and former Whig politician, had served four terms in the Illinois legislature before being elected to Congress in 1847. As a Republican, he achieved national prominence during his unsuccessful 1858 campaign against Stephen A. Douglas for the U.S. Senate. His election to the presidency in 1860 triggered southern secession and the coming of the Civil War. Lincoln is remembered for his vigorous conduct of the war, his commitment to preserving the Union, and his Emancipation Proclamation. Stephen B. Oates, *With Malice toward None: The Life of Abraham Lincoln* (New York, N.Y., 1977).

9. During the late 1850s, members of the Republican party often invoked the political legacy of the Founding Fathers. Abraham Lincoln asserted that Republican principles were identical to those of "the men who made the Union" and that the party sought to "restore the government to the policy of the fathers." George B. Forgie, *Patricide in the House Divided: A Psychological Interpretation of Lincoln and His Age* (New York, N.Y., 1979), 275–76.

10. Douglas refers to a 30 October 1859 sermon by Henry Ward Beecher at Plymouth Congregational Church in New York City. Beecher expressed admiration for John Brown's cause, but deplored his actions. "His soul was noble," Beecher proclaimed, "his work miserable." James Redpath, *Echoes of Harper's Ferry* (Boston, Mass., 1860), 257–79.

11. In 1858, while laboring against the Illinois black laws, Douglas circulated a petition asking the legislature to overturn a state statute prohibiting black testimony in cases involving whites. Several prominent Illinois Republicans, including Abraham Lincoln and Lyman Trumbull, refused to sign. Trumbull (1813–1896), a conservative jurist and politician, served from 1855 to 1873 in the U.S. Senate. Although he opposed slavery, he advocated enforcement of the Fugitive Slave Law and opposed equal rights for blacks until the Civil War. A reluctant Radical Republican, he proved a key supporter of the Thirteenth Amendment in

the Senate. *Lib*, 13 July 1860; Litwack, *North of Slavery*, 93, 276; Mark M. Krug, *Lyman Trumbull: Conservative Radical* (New York, N.Y., 1965).

12. Douglas refers to the commitment of Garrisonian abolitionists to disunionism and nonresistance principles.

13. Douglas suggests that slavery had corrupted the soul of the nation. He argues that it would be more in keeping with the American character to commemorate Herod (37–4 B.C.), a ruthless king of ancient Judea, and the notorious English pirate William Kidd (ca. 1645–1701) than to sponsor searches for the remains of Sir John Franklin (1786–1847), an English explorer who led a heroic but ill-fated Arctic expedition in 1846–47. *DNB*, 7:631–36.

14. Douglas refers to the English Civil War of the 1640s—a struggle between parliamentary and royalist factions. It ended in 1649 with the execution of Charles I (1625–49) on charges of being a tyrant, traitor, murderer, and enemy of the English people. The truculent Stuart monarch had been a staunch defender of the theory that kings ruled by divine right. Douglas's reference to "the government of 1678" probably alludes to the Glorious Revolution (1688) in which Parliament forced James II (1685–88), another Stuart, from the English throne and replaced him with William of Orange.

18.
Editorial by Thomas Hamilton
22 December 1860

South Carolina's withdrawal from the Union on 20 December 1860 reinforced black fears of the slave power conspiracy. The state's petulant
action in response to Republican electoral victories demonstrated that
the South would go to any length to keep slavery secure. Garrisonian
abolitionists, who had clamored for disunionism since the 1840s, believed that slavery could not survive outside the Union, and they welcomed the peaceful separation of the South as the beginning of the end
for black bondage. But black abolitionists maintained a more pessimistic view. Thomas Hamilton's editorial in the *Weekly Anglo-African*,
published two days after South Carolina seceded, expressed the fear
that an independent South might strengthen the institution of slavery.
According to Hamilton, secession merely formalized a state of affairs
that had existed for years; but the South, now fully free of the federal
government, could reopen the international slave trade, which would
increase the region's black population and likely lead to full-scale slave
insurrection. Hamilton predicted that the federal government would
intervene on the side of slaveholders if such a revolt took place.

Secession

People talk of secession as an event about to happen. The truth is, it
happened long ago, and what remains to be done is the mere formality
of sealing by legislative act what the people of several of the cotton States
have long since effected in fact. When South Carolina sent Mr. Hoar
back to Massachusetts, she did, to all intents and purposes, secede from
the Union and the Constitution; and the President of the United States,
who suffered the act to go unpunished, consented to secession as plainly
as Buchanan does today.[1]

For years past, South Carolina and the other cotton States have ceased
to be members of the Union, and have maintained towards the free States
the relation of victors over conquered States.

They have compelled the free States to maintain a standing army for
their protection against slave insurrections.

They have compelled the free States to pay for the carrying of their
mails, and have exercised the tyrannical power of opening letters from
the said free States when found in the mails aforesaid.

They have exercised the right of way through the free States, and the
right to utter in them whatever opinions they chose, no matter how ab-
horrent to their free State audiences.

They have denied the right of way for free State men through the cotton States aforesaid, have arrested them on mere suspicion of holding free State opinions, have robbed them, beaten them, and even murdered them for holding opinions favorable to human freedom.

In short, so far from fulfilling the duties of members of the same Union, these cotton States have acted worse than if they were foreign sovereignties, having relations but one remove from actual hostilities with the Northern States of the Union.

To crown all, these cotton States have the brazen effrontery to whine and howl about their rights overthrown, grievances unredressed, as the reason for their threatened secessions!

The real reasons for secession may be summed up as follows:

1. The cotton States have got from the Union all that the Union can give them and they hope to obtain some new advantages *outside* which they could not gain if inside the Union.

2. The cotton States owe the Northern merchants and capitalists more than the entire States are worth or can yield for years to come. They wish to repudiate this debt. Having lived for years on the unpaid labor of black men, they are educated up to the point of appropriating the unpaid capital of white men—for a man is a man.

3. "Two who do not agree cannot walk together." Charles O'Conor says truly, "When the utter detestation of the life and morals of the people of Carolina have made the basis of a political party in New York, and that political party acquire but ascendency in the political affairs of the government, these two States cannot live together except in the relation of oppressor and oppressed."[2] The cotton States regard as a hopeless task the effort to convince the North that slavery is a blessed and divine institution; hence they coldly, not to say cruelly, abandon the North to the outer darkness of hopeless infidelity.

If these things be so, secession must soon triumph. The Republican party may, by bowing down to the required depth, stave off for a month, or a year, or two years, the formal withdrawal of these cotton States; but the event is as certain as the sunshine and the rain, and depends upon laws as inevitable as the laws of nature. We have no tears to shed on the occasion. Nor do we give vent to expressions of joy, for we cannot tell the issue of the event, when, as a necessary consequence of secession and a renewal of the African slave trade, insurrection of the slaves must follow.

The South cannot keep down their slaves without a standing army. They cannot pay for a standing army except, as in Cuba, by a constant sacrifice of life on the part of the slaves,[3] which will require a renewal of the slavetrade on a scale greater than anything hitherto dreamed of, and which will be arrested by the common act of all Christendom.

Then the South will have to abandon a standing army; then the slaves will increase fourfold more rapidly than the whites; and the slaves, knowing or believing that no Northern army will come down to interfere, will raise the arm of rebellion.

What will the North do then? Will they stand idle and see the masters butchered or driven away from the cotton States? Could they, if they would, reduce the slaves back to slavery?

Weekly Anglo-African (New York, N.Y.), 22 December 1860.

1. In November 1844, Massachusetts sent Concord attorney Samuel Hoar (1778–1856) to South Carolina to protest the imprisonment of free black sailors under the state's Negro Seamen's Act. When a Charleston mob forced him to flee the state before he could challenge the odious practice in the courts, President John Tyler refused to intervene. Hamilton compares Tyler's inaction to that of President James Buchanan in the wake of southern secession. *DAB*, 9:89–90; Philip M. Hamer, "Great Britain, the United States, and the Negro Seamen Acts, 1822–1848," *JSH* 1:22–23 (February 1935).

2. Hamilton quotes from an attack on the Republican party by Charles O'Conor (1804–1884), a successful New York City attorney who frequently represented claimants in fugitive slave cases. O'Conor argued that "amazing, dangerous, and unconstitutional aggression" against slavery by abolitionists and Republicans had left the South with little choice but to secede. *DAB*, 13:620–21; Paul Finkelman, *An Imperfect Union: Slavery, Federalism, and Comity* (Chapel Hill, N.C., 1981), 302, 304–7, 319, 330; *NYT*, 24, 26 December 1859.

3. Cuban sugar growers imported thousands of African slaves annually until the 1860s. Because the vast majority of these were adult males, and most of the females were well along in their childbearing years, the slave population could be sustained only through continued importation. Hamilton compares this to the situation in the South. He argues that, although Congress had prohibited the importation of African slaves into the United States in 1808, secession would force the South to renew the exchange. Throughout the 1850s, a growing number of southern politicians had called for reopening the African slave trade. But when delegates met at Montgomery, Alabama, in February 1861 to draft a constitution for the newly formed Confederacy, they rejected these appeals. Herbert S. Klein, *African Slavery in Latin America and the Caribbean* (New York, N.Y., 1986), 148–49, 248; Ronald T. Takaki, *A Proslavery Crusade: The Agitation to Reopen the African Slave Trade* (New York, N.Y., 1971).

19.
James McCune Smith to Henry Highland Garnet
30 December 1860
5 January 1861

Although emigration advocates found their greatest support on the eve of the Civil War, a majority of black abolitionists remained skeptical. Many black leaders saw little difference between West African and Haitian settlement programs and the older, white-led colonization movement; they argued that emigration meant forsaking the antislavery struggle, the slave, and any claims to American nationality. James McCune Smith brought extraordinary skills and an unshakable commitment to black American citizenship to his analysis of emigration programs. Together with the "Smith clique" of George T. Downing and J. W. C. Pennington, he led the antiemigrationist attack. His caustic critiques of the emigration movement regularly appeared during 1860–61 in the *Weekly Anglo-African*. The following two letters to Henry Highland Garnet, the moving force behind the African Civilization Society and an agent of the Haytian Emigration Bureau, illustrate Smith's efforts to discredit black settlement beyond the United States. He equated emigration to colonization and contrasted the failures of those movements with black achievements in the United States. Smith, fearful that the endorsement of black leaders gave the movement unwarranted credibility, expressed dismay that Garnet, "an acknowledged leader among us," embraced emigration. Smith's sarcastic comments were infused with bitterness and a sense of betrayal, while also expressing the hope that Garnet might abandon "these migrating phantasms" and join the antiemigrationist ranks. Miller, *Search for a Black Nationality*, 241–43; Ripley et al., *Black Abolitionist Papers*, 2:38, 3:56; Dean, *Defender of the Race*, 35–36, 116–18n.

New York, [New York]
Dec[ember] 30*th*, 1860

REVEREND AND DEAR SIR:

The diamond owes its brilliancy to the numerous facets which it presents, and doubtless, in like manner, is your reverence indebted for the manifold luster with which you illuminate your times. There is scarcely a subject, or any side of a subject, connected with the recent history of us blacks for which you have not a corresponding face. Hence you rather astonished your admirers when you began your last manifesto with the ominous assertion, "*No change*."[1] We all knew very well that there was *some change*, present or prospective, in the matter, *or* your reverence would not have been interested.

The sudden agility with which you wheeled about from African civilization to Haytian emigration was not at all surprising to those familiar with your antecedents. One morning, a dozen years ago, while comfortably sitting at breakfast with your coffee sweetened—for you can sweeten coffee—with slave-grown sugar, as it had been for years before, and is again sweetened today—a sudden light broke upon you, that the best and only way to abolish slavery was to refuse to use the products of slave labor; the source of this light came, not by any process of reasoning on your part, but came, like your recent light about Hayti, from an appointment as agent to a Free Produce Association, with such salary as in your judgement constituted a "call." [2] For your reverence, like the rest of your cloth (and of mine), regards the trimmings or fixings—in short, filthy lucre—as an essential in determining the validity of a "call." Yet I exonerate you from mere mercenary motives. When you exchanged the ample salary and comfortable surroundings of your mission in Jamaica for the hard work and moderate pay of Shiloh, it was the jewel in your head rather than avarice in your heart which dictated the change. You doubtless felt that you could live easily and wax fat, but could you shine in Jamaica? Would the reporters of the New York *Herald*, and *Tribune*, and *Times* ever find their way to your remote parish church and essay to report your burning eloquence or flashing wit?

And now, my dear Sir, if Jamaica, with a fine church and ample salary, was not a fit place for you to shine in, why do you urge upon us, your brethren, to go to Abbeokuta, or Hayti, or any other climate equally hot, or hotter? Are we not constituted like you? Have we any qualities or abilities which will enable us, dumped on the shores of Hayti, indebted to the government for our passage-money, have we any qualities so superior to yours that we will be able, under circumstances where you failed, to shine generally and abolish slavery in particular? Or did your reverence leave something behind you in that torrid fox-trap which you would like us to go out and admire?

For my own part, I ask to be excused from emigrating either to Abbeokuta or Hayti, and for the following reasons:

More than a quarter of a century ago, you and others, among whom I was the humblest, pledged yourselves to devote life and energies to the elevation and affranchisement of the free colored people on this, the soil which gave them birth, and through their affranchisement, the emancipation of the slaves of the South. [3] This may be called old-fashioned doctrine; but it is none the less sound, and our pledges are none the less binding on that account. We are bound by these pledges until one of two things occurs. Either the elevation and affranchisement of our brethren, free and enslaved, must be accomplished, or the attempt must be proven useless because impossible of accomplishment.

You know that neither of these things have happened; we are not elevated to affranchisement and equality; and this elevation and affranchisement is not impossible. So that we are still bound by the pledge of our young enthusiasm to labor in this land and for this land.

So far from being released, we are more solemnly bound by those pledges today than at any time since we made them; for we are hourly approaching that affranchisement for which we are bound to struggle. Look at the advancement in wealth, intelligence, and esteem that our people have made within the last ten years. In one of the eastern states (Massachusetts) we have advanced from step to step until we stand on equal citizenship. In Philadelphia, there is a school taught exclusively by colored teachers,[4] in which youth pursue studies as far and with greater thoroughness than was taught in colleges from which you and I were excluded on account of our complexion. In New York City, in that very neighborhood through which we often fought our way to school and from school, an *Irish constituency* has erected on the old site a splendid new schoolhouse for colored children.[5] In the recent election in our State, although opposed by the leaders of both political parties, for political reasons, we obtained seventy thousand more votes for the elective franchise than we obtained fourteen years ago;[6] and we are assured by those who know, that if the vote shall be taken at an election not Presidential, we can carry the State! Do you ever go into Wall Street? Have you noticed quite a number of colored youths, neatly dressed, hurrying from bank to bank with vast sums of money in their hands? Do you not know as well as I that it only requires dash and pluck for these young men to rise higher and higher?

Is it right, my dear Sir, or is it not rather a wanton shame, when the work goes so nobly on, while the goal is within our reach, is it not a shame that you should lend the weight of your name and the luster of your talents to divert us to other and distant fields of labor? I admit that at this moment our enemies are neither idle nor silent. They see our advancement, know its force and bearings, and were never so boisterous as now in overwhelming us with bitter abuse and hard names, asserting our natural inferiority, and that we cannot live on equal terms in the white man's country. Let them howl. But is it right in you, my dear Sir, is it in accordance with the pledges of your youth to seize this moment to give aid and comfort to their devilishness, by not only advising us to leave the *white man's country*—which is our country before God—but even accepting yourself the appointment of "agent" to lead and direct us how and when we shall desert our homes, our duties, and our destinies?

Our Henry Highland Garnet, whose anti-colonization eloquence had spread throughout both hemispheres, our Henry Highland Garnet, an acknowledged leader among us, long known, well tried through many a gallant fight, in this our present hour, half of trial, half of triumph, to accept an agency to drive us out—for you will not lead—from our chosen field of battle! An agency? appointed by whom? By a "Roving Editor" who recently passed through Hayti, and sent to the New York *Tribune* such grotesque, forbidding, hopeless pictures of the Haytians in the rural districts, as leads anyone who has read them to wonder how he could have accepted for himself the appointment of Commissioner from a people such as he described.[7]

Nobody, my dear Sir, marvels at your appointment—but a good many wonder at your acceptance. Next week, with the indulgence of the Editor, I will try and finish my say. In the meantime believe me, reverend and dear Sir, faithfully yours,

JAMES MCCUNE SMITH

Weekly Anglo-African (New York, N.Y.), 5 January 1861.

New York, [New York]
Jan[uary] 5*th*, 1861

REVEREND AND DEAR SIR:

Your schemes of emigration have neither the charm of novelty nor the prestige of success.

The African Civilization scheme is a feeble attempt to do what the American Colonization Society has failed to do; witness Liberia. After forty years of incessant labor, at an expense of one hundred thousand dollars a year—to say nothing of the sacrifice of precious lives and the immolation of brilliant talents and acquirements—we have the admission, through a recent number of the *Liberia Herald*,[8] that if the colonization funds were withheld, Liberia would be unable to support itself. And it is in consequence of their utter dependence on the Colonizationists of this land for their support that the Liberians are obliged to admit into their borders the thousands of recaptured Africans sent there by the United States Government.

I do not see in your African Civilization scheme anything different in character or at all equal in force and power to the American Colonization Society. Yes, there is this difference: the Liberians, by their Constitution, prohibit slavery and the slave trade within their borders;[9] your commissioners—Messrs. Campbell and Delany—in their treaty with the chiefs of Abbeokuta, agree in one of their articles to "*respect the domestic institutions of the country.*" One of those institutions—I have it from Mr. Campbell's own lips—is "THE INSTITUTION OF SLAVERY."[10] You, therefore, as president of an association, one professed object of which is to abolish slavery in America, are joined, without protest, in a league to respect the institution of slavery in Africa. Does your reverence see more than one face in this matter? It shines double to the world without you. Mr. Campbell mildly interposes the statement that the slavery of Abbeokuta "is of the mildest form," &c. Did you ever hear a slaveholder or his apologist admit of any other kind of slavery? But I forget. You have recently sent out pioneers into the land of Abbeokuta. They may change the face of matters. Yet they must be mighty men to do so, being themselves, all told, two barbers and a poet![11] In the meantime, you owe it to your own fair fame to wash your hands of that treaty, which commits your association to "respect the institution" of domestic slavery.

In like manner, the Haytian emigration scheme is an attempt at an experiment which was made, and failed, thirty years ago. At that time the Haytian government sent to the United States one of its most honored citizens—M. Granville—who laid before the colored people proposals for their emigration. Between two and four thousand of our people migrated to Hayti, and within six or ten months nearly all who survived or could get away from Hayti returned to the United States. The Haytian government was unwilling to allow them to leave, and the Rev. Peter Williams and another were obliged to go to Port-au-Prince to plead for the release of their disappointed, distressed, and dissatisfied brethren.[12]

I do not see any reason to believe that the present experiment will be any more successful, because—

1. While the Haytian government *then* gave emigrants six months' board and shelter, the same government *now* offers emigrants only eight days' board and lodging (see Redpath's *Guide to Hayti*, p. 94).

2. Dissimilarity of language is the same now as in 1824. Our people do not understand French; the Haytians do not speak English. "A knowledge of the French language," says Mr. Redpath (p. 131), "is absolutely essential to every one who intends to reside in Hayti." He afterwards proves that a knowledge of Creole is equally necessary. How many of the emigrants whom you prayerfully dismissed to Hayti the other day knew anything of French? How many "text-books and dictionaries" were furnished them by the "Bureau of Emigration"?[13]

3. Dissimilarity of manners and morals. Thirty years have made a vast difference in the manners and morals of the free colored people of the United States—especially in the now free States. We are almost exclusively of the Protestant faith, and live and believe according to that faith. We believe, as you know, in the marriage relation, and are accustomed to the proprieties, the joys, and the responsibilities that spring therefrom. Hayti, according to Mr. Redpath's own showing in his letters to the *Tribune*, is half Romanist, half fetich; not only among the masses, but even in the upper classes—reaching until recently to the very head of the government—there is no such rule as marriage. There are a few noble exceptions. Can there be, will there be, any cordial sympathy between such a people and ours? Will not our young women, married or single, ask to be delivered from such a contact?

4. In your manifesto you say that Hayti needs population, and that you propose to remedy this want by sending thither our colored pop-

ulation. The bureau of emigration is happily located, with this view, in Boston, where, among the colored people, in the year 1859 (see last week's Boston letter in the *Weekly Anglo-African*), there were 326 deaths, and only 183 births![14] How long would it take this class to populate Hayti—or Hades? The true remedy for sparseness of population in Hayti is, that the Haytians should become so far Christians as to respect the marriage relation; and this, I take it, could be done by the preaching of one apostle (such as your reverence, speaking French) sooner than by the landing of a few hundred emigrants, which will be the extent of your labors.

Your duty to our people is to tell them to aim higher. In advising them to go to Hayti, you direct them to sink lower. You and those with whom you are immediately identified—nay, the most, if not all, of our people in the free States—believe themselves of equal force and ability with the whites, come whence they may. We affirm by our lives and conduct that, if degraded, it is not by our innate inferiority, but by the active oppression of those who outnumber us. The Haytians have a proverb, universal among the masses, "*Aprez bon Jo-blanc*"—"*Next to God is the white man.*" The Haytians, too, like the Liberians, further admit their inferiority by making it an article of their constitution that "no white man can become a Haytian (or Liberian) citizen."[15]

No, my dear sir, the free blacks of the United States are wanted in the United States. The people of Maryland said so the other day when they voted that they should not be reduced to slavery. Even the people of Charleston, S.C., say that they cannot spare them as freemen, even to be converted into slaves.[16] And our people want to stay, and will stay, at home; we are in for the fight, and will fight it out here. Shake yourself free from these migrating phantasms, and join us with your might and main. You belong to us, and we want your whole soul. We have lost Crummell, and we have lost Ward, and Frederick Douglass's eyes appear dazzled with the mahogany splendor of the Boston "bureau."[17] Do not, I beseech you, follow their example, and leave an earnest and devoted people without a leader.

As the beloved pastor of a large and intelligent people in the centre of a metropolis which appreciates your talents and acknowledges your genius, you have ample room and verge enough for the marked abilities with which it has pleased God to endow you, without wasting your vigor in the vain attempt to people an island within the tropics. Sincerely and faithfully yours,

JAMES MCCUNE SMITH

Weekly Anglo-African (New York, N.Y.), 12 January 1861.

1. Smith refers to an essay by Henry Highland Garnet entitled "No Change—A Word to My Friends and Foes," which appeared in the 22 December

1860 issue of the *Weekly Anglo-African*. Garnet assured readers that he had not altered his views on emigration, "turned [his] back upon the African cause," or forsaken the Haitian movement. *WAA*, 22 December 1860 [13:0059].

2. At the invitation of English abolitionists, Henry Highland Garnet toured the British Isles from 1850 to 1852 as a lecturing agent for the Free Produce Association, which he helped reactivate in Britain. Smith's criticism of Garnet's free produce activity abroad was probably influenced by Frederick Douglass, who charged in 1849 that Garnet had never supported the movement in the United States. To counter this claim, Garnet had embarked on a free produce tour of the North before leaving for Britain. R. J. M. Blackett, *Building an Antislavery Wall: Black Americans in the Atlantic Abolitionist Movement, 1830–1860* (Baton Rouge, La., 1983), 119–23, 143–44; *NSt*, 7 September 1849.

3. In 1837 Smith, Henry Highland Garnet, George T. Downing, Charles L. Reason, John J. Zuille, and other local black leaders formed the Colored Young Men of New York City to flood the state legislature with petitions asking for equal suffrage. At a 21 August meeting at Philomathean Hall, members adopted a resolution pledging themselves to continue the fight for equal suffrage until it was achieved. This organization prompted the formation of the New York Political Association the following year. *CA*, 19 August, 2, 9 September 1837, 10 February 1838.

4. Smith refers to the Institute for Colored Youth.

5. Smith and Henry Highland Garnet attended African Free School No. 1 at 135 Mulberry Street in New York City from 1826 to 1828. In 1859 the forty-year-old building—by then a public school—was demolished and replaced by a "new and elegant structure, replete with all the modern furniture and equipment." Henry Highland Garnet, *A Memorial Discourse* (Philadelphia, Pa., 1865), 20–23; Freeman, "Free Negro in New York City," 343, 357, 362.

6. In an 1846 referendum, voters in New York state defeated a proposal to enfranchise all adult black males by a vote of 224,336 to 85,406. Equal suffrage was again rejected by a vote of 375,791 to 197,889 in 1860. Black leaders were somewhat encouraged that the proportion of the electorate opposed to extending black suffrage had declined from 72.8 to 63.6 percent. Field, *Politics of Race*, 59–64, 126–27.

7. In late 1860, Henry Highland Garnet became an agent of the Haytian Emigration Bureau, which was directed by Scottish-born journalist James Redpath (1833–1891). As a correspondent for the *New York Tribune* during the 1850s, Redpath covered the fighting between free-state and slave-state forces in Kansas. He also toured the South and published an account of his travels entitled *The Roving Editor, or Talks with Slaves in the Southern States* (1859). An ally and acquaintance of John Brown, he lionized the abolitionist in two books about his life. After accepting an appointment from the Haitian government in mid-1860, Redpath worked tirelessly for the emigration movement. Smith refers to several accounts of Haitian life that Redpath wrote for the *Tribune* late in the year. Although they minimized the level of Haitian political violence and defended the rule of President Fabre Nicholas Geffrard, many blacks found his reports troubling. Redpath continued his reportage for the *Tribune* during the Civil War. After the conflict, he served as commissioner of education in Charleston, South Carolina, and founded the Boston Lyceum to encourage and manage public lec-

tures. *DAB*, 15:443–44; Miller, *Search for a Black Nationality*, 236–47; *NYT*, 17 December 1860.

8. The *Liberia Herald*, a monthly journal published in Monrovia by the Liberian government, was the only newspaper in the republic at this time. Founded in 1830, it had several editors, including John B. Russwurm and Edward W. Blyden. During 1860–61, the *Herald* published a series of appeals imploring black Americans to settle in the African nation. Hollis R. Lynch, *Edward Wilmot Blyden: Pan-Negro Patriot, 1832–1912* (London, 1967), 9, 15, 25, 255.

9. The 1847 constitution of Liberia expressly prohibited slavery and slave trade within the republic's borders. C. Abayomi Cassell, *Liberia: History of the First African Republic* (New York, N.Y., 1970), 415–30.

10. Smith confuses the African Civilization Society with Martin R. Delany's Niger Valley Exploring Party; both organizations advocated African immigration in the late 1850s. Delany established the NVEP in early 1858 to facilitate Afro-American settlement in the Niger valley region of West Africa. He hoped to recruit black scientists, doctors, and businessmen to conduct the necessary exploration and arrange treaties with the indigenous peoples, but his inability to attract financial support all but destroyed the NVEP within six months. Finally in May 1859, Delany and black Philadelphian Robert Campbell undertook an expedition to explore the Niger valley and find a suitable location for settlement. On 27 December, they signed a treaty with the tribal leaders of Abeokuta that provided land and stated that "the laws of the Egba people shall be strictly respected by the settlers." Delany and Campbell toured Britain to gain backing for their proposed colony early the next year. Campbell's comment on slavery in Abeokuta may have come from one of his lectures in England. Delany also issued the *Official Report of the Niger Valley Exploring Party* (1861), a summary of his and Campbell's findings as NVEP representatives. But these efforts failed to generate the needed funds and the NVEP ceased to exist by mid-1860. Smith's inability to distinguish between the NVEP and AfCS is understandable. AfCS officials, including Henry Highland Garnet and Theodore Bourne, sometimes referred to Delany and Campbell as "our commissioners in Yoruba." Miller, *Search for a Black Nationality*, 170–231, 250–61.

11. In early November 1860, the African Civilization Society sent three agents to Yoruba to investigate the feasibility of establishing a black American settlement there. They carried with them a large supply of Bibles and an assortment of agricultural tools. The mission was headed by Elymus P. Rogers, pastor of the Plane Street Presbyterian Church in Newark, New Jersey. Renowned for his "ripe scholarship and poetical talents," he had published several abolitionist satires in verse. Accompanying him were black barbers John B. Simpson of West Point, New York, and Stephen V. Douglass of New York City. The latter was the brother-in-law of *Weekly Anglo-African* editor Thomas Hamilton. All three men were active in the antislavery movement. Rogers and Douglass were also members of the AfCS board of directors. They arrived in Sierra Leone in early December, then traveled on to Liberia. Although Rogers died of malaria on 20 January 1861, Douglass and Simpson initially hoped to continue the expedition. But they soon abandoned the idea and returned home. Miller, *Search for a Black Nationality*, 230–31, 258; *NYCJ*, December 1860, April 1861; *WAA*, 23 July 1859, 28 January, 28 April 1860, 19 January, 2 February, 6 April 1861, 3, 24 January 1863

[12:0450, 0661]; Circular of the African Civilization Society, 16 February 1859, Gerrit Smith Papers, NSyU [11:0588]; S. V. Douglass to George Whipple, 20 February 1861, AMA-ARC.

12. The government of Haiti sparked an immigration movement in 1824 by offering to provide transportation and grant homesteads to black Americans willing to settle in the island nation. President Jean-Pierre Boyer dispatched Jonathan Granville (1785–1839), a French-educated official, to the United States to promote Haiti and recruit settlers in northern black communities. Some black leaders rushed to embrace the scheme, and emigration societies were soon formed in Philadelphia, New York City, and Baltimore. According to official estimates, nearly six thousand black Americans settled in Haiti during the mid-1820s. But legal barriers, the climate, disease, and differences in religion and language proved more burdensome than most emigrants had expected. Beginning in early 1825, they began to return to the United States, bearing complaints and pessimistic reports about Haitian life. Despite Smith's assertion to the contrary, the Haitian government permitted them to leave. At least one-third of the settlers eventually returned home. Peter Williams, Jr., the pastor of St. Philip's Episcopal Church in New York City, went to Haiti in April to investigate conditions among the emigrants. Fifty-six settlers returned with him to the United States. Disillusioned, the Boyer government withdrew its offer of travel stipends and land grants. Miller, *Search for a Black Nationality*, 74–82; Julie Winch, *American Free Blacks and Emigration to Haiti*, Centro de Investigaciones del Caribe y América Latina Working Paper no. 33 (Río Piedras, Puerto Rico, 1988), 9–11, 19–20.

13. Smith refers to the Haytian Emigration Bureau. In order to stimulate black American settlement in Haiti, the Haitian government appointed James Redpath as its commissioner of emigration in the United States in mid-1860. Armed with a $20,000 annual budget, he set about the task of recruiting emigrants. Redpath soon established the HEB, with headquarters in Boston and a branch office in New York City. These offices directed publicity efforts, processed applications from potential emigrants, and arranged their passage. To spread word of Haiti's advantages, Redpath enlisted a number of lecturing agents—including Henry Highland Garnet, William Wells Brown, H. Ford Douglas, James T. Holly, William J. Watkins, and John Brown, Jr.—to tour black communities throughout Canada West and the northern United States. He also initiated a publication program. The bureau printed and circulated *A Guide to Hayti* (1860), a pamphlet by Redpath enumerating the benefits of Haitian settlement. In early 1861, Redpath purchased the *Weekly Anglo-African* from Thomas Hamilton and made it an HEB organ. Renamed the *Pine and Palm*, it appeared under the editorship of George Lawrence, Jr., from May 1861 until September 1862. The HEB eventually persuaded some two thousand blacks to settle in Haiti. But reports from disillusioned emigrants, growing opposition on the part of black leaders, and the coming of the Civil War destroyed support for the Haitian movement by autumn 1862. The HEB soon closed its doors. Dean, *Defender of the Race*, 34–37, 118n; Miller, *Search for a Black Nationality*, 236–47.

14. Smith refers to a letter by George W. Potter in the 5 January 1861 issue of the *Weekly Anglo-African*. Potter, the paper's regular Boston correspondent, cited the city registrar's report for 1859, which indicated that 46 black children

had been born that year—22 more than the previous year. The registrar also reported that there had been 183 births and 326 deaths among local blacks over the past five years.

15. Article 5, section 13, of Liberia's 1847 constitution limited citizenship to "persons of color." Other provisions in the document mandated that only citizens could own property, vote, or run for political office. The 1804 constitution of Haiti denied the right of property ownership to whites. Cassell, *Liberia*, 415–30; H. P. Davis, *Black Democracy: The Story of Haiti* (New York, N.Y., 1967), 96.

16. In the wake of John Brown's raid, most southern state legislatures considered proposals to expel or enslave their free black population. Arkansas legislators approved a bill requiring free blacks to leave the state by 1 January 1860. But a backlash of white opinion soon doomed similar measures. Maryland voters overwhelmingly rejected an enslavement statute in a November 1860 referendum. The South Carolina legislature considered expulsion bills in 1859 and again in 1860, but opposition led by Charleston representatives prevented their passage. Berlin, *Slaves without Masters*, 370–80; Michael P. Johnson and James L. Roark, *Black Masters: A Free Family of Color in the Old South* (New York, N.Y., 1984), 166–68.

17. After living in Britain for several years, black abolitionists Alexander Crummell and Samuel R. Ward declined to return to the United States. Crummell immigrated to Liberia in 1853, and Ward settled in Jamaica two years later. Frederick Douglass abandoned his opposition to Haitian immmigration in January 1861, saying that it "may prove advantageous to many families." He intended to visit Haiti, but changed his mind with the outbreak of the Civil War. Ripley et al., *Black Abolitionist Papers*, 1:147–48, 301; Miller, *Search for a Black Nationality*, 239–40.

20.
Editorials by George Lawrence, Jr.
13 April 1861
27 April 1861

"We want Nat Turner—not speeches; Denmark Vesey—not resolutions; John Brown—not meetings," announced an April 1861 editorial
in the *Weekly Anglo-African*. After more than a decade of pessimism
and despair, many black abolitionists viewed armed insurrection, guerrilla warfare, and revolution as the only effective means for ending slavery. The failure of moral suasion and political abolitionism to arrest the
growth of the institution, coupled with the South's growing militancy,
compelled a large number of blacks to endorse violence. The following
editorials by George Lawrence, Jr., the new editor of the *Weekly Anglo-
African*, express the black community's most bellicose sentiments. Lawrence, the son of a prominent local black abolitionist, was the New
York City agent for the Haytian Emigration Bureau and later coedited
the *Pine and Palm* with James Redpath. The first editorial was probably
written a matter of hours before South Carolina's attack on Fort Sumter; the second was published shortly after the outbreak of the Civil
War. Both called for the violent overthrow of slavery and urged blacks
to kill the tyrants that oppressed them. They reflect the widely held
conviction among black leaders that only through war or insurrection
could "the sins of this demonized people be washed away." Ripley et al.,
Black Abolitionist Papers, 3:56–57; Miller, *Search for a Black Nationality*, 242; FDP, 15 December 1854 [9:0285]; WAA, 16 March 1861,
12 April 1862, 3 January, 11 April 1863 [14:0238].

A CARBONARI WANTED

CHICAGO, April 3, 1861.—A colored man named Harris, and his
wife and two children were arrested here this morning, on a warrant issued by United States Commissioner Corneau, and sent by
special train to Springfield, where they will be examined tomorrow.
The man is claimed by Mr. Patterson, of St. Louis County, Mo.,
and the woman and children by Mr. Veil of the same county, from
whence they have escaped. As it was almost entirely unknown that
warrants were issued, they were executed with little difficulty but
after the affair became known the most intense excitement pre-
vailed among the colored portion of the community, and large numbers gathered at the depot at the time the regular morning train left,
the crowd supposing the fugitives to be on board. One or two shots
were fired at the train. Beyond this there was no disturbance.[1]

The only way to stop scenes like the above is to make the slave-hounds *personally responsible*. We want a Carbonari, as swift and terrible as that which has been the terror of European tyrants.[2] We want men like Orsini who will dare to go through all guards to strike at the oppressor's heart.[3] Every wretch who dares to defile himself by kidnapping must be held accountable to outraged humanity *with his life*. Until the whole pack of panting bloodhounds of Commissioners, Marshals and Deputies *know* that for every unfortunate returned to bondage, some *one* of their number will fall under the pistol, knife, or poison of the Avenger, there will be no peace for the poor; no security for the oppressed. Let the infamous wretches understand that the issues between freedom and slavery are the broad issues of life and death, and these damnable scenes of diabolism will cease. If we are not strong enough openly to *resist*, we are strong enough to *conspire*. "One or two shots were fired at the train." What imbecility? Why not have saved the powder and ball and fired them through the corrupt heart of the manstealer, Commissioner Corneau? Until these things are done there will be no security in the land.

If we are not prepared to act upon the idea that "man must be free, if not within the law, then above the law," in these demonized States, then let us prepare to go where we can be free, and untrammeled live out our lives.

P.S. Since the above was written the tragedy has been consummated, and the husband, wife, and children sent back to bondage in Missouri. There they will without doubt be sold into the Cotton States. Springfield, Ill., the home of President Lincoln, has the infamy of consummating this tragedy. God pity the victims, and punish the Oppressor. Only through the Red Sea of civil war and insurrection can the sins of this demonized people be washed away.

Weekly Anglo-African (New York, N.Y.), 13 April 1861.

"One man in the right is a majority." Frederick Douglass crystalized the heroism that animates practical Abolitionists in those ringing words. They were forcibly brought to our minds by hearing a prominent orator say, that, being in the minority, it was no use trying, for colored men to attempt stemming the current. We wonder if he thought *that*, when, but a few years since, as a slave, he fled the land of bondage. Five hundred black men, divided into guerilla bands, and working their way through the mountain Ranges of Virginia, Kentucky, Tennessee, Arkansas, and the swamps of the Atlantic Coast, can do more to destroy slavery than five-thousand Regulars. It only wants men determined to do or die. White men had this spirit at Harpers Ferry on that memorable October morn.

We want Nat Turner—not speeches; Denmark Vesey—not resolutions; John Brown—not meetings.

Weekly Anglo-African (New York, N.Y.), 27 April 1861.

1. On the morning of 3 April 1861, a fugitive slave named Harris and his wife and three children were arrested in Chicago by the local U.S. marshal on a warrant issued by Stephen A. Corneau of Springfield, the federal fugitive slave commissioner for Illinois. Despite public protest by several hundred Chicago blacks and the condemnation of the local press, the Harris family was taken by train to Springfield. After a hearing before Corneau the following day, they were remanded to two slaveowners from St. Louis County, Missouri. Such aggressive enforcement of the Fugitive Slave Law sparked a mass exodus of black residents from Chicago; in the week following the Harris family's arrest, three hundred blacks left the city for Canada West. *CT*, 4, 6 April 1861; *NASS*, 13 April 1861; *DM*, May 1861; Paul M. Angle, *"Here I Have Lived": A History of Lincoln's Springfield, 1821–1865* (New Brunswick, N.J., 1935), 226.

2. The *Carbonari* (which means "charcoal-burners" in Italian) were members of a secret society dedicated to the violent overthrow of authoritarian rule and the establishment of constitutional government in Italy.

3. Felice Orsini (1819–1858), an Italian revolutionary, attempted to assassinate Napoleon III in 1857 by throwing a bomb at his carriage as he rode through the streets of Paris. The emperor escaped unharmed but many bystanders were killed. Orsini was executed for this act in 1858. *CBD*, 1007.

21.
James McCune Smith to Gerrit Smith
22 August 1861

Black abolitionists were the conscience of the antislavery movement. They continually challenged their white colleagues to stay focused on the proper goals—an unequivocal commitment to ending slavery and fighting prejudice. With the outbreak of the Civil War, many white abolitionists rallied behind the Lincoln administration, despite its ambiguous position on the slavery issue. James McCune Smith saw a wavering of antislavery resolve and feared that the clamor to save the Union would muffle the call for emancipation. His 22 August 1861 letter to Gerrit Smith accused the New York philanthropist of being "unequal to the exigency of the hour." The two reformers had cooperated on a wide range of issues since the 1830s, but this long-standing friendship did not deter James McCune Smith from expressing his disappointment. He called on Gerrit Smith to make slavery the focus of political debate and to keep emancipation central to a resolution of the nation's political crisis. James M. McPherson, *The Struggle for Equality: Abolitionists and the Negro in the Civil War and Reconstruction* (Princeton, N.J., 1964), 47–60; Ripley et al., *Black Abolitionist Papers*, 3:479–81, 482n; 4:42–45, 274–75.

New York, [New York]
Aug[ust] 22, 1861

Dear friend:

I thank you for a copy of your letter to the "Dem. State Comee,"[1] and proceed to be faithful to you about it.

I do not like the heading of it: it has not the ring of your metal: it hides the issue, and does not express the only terms in which peace can be made—emancipation.

I charge you therefore, and charge the Garrison party likewise with being unequal to the exigency of the hour. After lives spent in signal devotion to the cause of the slave you farily abandon that cause in the hour of its trial and triumph. A sort of Bull's Run phrenzy seems to have seized on you inasmuch as you are fleeing from a half won field.[2]

This is strong language: what are the facts: because the South chose to storm Sumter and rave generally, the Garrison host abandoned its May meeting in New York;[3] and you cried hosanna to the coming hour of Emancipation: you lent the sanction of your great name to the support of an Administration which, with trembling knees and in the face of the enemy endeavered to pacify the South by returning Fugitive slaves![4]

And, to day, when ever since the Bull Run panic, a field has been opened for you to do most effectual Anti-Slavery work with the masses, you bandy words with a dead Democratic Committee! A Single sentence from that letter shows that you fail to see "the Situation." You say "for whilst the other President (Davis)[5] is cheered and strengthened by the entire devotion ~of all~ to his cause of all around him." &c. &c.

Is this true? is it not virtually ignoring one half of those around Jeff Davis (I mean the Slaves)? I know that you allude to them, but only hypothetically, in a preceding sentence: but that does not cover the ignoring in the sentence quoted.

Let me tell you how I see this "situation": and what I expect from you.

First. The whole nation is upon the "Anxious seat," enquiring "what shall we do to be Saved?"[6]

Second. The only salvation of this nation is <u>Immediate Emancipation</u>.

Third. As soon as the people are convinced of this great truth, they will ordain and carry out <u>Immediate Emancipation</u>.

Fourth. You are the man to convince the people of this great truth by shouting it in their ears throughout the land by voice and pen.

You can write in your own strong style, one pamphlet entitled "Slavery the sole cause, Emancipation the sole remedy for the Rebellion."[7] You may Appendix it with a paragraph or two showing the entire safety of Immediate Emancipation: and let this pamphlet be showered in millions of copies through every household in the North, and wherever it can reach in the South.

The people thus moved would cause the Administration and Congress to move; and if these last moved too slowly they would topple in the mud and leave room for veteran Anti-Slavery men to do all the good work.

In addition, let the tables of the coming Congress groan with the weight of petitions urging Immediate Emancipation. Sincerely, your loving friend,

James McCune Smith

Gerrit Smith Papers, George Arents Research Library, Syracuse University, Syracuse, New York. Published by permission.

1. Smith refers to Gerrit Smith's 13 August 1861 letter to the New York State Democratic Committee, which was reprinted ten days later in the *Liberator* under the heading, "No Terms with Traitors: The Submission of the Rebels the Sole Condition of Peace." The letter criticized Democrats for failing to join with Republicans in a show of political unity against the Confederacy. Although Gerrit Smith never directly raised the issue of emancipation, he did mention the slavery question, noting that "whilst the South is wholly and hotly determined to maintain Southern Slavery and kill Northern Liberty, the North is half-heartedly in the work of maintaining both." Smith questioned whether continued Union neglect of emancipation and equal rights for blacks might not

"bring this mighty element into a sincere . . . identification with our foe." *Lib*, 23 August 1861.

2. Smith compares Gerrit Smith's behavior to the actions of Union soldiers at the first battle of Bull Run, which was fought on 21 July 1861 at Manassas Junction, Virginia. Confederate forces won a decisive victory, routing the inexperienced Union troops and forcing them to flee panic-stricken back to Washington, D.C. *HTECW*, 91–92.

3. On 14 April 1861, the commander of Fort Sumter, a Union garrison in Charleston harbor, surrendered to Confederate forces after two days of artillery bombardment. The fall of Sumter signaled the beginning of the Civil War. In response to the attack, William Lloyd Garrison and the executive committee of the American Anti-Slavery Society took the unprecedented action of canceling the organization's annual May meeting, believing that antislavery sentiment would sweep across the North. Garrison misjudged popular sentiment during the early stages of the Civil War; many abolitionists disagreed with the decision, arguing that events demanded more agitation, not less. Wendell Phillips Garrison and Francis Jackson Garrison, *William Lloyd Garrison, 1805–1879: The Story of His Life*, 4 vols. (New York, N.Y., 1885–89), 4:20–22; McPherson, *Struggle for Equality*, 55–58.

4. The Lincoln administration's policy on fugitive slaves was driven by political demands and characterized by varying degrees of enforcement. Hoping to strengthen Unionist sentiment in the border states, Attorney General Edward Bates instructed federal marshals to faithfully execute the Fugitive Slave Law in that region. Washington jails filled up with escaped slaves waiting to be claimed by their masters. Federal commissioners and Union army officers returned runaways to loyal slaveowners in Missouri, Kentucky, Delaware, and Maryland. But further South, the fate of slaves taking refuge behind Union lines often depended on military exigencies and the views of individual commanders. On 6 August 1861, Congress passed the First Confiscation Act, giving Union commanders the authority to protect the slaves of disloyal owners who had escaped to their lines. These runaways were now defined as contrabands of war. But the Fugitive Slave Law remained in force in the border states until repealed by Congress in June 1864. Benjamin P. Thomas, *Abraham Lincoln* (New York, N.Y., 1952), 310–11; Stanley W. Campbell, *The Slave Catchers: Enforcement of the Fugitive Slave Law, 1850–1860* (Chapel Hill, N.C., 1968), 188–94.

5. Jefferson F. Davis (1808–1889), an outspoken and persistent champion of slavery and the South, was president of the Confederacy during the Civil War. Prior to the war, he had represented Mississippi in the U.S. House of Representatives (1845–46) and the Senate (1847–51, 1857–61) and served as secretary of war in the administration of President Franklin Pierce. Despite Davis's undisputed commitment to Southern independence, his inflexibility and poor judgment hampered the Confederate war effort. He was captured on 10 May 1865 and confined for two years to Fortress Monroe, Virginia. The federal government later abandoned plans to try Davis for treason, and he spent his last years traveling and writing his apologia, *The Rise and Fall of the Confederate Government* (1881). *HTECW*, 208–9.

6. The "anxious seat"—a bench placed near the front of the congregation in

revival meetings—was a common feature of American evangelicalism. It was reserved for individuals concerned about their spiritual welfare. Mitford M. Ma-
thews, *A Dictionary of Americanisms on Historical Principles* (Chicago, Ill.,
1951), 36.

    7. Gerrit Smith never wrote a pamphlet with this title.

22.
The Black Role in the Civil War

"R. H. V." to Robert Hamilton
September 1861

Alfred M. Green to Robert Hamilton
October 1861

After the fall of Fort Sumter, thousands of northern blacks rallied to the Union cause. Groups of black men in Boston, New York City, Philadelphia, and other cities organized independent militia units and volunteered for service, only to be rebuffed by the Lincoln administration. During the months that followed, the black community debated its proper role in the conflict. Many black leaders were convinced that nothing could be gained by supporting the war effort. The African Methodist Episcopal church declared that blacks had no responsibility to fight for a country that oppressed them. Others believed that black support might move the nation toward emancipation and ease racial tensions. By the close of 1861, most blacks resolved to withhold their support for the Union until the destruction of slavery became its central aim, pledging to labor "for the slave, and the slave alone." The *Weekly Anglo-African* urged blacks to organize, drill, and stand ready, but to respond only "when the slave calls." The following letters by "R. H. V."—most likely Robert H. Vandyne, a New York City correspondent and financial contributor to the *Anglo-African*—and Alfred M. Green of Philadelphia were part of a lengthy exchange in the paper during the fall of 1861 and reflected the debate in northern black communities. *Lib*, 10 May 1861 [13:0525]; *WAA*, 20, 27 April, 4, 11 May, 14, 28 September, 5, 12, 19, 26 October 1861 [13:0475, 0486–87, 0490, 0500–501, 0536, 0755, 0779, 0781, 0804, 0816–17]; Clarence E. Walker, *A Rock in a Weary Land: The African Methodist Episcopal Church during the Civil War and Reconstruction* (Baton Rouge, La., 1982), 31–34; Ripley et al., *Black Abolitionist Papers*, 3:58–59.

FORMATION OF COLORED REGIMENTS
MR. EDITOR:

The duty of the black man at this critical epoch is a question of much importance, deeply interesting the friends of liberty, both white and black. The most imposing feature of this duty, I am told, is in relation to military organizations. This question, I am told, is forced upon us by our eminent, educated, farsighted leaders, who, anxious for our elevation and zealous for our reputation, in connection with our white brothers would have us write our names side by side with them upon the immortal book of fame, won by well-contested and desperate encounters upon the battlefield. Claiming that any omission on our part to exhibit that patriotism so noticeable in the whites, will, when history shall record the doings of this memorable country, leave our names without one deed of patriotism or expressed desire for the success of the cause of liberty; not one laurel to entwine the brows of those whose valor like blazing stars upon the battlefield would, no doubt, have eclipsed those whom we now are satisfied to acknowledge as superiors and protectors. Is this all wisdom, this mode of reasoning; or is it a mistaken idea, called into existence by a desire for fame? Is it a demanding necessity that the world will decide belongs to us to meet, thus to prove our manhood and love of liberty? Have not two centuries of cruel and unrequited servitude in this country, alone entitled the children of this generation to the rights of men and citizens? Have we not done our share towards creating a national existence for those who now enjoy it to our degradation, ever devising evil for our suffering, heart-crushed race?

Who that will carefully note the many historical reminiscences, made mention of by those who are ready to do justice to us, can doubt our bravery? Who that has heard of the many privations, hair-breadth escapes, and the unflinching determination of our enslaved brethren seeking the free shores of Canada, can doubt our love of liberty? True patriotism does not consist in words alone, neither do patriotic demonstrations always contribute to the end alone, independent of material aid. I do not suppose any people have been taxed heavier or more than the poor colored people for the cause of liberty, with such small results to themselves. Now, if we have contributed our share to support and establish a government, that we are not entitled to a share in the benefits thereof, what becomes our duty when that government is menaced by those they have cherished at the expense of our blood, toil and degradation?

Let your own heart answer this question, and no regiments of black troops will leave their bodies to rot upon the battlefield beneath a Southern sun—to conquer a peace based upon the perpetuity of human bondage—stimulating and encouraging the inveterate prejudice that now bars our progress in the scale of elevation and education.

I claim that the raising of black regiments for the war would be highly impolitic and uncalled for under the present state of affairs, knowing, as we do, the policy of the government in relation to colored men. It would show our incompetency to comprehend the nature of the differences existing between the two sections now at variance, by lending our aid to either party. By taking such measures, we invite injustice at the hands of those we prefer to serve; we would contribute to the African colonization scheme, projected a half century ago,[1] by ridding the country of that element so dangerous to the charming institution of negro slavery.

Entertaining the sentiment and determination that they do, would it not be unjust in them to accept our service? Would we still invite them to cap the climax by forcing us to the cannon's mouth to save the destruction of those whose whole existence should be merged in with their country's weal and woe? That death should be the readiest sacrifice patriotic citizens could offer to uphold the people's hope, the people's palladium, no one should deny. But what do we enjoy, that should inspire us with those feelings towards a government that would sooner consign five millions of human beings to never-ending slavery than wrong one slave master of his human property? Does not the contemplation of so flagrant a wrong cause your blood to boil with Christian indignation, or bring tears to the eyes of your brokenhearted old men, whose heads, now silvered by time or bleached by sorrow, can no longer shoulder the weightier responsibilities of a young man's calling?

Not only that. Any public demonstration (for this could not well be done in a corner) would only embarrass the present administration, by stirring up old party prejudices which would cause the loss of both sympathy and treasure, which the government cannot well afford to lose at present. By weakening the arm of the government, we strengthen that of the slave power, who would soon march through these States without fear of forcible resistance.

It would be contrary to Christian humanity to permit so flagrant an outrage in silence to be perpetuated upon any people, especially a class who have known naught else but wrong at their hands, whom they would so gloriously serve in time of danger to their own liberties and sacred rights, proffering now their services to uphold a government leagued with perdition, upon which the doom of death is written, unless they repent, in letters so plain that he who runs may read. Let us weigh well this thing before taking steps which will not only prove disastrous to the cause we would help, but bring suffering and sorrows upon those left to mourn unavailingly our loss.

I maintain that the principle of neutrality is the only safe one to govern us at this time. When men's lives are in their hands, and so little inducement as there is for us to cast ourselves into the breach, our work for the present lies in quite a different channel from assuming war responsibilities uninvited, with no promised future in store for us—a dilemma inviting enmity and destruction to the few, both North and South, among our people, enjoying partial freedom.

The slave's only hope—his only help—is his suffering brother at the North. When we are removed, the beacon light which directs and assists the panting fugitive is darkened and obscured—his once bright hope, that gave comfort to him as he pressed on to liberty's goal, is shadowed o'er forever. Our own precipitous, unwise zeal must never be the cause to stay the car of freedom, but ever let it roll onward and upward until earth and heaven united shall become one garden of paradisal freedom, knowing no color, no clime, but all one people, one language, one Father, Almighty God.

Once under army discipline, subject to the control of government officers or military leaders, could we dictate when and where the blow should be struck? Could we enter upon Quixotic crusades of our own projecting, independent of the constituted authorities, or these military chiefs? Will the satisfaction of again hearing a casual mention of our heroic deeds upon the field of battle, by our own children, doomed for all that we know to the same inveterate, heart-crushing prejudice that we have come up under, and die leaving as a legacy unto our issue—all from those for whom you would so unwittingly face the cannon's mouth to secure to them a heritage denied you and yours.

Is this country ready and anxious to initiate a new era for downtrodden humanity, that you now so eagerly propose to make the sacrifice of thousands of our ablest men to encourage and facilitate the great work of regeneration? No! no!! Your answer must be: No!!! No black regiments, unless by circumstances over which we have no option, no control; no initiatory war measures to be adopted or encouraged by us. Our policy must be neutral, ever praying for the success of that party determined to initiate first the policy of justice and equal rights.

Who can say that in another twelve months' time the policy of the South will not change in our favor, if the assistance of England or France will by it be gained, rather than submit to Northern dictation or subjugation?[2] Did that idea ever suggest itself to your mind? Strange things happen all the while. Look back for the last twenty-four months, and ask yourself if you could have foretold what today you are so well informed has actually transpired when coming events cast their shadows before?

In these days, principle is supplanted by policy, and interest shapes policy, I find by daily observation, both in high and low places. Although to many the above idea may seem idle and delusory, inconsistent with the present spirit and suicidal policy of the South, yet I for one would feel justified in entertaining it equally with the idea that the North would proclaim a general emancipation so long as she supposed it a possibility to reclaim the disaffected States of the Southern Confederacy.

And, if an impossibility, what would all proclamations to that effect avail?

I believe with the act of emancipation adopted and proclaimed by the South, both England and France (and in fact, I might safely say, all Europe) would not only recognize their independence, but would render them indirectly material aid and sympathy.

To get the start of the Northern slave-worshippers, as they are sometimes termed, who can say that, as a last resort, these rebel leaders have not had that long in contemplation, knowing that should they succumb to this government through force of circumstances, or the uncertain chances of war, their lives would be valueless only as a warning to future generations.

Then, why may we not hope that such is their ultimatum in case of a series of defeats—the liberation of four millions of our poor, heart-crushed, enslaved race. One or two large battles will decide the future policy of both the contending parties—the sooner it comes, the sooner we will know our fate. It is in that scale it hangs.

Then let us do our duty to each other—use care in all our public measures—be not too precipitous, but in prayer wait and watch the salvation of God.

R. H. V.

Alfred M. Green, *Letters and Discussions on the Formation of Colored Regiments, and the Duty of the Colored People in Regard to the Great Slaveholders' Rebellion, in the United States of America* (Philadelphia, Pa., 1862), 13–17.

REPLY

MR. EDITOR:

In your issue of September 28th appears an able and elaborate article on the "Formation of Colored Regiments." I have no desire for contention at a time like this with those who differ honorably from me in opinion; but I think it just, once in a while, to speak out and let the world know where we stand on the great issues of the day, for it is only by this means that we can succeed in arousing our people from a mistaken policy of inactivity, at a time when the world is rushing like a wild tornado in the direction of universal emancipation. The inactivity that is advocated is the principle that has ever had us left behind, and will leave us again, unless we arouse from lethargy and arm ourselves as men and patriots against the common enemy of God and man. For six months, I have labored to arouse our people to the necessity of action, and I have the satisfaction to say not without success. I have seen companies organized and under the most proficient modern drill in that time. I have seen men drilled among our sturdy-going colored men of the rural districts of Pennsylvania and New Jersey, in the regular African Zouave drill,[3] that would make the hearts of secession traitors or prejudiced Northern Yankees quake and tremble for fear.

Now, I maintain, that for all practical purposes, whatever be the turn of the war, preparation on our part, by the most efficient knowledge of the military art and discipline, is one of the most positive demands of the times. No nation ever has or ever will be emancipated from slavery, and the result of such a prejudice as we are undergoing in this country, but by the sword, wielded too by their own strong arms. It is a foolish idea for us to still be nursing our past grievances to our own detriment, when we should as one man grasp the sword—grasp this most favorable opportunity of becoming inured to that service that must burst the fetters of the enslaved and enfranchise the nominally free of the North. We admit all that has been or can be said about the meanness of this government towards us—we are fully aware that there is no more soul in the present administration on the great moral issues involved in the slavery question, and the present war, than has characterized previous administrations; but, what of that; it all teaches the necessity of our making ourselves felt as a people, at this extremity of our national government, worthy of consideration and of being recognized as a part of its own strength. Had every State in the Union taken active steps in the direction of forming regiments of color, we should now, instead of numbering eight regiments or about eight thousand five hundred men, have numbered seventy-five thousand—besides awakening an interest at home and abroad, that no vacillating policy of the halfhearted semi-secessionists of the North could have suppressed.

It would have relieved the administration of so much room for cavil on the slavery question and colored men's right to bear arms, &c. It is a strange fact that now, when we should be the most united and decided as to our future destiny, when we should all have our shoulders to the wheel in order to enforce the doctrine we have ever taught of self-reliance and ourselves striking blows for freedom, that we are most divided, most inactive, and in many respects most despondent of any other period of our history. Some are wasting thought and labor, physical and intellectual, in counseling emigration (which I have nothing against when done with proper motives); others are more foolishly wasting time and means in an unsuccessful war against it; while a third class, and the most unfortunate of the three, counsel sitting still to see the salvation of God. Oh, that we could see that God will help no one that refuses to help himself; that God will not even help a sinner that will not first help himself. Stretch forth thy hand, said the Saviour to the man with a withered hand. He did so and was healed. Take up thy bed and walk, said he, and the man arose; go and wash, said he to the blind man, and he did it.[4] How many are the evidences of this kind. God is saying to us today as plainly as events can be pointed out, stretch forth thy hand; but we sit idly, with our hands folded, while the whole world, even nations thousands of miles distant across the ocean, are maddened by the fierceness of this American strife, which after all is nothing less than God's means of opening the way for us to free ourselves by the assistance of our own enslavers, if we will do it.

Can we be still or idle under such circumstances? If ever colored men plead for rights or fight for liberty, now of all others is the time. The prejudiced white men, North or South, never will respect us until they are forced to do it by deeds of our own. Let us draw upon European sentiment as well as unbiased minds in our own country by presenting an undaunted front on the side of freedom and equal rights; but we are blindly mistaken if we think to draw influence from any quarter by sitting still at a time like this. The world must know we are here, and that we have aims, objects and interests in the present great struggle.

Without this we will be left a hundred years behind this gigantic age of human progress and development. I never care to reply to such views as those which set up the plea of previous injustice or even of present injustice done to us, as a reason why we should stand still at such a time as this. I have lived long enough to know that men situated like ourselves must accept the least of a combination of difficulties; if, therefore, there is a chance for us to get armed and equipped for active military service, that is one point gained which never could be gained in a time of peace and prosperity in this country; and that could have been done months ago, and can now be done in a few weeks, if we adopt the measure of united effort for its accomplishment.

Does anyone doubt the expediency of our being armed and under military discipline, even if we have always been sufferers at the hands of those claiming superiority? But enough of this. As to public demonstrations of this kind weakening the arm of the Federal Government, I must say that I was prepared to hear that remark among Democratic Union-savers, but I am startled to hear it from among our own ranks of unflinching abolitionists.

Indeed, sir, the longer the government shirks the responsibility of such a measure, the longer time she gives the rebel government to tamper with the free colored people of the South, and prompt and prepare their slaves for shifting the horrors of Saint Domingo from the South to the North;[5] and, in such an event, could we rid ourselves from the responsibility of entering the field more than any other Northern men whom the government chose to call into active service?

Could we more effectually exercise proper discretion without arms, without drill, without union, than by availing ourselves of all these at the present time, looking boldly forward to that auspicious moment.

The South (as I have said in an article written for the Philadelphia *Press*, and copied into several popular journals)[6] can mean nothing less than emancipation, by the act of her having thousands of free colored men, as well as slaves, even now under the best military discipline. England and France of course would favor such a project should the South thus snatch the key to a termination of this rebellion from the hands of the Federal Government. But how much better off would we be, sitting here like Egyptian mummies till all this was done, and then drafted and driven off, undisciplined, to meet well-disciplined troops, who will then truly be fighting for freedom; and while we could have no other motive than to help conquer a peace for the "*Union still!*" in its perfidious unregenerate state? Tell me not that it will be optional with us, in the event of emancipation by the South, whether we fight or not. On the contrary, there is no possible way to escape it but to either commit suicide or run away to Africa, for even the climate of Canada, in such an event, would not be cool enough to check the ardor of fighting abolitionists against the hell-born prejudice of the North, and the cowardly black man would sit here quietly with his arms folded, instead of taking advantage of the times, till even the emancipated slaves of the South, rigorous in their majesty, force him to rise and flee to Canada to save his unsavory bacon. Let us then, sir, hear no more of these measures of actual necessity inaugurating a "dilemma, inviting enmity, and destruction to the few, both North and South, among our people enjoying partial freedom." That is a work that cannot be accomplished by loyal patriotic efforts to prepare a hundred thousand men to do service for God, for freedom, for themselves. Sitting still, shirking the responsibility God has thrown upon our shoulders, alone can engender such a dilemma.

Your correspondent also asks whether: "Once under army discipline, subject to the control of the government officers or military orders, we could dictate when and where the blow should be struck. Could we enter upon Quixotic crusades of our own projecting, independent of the constituted authorities or these military chiefs?" Sir, it appears to me that, under whatever changes of governmental policy, our favor would be courted more under such circumstances, and our dictation received with more favor and regard, both by the authorities, chiefs, and the people at large, than by our weak, effeminate pleadings for favor on the merits of our noble ancestry, rather than nerving our own arms and hearts for a combat that we have long halfheartedly invited by our much groanings and pleadings at a throne of grace.

The issue is here; let us prepare to meet it with manly spirit; let us say to the demagogues of the North, who would prevent us now from proving our manhood and foresight in the midst of all these complicated difficulties, that we will be armed, we will be schooled in military service, and if our fathers were cheated and disfranchised after nobly defending the country, we, their sons, have the manhood to defend the right and the sagacity to detect the wrong; time enough to secure to ourselves the primary interest we have in the great and moving cause of the great American Rebellion. I am, as ever, yours, for truth and justice,

ALFRED M. GREEN [7]

Alfred M. Green, *Letters and Discussions on the Formation of Colored Regiments, and the Duty of the Colored People in Regard to the Great Slaveholders' Rebellion, in the United States of America* (Philadelphia, Pa., 1862), 17–22.

1. "R. H. V." refers to the formation of the American Colonization Society in 1816.
2. The major diplomatic objective of the Confederacy was to persuade Euro-

pean governments, especially Britain and France, to recognize the seceded states as an independent nation. But both Britain and France adopted an official policy of neutrality at the beginning of the Civil War. Union military successes after 1862 and the Emancipation Proclamation encouraged European governments to remain neutral, despite the efforts of Confederate diplomats and propaganda agents. The prediction of "R. H. V." anticipated a late foreign policy initiative by the Confederacy, when, in December 1864, Jefferson Davis unsuccessfully sought to win British and French recognition by promising to abolish slavery in the South. Frank L. Owsley, *King Cotton Diplomacy: Foreign Relations of the Confederate States of America* (Chicago, Ill., 1931), 550–61.

3. Responding to the attack on Fort Sumter, Green and other leading black Philadelphians called in late April 1861 for the formation of independent black regiments. Within a month's time, six local companies were organized, equipped themselves, and prepared to fight. A Philadelphia correspondent reported to the *New York Tribune* that "the blacks here are drilling on their own hook. They could muster 5000 here easily." As Green noted, one of these companies wore the exotic uniforms of the Zouaves, Algerian tribesmen who fought with the French army in several European conflicts during the 1850s. Their colorful attire—which consisted of a red fez, white leggings, baggy red pants, a blue sash, and a blue vest—had been popularized by dozens of Union and Confederate Zouave regiments during the first months of the Civil War. But like other Northern states, Pennsylvania refused to accept black volunteers. *PP*, 4, 25 May 1861 [13:0503, 0545]; Benjamin Quarles, *The Negro in the Civil War*, 2d ed. (Boston, Mass., 1969), 27; *HTECW*, 850; James M. Gallman, *Mastering Wartime: A Social History of Philadelphia during the Civil War* (Cambridge, England, 1990), 45.

4. Green refers to three miracles attributed to Jesus in the New Testament. The healing of a man with a withered hand is described in Matthew 12:9–14, Mark 3:1–6, and Luke 6:6–11. Mark 2:1–12 provides an account of Jesus telling a man with the palsy to "take up thy bed, and walk." The healing of a blind man is recorded in John 9:1–7.

5. Green alludes to the Haitian Revolution to suggest that, because of Union refusals to enlist black troops, the Civil War might be prolonged to the point that the Confederacy would arm slaves and free blacks. As he predicts, the Confederate Congress approved the recruitment of black troops in March 1865, less than a month before the end of the war. *HTECW*, 63–64.

6. Green published an article in the 22 April 1861 issue of the Philadelphia *Press*, the leading Republican newspaper in Pennsylvania during the Civil War. But the piece to which he probably refers appeared under the pseudonym "Hamilcar" in the weekly Philadelphia *Sunday Transcript* in May. Alfred M. Green, *Letters and Discussions on the Formation of Colored Regiments, and the Duty of the Colored People in Regard to the Great Slaveholders' Rebellion, in the United States of America* (Philadelphia, Pa., 1862), 1–6; Frank Luther Mott, *American Journalism: A History, 1690–1960* (New York, N.Y., 1962), 347.

7. Alfred M. Green (1833–?), the son of noted African Methodist Episcopal clergyman Augustus R. Green, was born in Pennsylvania but spent much of his youth in Windsor, Canada West. He settled in Philadelphia, advertised his services as a speaker, and lectured widely on subjects ranging from mythology to

temperance to "the Destiny of the Colored People on the American Continent"—sometimes traveling with a twenty-scene "chemical diorama." Green also organized First of August celebrations and joined several local black organizations, including the Banneker Institute and the Philadelphia Library Company of Colored Persons. He joined the antislavery movement in the late 1850s, supported John Brown's call for slave insurrection, and coauthored a letter to Governor Henry Wise of Virginia asking for compassion for the abolitionist martyr and his men. In 1860 Green and eight other Philadelphia blacks were arrested and sentenced to federal prison for the attempted rescue of fugitive slave Moses Horner.

Immediately following the fall of Fort Sumter, Green called for black enlistment and helped form two "home guard" regiments to defend Philadelphia from possible Confederate attack. In early 1863, he recruited black soldiers for the Fifty-fourth Massachusetts Regiment. Green enlisted in the 127th U.S. Colored Troops in August 1864, was promoted to sergeant major, resumed recruiting duties, and addressed war meetings throughout the North. He pressed federal officials to commission black officers and guarantee equal treatment for black regiments and joined in local efforts to aid contrabands in the South. A delegate to the 1864 black national convention in Syracuse, he supported the formation of the National Equal Rights League, arguing that racially distinctive organizations were the best means to obtain black rights. In 1865 he accepted an appointment as solicitor and general agent for the Pennsylvania State Equal Rights League, an NERL auxiliary; in this capacity, he lectured throughout the state and helped lead the battle to end racial segregation on Philadelphia's streetcars. Green also served as secretary of the local Union League.

Green entered the AME ministry and accepted a pastorate in Washington, D.C., in the late 1860s. While living in the district, he joined the Colored National Labor Union, became involved in local politics, and attended the 1869 and 1872 black national conventions. In 1872 Green was transferred to the AME's Louisiana Conference and stationed as a missionary in New Orleans. He later served as pastor of the city's St. James AME Church (1881–83) and principal of the St. James Academy (1884–87), a private school operated by the congregation. A leading AME spokesman during the 1890s, he represented the denomination at the worldwide Second Ecumenical Methodist Conference (1891), edited the church's *Southern Christian Recorder* (1892–96), and participated in attempts to unite the AME and African Methodist Episcopal Zion bodies. Green continued to serve in the Louisiana Conference through 1908. Compiled Military Service Records, RG 94, Adjutant General's Office, U.S. Colored Troops, DNA; Alexander W. Wayman, *Cyclopaedia of African Methodism* (Baltimore, Md., 1882), 68; *WAA*, 17, 24 September, 19 November, 17, 24, 31 December 1859, 9 June, 14 July 1860, 26 January, 2 February, 4 May, 7 December 1861, 25 January, 12 April 1862, 7, 14, 28 February, 11, 18 April, 11 July 1863, 4 February 1865 [12:0048, 0302, 0319, 0590, 0769, 0875, 13:0230, 0262]; *PP*, 25 May, 22 June, 10 August 1861, 5 June 1862; Green, *Letters and Discussions on the Formation of Colored Regiments*; Luis F. Emilio, *History of the Fifty-Fourth Regiment of Massachusetts Volunteer Infantry, 1863–1865*, 2d ed. (Boston, Mass., 1894; reprint, New York, N.Y., 1968), 12; *PA*, 27 September 1862 [14:0516]; *Lib*, 5 August 1864 [15:0476–77]; *CR*, 27 August 1864; Philip S.

Foner and Ronald W. Lewis, *The Black Worker: A Documentary History from Colonial Times to the Present*, 8 vols. (Philadelphia, Pa., 1978–84), 2:42–43, 94; James H. Whyte, *The Uncivil War: Washington during the Reconstruction, 1865–1879* (New York, N.Y., 1958), 97; *Louis*, 14 April 1872, 23 July 1881; *New Orleans City Directory*, 1881–87; Charles S. Smith, *A History of the African Methodist Episcopal Church* (Philadelphia, Pa., 1922; reprint, New York, N.Y., 1968), 131–32, 143, 162, 169–70, 202, 208, 218, 256, 342, 383–85.

23.
Petition of William E. Walker to the
United States Congress
December 1861

Most calls for black resettlement involved migration beyond the borders of the United States—to West Africa, Latin America, or the Caribbean. But from the 1830s on, a few black abolitionists encouraged resettlement on the American frontier. They claimed that separate communities there would offer blacks a sanctuary from discrimination without abandoning their American birthright. This idea was revisited after the outbreak of the Civil War in the hope that it might yield an answer to the question of what to do with the freedmen. In December 1861, Baptist clergyman William E. Walker from Trenton, New Jersey, circulated a petition asking the U.S. Congress to designate Florida as a territory reserved for blacks. Walker printed the petition in the *Pine and Palm* and *Weekly Anglo-African* and persuaded several congressmen to back the program. Frederick Douglass supported the idea in the pages of *Douglass' Monthly* with the prediction that Florida would attract 150,000 freedmen from neighboring Georgia and South Carolina over a twelve-month period. *CA*, 18 November 1837, 31 August 1839, 17 April 1841; *PP*, 28 December 1861; *DM*, November 1862.

PETITION
TO THE SENATE AND HOUSE OF REPRESENTATIVES OF
THE UNITED STATES, IN CONGRESS ASSEMBLED

We the undersigned, confidently trusting in the wisdom, justice and magnanimity of your honorable bodies, beg leave to ask respectfully that you grant all that portion of the country, designated by the name and title of the State of Florida, originally purchased from Spain by the United States of America, and annexed to the United States by an act of Congress as one of the sovereign states of the Union.[1]

Your petitioners request that said act by which she became a state be repealed, and that said state be restored to its original condition of a territory, and that said territory be granted for the use, benefit, and occupation of the free colored population of the United States, their descendants, and all others who may hereafter become free by confiscation,[2] emancipation, or otherwise.

Your petitioners further pray that grants of land be given to each family and adult respectively, (of the aforesaid class), as an inducement and encouragement to emigration, and that said territory be under the protection of the government of the United States until such time as the people of said territory shall show themselves capable of making their own laws and administering their own government.

Your petitioners further pray that nothing herein contained may be so construed as to require any compulsory emigration on the part of the said people of color of the United States to the aforesaid territory.

Your petitioners ask this for the following reasons, and others which may address themselves to your minds:

1. Florida has by a deliberate act of her own seceded from the United States, by which act she has forfeited all *claim, right* and *title* to all lands within said state.

2. The free colored population of the United States, their ancestors and brethren who are in bonds, have helped to make the government what it is in wealth and power. This surely will not be denied.

3. The free colored population of the United States own a vast amount of property, which property is taxed annually, and a vast amount of revenue obtained to help support and defray the expense of government.

4. In every state in the Union the free colored people are proscribed to a greater or lesser extent; their presence is obnoxious to the masses of the whites; they, the whites, will not submit to living with them on terms of equality under the same government. Surely, then, this little spot of six thousand square miles (her resources yet undeveloped), is the place for them (and this is all that is appropriated to one sixth of the whole population of the Union—including slaves).

5. In the colored people of the United States the love of home is inherent, they know no other—no other they want—this place would be congenial to their feelings, sentiments and pursuits, hence they would migrate there, and soon show their capacity for self-government, and become respectable and respected.

6. There are many slaves, and the probability is there will be many more slaves who will be confiscated and set free by the acts of Congress; this territory, then, will be an asylum for that class which would be unacceptable to the free states.

7. The general government has never yet granted to this class a homestead,[3] or permitted them to settle on the public lands; nor have they been allowed the same privileges in common with others which tend to their elevation in the scale of being. Besides this portion of the country, with its climate and other advantages, would alike meet the wishes of both black and white, and in the judgement of your petitioners be a wise and just measure.

These, with many other reasons which might be assigned, your petitioners conceive would justify and secure the passage of such an act, for which your petitioners will ever pray.

Dated Trenton, N.J., December 1861.

                                        Wm. E Walker[4]

Pine and Palm (Boston, Mass.), 28 December 1861.

1. Spain ceded the territory of Florida to the United States in 1819 under the terms of the Adams-Onís Treaty. Spain received no payment, but the United States

settled several boundary questions and assumed $5,000,000 in claims by American citizens against the Spanish government. In 1845 Florida was admitted to statehood.

2. The U.S. Congress approved two confiscation acts during the Civil War. The First Confiscation Act (1861) provided for the seizure of all property, including slaves, used directly in the Confederate war effort. The Second Confiscation Act (1862) established penalties for those convicted of treason against the United States and subjected individuals in "rebellion or insurrection" to fine, imprisonment, and the liberation of their slaves. J. G. Randall and David Donald, *The Civil War and Reconstruction*, 2d ed. (Lexington, Mass., 1969), 283–84.

3. Walker alludes to homestead bills pending before the U.S. Congress. The Republican party platform of 1860 endorsed legislation creating free homesteads on the vast public lands in the American West. In 1862 Congress approved the Homestead Act, which permitted any adult citizen (or future citizen) to claim 160 acres in government land. This act accelerated the settlement and agricultural development of the Great Plains. *HTECW*, 3667–68.

4. William E. Walker, a black Baptist clergyman, was a native of Fredericksburg, Virginia. After attending Oberlin College in the early 1840s, he moved to Cincinnati, where he did missionary work, joined the antislavery movement, and participated in the struggle for equal rights. He later studied at the Western Theological Seminary in Allegheny, Pennsylvania. Walker returned to Fredericksburg in the 1850s as pastor of the black branch of the city's First Baptist Church. He frequently traveled back and forth across the Mason-Dixon line to attend meetings of the American Baptist Missionary Convention, a quasi-denominational assembly of black churches. When the ABMC disfellowshipped white Baptist churches in the South in 1859, he dissented, fearing that it would impede his travels and provoke attacks on his church. But he accepted an appointment as ABMC missionary agent and, in this role, visited black churches and conventions throughout the North. In 1861 he married Procena Arnold of Trenton, New Jersey, and settled in that city. He gained a reputation as a church historian when his "History of the Church in Africa" appeared in the *Anglo-African Magazine* in February 1860.

Walker, a black cultural nationalist, hoped that an independent black nationality could be established in the Western hemisphere. After 1854 he lectured widely on the plans, prospects, and probable success of the emigration movement and "The Destiny of the Colored Race." Walker endorsed Haitian immigration by the end of the decade, and he settled there briefly. In late 1861, he began circulating a petition urging Congress to reserve Florida for black homesteaders. With the coming of emancipation, Walker redirected his energies toward aiding the freedmen in the upper South. In 1863 he organized a Contraband's Relief Association in Trenton. He also visited contraband camps in Baltimore, Alexandria (Va.), and Washington and organized Baptist congregations, Sunday School unions, and missionary societies in those cities.

Walker returned again to Virginia near the end of the war. Although viewed as a black carpetbagger by many former slaves, he became a major figure at the 1865 black state convention, serving as secretary of the gathering. Walker lived in Trenton throughout the 1870s. He became the political voice of the local black community, urging his constituents not to blindly follow the Republicans, but to vote their own interests. He often corresponded with the *New National Era*, a black paper, on political subjects. Walker implored blacks to press militantly for their rights, reminding them that "rights can never be secured or obtained by passiveness, inactivity, or indifference." At the request of New Jersey's black leaders, he lobbied members of Congress for passage of the Civil Rights Act of 1875. James Melvin Washington, *Frustrated Fellowship: The Black Baptist Quest for Social Power* (Macon, Ga., 1986), 41–42, 120–21; Mechal Sobel, *Trabelin' On: The Slave Journey to an Afro-Baptist Faith* (Westport, Conn., 1979), 208, 290–91, 293; *P*, 15 March 1843 [4:0542–43]; Oberlin College Catalog & Record of Colored Students, 1835–62, William E. Walker to Hamilton Hill, 28 March, 7 October 1842, Cowles Papers, OO [1:0543, 4:0393–94, 0472–74]; *FDP*, 29 December 1854, 4 January 1855 [9:0362]; *WAA*, 1, 7, 15, 22 October 1859, 11 February, 14 July 1860, 2, 9 February, 17 August, 12, 19 October 1861, 11 January, 1 February 1862, 17 January, 18 April 1863, 20 August 1864, 15 April, 12, 19 August 1865 [12:0014, 0092, 0129, 0145, 0480, 13:0254, 0692, 0815, 0838, 14:0068, 16:0058, 0096]; *PP*, 17 August, 28 December 1861, 2, 23 January 1862 [13:0692]; Foner and Walker, *Proceedings of the Black State Conventions*, 2:259–66, 273; *Louis*, 5 February 1876; *NEW*, 3 March, 21 April 1870.

24.
Robert Hamilton to John Jay
27 January 1862

Black newspapers such as the *Weekly Anglo-African, Christian Recorder, Pacific Appeal,* and Cincinnati *Colored Citizen* took on new importance in the black community as the Civil War progressed. The columns of the *Weekly Anglo-African* became a forum for public debate on black involvement in the war, emancipation, and Reconstruction issues. The paper also served as a communications link for displaced fugitive slaves, families separated by the war, and lonely black soldiers; its black correspondents provided firsthand accounts of Union military campaigns and the conduct and treatment of black troops. A national network of subscription agents enabled it to circulate widely among black regiments in the field and southern blacks in Union-held territory. Beginning in 1863, the offices of the paper doubled as a recruiting station for black soldiers. Despite financial hardships, editor Robert Hamilton published the *Weekly Anglo-African* throughout the war. He appealed for funds to sustain the paper in a 27 January 1862 letter to John Jay, a longtime friend of New York City blacks. Hamilton told Jay of his journal's special role in informing the black community about relief efforts among the contrabands and collecting and forwarding supplies for the freedmen. James M. McPherson, *The Negro's Civil War* (New York, N.Y., 1965), 346–47; *WAA*, 23 July, 29 October 1859, 17 March 1860, 27 April 1861 [11:0877, 12:0163–64, 0579, 13:0486–87].

Off[ice] of Anglo African
New York, [New York]
Jan[uary] 27, [18]62

Dear Sir:

From your welknown sympathy for my people, I have taken the liberty of sending to your address a copy of my paper, hoping that you will give it a perusal. A paper of this kind is very much needed at the present time, if for no other purpose than to keep our people advised of all movements in relation to their southern brethren, and to instruct them as to their duties toward the same. As the result of such instruction we have been able to foward to Fortress Monroe through the Am. Missionary Asso. and which will be acknowledged in the Am. Missionary for Feb. nearly $300 worth of clothing. Much more will be collected during the present month for said mission and that of Port Royal.[1]

My object in writing this is to ask from you a contribution in aid of my paper. What ever you may be inclined to give will be promptly acknowledged and a copy of the paper will be sent regularly to your address if such is your pleasure.

Hoping to hear from you at your earliest convenience, I am, Yours truly,

Robt Hamilton

Jay Family Papers, Rare Book and Manuscript Library, Columbia University, New York, New York. Published by permission.

1. Fortress Monroe, Virginia, located on a narrow peninsula near the mouth of the James River, became a key garrison in Union efforts to control the Chesapeake Bay and the Virginia coast during the Civil War. Beginning in May 1861, escaped slaves fled to the fort seeking protection behind Union lines. By July more than nine hundred had found temporary refuge there. Within three months, the American Missionary Association began relief and missionary work among the contrabands at Fortress Monroe. Robert Hamilton and Charles B. Ray soon collected $275 worth of clothing from blacks in New York City for the former slaves at Fortress Monroe and Port Royal, South Carolina. The AMA acknowledged these donations in the February and March 1862 issues of the *American Missionary*. Robert F. Engs, *Freedom's First Generation: Black Hampton, Virginia, 1861–1890* (Philadelphia, Pa., 1979), 3, 7, 18–22, 29.

25.
John Oliver to William L. Coan
5 February 1862

Thousands of contrabands began the process of emancipation by fleeing to Union lines during the first months of the Civil War. They usually arrived with little more than their clothes and a desire for freedom and were often met by a Union army that had neither a policy nor the resources to accommodate them. Many black abolitionists redirected their energies toward aiding these freedmen. Dozens of northern blacks applied to evangelical, educational, and freedmen's aid organizations for posts as teachers, relief workers, and missionaries in the South. One of the first was John Oliver, a Virginia-born Boston carpenter and antislavery activist. After hearing former slave William Davis speak in Boston on the condition of the contrabands streaming into Fortress Monroe, Virginia, he "felt a desire to go and help teach them." Oliver's application to a Boston educational association was rejected because it refused to hire blacks. On 5 February 1862, he wrote a hasty note to William L. Coan, an American Missionary Association official, requesting a post at Fortress Monroe. Impressed with Oliver's qualifications and enthusiasm for the work, Coan arranged an AMA appointment. Oliver arrived at Fortress Monroe that May. Like many of the blacks who went South, he viewed missionary work as an extension of his abolitionism. "The work of Anti-Slavery men is not yet compleat," he informed Coan. De Boer, "Afro-Americans in American Missionary Association," 247–48.

Boston, [Massachusetts]
Feb[ruary] 5th, 1862

Dear Brother: [1]

Since I have heard Mr. Davis speak of the condition and Educational wants of the Slaves who are constantly coming into Fortress Monroe and other places along the line of our army,[2] I have felt a desire to go and help teach them. And with my knowledge of both Slavery and the Slave and the condition in which the former has left the latter, I Beleve that I would be of great service to that people. The work of Anti-Slavery men is not yet compleat, and, now that they have melted away the little end of the Chain that has so long heald that people in Slavery, They must also at this very begining prepare their minds for this new berth the crisis upon which they have already entered.

Please let me know what ferther stepts are necessary to obtain a place in the above capacity at Fortress Monroe and the conditions.

Rev. L. A. Grimes will call to see you,[3] Yours very truly,

John Oliver[4]

American Missionary Association Archives, Amistad Research Center, Tulane University, New Orleans, Louisiana. Published by permission.

1. William L. Coan of Chelsea, Massachusetts, was an agent and missionary for the American Missionary Association during the Civil War and early years of Reconstruction. He began work among the contrabands at Fortress Monroe in December 1861. His wife, J. N. Coan, also taught for the AMA and kept a boardinghouse for teachers in nearby Hampton. During 1862–63, Coan promoted the society's work among the freedmen in churches across the North; he raised funds and collected hundreds of barrels of clothing for distribution at Fortress Monroe and Port Royal, South Carolina. Coan supervised an AMA school in Norfolk from April 1863 through the end of the war. He insisted that "there should be no discrimination in employment and remuneration of service on account of color" and advised the association to dismiss whites who violated this rule. But his opposition to social interaction and physical contact between teachers of different races drew criticism from blacks. In 1865 Coan became superintendent of AMA schools in Richmond. From 1866 to 1870, he labored at the Stanton Normal Institute, an AMA school in Jacksonville, Florida. At both places, he worked with local blacks to establish branches of the Freedman's Savings Bank. Richardson, *Christian Reconstruction*, 5, 59, 95–96, 204–5; Sing-Nan Fen, "Notes on the Education of Negroes at Norfolk and Portsmouth, Virginia, during the Civil War," *Phy* 28:204–7 (1967); Carl R. Osthaus, *Freedmen, Philanthropy, and Fraud: A History of the Freedman's Savings Bank* (Urbana, Ill., 1976), 18, 24, 231.

2. William Roscoe Davis (ca. 1812–1904), a former slave and American Missionary Association agent, spoke several times in Boston during late January 1862. Oliver apparently attended one of these meetings. Davis, the son of a slave woman smuggled into Virginia from Madagascar, was born and reared in Norfolk. He learned to read and write with the help of his master's son. Later sold to a planter near Hampton, he worked for a time as a slave overseer and became a Baptist exhorter in the quarters. From the mid-1850s until the Civil War, he hired his time as the operator of a pleasure boat at Old Point Comfort. When the Union army occupied the Hampton area in 1861, Davis remained and found employment dispensing rations to the contrabands at Fortress Monroe. But the American Missionary Association soon recruited him to accompany Rev. Lewis C. Lockwood and William L. Coan on fund-raising tours of the North. Davis informed audiences about the condition of the contrabands and solicited contributions and collected clothing to send South. Listeners thrilled to his lectures, and some reporters compared his oratory to that of Frederick Douglass. Davis returned to Hampton at the end of the Civil War and distinguished himself as a spokesman for local blacks. He established a Baptist congregation, served briefly on the city council, and was rewarded for his involvement in Republican politics with an appointment as a lighthouse keeper. Black education was of particular concern to Davis—he established an elementary school at his church and advocated a traditional liberal arts curriculum over vocational training. Proud, outspoken, physically imposing, and a stern moralist, he came to be regarded in his later years as a patriarch of the local black community. Arthur P. Davis, "William Roscoe Davis and His Descendants," *NHB* 17:75–89 (January 1950); Richard-

son, *Christian Reconstruction*, 59, 95–96; Engs, *Freedom's First Generation*, 16–17, 26, 31, 89, 91, 134–35, 192; *WAA*, 25 January 1862, 21 March 1863 [14:0087].

3. Beginning in early 1862, Rev. Leonard A. Grimes and his congregation, the Twelfth Baptist Church of Boston, regularly collected clothing and other supplies for the contrabands at Fortress Monroe. This was probably Grimes's reason for wanting to meet with Coan. John Oliver to Simeon S. Jocelyn, 25 November, 5 December 1862, AMA-ARC [14:0592, 0602].

4. John Oliver (1821–1899), a free black carpenter, came to Boston in 1853 from Petersburg, Virginia. He was married to dramatic reader Louise DeMortie, but they divorced after he went West to the California gold fields. Oliver returned East by 1856, studied at Oberlin College and Folsom's Commercial College in Cleveland, then taught school in Massachusetts. Although he flirted with spiritualism, he became a respected member of Boston's Twelfth Baptist Church, belonged to the American Baptist Missionary Convention, and prepared for the ministry. Near the end of the decade, he joined the antislavery movement and participated in a campaign to strike the word "white" from the state statutes. Oliver aided the Boston Vigilance Committee, boarded fugitive slaves in his home, and transported many of them to Canada East. An outspoken antiemigrationist, he labeled the African Civilization Society "an infernal enemy in our midst."

In early 1862, Oliver secured a teaching appointment from the American Missionary Association. Working in the contraband camps in eastern Virginia, he founded and taught schools and Sabbath schools, organized local aid societies, acted as a conduit for relief from the North, and worked to protect the freedmen from racist mistreatment by Union soldiers and southern whites. His frequent letters to AMA officials offer an outstanding record of life in the camps. In mid-1863, he left for Philadelphia, where he directed an employment office for freedmen coming into the city. Joining the campaign to integrate local streetcars, he lobbied the state legislature for a law prohibiting segregation on public transportation and became a leading member of the Pennsylvania State Equal Rights League.

Oliver came to Richmond in 1865 to observe the situation of local blacks, but the racism he encountered prompted him to stay and fight for equal rights. He personally shattered many of the city's racial barriers. In 1867 he was one of six black jurors on the federal grand jury that indicted Jefferson Davis for treason. He became the first black notary public in the state, and as messenger of the city council in 1868, was the highest-ranking black political appointee in Richmond. He later served on the council (1872–73) and was named a deputy U.S. marshal. A prominent Republican, he criticized the racism of the party's white leaders and urged blacks to vote as an independent bloc to better influence elections and to win concessions from both parties. Oliver organized black workers in the city to push for better working conditions and presided over an interracial labor convention in 1870—the first of its kind in the nation. He served as president of the local chapter of the Colored National Labor Union from 1870 to 1878. Turning his attention to black education in the mid-1870s, he helped establish the city's Moore Street Industrial School, taught classes, acted as superintendent, and made fund-raising tours of the North. To publicize his views on politics, labor, and education, he edited a local paper called the *Industrial Herald* in the 1880s. Peter J. Rachleff, *Black Labor in the South: Richmond, Virginia, 1865–1890* (Philadelphia, Pa., 1984), 36, 41, 56, 61, 65, 68–69, 90, 93, 99, 103, 187; *RP*, 2, 30 December 1899; Michael B. Chesson, "Richmond's Black Councilmen, 1871–96," in *Southern Black Leaders of the Reconstruction Era*, ed. Howard N. Rabinowitz (Urbana, Ill., 1982), 191, 199, 213, 220; De Boer, "Afro-Americans in American Missionary Association," 247–53, 653n; Betty Mansfield, "That Fateful Class: Black Teachers of Virginia's Freedmen, 1861–1882" (Ph.D. diss., Catholic University of America, 1980), 85; John Oliver to Wendell Phillips, 9, 12 October 1856, 11 January, 1 February, 5 August 1857, Crawford Blagden Collection of the Papers of Wendell Phillips, MH [10:0311, 0314–15, 0492–93, 0528–29, 0722]; *WAA*, 9 June 1860, 12 October 1861, 28 March, 23 May 1863 [12:0765, 13:0816]; William C. Nell to Amy Post, 26 October 1860, Post Papers, NRU [12:1055]; *Lib*, 20 January 1860 [12:0436]; Philip S. Foner, *Essays in Afro-American History* (Philadelphia, Pa., 1978), 35–36, 57; Alrutheus A. Taylor, *The Negro in the Reconstruction of Virginia* (Washington, D.C., 1926), 214, 216, 220, 261, 277; *NNE*, 21 April 1870; *G*, 12 July 1884.

26.
"What Shall We Do with the Contrabands?"
by James Madison Bell

The flight of thousands of fugitive slaves to the Union lines during the
Civil War raised unanticipated political and military questions. In August 1861, as part of the First Confiscation Act, the U.S. Congress defined these refugees as contrabands of war, a term normally reserved
for property and war matériel. As federal officials struggled with the
issue of what to do with the contrabands, abolitionists—black and
white—viewed the matter as a test of the Lincoln administration's anti-
slavery commitment. Many black leaders urged that the contrabands be
"CALLED INTO SERVICE, AND FORMED INTO A LIBERATING
ARMY." In the following poem from the *Pacific Appeal*, James Madison Bell, one of the foremost black poets of the nineteenth century, offered his response to the contraband question. He pressed the federal
government to arm the former slaves and to make the conflict a war
for freedom. *HTECW*, 161–62; McPherson, *Struggle for Equality*,
69–70n; Dudley Taylor Cornish, *The Sable Arm: Negro Troops in
the Union Army, 1861–1865* (New York, N.Y., 1966), 4–6, 36–37.

What Shall We Do with the Contrabands?

Shall we arm them? Yes, arm them! give to each man
A rifle, a musket, a cutlass or sword;
Then on to the charge! let them war in the van,
Where each may confront with his merciless lord,
And purge from their race, in the eyes of the brave,
The stigma and scorn now attending the slave.

I would not have the wrath of the rebels to cease,
Their hope to grow weak nor their courage to wane,
Till the Contrabands join in securing a peace,
Whose glory shall vanish the last galling chain,
And win for their race an undying respect
In the land of their prayers, their tears and neglect.

Is the war one for Freedom? Then why, tell me why,
Should the wronged and oppressed be debarred from the fight?
Does not reason suggest, it were noble to die
In the act of supplanting a wrong for the right?
Then lead to the charge! for the end is not far,
When the Contraband host are enrolled in the war.

J. M. B.[1]

Pacific Appeal (San Francisco, Calif.), 24 May 1862.

1. James Madison Bell (1826–1902), a poet and political activist, was born to free black parents in Gallipolis, Ohio. While living in Cincinnati from 1842 to 1854, he attended a private high school, worked as a plasterer, married and had a family, and was indoctrinated "into the principles of radical antislaveryism." In 1854 he settled in the thriving black community at Chatham, Canada West. Bell became a spokesman for Chatham blacks, participated in local antislavery meetings, served as secretary of the Chatham Vigilance Committee, and began writing and reciting reform poetry. He published some of his verse in the *Provincial Freeman.* John Brown used Bell's home as his headquarters during the 1858 Chatham Convention, which designed a government to be established in the Appalachian Mountains following the Harpers Ferry raid. Bell participated in the gathering and later recruited men and solicited funds for Brown's raid.

Bell moved to San Francisco in 1860. He again plied his trade and wrote poetry that often appeared in two local black newspapers—the *Elevator* and *Pacific Appeal.* He also published several volumes of verse. Bell again participated in community affairs, reading his poems on public occasions, serving as president of a music association, and becoming a lay leader in the African Methodist Episcopal church. He agitated for better black schools and equal rights, led protests against minstrel shows and color restrictions in public facilities, and joined the statewide fight for black suffrage. In 1866 Bell returned briefly to Canada West, then made his home in Toledo, Ohio, where he joined in local Republican party politics and was elected to the 1872 state and national nominating conventions. He supported his family for a decade by giving poetry readings in cities across the North. In 1901 he collected and published his verse in a volume entitled *Poetical Works,* which conveys his views on slavery, the Civil War, emancipation, and Reconstruction. Bell is remembered as one of the foremost black poets of the nineteenth century. *DANB*, 38; Joan R. Sherman, *Invisible Poets: Afro-Americans of the Nineteenth Century*, 2d ed. (Urbana, Ill., 1989), 80–87; *PFW*, 16 June 1855, 8 March, 19 April 1856, 24 January 1857 [9:0699, 10:0075, 0112, 0516]; *PA*, 12 April, 24 May, 28 June, 5 July, 2 August, 27 September, 27 December 1862, 10 January, 16 May, 22 August, 3 October 1863 [14:0242, 0321, 0323, 0373, 0381, 0422, 0514, 0624, 0690, 1018, 1077]; *ESF*, 7, 21 April 1865 [15:0803, 0835, 0836]; Quarles, *Allies for Freedom*, 43–45, 74–75, 131.

27.
Report by William Still
22 May 1862

Although the Civil War eliminated the need to smuggle slaves out of the
South, recently freed blacks required enormous assistance. Black abolitionists met this wartime challenge by transforming local vigilance committees and the underground railroad into a contraband relief network.
With the support of the Pennsylvania Abolition Society, black leaders in
Philadelphia opened an employment office for contrabands in April
1862. William Still, the dominant figure in local underground railroad
activities before the war, headed the new agency. Under his guidance,
the office helped hundreds of former slaves locate lost relatives, obtain
housing, and find work. Still's hastily scrawled report of 22 May to Joseph M. Truman, a PAS official, provides a rare firsthand account of
black efforts to assist the contrabands. Still was so successful that he
became overwhelmed by the demand for his services and resigned in
September. John Oliver, an American Missionary Association teacher
from Virginia, carried on the agency's important work. Still's and Oliver's
efforts demonstrated the continuity of black abolitionism through the
war years. William Still to Joseph M. Truman, 13 March, 8 May, 15
September 1862, Pennsylvania Abolition Society Papers, PHi [14:0184,
0285, 0500–502]; CR, 1 November 1862 [14:0568]; John Oliver to
Simeon S. Jocelyn, 26 September 1863, AMA-ARC [14:1071].

Philadelphia, [Pennsylvania]
May 22, 1862

"The Office for obtaining Employment for Colored Persons &c."[1]
would respectfully report that the enterprise up to the present time has
been quite successfull.

Although no public notice has been made concerning the agency a
knowledge of the Office has been considerably spread by Cards &c.
which has induced many to call for all kinds of help—men & women—
and boys & girls both for the City & Country.

By the Register, I find that 193 persons have applied for help or servants. In some instances individuals have wanted 2 or 3—as high as Fifteen in one case—hence the actual number of persons that have been
demanded very far exceed the number of applicants.

According to the Register places have been obtained for only 74 persons. This is less than the number, however, that has found situations
through this channell.

For instance, some are directed to places, without knowing whether
they ~~can~~ will suit, or whether ~~they~~ parties have been previously accom-

modated, hence such are not intered as having been provided for, ~~al-~~
~~though they~~ as they do not always report their success.

With regard to ~~prices~~ wages, it is difficult for the agent to gain this
information in many instances at least. For the very good reason that the
parties in many cases can not have the chance of interviews before hand,
and before a trial but few are willing to make substantial bargains. Nevertheless as a general thing s the class of persons who apply seem disposed to pay whatever they are worth, from seven to Twelve Dollars per
month for men & from 75 cents to $1.50 per week for women.

The agent has been solicited frequently to make efforts to obtain supplies from Washington. As but few have been coming as of late.

The Freedmen's Association of Washington sent an agent here the for-
part of this week to try ~~and~~ to effect an arrangement with parties ~~here~~ by
which a number might be sent on soon.[2] But the agent was not altogether
successfull in this matter, yet it is to be presumed ~~that~~ the object aimed
at will not utterly fail. Respectfully,

Wm. Still

Agt

Pennsylvania Abolition Society Papers, Historical Society of Pennsylvania, Philadelphia, Pennsylvania. Published by permission.

1. In April 1862, the Pennsylvania Abolition Society opened an office in Philadelphia to help locate housing and employment for contrabands arriving in the
city. William Still managed the agency during its first months, until he was overwhelmed by the number of applicants and was replaced in 1863 by John Oliver,
an American Missionary Association teacher. Still and Oliver placed hundreds of
refugees in jobs, primarily as domestic servants. But by 1865 the task had become
too great a financial burden for the PAS alone. It joined with the Pennsylvania
Freedmen's Relief Association and two Quaker bodies to establish the Freedmen's
Employment Agency, which continued until 1867. Jeffrey N. Bumbrey, *A Guide
to the Microfilm Publication of the Papers of the Pennsylvania Abolition Society*
(Philadelphia, Pa., 1976), 14, 42; William Still to Joseph M. Truman, 13 March,
15 September 1862, Pennsylvania Abolition Society Papers, PHi [14:0184,
0500–502]; John Oliver to Simeon S. Jocelyn, 26 September 1863, AMA-ARC
[14:1071].

2. Still refers to the National Freedmen's Relief Association, which was
founded in Washington, D.C., during March 1862. For nearly a decade, the organization furnished local contrabands and freedmen with food, clothing, shelter,
medical care, employment, and schooling and worked to "bring them under
moral influences." Still cooperated closely with the NFRA and its fund-raising
agent, Edward M. Thomas (1821–1863), a native of Philadelphia. After moving
to Washington, Thomas had worked as a messenger in the U.S. House of Representatives. He led the national Order of Good Samaritans and Daughters of Sa-
maria and was an official in several other black fraternal organizations. Thomas
owned sizable collections of fine art and rare coins and a personal library
of nearly six hundred volumes. In early 1863, he organized the New York

City–based Anglo-African Institute of Industry and Art, a national exposition of black talent. Constance McLaughlin Green, *The Secret City: A History of Race Relations in the Nation's Capital* (Princeton, N.J., 1967), 61–62, 65–68; CR, 1 November 1862 [14:0568]; *WAA*, 13 August 1859, 14, 28 March, 18 April 1863 [13:0010]; Paul Jennings, *Colored Man's Reminiscences of James Madison* (Brooklyn, N.Y., 1865), vi [15:0362].

28.
Editorial by Philip A. Bell
14 June 1862

From the first clash of arms, black abolitionists struggled to make emancipation the focus of the Northern war effort. Their message was unequivocal and persistent—only by destroying slavery could the conflict be ended and the Union restored. But the Lincoln administration's cautious, halting movement toward freedom frustrated black leaders. Their disillusionment grew as they watched the president rebuke Union military commanders who interfered with slavery in areas under their jurisdiction. In September 1861, Lincoln overturned an order by General John C. Frémont that emancipated slaves in Missouri. The following May, when General David Hunter freed all slaves in the Department of the South, Lincoln issued a proclamation revoking the action. Philip A. Bell's 14 June 1862 editorial in the *Pacific Appeal* conveyed the disappointment of black leaders with the president's "pro-slavery proclamation." Arguing that the federal government had the constitutional authority to abolish slavery in the rebellious states, Bell charged that the failure to adopt emancipation as a Union war aim encouraged slaveholders, perpetuated slavery, and supported the Confederacy. McPherson, *Struggle for Equality*, 102–11; Cornish, *Sable Arm*, 12–13, 34–36.

We have refrained, hitherto, from commenting on President Lincoln's Pro-slavery Proclamation in reference to the proclamation issued by Gen. Hunter, declaring the slaves free in the department of the South, over which he had military command, in hopes that the President only denied that Gen. Hunter had "been authorized by the Government to make any proclamation declaring slaves free," in order that action in the premises might come from the highest source, *i.e.* the President himself, moreover, he intimates in his proclamation that he is yet undecided. He says "whether it is competent for him, as Commander-in-Chief of the army and navy, to declare slaves in any State free, and whether at any time it shall become necessary and indispensible for the maintenance of Government to exercise such supposed power, are questions which he reserves to himself, and which he cannot feel justified in leaving to the decision of commanders in the field."[1]

The President exhibits as much tergiversation as ever did our New York Magician, as Martin Van Buren was called, in former days. He is as noncommittal as that "Northern man with Southern principles."[2]

Recent dispatches, however, have given us to understand that the Cabinet has revoked Gen. Hunter's proclamation, and hence slavery is still

5. Philip A. Bell
From I. Garland Penn, *The Afro-American Press and Its Editors*
(Springfield, Mass., 1891)

recognized in the department of the South. We thought from President Lincoln's confiscation messages, his emancipation recommendations and other liberal actions, that it was his intention to strike at the root of the tree of strife.[3] We supposed he was possessed of judgment sufficient to know that it was useless to lop off the extraneous branches, and leave the trunk of the Upas of discord and disunion—slavery—still standing to branch forth again and diffuse its malignant and pestiferous poison over the land; and we still hope he will abide by the principles he has hitherto avowed, on the strength of which he was elected.

The success of the Republican party in the Presidential election of 1860 was predicated on the resolutions passed by the Convention which nominated Mr. Lincoln, commonly called the Chicago Platform,[4] and on the principles therein enunciated, and the President has frequently declared that he would abide and be governed in his administration by these principles.

How does the present action of President Lincoln agree with the Chicago Platform? The 7th and 8th resolutions of that Convention, passed unanimously, read as follows:

> 7. That the new dogma, that the Constitution, of its own force, carries slavery into any or all of the Territories of the United States, is a dangerous political heresy, at variance with the explicit provisions of that instrument itself, with contemporaneous expositions, and with legislative and judicial precedent, is revolutionary in its tendency, and subversive of the peace and harmony of the country.
>
> 8. That the normal condition of all the territory of the United States is that of freedom: That as our Republican fathers, when they abolished slavery in all our national territory, ordained that "No person should be deprived of life, liberty or property, without due process of law," it becomes our duty, by legislation, whenever such legislation is necessary, to maintain this provision of the Constitution against all attempts to violate it; and we deny the authority of Congress, of Territorial Legislature, or of any individuals, to give legal existence to slavery in any Territory of the United States.

An adherence to these resolutions gives the President power over the institution of slavery in the Territories, as they declare freedom to be the "normal condition of all the territory of the United States." The action of the President in appointing Military Governors over the rebellious States, and subjecting them to martial law, reduces such States to the condition of Territories,[5] the "normal condition" of which is "freedom."

We fear the Administration is pursuing a course detrimental to the best interests of the country, and encouraging the Rebels in their efforts to overthrow the Union, and perpetuate slavery.

Generals who are on the ground where slavery exists, and see what effects emancipation would produce, are the best judges when to strike the blow, and, by eradicating the evil, end the war.

We also fear, by the course he is pursuing, the President will alienate his ablest generals from him, and he will be unable to find capable men to take command of departments most infected with the evil. He must either grant them unrestricted power, or appoint such ingrates as Edward Stanly.[6]

Pacific Appeal (San Francisco, Calif.), 14 June 1862.

1. On 9 May 1862, General David Hunter, the military commander of the Department of the South, ordered all slaves to be freed in South Carolina, Georgia, and Florida. President Abraham Lincoln disappointed abolitionists by revoking the order eleven days later, arguing that Hunter had exceeded his authority. Willie Lee Rose, *Rehearsal for Reconstruction: The Port Royal Experiment* (New York, N.Y., 1964), 144–52.

2. Martin Van Buren (1782–1862), the president of the United States from 1837 to 1841, dominated New York state politics during the Jacksonian era and contributed to the rise of modern political parties. His reputation as the "Little Magician" testified to his political skill, but revealed widespread mistrust. Although Van Buren was the presidential candidate of the Free Soil party in 1848, many abolitionists characterized him as a "doughface"—a northern politician who sympathized with the principles of proslavery southern politicians. John Niven, *Martin Van Buren: The Romantic Age of American Politics* (New York, N.Y., 1983).

3. President Abraham Lincoln moved toward a stronger antislavery position during the spring and early summer of 1862. In his 6 March annual message to Congress, he asked the body to consider compensating slaveholders in any slave state enacting gradual emancipation. One week later, the federal government issued an article of war expressly forbidding Union commanders to return contrabands to their masters. Lincoln signed into law in April an act emancipating slaves in Washington, D.C. When Congress passed the Second Confiscation Act in July, Lincoln implemented the law with haste. On 22 July, he ordered Union commanders to seize and use any property (including slaves) necessary to the war effort and urged them to employ black laborers and pay them reasonable wages. James M. McPherson, *Battle Cry of Freedom: The Civil War Era* (New York, N.Y., 1988), 496–99.

4. Abraham Lincoln was nominated as the presidential candidate of the Republican party at its national convention in Chicago during 16–18 May 1860. The gathering also drafted a platform that reaffirmed the party's opposition to the extension of slavery, rejected the concept of popular sovereignty, called for the admission of Kansas as a free state, and denounced calls for secession and attempts to reopen the African slave trade. The party also tried to broaden its popular appeal by advocating free homesteads in the West, tariff revision, daily overland mail, and a transcontinental railroad. Allan Nevins, *The Emergence of Lincoln*, 2 vols. (New York, N.Y., 1950), 2:229–60.

5. Bell's comments on the status of the seceded states raise a central constitutional question of the Civil War era. Peace Democrats, eager to repair the party's

historic base in the South, urged that the rebel states be restored to their antebellum position, thus preventing Congress from implementing an effective Reconstruction program. Radical Republicans argued that the states had committed constitutional "suicide" by seceding, thus reducing them to territories subject to complete federal authority. The Lincoln administration's policy on the constitutional status of these states developed haltingly during the war. By late 1862, Lincoln had appointed military governors in occupied portions of Louisiana, Mississippi, Tennessee, Arkansas, and North Carolina. As the conflict wore on, Lincoln appeared increasingly tolerant of Radical Republican policies in those areas. But his only comprehensive program, outlined in his 8 December 1863 Proclamation of Amnesty and Reconstruction, called for rebel states to be restored to the Union whenever 10 percent of their electorate took an oath of loyalty to the United States. This anticipated a brief and lenient Reconstruction. Harold Hyman, *A More Perfect Union: The Impact of the Civil War and Reconstruction on the Constitution* (Boston, Mass., 1975), 82, 141–47, 156–70, 195–211; C. Peter Ripley, *Slaves and Freedmen in Civil War Louisiana* (Baton Rouge, La., 1976), 160–80.

6. Edward Stanly (1810–1872), a North Carolina lawyer and Whig politician, served in the state legislature and the U.S. Congress (1837–43, 1849–53). After moving to San Francisco in 1853, he practiced law, joined the Republican party, and waged an unsuccessful 1857 campaign for governor of California. Stanly was appointed military governor of eastern North Carolina in May 1862. He hoped to cultivate Unionist sentiment there by returning fugitive slaves to their masters, but was prevented from doing so by Congress. Critical of this action, he resigned the following year and returned to California. *BDAC*, 1743.

29.
William H. Parham to Jacob C. White, Jr.
7 September 1862

The Civil War broke the national impasse on the slavery issue and produced new possibilities for racial progress. Yet the war also created economic hardship and dislocation that turned northern white workers
against blacks. Union military conscription and pro-Confederate propaganda heightened racial animosity and provoked vicious race riots in
several northern cities. William H. Parham's assessment of conditions in
Cincinnati conveyed the anxiety and pessimism shared by many blacks.
Writing to his good friend Jacob C. White, Jr., on 7 September 1862, he
noted the tensions between Irish and black workers on the city's river-
front and described the climate of fear and persecution created by rumors of an impending Confederate attack on the city. Amid the turmoil
of the moment, Parham's thoughts briefly turned to emigration, and he
expressed a desire "to get out of this slavery-cursed and Negro-hating
country." V. Jacques Voegeli, *Free but Not Equal: The Midwest and the
Negro in the Civil War* (Chicago, Ill., 1967), 34–35, 60–67, 82–89;
Williston Lofton, "Northern Labor and the Negro during the Civil
War," *JNH* 34:251–73 (July 1949).

286 West Front St[reet]
Cin[cinnati], [Ohio]
Sep[tember] 7, 1862

Friend White:

Your letter of the 13th ult. was duly received, and found me in my
usual good health.

You have, of course, already seen by the papers that we are at present,
to all appearances, in imminent danger of an attack from the Confederates.[1] At present it is impossible for me to tell you more than you have
already learned; as, owing to the cessation of telegraphic communications, we are unable to learn anything definite; there are rumors enough,
but nothing reliable. Last night it was rumored that the "rebs" had made
their appearance within 5 miles of this city; and when I retired to rest, I
knew not whether I should wake up a subject to Jeff Davis or Abe Lincoln; however, the rumor proved unfounded, and I, therefore, find myself
still under the government of the colonizer.

Never in all my life, my dear friend, have I witnessed anything which
approximated the scenes of the eventful past week. Since Tuesday morning last, preparations for defence have absorbed everything else. All
places of business have been closed—butchers, bakers, and apothecaries

excepted—likewise all places of amusement or recreation. Every able-bodied man was expected to do something toward placing the city in an attitude of defence—some to dig trenches[,] others to shoulder muskets. When I say "was expected" I do not use language sufficiently forcible, as every one was <u>compelled</u> to render aid. Those who failed to come forward and volunteer, were taken from their homes, or wherever found, at the point of the bayonet. Your humble friend was taken at the point of the bayonet, but afterward discharged; schoolteachers being exempt from duty.

Things are more settled at present, yet no one can tell "what a day may bring forth."

I do not take any of the papers of which you speak; if, therefore, you should, as you propose, send me an occasional copy, I shall feel myself under renewed, and additional obligations to you.

After much deliberation, I have almost concluded to go to Jamaica. What think you of it? I should like to have you answer this question at your earliest convenience, as I shall, unless my mind should undergo a very sudden & radical change, make an effort to get out of this slavery-cursed and Negro-hating country as soon as I can make it expedient so to do. My dear friend, you do not know how much I yearn to be a <u>man</u>, and having found that I can only be so by leaving the country, I am willing to accept the conditions.

The communication of which you speak, was, as far as I can learn, written by the Rev. Grafton Graham of the A.M.E. Church of this city.[2] He is not, to my knowledge, much of a scholar, but he is a man of great good sense & a gentleman. As a speaker he is very felicitous; as a writer I know nothing of him.

Your promise of reciprocation, I receive as made in good faith, as a matter of course.

Our troubles with the Irish are not yet wholly at an end. On Friday a party of them attacked a house occupied by a colored family on Commercial Street, when one of the inmates appeared at the door, gun in hand, and requested them to desist; this had no other effect than to increase their violence, when one of them rushing up to him, seized and wrested the weapon from his grasp, and commenced beating him with it; the shock occasioned by the blows given, caused the gun to go off, killing the assailant instantly.[3]

J. P. Sampson has rendered himself quite unpopular among the colored people of this city, by a communication written by him a few days since and published in the "Cincinnati Enquirer," a paper more notorious for secession & pro slavery proclivities[4] than even the "N.Y. Herald." In this communication he said if black men were employed as soldiers that it would bring down the indignation of foreign powers. Upon the whole, I think he showed himself an ass, & extremely lacking in "horse sense." Answer soon & oblige, Your Friend,

Wm. H. Parham[5]

Jacob C. White, Jr., Papers, Moorland-Spingarn Research Center, Howard University, Washington, D.C. Published by permission.

1. As part of a Confederate strategy to rid Kentucky of Union troops, General Edmund Kirby Smith and an army of twenty-one thousand men occupied the Lexington area in August 1862, bringing them within seventy-five miles of Cincinnati and alarming the city's residents. The Confederate threat to Cincinnati ended when Union forces regained control of Kentucky in October. *HTECW*, 414–15.

2. Parham probably refers to a 2 August 1862 letter in the *Christian Recorder*. Written from Cincinnati, it appeared under the pseudonym "Aleph" and was probably written by Grafton H. Graham, a local African Methodist Episcopal clergyman and one of the *Recorder*'s corresponding editors. The letter recounted recent Irish rioting against blacks in the city, including the sacking of Allen Chapel, which housed an AME congregation. It blamed Peace Democrats for provoking racial violence. Graham was originally from Maryland. A barber by trade, he settled in Allegheny, Pennsylvania, attended Avery College, and became a minister in the African Methodist Episcopal Zion denomination. He joined the AME church in 1854. Graham was pastor of Allen Chapel from 1861 to 1863, then ministered to congregations in Columbus and Delaware, Ohio, during the latter part of the Civil War. After the war, he served in Kentucky and was a delegate to the 1867 black state convention. Graham was described as an "urbane gentleman" with a "pulpit ability beyond any of his compeers." *CR*, 28 March, 16 May 1863 [14:0776]; Wayman, *Cyclopaedia of African Methodism*, 67–68; Smith, *African Methodist Episcopal Church*, 97; *Lib*, 15 August 1856 [10:0278]; *WAA*, 4 April, 9, 23 May 1863, 4 February 1865; Philip S. Foner and George E. Walker, eds., *Proceedings of the Black National and State Conventions, 1865–1900*, 1 vol. to date (Philadelphia, Pa., 1986–), 309–10, 317.

3. The loss of river trade with the South disrupted Cincinnati's economy during the Civil War. Growing competition for scarce employment exacerbated tensions between Irish and black stevedores on the Ohio River docks. Violence erupted in July 1862 as Irish mobs attacked black neighborhoods, destroying homes and businesses and assaulting residents. Many blacks fled the city. Civil authorities restored order after two weeks and most blacks returned to their homes, but incidents such as the one Parham describes were repeated. The rioting triggered a permanent decline in black employment on the river. Leonard Harding, "The Cincinnati Riots of 1862," *CHSB* 25:229–39 (October 1967).

4. Parham refers to a letter by John P. Sampson in the 16 August 1862 issue of the *Cincinnati Enquirer*, a Democratic daily founded in 1841 and known for its sensationalistic and racist journalism. The letter opposed black enlistment in the Union army, arguing that it would alienate the border states and arouse pro-Confederate sympathy in Europe. It maintained that emigration offered the only hope for racial progress and had widespread black support. Sampson (1838–?), a local journalist, was born to free black parents in Wilmington, North Carolina.

His father, a man of means, sent him North to be educated. After graduating from Comer's Commercial College in Boston in 1856, he taught for several years in the public schools of Long Island. Sampson edited and published the *Colored Citizen* in Cincinnati during the Civil War. Although initially opposed to black enlistment, he soon devoted the weekly to the "interests of colored soldiers."

He returned to Wilmington at the end of the war to accept appointments as tax assessor and superintendent of local schools for the freedmen. Sampson was a Republican candidate for Congress in 1867, but after failing to win a seat, he accepted a clerkship in the Department of the Treasury at Washington, D.C. Over the next few years, he also read law and briefly studied theology at the Western Theological Seminary in Allegheny, Pennsylvania. He was admitted to the D.C. bar in 1873 and served for five years as a judge in the city's civil courts. In 1882 Sampson abandoned law and politics to enter the African Methodist Episcopal ministry. From that point until his retirement in 1917, he pastored AME congregations in New Jersey, Pennsylvania, and Massachusetts, serving for a time as superintendent of the New England Conference. He received a doctor of divinity degree from Wilberforce University in 1888. Sampson became a noted author and lecturer on a variety of social and scientific subjects. Of his five books, his *Temperament and Phrenology of Mixed Races* (1884) was widely reprinted. Mott, *American Journalism*, 283n, 357, 442, 459; NCAB, 4:379; ACAB, 5:382–83; Frank Mather, ed., *Who's Who of the Colored Race* (Chicago, Ill., 1915), 236–37.

5. William H. Parham (1839–?), a Cincinnati educator and lawyer, was born to free black parents in Virginia. As a young child, he was sent to Philadelphia for a public school education. Then at age nineteen, he moved to Cincinnati, earned a teaching certificate, and obtained employment in the city's black schools. Parham initially opposed black involvement in the Civil War, arguing that racial prejudice would persist even if slavery were destroyed. Because of his pessimistic assessment of American race relations, he briefly considered immigrating to the Caribbean. After the war, Parham served as superintendent of Cincinnati's black schools (1866–87) and principal of Gaines High School (1887–90). He also achieved distinction as the first black graduate of Cincinnati Law School (1874) and the first black notary in Ohio. Parham left his career in education and established a law practice in the 1890s. Through involvement in local Republican party politics, he became a strong political voice for the black community, and he later became a member of the state legislature. Parham withdrew from politics after the 1890s, but continued his law practice. Gerber, *Black Ohio and the Color Line*, 41–43, 160, 169–70, 334, 341–48, 362–64; William H. Parham to Jacob C. White, Jr., 12 October 1862, Moorland-Spingarn Research Center, DHU [14:0168]; Wendell P. Dabney, *Cincinnati's Colored Citizens: Historical, Sociological and Biographical* (Cincinnati, Ohio, 1926; reprint, New York, N.Y., 1970), 108–9, 116, 200–201.

30.
George B. Vashon to Abraham Lincoln
[September 1862]

Blacks had to fight for the right to live on American soil even in the
midst of the Civil War. Since the founding of the American Colonization
Society in 1816, black abolitionists contested repeated attempts to make
colonization the official policy of the nation. When President Abraham
Lincoln outlined plans in August 1862 to settle freed slaves in the Chiriquí region of Central America, black leaders again organized in protest.
Speaking at an anticolonization rally in New York City, Rev. William T.
Catto accused Lincoln of "pandering to the mob spirit." Frederick
Douglass called the president "a genuine representative of American
prejudice and Negro hatred." George B. Vashon opposed the policy in
the following open letter to Lincoln. Vashon, who had lived briefly in
Haiti, argued that the forced expatriation of Afro-Americans was neither ethical nor expedient. He refuted the president's assertion that
blacks were the cause of the Civil War, charging instead that white racial oppression had corrupted society and provoked the conflict. When
Lincoln later tried to colonize blacks on the Ile á Vache in the Caribbean, blacks resisted once again. Both of Lincoln's colonization projects
ended in failure. *DM*, September 1862; *PA*, 20 September, 11, 18 October 1862 [14:0506, 0543, 0549]; *CR*, 27 September, 4 October 1862
[14:0511, 0512, 0528]; Benjamin Quarles, *Lincoln and the Negro*
(New York, N.Y., 1962), 108–20.

To His Excellency ABRAHAM LINCOLN, President of the United States
of America
HIGHLY HONORED AND RESPECTED SIR:
    The papers announce that on the 14th of August you had an interview
with a committee of colored men, and addressed them in reference to the
propriety of the expatriation of their class.[1] As a colored man, I am
deeply interested in this matter; and feel that under the circumstances, I
ought to be excused for the liberty which I take in making answer to you
personally.
    In the first place, sir, let me say, that I do not put myself in opposition
to the emigration of Colored Americans, either individually, or in large
masses. I am satisfied, indeed, that such an emigration will be entered
upon, and that too, to no inconsiderable extent. Liberia, with the bright
and continually growing promise for the regeneration of Africa, will allure many a colored man to the shores of his motherland. Haiti, with her
proud boast, that, she alone, can present an instance in the history of the
world, of a horde of despised bondmen becoming a nation of triumphant

freemen, will by her gracious invitation, induce many a dark hued native of the United States to go and aid in developing the treasures stored away in her sun-crested hills and smiling savannahs. And, Central America, lying in that belt of empire which Destiny seems to promise to the blended races of the earth, will, no doubt, either with or without federal patronage, become the abiding place of a population made up, in great measure, of persons who will have taken refuge there from the oppression which they had been called upon to undergo in this country.

But, entertaining these views, and almost persuaded to become an emigrant myself, for the recollections of a thirty months' residence in Haiti still crowd pleasantly upon my memory.[2] I am confident that, in thus feeling, I am not in sympathy with the majority of my class—not in sympathy either with the great body of them. Those men are doubtless aware that many comforts and advantages which they do not now enjoy here, await them elsewhere. No feeling of selfishness, no dread of making sacrifices (as you intimate), detains them in the land of their birth. They are fully conscious of the hatred to which you have adverted, they endure its consequences daily and hourly; tremblingly too, perhaps, lest the utterances of their Chief Magistrate may add fuel to the fire raging against them, but buoyed up by the knowledge that they are undeserving of this ill usage, and sedulously endeavoring to perform the various duties that are incumbent upon them, they enjoy, amid all their ill, a species of content, and echo back, by their conduct, your own words, that "It is difficult to make a man miserable while he feels he is worthy of himself, and claims kindred to the great God who made him." Thus, they have schooled themselves "to labor and to wait," in the hope of the coming of a better time. And, this hope is based in the innermost convictions of their religious nature, in the trust which is not to be shaken, that the God who rules the Universe is a God of fixed, and immutable justice, under whose dispensations the proud and defiant ones of today become invariably the peeled and broken ones of the morrow; while those who were despised and rejected, find themselves, in turn, the recipients of abundant and overflowing "mercies."

These men, too, have another reason for clinging to the land of their nativity; and that is, the gross injustice which inheres even in the slightest intimation of a request, that they should leave it, an injustice which must necessarily be, in the highest degree, revolting to their every sense of right. Who and what are these men? Their family records in this land, in almost every instance, antedate our revolutionary struggle, and you, sir, will read in your country's history, unlike the ignorant and rapid reporters, who, from time to time, in their marketless and pen free calumny of a race, detail from our camps the lie that "the negro will not fight"[3]—you, sir, know that black Americans fighting shoulder to shoulder with white Americans, in the contest which confirmed our nationality, merited and received the approbation of Washington;[4] and that the zealous and fleet-footed slave of that time did, for the partizan bands of Sumter and Marion, the same kind offices which the travel-worn and scarcely tolerated "contraband" of our days has done for the armies of Burnside and McClellan.[5] And now, what reward is offered by republican gratitude? Now, forsooth, when the banquet of Freedom has been spread, when the descendants of the men who fought under Howe and Clinton, under Cornwallis and Burgoyne, have with ostentatious liberality been invited to the repast, the children of the patriotic blacks who periled their lives at Bunker Hill, at Red Bank, and on many another hard fought field, must be requested, not merely to take a lower seat, but to withdraw entirely from the table.[6]

But setting aside the injustice of a policy which would expatriate black Americans, let us examine for a moment its expediency. Cicero has declared, in his principal ethical treatise, that, "no greater evil can happen to humanity than the separation of what is expedient from that which is right."[7] Let us suppose, however, that he was wrong in thus teaching; and that the antipathy existing between the white and black races—somewhat of a one-sided antipathy, by the by—would justify the removal of the latter one from this country. It might be, indeed, a matter for discussion, whether this antipathy is as extended and as exacting as you allege; whether, instead of being a permanent instinct, it is not rather a temporary sentiment which will gradually pass away, when once its cause—the slavery and wrong imposed upon the descendants of Africa—will have been removed. But, let that pass. Would it be wise, sir, when Denmark and France and England are looking with envious eyes upon our liberated slaves, and regarding them as important acquisitions to their West India possessions, to denude our southern States of that class of laborers?[8] Has not the experience of our heart-stricken armies—an experience which has prompted the yielding up of the spade to the black man, while the musket is withheld from him—sufficiently indicated that negro cultivators are absolutely required for that portion of the Union?

But, sir, it is not enough that the policy which you suggest should be expedient. It must also be feasible. You have, doubtless, looked at this matter with the eye of a statesman. You have reflected, that to remove entirely this "bone of contention" demands the expatriation of nearly one-sixth portion of the Union. You have, after mature thought, settled the physical possibility of so large an expatriation; and calmly calculated the hundreds of millions of dollars which its accomplishment will add to our national liabilities—large now, and growing larger daily under the exigencies of our civil war. Have you also considered that the meagre handful of negroes under Federal rule constitutes, so to speak, only the periosteum, while "the bone" itself projects over into territory arrayed against your authority, and may yet be employed by unhallowed Rebellion, grown desperate in its extremity, as a vast and terrible weapon for the attainment of its ends? Whether this be a probability, or not, it is clear that the difficulties in the way of your suggested enterprise are such as entitle it to be termed Herculean. Herculean? I fear, sir, that we must glance at another of the pages of mythology to find an epithet with which to characterize it. Africa, in the days of your administration, as in those of the line of Belus, may be called upon to witness the retribution dealt out to wrong by the Eternal Powers. The States of this Union, having assassinated in the person of the negro all of the principles of right to which they were wedded, may, like the Danaides, be condemned to expiate their crime; and this scheme of expatriation may prove, for them, the vain essay to fill a perforated "cistern which will hold no water."[9]

President of the United States, let me say in conclusion that the negro may be "the bone of contention" in our present civil war. He may have been the occasion of it; but he has not been its cause. That cause must be sought in the wrongs inflicted upon him by the white man. The white man's oppression of the negro, and not the negro himself, has brought upon the nation the leprosy under which it groans. The negro may be the scab indicative of the disease, but his removal, even if possible, will not effect a cure. Not until this nation, with hands upon its lips, and with lips in the dust, shall cry repentantly, "Unclean! unclean!" will the beneficent Father of all men, of whatever color, permit its healing and purification.[10]

I have the honor, sir, to be, with all the consideration due to your high office, Most Respectfully, Your Obedient Servant,

GEORGE B. VASHON

Douglass' Monthly (Rochester, N.Y.), October 1862.

1. On 14 August 1862, President Abraham Lincoln met with Edward M. Thomas, John F. Cook, Cornelius C. Clark, John T. Costin, and Benjamin McCoy—leaders of the Washington, D.C., black community—at the White House. Lincoln asked for the meeting to encourage black settlement in the Chiriquí region of Central America after Congress appropriated $600,000 to aid colonization efforts. The president's request was first announced on 10 July in the city's black churches. Local blacks quickly assembled to discuss strategy, to name a committee, to adopt resolutions opposing colonization, and to allay fears that the federal government planned to expel blacks by force. When the committee members assembled at the White House nearly a month later, Lincoln told them that their race was "suffering . . . the greatest wrong inflicted on any people." He expressed his belief that it was impossible for whites and blacks to live together and declared that without "the institution of Slavery and the colored race as a basis, the war could not have an existence." Lincoln claimed that it would be best for both races if blacks were removed from the country. He proposed Chiriquí as the best location for black resettlement as newly discovered coal deposits

there would provide the basis for a sound economy. The president's remarks were widely reprinted in the northern press and outraged black leaders. Even those sympathetic to emigration, such as Henry Highland Garnet, were angered by Lincoln's inference that blacks were responsible for the war. One New Jersey black exclaimed: "Coal land, sir! If you please, sir, give McClellan some, give Halleck some, and by all means, save a little strip for yourself." Lincoln interested five hundred blacks in his Chiriquí scheme, but later abandoned it when his cabinet turned against the plan and the coal deposits proved worthless. *PA*, 20 September, 11 October 1862 [14:0507–8, 0543]; *CR*, 30 August, 6 September 1862; Abraham Lincoln, *Speeches and Writings, 1859–1865*, ed. Don E. Fehrenbacher (New York, N.Y., 1989), 353–57; McPherson, *Negro's Civil War*, 91–97.

2. Vashon taught at the Collège Faustin in Port-au-Prince, Haiti, from February 1848 to the fall of 1850. Catherine M. Hanchett, "George Boyer Vashon, 1821–1878: Black Educator, Poet, Fighter for Equal Rights," *WPHM* 68:208–9 (July, October 1985).

3. At the beginning of the Civil War, Union military leaders, common soldiers, politicians, and the press all questioned the value of black enlistment. Reflecting popular stereotypes, they argued that blacks belonged to an inferior and degraded race and lacked the intelligence and courage to perform the duties of a soldier. But public opinion changed in 1863 as more and more troops were needed and black soldiers proved themselves on the battlefield. Quarles, *Negro in the Civil War*, 13, 21, 29–32, 183–84.

4. George Washington commended the military service of several black soldiers during the American Revolution, although he initially opposed the enlistment of free blacks and slaves in the Continental army. Foner, *History of Black Americans*, 1:311–43.

5. Vashon compares the contributions made by contrabands to the Union war effort with those of blacks to rebel forces in the South during the American Revolution. Southern slaves and free blacks assisted American and French forces as spies, messengers, and scouts. South Carolina generals Francis Marion (ca. 1732–1795) and Thomas Sumter (1734–1832) used black labor to assist their military operations. During the Civil War, southern blacks furnished Union forces with indispensable information concerning local terrain, the length and direction of navigable rivers and roads, and Confederate troop movements and fortifications. Jefferson Davis's personal coachman, William A. Jackson, provided an intimate report of Davis's relationship with his generals. Another fugitive, Nathaniel Evans, gave Union troops a detailed description of Richmond's defenses. Union commanders quickly discovered the military value of black teamsters, pilots, and scouts. Blacks in the North Carolina Tidewater provided vital information to General Ambrose E. Burnside (1824–1881) in his campaign against New Bern in early 1862. Burnside, an arms designer and manufacturer born to a South Carolina slaveholder, entered the Union army as a colonel in the First Rhode Island Volunteers. Early military successes brought his rapid advancement to brigadier general and command of IX Corps under Major General George B. McClellan (1826–1885). Although McClellan lacked sympathy for blacks and supported the return of runaway slaves to their owners, he too admitted that his most reliable military intelligence "comes from fugitive

slaves." His intelligence service filed daily reports based upon interrogation of those fugitives who entered Union lines. McClellan, a member of the Philadelphia elite and a military engineer with distinguished service in the Mexican War, led the Army of the Potomac after the disastrous Union defeat at the first battle of Bull Run. Later removed from this command, he became the Democratic challenger to Lincoln in the 1864 election. Benjamin Quarles, *The Negro in the American Revolution* (Chapel Hill, N.C., 1961), 94–97, 103, 105, 108; Ezra J. Warner, *Generals in Blue: Lives of the Union Commanders* (Baton Rouge, La., 1964), 57–58, 290–92; Ira Berlin et al., eds., *Freedom: A Documentary History of Emancipation, 1861–1867,* 2 ser. to date (Cambridge, England, 1982), 2:17–18, 23–24, 32, 80–81, 297–98; Quarles, *Negro in the Civil War,* 78–79, 81–82, 84–85, 318.

6. Of the thousands of immigrants from Britain who settled in the United States between 1783 and 1840, many were the children and grandchildren of soldiers who had fought in the American Revolution under British generals Charles Cornwallis (1738–1805), William Howe (1729–1804), Henry Clinton (ca. 1738–1795), and John Burgoyne (1722–1792). Vashon compares the treatment accorded them with that received by the descendants of blacks who fought with the American forces in several key battles of that conflict. In June 1775, blacks fought at the battle of Bunker Hill, which took place on the heights overlooking Boston harbor. At the battle of Red Bank in October 1777, black soldiers from Rhode Island turned back an attack of fifteen hundred Hessian troops on Fort Mercer, New Jersey. Vashon reminds Lincoln that while British immigrants were granted American citizenship, black Americans were denied the rights of citizens. Mark M. Boatner, ed., *Encyclopedia of the American Revolution* (New York, N.Y., 1966), 382–83.

7. Vashon quotes from the third book of *On Duties,* a commentary on expediency and morality by Marcus Tullius Cicero (106–43 B.C.), a Roman philosopher and statesman.

8. Britain, France, and Denmark ended slavery in their West Indian colonies between 1834 and 1848. Many former slaves left the sugar plantations, causing chronic labor shortages and prompting colonial governments to recruit new workers in Africa, Asia, and elsewhere. Although most of the labor needs were met by immigrants from India, emigration agents persuaded several thousand blacks to leave Sierra Leone and the United States and settle in Jamaica, Guiana, Trinidad, and the French sugar islands. Cyril Hamshere, *The British in the Caribbean* (Cambridge, Mass., 1972), 158; McCloy, *Negro in the French West Indies,* 160.

9. Vashon refers to the ancient Greek myth of Belus, whose twin sons, Aegyptus and Danaus, vied for their father's inheritance. As a gesture of reconciliation, a marriage was arranged between Aegyptus's fifty sons and Danaus's fifty daughters—the Danaides. Danaus feared a conspiracy and persuaded his daughters to kill their husbands on their wedding night. For their crime, the Danaides, who were renowned for drilling wells, were condemned by the Judges of the Dead to an eternity of carrying water in perforated jars. Robert Graves, *The Greek Myths* (Mt. Kisco, N.Y., 1988), 200–203.

10. Vashon uses the ancient condition called leprosy as a metaphor for the division of the nation by the Civil War. He alludes to the regulations concerning

lepers in Leviticus 13–14. In ancient Jewish culture, lepers were required to dwell alone, to rend their clothes, to leave their heads uncovered, to cover their upper lips, and to warn others of their condition by crying "Unclean, unclean," as they approached. Healing from leprosy had to be certified by the priests, who conducted extensive purification rites.

31.
John Oliver to Simeon S. Jocelyn
25 November 1862
17 February 1863

Slaves who escaped to Union lines during the early years of the Civil War rarely found the freedom and protection that they sought. White Southerners and racist Union troops hindered relief efforts and endangered black lives. Rebel sympathizers burned freedmen's schools and churches and whipped or murdered blacks who spoke too loudly of Northern victory. The vast majority of white Union soldiers denied that they were fighting to end slavery and blamed blacks for causing the conflict; they vented their anger and frustration by committing barbarous crimes against the freedmen, including physical mutilation, rape, and murder. One Massachusetts officer characterized contraband children as "little vermin" to be crushed underfoot. As the war ground on, a growing number of fugitives became dependent upon northern relief workers for aid and protection. The following two letters by missionary teacher John Oliver to the American Missionary Association offer an insightful view of the organization's work and the plight of the freedmen in eastern Virginia. Leon F. Litwack, *Been in the Storm So Long: The Aftermath of Slavery* (New York, N.Y., 1979), 10, 30, 122–33; Berlin et al., *Freedom*, 1(1):59–70.

Newport News, [Virginia]
Nov[ember] 25<u>th</u>, 1862

My Dear Beloved Brother:

Your kind letter of the 18<u>th</u> has been received. I went to Yorktown last week with the full expectation of what General E. [D.] Keyes hade promised me to open a school. But I was disappointed, General Keyes was in newyork. And General H. M. Nagler informed me that no school could be hade at Yorktown, that all persons who are in gaged in this enterprise are ruining the Colored people, and retarding the progress of the Government. He would not think of alowing a school at Yorktown, as he Expected to have them all sent away.[1] I went from their to Suffolk[,] here I fould a man by the name of Williams teaching a little pay School of about 30 Children. I could gete up a good school here. But there is an order tomove all the Colored people from there to Cranny Island, as soon as there is room. Carpenters are at work Erecting barrcks for them there. But much time must elapse and much painful suffering, before they are setteled. And this Island will be to them what Elba was to Nepolean[,] aplace of confinement and hard bread.[2] It is an Island of 1/4 of amile wide by 3/4 long surrounded with warter. General Mansfeild[3] said tome,

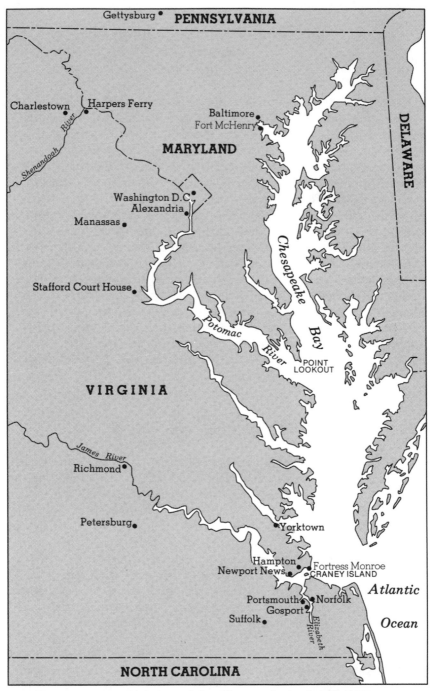

Fig. 1. Eastern Virginia and the Chesapeake in the Civil War era

I will give their people <u>Slaves</u> every opportunity I can to learn how tobe-come self sustaining. Craney Island is just the place to prevent it. They are Cut off from Every facility of aiding themselves only to depend upon the commesery[,] they are soplaced for an Easy speculation for bade men this winter in Congress Either of Compromise or Colonization. But Mr. Wilder[4] thinks that I am an injury to the mission from being out Spoken about things that Cannot be remedied.

I Cannot help speaking against Slavery and the cruelty of Slaveholders, and all men who are in sympathy with them, and I cannot go amiss for our army swarm with them.

Yesterday and today the colored people have been in the wildist state of confussion. By order of Gen. John A. Dix, General Corcoran has his wild Irish gards hunting every one, man, women, and Child, putting them on board the steemer Express, to be sent to the Island,[5] the Exposeer of the is too terable to think of. A Mother is just passing with her daughter of 13 years upon her Shoulder, and a gard behind forcing her on. Those that were not sent last night were put into the Commicery building where they remaine[d] all night, I have just been in to see them and I found the little ones satting around on the floor and not one spark of fire alowed in the place. Between 40 and 50 of these Men left Sunday night, when they know what was to take place, saying good by union I never will come within your lines again. I shall leave as soon as I can[.] I have just received a letter from Brother Grimes[6] at Boston. My friends have sent 5 Bbl of Clothing, as soon as they come I shall give them out at fort Norfolk and the pes[t] house, and come home untill the people are setteled, there is noplace for me at Crany Island. Please send me $30 to Norfolk by Adams Express[7] in many yours in pray for the Slave,

John Oliver

American Missionary Association Archives, Amistad Research Center, Tulane University, New Orleans, Louisiana. Published by permission.

Portsmouth, V[irgini]a
Feb[ruary] 17<u>th</u>, 1863

Dear Brother Jocelyn:

Your kind letter of Jan. 29" was received[,] also one of Feb 10" containing a check for $30. for all of which you will now please except sincere thanks. It is not plesent for one whos heart is in his work tofeel that he has not been able to give Satisfaction to those interrested in his labors. I Cannot conceive that there are worst difficulties any where for missionary to condend with than there are here. At Hamption the School[8] is hardly in the way or under the notice of the military nor are there there but few of the original white inhabitance to make the success of the School there diffcult. While here we are surrunded with the Southern people[,] southern feeling and the prejudice of the army because

of the Extent of that southern feeling. I Left Newport News on the 27"
Nov. when I found it nolonger posable for me to continue or keep up a
school there with successful results, And After various unsuccessful efferts at various places to gete up a school, and of which efferts I have
informed you. Any where among the army would have been perferable
to this place or Norfolk because of the feeling. I Returned to Norfolk
determin to open a school any where in this neighborhood I could gete
up one. If the mission could afford to higher building for schools you
could not higher one for that perpous here, the owners hade rather burn
them down. Between that difficulty and the Slaveish fears of the colored
people on the other hand, who have Churches but fear to let us have
them for school houses, I was without a school some few weeks. This I
could not over come in a day, you could not if you hade been here. Main-
time however, I busied myself as far as it was in my power to do what I
could for the distitute at Pest house and Fort Norfolk.[9] I wrote may letter
about there condition, and left no one uninformed, and If any clothing
hade been sent to me even with or without instruction from the Fortress,
or New York, I could have covered many a nacked brest at the above
places which was bare and Exposed to the Elements, while much of the
clothing which was sent to Norfolk was given to those who were handy
and in better circomstances. The society which I brought into Existence
in this time for the aid of this poor, I will put others in the way to see its
workings that you may be still further informed about it. Hade I have
hade the Old South at Boston[10] for a school house I do not think I could
have held a school in it, if the condition of the Children hade been that
of those at the above named places. But I know it is imposable for those
who have the will far of those people at heart, to foresee every thing just
as they would have it, and though humanbeings and under the head of
the highest objects of our intrest, yeat like all things in natures, there has
been at times an unavoidable unjust disposition of what in justice they
would seem to be intitle to.

I Pass now to my present location and labors. I have not seen Miss
Smith[,][11] I have written to her. My School at Portsmouth is composed
of the very class whom I supposed, I was sent to Virginia to teach.[12]
Many of them are from the country[,] 3/4 of the school however I beleave
belong in this neighborhood, many of their Masters are here, others
are in the southern army. There are over 200 Children in the school. Ages
from 3 to 15 years, there has been two conversion in the school, and we
are confidently expecting others Every days.

On the 11th instent Brothern J. P. Bardwell,[13] and Palmer Litts,[14] made
me very plesent Call. Each passed afew plesent moments in addressing
the school. I have no doubt but they will inform you of their visits.
Brother Greely[15] arived on monday on the 16th who handed me your
friendly note. I shall be trully happy if in any way I can assist in making

him comfitable. At present he is with me, and I am happy of the opportunity of receiving him. I Have shown him to the Brethren, and have no doubt but they will soon become much attached to him. We have a good many incendiary fires both here and in Norfolk, none of which are Ever checked, untill the buildings in which they occur are burned to the ground, as soon as the fires engines begin to work some one always manages to cut the hose. I will see Miss Smith as soon as I can, as I think I can arrange for a school for her in Norfolk, Yours Very trully,

John Oliver

P.S. we have just gote a Post office this side. Within a week, you can adress here. I have settled with Mr Cook,[16] for the amout you stated. I Have by some means taken a heavy cold, which I cannot for, I can hardly speak so as to be heard.

J. O.

American Missionary Association Archives, Amistad Research Center, Tulane University, New Orleans, Louisiana. Published by permission.

1. In October 1862, Oliver and American Missionary Association agent Lewis C. Lockwood visited Yorktown, Virginia, and obtained permission from Brigadier General Erasmus D. Keyes (1810–1895) to open a school for the large contraband camp there. Keyes, a former West Point instructor, commanded the IV Corps of the Army of the Potomac. When Oliver returned to Yorktown the following month, Brigadier General Henry Morris Naglee (1815–1886), the new commander, informed him that no schools could be opened. He also advised Oliver that such schools were unnecessary, as he intended to remove all contrabands from the area. Naglee, a Mexican War veteran and civil engineer from California, was removed from command and resigned his commission in April 1864, after clashing with the military governor of "restored" Virginia over oaths of allegiance. Mansfield, "That Fateful Class," 92–93; Warner, *Generals in Blue,* 264–65, 340–41; *WWWCW,* 466–67.

2. Following his abdication in 1814, Napoleon Bonaparte of France was confined to Elba, a small island off the Italian coast.

3. Joseph K. F. Mansfield (1803–1862), a brigadier general, served at Fortress Monroe, Virginia, from March to September 1862. He had been General Zachary Taylor's chief engineer during the Mexican War and assumed command of the Department of Washington, D.C., at the beginning of the Civil War. That September, while leading the XII Corps of the Army of the Potomac, he was killed in action at the battle of Antietam. *HTECW,* 473.

4. Charles B. Wilder, a Boston businessman, abolitionist, and member of the American Missionary Association executive committee, served as superintendent of relief operations for the contrabands at Fortress Monroe, Virginia, from March 1862 through the end of the Civil War. He regularly reported to AMA headquarters on conditions at the camp and the mistreatment of the contrabands by Union troops. He thought Oliver "too outspoken" and advised the black teacher to change his behavior or risk dismissal. In 1865 Wilder was named as-

sistant subcommissioner for the Freedmen's Bureau at nearby Hampton. After persuading military authorities to settle freedmen on confiscated lands, he vigorously resisted orders to dispossess them and enforce labor contracts. The latter action earned him a court martial for malfeasance in office. Although acquitted of these charges, Wilder was mustered out of service in 1866 and accepted an AMA post at Jacksonville, Florida. Richardson, *Christian Reconstruction*, 7–9, 59–61, 219; De Boer, "Afro-Americans in American Missionary Association," 245; Engs, *Freedom's First Generation*, 32, 35–39, 77, 86–87, 100–111, 212n; Mansfield, "That Fateful Class," 100–101.

5. In November 1862, Major General John A. Dix (1798–1879), the commander of the Department of Virginia, ordered the removal of contrabands from Newport News to Craney Island to make room for the Corcoran Irish Legion, a unit of Irish immigrant volunteers assigned to the department's IV Corps. The legion was organized and led by Brigadier General Michael Corcoran (1827–1863), a colorful Irish immigrant who had spent more than a year as a Confederate prisoner of war following the first battle of Bull Run. Corcoran supervised the forced removal of the contrabands to Craney Island. Like most Irish units, his troops were notorious for their racism and abuse of contrabands. Dix, a leading Democrat from New York, had been a member of the U.S. Senate and secretary of the treasury in the administration of James Buchanan. Although usually assigned to garrison duty during the Civil War, he was sent to quell the New York City draft riots in July 1863. After the war, he served as minister to France (1866–69) and governor of New York (1872–74). *HTECW*, 165–66, 222–23; Lawrence F. Kohl and Margaret Cossé Richard, eds., *Irish Green and Union Blue: The Civil War Letters of Peter Welsh, Color Sergeant, 28th Regiment Massachusetts Volunteers* (New York, N.Y., 1986), 9, 62–63; Mansfield, "That Fateful Class," 91.

6. Leonard A. Grimes.

7. Adams Express Company, one of the largest independent couriers of the nineteenth century, delivered parcels, money, and military pay warrants along the Atlantic seaboard and throughout the South. Wayne E. Fuller, *The American Mail: Enlarger of the Common Life* (Chicago, Ill., 1972), 162–63, 181.

8. In September 1861, the American Missionary Association founded a school for contrabands on the grounds of the Chesapeake Female Seminary at Hampton, Virginia. It developed into the Hampton Institute after the Civil War. De Boer, "Afro-Americans in American Missionary Association," 240–43; Engs, *Freedom's First Generation*, 145–47.

9. After Norfolk, Virginia, fell to Union troops in May 1862, nearly twenty thousand contrabands fled to the city for refuge. Most congregated in camps at nearby Fort Norfolk and the Pesthouse Barracks. Fort Norfolk was a Union garrison at the mouth of the Elizabeth River. The Pesthouse Barracks was an infirmary for those infected with contagious diseases. The local black community founded schools at each of these camps; in September the American Missionary Association commissioned a black teacher, George W. Cook, to take charge of these two schools. Because of Cook's mismanagement and frequent absences, Oliver dismissed him early the following year. Mansfield, "That Fateful Class," 94–98; Henry L. Swint, *Dear Ones at Home: Letters from Contraband Camps* (Nashville, Tenn., 1966), 72n.

10. Oliver refers to the Old South Meeting House in Boston. Built in 1729 to accommodate the city's Third Congregational Church, it often hosted public meetings too large for Faneuil Hall. Since 1876 it has been preserved as a historical monument. Carl Seaburg, *Boston Observed* (Boston, Mass., 1971), 202.

11. R. W. Smith of Philadelphia taught for the American Missionary Association from February to November 1863 at contraband camps in the Norfolk-Portsmouth area. She worked at AMA schools in New Bern, North Carolina, and Yorktown, Virginia, during the remainder of the Civil War. Henry L. Swint, *The Northern Teacher in the South, 1862–1870* (Nashville, Tenn., 1941), 196; *Seventeenth Annual Report of the American Missionary Association* (New York, N.Y., 1863), 41.

12. In mid-January 1863, Oliver opened an American Missionary Association school in the basement of the Emanuel African Methodist Episcopal Church in Portsmouth, Virginia. Most of his students were local contrabands, although a few had followed the Union army from North Carolina. Local whites fiercely opposed the school's existence. Mansfield, "That Fateful Class," 121–22.

13. John P. Bardwell (1803–1871), a clergyman from Oberlin, Ohio, worked as a school inspector for the American Missionary Association during the Civil War. In 1866, while serving as an AMA principal in Grenada, Mississippi, he was beaten and his assistant murdered by a white mob intent on closing his black school. Bardwell was later made superintendent of missions in Minnesota, where he managed the organization's work among the Chippewas. *AM*, October 1871; Swint, *Northern Teacher in the South*, 123, 176; Richardson, *Christian Reconstruction*, 181, 200, 205, 220.

14. Palmer Litts, a theology student at Oberlin College, was assigned to teach at an American Missionary Association school at Fortress Monroe, Virginia, in late 1862. He also instituted religious revivals and instructed a night school for adults at nearby Hampton. Litts was transferred by early 1864 to an AMA post in Natchez, Mississippi. Swint, *Northern Teacher in the South*, 190; Testimonial letters by J. M. Ellis and John Morgan, 20 October 1862, AMA-ARC; De Boer, "Afro-Americans in American Missionary Association," 256–57.

15. Gorham Greely, a white Methodist clergyman from Albany, New York, arrived at Portsmouth, Virginia, in January 1863 to become Oliver's assistant. Upon the recommendation of Bishop Daniel A. Payne, he also served as pastor of the city's Emanuel African Methodist Episcopal Church, which housed Oliver's school. Oliver had originally requested that the American Missionary Association send him a black clergyman; he was further disappointed to discover that Greely's partial deafness prevented him from maintaining classroom discipline. In 1864 Greely was transferred to St. Augustine and Jacksonville, Florida, where he continued to work for the AMA until 1867. De Boer, "Afro-Americans in American Missionary Association," 251–52; Daniel A. Payne to Simeon S. Jocelyn, 29 April 1864, AMA-ARC [15:0324]; *WAA*, 23 May, 24 October 1863, 9 April, 25 June 1864; Wayman, *Cyclopaedia of African Methodism*, 129–30; Mansfield, "That Fateful Class," 122–23.

16. George W. Cook.

32.
H. Ford Douglas to Frederick Douglass
8 January 1863

When Abraham Lincoln issued the Emancipation Proclamation on
1 January 1863, black abolitionists claimed the Civil War as their own
struggle—finally the conflict was a battle for liberation. Despite its
bland language and its failure to end slavery in some parts of the South,
the document offered reasonable hope that the institution was coming
to an end. For blacks such as H. Ford Douglas, Lincoln's declaration
had "laid bare the naked issue of freedom on one side and slavery on
the other." Douglas, who escaped from slavery in 1846 and became a
brilliant antislavery lecturer, had traveled the full range of black anti-
slavery thought—from Garrisonianism to emigration and disillusionment—by the eve of the Civil War. In July 1862, he joined the Ninety-
fifth Illinois Regiment of Infantry Volunteers, becoming one of the few
blacks to serve in a white regiment. A week after the Emancipation
Proclamation, Douglas wrote the following letter to Frederick Douglass
to express his excitement and to encourage the black editor to "finish
the crowning work of your life" by recruiting black troops. This dispatch from the front provides a moving black response to the central
event of the war. Robert L. Harris, Jr., "H. Ford Douglas: Afro-American Antislavery Emigrationist," *JNH* 62:217–29 (July 1977).

COLLIERSVILLE, TENNESSEE
Jan[uary] 8th, 1863

My Dear Douglass:

My wife[1] sent me this morning the *Monthly* for December containing
your appeal to England to "*hands off*" in this fearful conflict for freedom.[2] It was indeed gratifying to me, who has always felt more than a
friendly interest in you and yours, to read your eloquent and manly
words of admonition to the old Saxon mother States to give no moral or
legal countenance to the claims of the impious Confederate States of
America in their attempt to set up a Government established upon the
idea of the perpetual bondage of the Negro. England has wisely with-
stood every temptation to do so. Abraham Lincoln has crossed the Ru-
bicon and by one simple act of Justice to the slave links his memory with
immortality.[3]

The slaves are *free*! How can I write these precious words? And yet it
is so unless twenty millions of people cradled in christianity and civilization for a thousand years commits the foulest perjury that ever blackened
the pages of history. In anticipation of this result, I enlisted six Months
ago[4] in order to be better prepared to play my part in the great drama of

the Negro's redemption. I wanted its drill, its practical details, for mere theory does not make a good soldier. I have learned something of war, for I have seen war in its brightest as well as its bloodiest phase and yet I have nothing to regret. For since the stern necessities of this struggle have laid bare the naked issue of freedom on one side and slavery on the other, freedom shall have in the future of this conflict, if necessary, my blood as it has had in the past my earnest and best words. It seems to me that you can have no good reason for withholding from the government your hearty cooperation. This war will educate Mr. Lincoln out of his idea of the deportation of the Negro, quite as fast as it has some of his other proslavery ideas with respect to employing them as soldiers.

Hitherto they have been socially and politically ignored by this government, but now by the fortunes of war they are cast morally and mentally helpless (so to speak) into the broad sunlight of our Republican civilization there, to be educated and lifted to a higher and nobler life. National duties and responsibilities are not to be colonized, they must be heroically met and religiously performed. This mighty waste of manhood, resulting from the dehumanizing character of slave institutions of America, is now to be given back to the world through the patient toil and self-denial of this proud and haughty race. They must now pay back to the Negro in Spiritual culture, in opportunities for self-improvement, what they have taken from him for two hundred years by the constant over-taxing of his physical nature. This law of supply and demand regulates itself. And so this question of the colonization of the Negro will be settled by laws over which war has no control. Now is the time for you to finish the crowning work of your life. Go to work at once and raise a Regiment and offer your services to the government and I am confident they will be accepted. They say we will not fight. I want to see it tried on. You are the one to me, of all others, to demonstrate this fact.

I belong to company G, 95th Regiment Illinois Volunteers—Captain Eliot N. Bush—a christian and a gentleman. You must pardon my miserable chirography. There is not in me one particle of mechanical genius, and it does seem to me that I can learn almost anything but to write a decent hand. If you can by what you see marked on this paper decipher my meaning, I shall be content. Very truly your friend,

H. Ford Douglas

Douglass' Monthly (Rochester, N.Y.), February 1863.

1. Sattira A. Douglas (1840–?), often called "Sattie," was born in Illinois to free black parents Alfred and Maria Steele. As an adolescent in Chicago, she participated in local antislavery activities and recruited subscribers for the *Provincial Freeman*. In 1857 she married black abolitionist H. Ford Douglas. Two years later, she gave birth to their only child, Helen Ford Douglas. After her husband's enlistment in the Union army in 1862, Sattie Douglas became a fre-

quent correspondent of the *Weekly Anglo-African* and *Christian Recorder*, urging other blacks to join up. She helped organize the Colored Soldier's Aid Society of Chicago, the first such organization in the West, and became an officer and tireless worker for the local Colored Ladies Freedmen's Aid Society. In July 1864, with the support of the CLFAS, she began teaching contrabands at a school run by Charles H. Langston in Leavenworth, Kansas. After H. Ford Douglas was mustered out one year later, they tried unsuccessfully to operate a restaurant in nearby Atchison. When he died that November, she returned to Chicago, remarried, and continued to live there into the 1890s. Harris, "H. Ford Douglas," 230, 233n; *WAA*, 2 May, 20 June, 1 August, 31 October, 12 December 1863, 4 June, 23, 30 July 1864; *CR*, 12 March, 24 October, 21 November 1863; Certificate of Military Enlistment for H. Ford Douglas, 9 April 1890, RG 94, Adjutant General's Office, U.S. Colored Troops, DNA.

2. Douglas refers to "The Slaves' Appeal to Great Britain," an editorial by Frederick Douglass in the 20 November 1862 issue of the New York *Independent*. Douglass urged the British government to resist appeals to extend diplomatic recognition to the Confederacy, fearing that such recognition would raise Southern hopes, extend the Civil War, and delay the complete emancipation of the slaves. Recounting past antislavery actions by the British government, Douglass implored officials in London to continue to "fix the burning brand of your reprobation upon the guilty brow of the whole slave system." He apparently reprinted this piece one month later in *Douglass' Monthly*.

3. Douglas refers to the Emancipation Proclamation signed by President Abraham Lincoln on 1 January 1863, which declared that slaves in those sections of the country in rebellion against the Union would be "thenceforward and forever free." Lincoln had been reluctant to consider emancipation for political reasons at the beginning of the Civil War. But moved by military necessity, abolitionist pressure, and his own sense of justice, he issued a preliminary emancipation proclamation on 22 September 1862. The final proclamation did not free slaves in Union-occupied areas of Louisiana and Tennessee, in the forty-eight loyal counties of Virginia, or in the border states, but it was a significant formal step in dismantling the institution of slavery. It tacitly recognized that the war was being fought for black freedom as well as to save the Union. Lincoln estimated that by early 1865 the document had freed some 200,000 slaves. John Hope Franklin, *The Emancipation Proclamation* (New York, N.Y., 1965), 13–134.

4. In July 1862, Douglas enlisted in Company G of the Ninety-fifth Illinois Regiment of Infantry Volunteers at Belvidere, Illinois. He was mustered into the Union army at Camp Fuller near Rockford that September. Because Douglas was light skinned, he may not have been questioned about his race. The men in his company later discovered that he was black, but continued to treat him with respect. He was transferred in June 1863 to the Louisiana Native Guards. Harris, "H. Ford Douglas," 228–29.

33.
H. Ford Douglas to Ralph Roberts
11 January 1863

Although the Emancipation Proclamation brought the hope of destroying slavery, black abolitionists understood that freedom could only be won on the battlefield. Facing the parapets at Vicksburg, Mississippi, H. Ford Douglas tempered his initial euphoric response to Lincoln's declaration. In an 11 January 1863 letter to the *Belvidere Standard* (Ill.), he expressed a determination to see the war through to final and complete victory. Douglas was buoyed by the belief that he fought under a flag that "*now* . . . means justice and liberty," but he counseled patience. He warned readers, especially those who passionately supported the Union cause, to appreciate "the magnitude of the struggle" and be prepared for a long war accompanied by painful losses. He could not have offered better advice. The bloody federal campaign against Vicksburg lasted the better part of a year and cost nearly ten thousand Union casualties. James M. McPherson, *Ordeal by Fire: The Civil War and Reconstruction* (New York, N.Y., 1982), 332–33.

CAMP NEAR MEMPHIS, [Tennessee]
Jan[uary] 11, 1863

Dear Sir:[1]

You will please send me your paper. There are several numbers received here by the boys, but not enough to supply the demand. Its local column affords us a pleasant entertainment, while in its editorials we are always sure to find a true exposition of the principles which underlie this fearful conflict.

We are on our way to Vicksburg, and shall in all probability face the music in the next (and third) assault upon that formidable rebel stronghold.[2] Others may despair, but I do not. We must be patient, however. Mr. Lincoln said to Wendell Phillips, a year ago, in homely but earnest phrase, that the subjugation of the Cotton States was a "big job." This does not fully express the magnitude of the struggle. The mind, the muscle, the unbounded resources displayed by both parties in this civil war surpass anything the world has ever witnessed. No thoughtful man, therefore, can reasonably expect to see the momentous issues which this war has raised to the surface of American society settled in one or two years; and yet it is this very class of men who are apt to be the first to find fault because our armies have not moved forward with more rapidity and better success. Thus it is ever with man. He is so constituted in his endless hopes and aspirations that the least object which confronts him with any apparent success of jostling them, fills him at once with doubts and apprehensions. It is not the noblest heroism that flings itself into the forlorn hope, nor yet the lowest exhibition of cowardice for one at times to take of his fears. In all things there is a happy medium. War is not an exception to this rule. And yet I must confess that of all other games in this world it is the most uncertain one that man ever played at. While I would not lightly undervalue the noble enthusiasm which the conscientiousness of right awakens in the bosom of a generous people, yet the simple fact of one being in the right has less to do with the success of a battle than the moralist is willing to admit.

In modern times, war has been reduced to a science, so that it is not altogether the righteousness of a cause, but the ability of the contending parties to make the right application of these principles, that wins.

Although we have met with reverses since the war commenced, reverses which have called forth our ever awaiting doubts and apprehensions, yet that happy medium which touches neither extreme should dispel from our minds every thought but that of success in crushing out this infernal revolt.

Strong in resources, in the means of hurling against the enemy every element known to civilized warfare, we are [illegible word] stronger in the righteousness of a just cause. If there is anything in such a conviction, then we may softly apply those words of Shakespeare,

That he is doubly armed who has his quarrel just.[3]

Certain it is, that in every encounter with the traitors, where there has been anything like an equality in numbers, we have always thoroughly whipped them. And so it will in the future. There is one thing you may be sure of, that the sons of Illinois who have gone forth to maintain the good old flag, which now, thank God, means justice and liberty, will not return home at the bidding of Northern traitors. They mean to put down treason wherever it may lift its bloody head, whether in Illinois or in Mississippi.[4] Yours,

H. FORD DOUGLAS

Belvidere Standard (Ill.), 27 January 1863.

1. Ralph Roberts (1822–?), a Connecticut-born printer, edited and published the *Belvidere Standard* (Ill.) from 1851 to 1877. He founded the weekly as a Democratic paper, but made it a Republican party organ in 1856. The *Standard* backed temperance reform, promoted fraternal societies, and ardently supported the Lincoln administration during the Civil War. It urged black enlistment and cited the early successes of the First South Carolina Volunteers as proof that "colored troops are more than a match for an equal number of the rebels." The *Belvidere Standard* continued publication until 1896. U.S. Census, 1850; Edmund J. James and Milo J. Loveless, eds., *Newspapers Published in Illinois Prior to 1860* (Springfield, Ill., 1899), 12; *BelSt*, 3, 17 February 1863; Gregory, *American Newspapers*, 117.

2. Early in the Civil War, the capture of Vicksburg, Mississippi, became a major objective of Union military leaders. A Union fleet bombarded the city during the summer of 1862. From October through December, land forces under Major General Ulysses S. Grant conducted a second but unsuccessful campaign. Douglas and his Ninety-fifth Illinois Regiment of Infantry Volunteers participated in the third and final assault on the Confederate stronghold that began in April 1863. After a lengthy and difficult siege, the city fell to Grant's troops that July. The surrender of Vicksburg gave Union forces virtual control of the Mississippi River and, coupled with the Union victory at Gettysburg, marked the turning point in the war. *HTECW*, 781–84.

3. Douglas loosely quotes from part 3 of William Shakespeare's play, *Henry VI* (1591):

> What stronger breastplate than a heart untainted!
> Thrice is he arm'd that hath his quarrel just.

4. Douglas compares the actions of Peace Democrats (often called "Copperheads") in the North to those of secessionists in the South. Peace Democrats, who urged reconciliation with the South and opposed the war policy of the Lincoln administration, often had to defend themselves against charges of disloyalty. They were most numerous in the Midwest, particularly in Illinois, where they gained control of the state legislature, dominated the 1862 state constitutional convention, and provoked several treason trials. The high point of their influence came at the 1864 Democratic national convention. Frank L. Klement, *The Copperheads in the Middle West* (Chicago, Ill., 1960), 27–28, 59, 199–202, 263–64.

34.
John Oliver to Simeon S. Jocelyn
14 January 1863

Black responses to the Emancipation Proclamation varied by place and circumstance. Although many northern black leaders criticized the document's galling limitations, those in slavery heralded Lincoln's proclamation as the day of jubilee. Even slaves in the deep South heard the news. Mississippi blacks organized a "loyal league" to spread word of the declaration. In one Kentucky town, slaves paraded in the streets. But blacks soon found that the coming of freedom could bring misery as well as jubilation. John Oliver's 14 January 1863 letter to Simeon S. Jocelyn, the corresponding secretary of the American Missionary Association, told of the huge celebration that Norfolk, Virginia, blacks had staged after learning of emancipation. But it also recounted the deplorable conditions they faced as a result of the proclamation. Many slaveholders responded by retreating with their human property from advancing Union forces; those who remained sometimes beat notions of freedom out of their slaves. When not facing the terrors of bondage, blacks suffered mistreatment at the hands of Union troops. "Human life," Oliver advised Jocelyn, "is most terabely insecure in Norfolk, for the Colored people." Eric Foner, *Reconstruction: America's Unfinished Revolution, 1863–1877* (New York, N.Y., 1988), 2–4; Berlin et al., *Freedom,* 1(1):1–56.

                                        Norfolk, V[irgini]a
                                        Jan[uary] 14th, 1863

Dear Brother Jocelyn:

It was my hope and pray that at this writing I might be able to Say to you, that I hade opened a School for the children of this city. But I am disappointed that my success, has not been more gratifying and have no doubt but what you will also Shiar the disappointment. I Have used every feasible means, to obtain a place in which to make a begining. When I last wrote to you, I hade almost been assured that I Should have one of the churches (colored) for a school house. But since than the secessionest have burned several building incendiarly that the government hade in use, caused them to recant least they too should losse their house in the same way. They knowing the temper of the people, perhapes better than I could judge, I thought that I would waight a while. Thought ancious to do all I can for the success of the mission, I did not wish to through away what might be an opportunity. I Have finnally obtained a place not in Norfolk, but in Portsmouth, which will lead to my getting a place in Norfolk here after. I shall open a school in the basement of the methodist church,

colored, in the city of Portsmouth[1] on Thursday 15" inst and if successfull it will bee the means of urging on the people of Norfolk to hazard
somthig for a School. You must remember that Presedent Lincoln leves
us as we were before his proclimation of freedom was issured, this will
be another cause of delay, in may things I fear. Wither this place is a
modern sodom not to be saved under the blessing of Abraham,[2] I am
Shoere I do not know. One thing however I do know and that is, the
Portsmouth Navy yard is in ashes,[3] and the Norfolkites are burning every
building that the Northern unionest have been using, and as they mean
to save their standing property from further use by Northern Soldiers,
they should not at least be aloward to save their moving slave property
from the edect of Emancipation. In contrary distinction to the proclimation however and not knowing what was coming, The Slaves to the number of more than 5000 from miles around celebrated in Norfolk, what
they supposed was their freedom on the forst day of January, last. But
since the proclimation has come to us the slaveholders have began again
to maltreat their slaves, at the same time tell them that no one on earth
has the power to free them. The slaves here are feeling the most intence
greaf from the efects of the proclimation. Now Brother Jocelyn human
life is most terabely insecure in Norfolk, for the Colored people. The
Southern people higher members of the New York 99' Regement, to mob
and robe the colored people at all times day or night[,] they also go to a
hose as gard and take from it the Slave of some slaveholder and carry
him or her out side of the lines for their masters or agents.[4] I Am afrade
to trust myself in the street after night. I will write soon again, please
write to Norfolk as before. Yours trully but much trubled about thing as
they are here,

John Oliver

American Missionary Association Archives, Amistad Research Center, Tulane
University, New Orleans, Louisiana. Published by permission.

1. Oliver opened a school for contrabands in the basement of the Emanuel
African Methodist Episcopal Church in Portsmouth, Virginia, during mid-January 1863. The school enrolled 430 students by November 1864. Emanuel, the
oldest black congregation in the city, began as the North Street Methodist Church
in 1857 and joined the AME during the Civil War. Gorham Greely, a white Methodist sent South by the American Missionary Association, served as its pastor
during 1863–64. The church became a meeting place for black political and
freedmen's aid associations during Reconstruction, and it still exists. Marshall W.
Butt, *Portsmouth under Four Flags* (Portsmouth, Va., 1961), 109; Wayman, *Cyclopaedia of African Methodism*, 129–30; *AM*, November 1864; *WAA*, 24 October 1863, 9 April, 22 June 1864; De Boer, "Afro-Americans in American Missionary Association," 251–52.
2. Oliver compares Norfolk to Sodom, a city in the ancient Middle East known
for the wickedness of its inhabitants. According to Genesis 18:20–19:25, the

patriarch Abraham repeatedly pleaded with God to spare Sodom for the sake of its few "righteous" residents; it was eventually destroyed by "brimstone and fire from the Lord out of heaven."

3. The Portsmouth Navy Yard on the Virginia coast was the largest of the federal shipyards. Occupied by Confederate forces in April 1861, it remained in Southern hands for over a year and represented a major loss to the Union navy. Confederates burned and abandoned the facility in the wake of Union advances in May 1862. Butt, *Portsmouth under Four Flags*, 14, 20–24.

4. The Ninety-ninth New York Regiment (also known as the "Union Coast Guard") was organized as a naval brigade to accompany Union gunboats along the Atlantic coast. It arrived at Fortress Monroe, Virginia, in May 1861 and was attached to the VII Corps of the Department of Virginia until February 1863. Whites in the area attempted to incite racial conflict between the unit and local blacks. The regiment served in Virginia and North Carolina throughout the Civil War. Frederick Henry Dyer, *A Compendium of the War of the Rebellion*, 3 vols. (Des Moines, Iowa, 1909; reprint, New York, N.Y., 1959), 3:1444; Mansfield, "That Fateful Class," 99–100.

35.
Editorial by Robert Hamilton
17 January 1863

As celebrations of the Emancipation Proclamation waned, northern blacks paused to consider the document's full meaning. Many viewed it as a call to action and an obligation to assist in transforming some four million slaves into American citizens. They felt a sense of unity with southern blacks and believed that the fate of the freedmen and the destiny of the race was in their hands. As a result, hundreds of northern blacks streamed southward to labor as relief workers, teachers, missionaries, and political organizers in areas occupied by Union forces. Thousands enlisted in the Union army. This was the subject of a forceful 17 January 1863 editorial by Robert Hamilton in the *Weekly Anglo-African*. Hamilton urged northern blacks to join in the war effort and to aid the newly emancipated slaves, thus carrying out "this labor of love and humanity . . . assigned to us." He declared that the critical moment had arrived. If northern blacks failed to act, Hamilton warned, "a century may elapse before another opportunity shall be afforded for reclaiming and holding our withheld rights." *WAA*, 3 January 1863; Richardson, *Christian Reconstruction*, 190–92; Walker, *Rock in a Weary Land*, 125–32.

The Present—and its Duties

After the feast, comes the reckoning. The good things served up to and by our people in the way of hearty and spontaneous rejoicing over the PROCLAMATION OF FREEDOM should be immediately followed by such practical results as will show that the rejoicing was not a mere outburst of feeling. Let us therefore endeavor to see our relations and duties in regard to this great event.

It is well known that in the great battle of Waterloo, Wellington held in reserve until late in the afternoon the bravest and most effective of his British troops, and when the final moment came to turn the doubtful fortunes of the day, he exclaimed to them, "*Up Guards, and at them!*"[1] We long ago took ground, that, in our present war, the black man is the "reserved guard," and the hour has come when our Commander-in-chief has exclaimed to them, "up blacks, and at them!"

What, therefore, the hour demands of us is action, immediate, pressing action! And the kind of action required is well described in one of the outbursts of Mr. Garnet's eloquent speech at the Cooper Institute—"We must fight! fight! fight!"[2] It is a fight for freedom and we are bound to go in. Let us organize one regiment in every large northern city, and send our offer of services directly to the President or the Secretary of War.[3] We have been pronounced citizens by the highest legal authority,[4] why should we not share in the perils of citizenship? What better field to claim our rights than the field of battle? Where will prejudice be so speedily overcome? Where will brotherhood be so quickly and firmly cemented? It is now, or never: now, if ever. A century may elapse before another opportunity shall be afforded for reclaiming and holding our withheld rights. If freedmen are accepted as soldiers to man the forts in the Mississippi and the Southern coast, why shall not free men be also accepted? If freedmen are accepted to man the fleets of the United States, why shall not free men also be received?[5]

Let us at this moment get rid of one great difficulty in our way; let us understand thoroughly that we have got to do our own work. It is no time to stop, with Professor Wilson,[6] and cast about in search of the duties of Abolitionists in the matter of our advancement; we must depend on no one under God for our elevation. It is our own work, and always has been. All we wanted was OPPORTUNITY, and that, blessed be GOD, has come! Freedom is ours. And its fruit, equality, hangs temptingly on the tree, beckoning our own brave arms to rise and clutch it. If we rise in tens of thousands, and say to the President, "here we are, take us!" we will secure to our children and children's children all that our fathers have labored and suffered and bled for! But if we tamely suffer this hour to pass, then will we sink, in the public estimation, lower down than the vilest slanders of our foes could carry us. We know that there are partial military organizations in most of our large cities, let those having them in charge bestir themselves, assured that this time they will work for something.

There are other labors also which we must undertake. The process of transforming three millions of slaves into citizens requires the aid of intelligent colored men and women. We are, and can be, nearer to them than any other class of persons; we can enter into their feelings and attract their sympathies better than any others can. We can more patiently help and teach, and more jealously defend them, than any others can. We are manifestly destined for this work of mercy. It is for this trial God has given us the partial freedom, and such education, and the irrepressible desire for equality which consumes our souls. This labor of love and humanity His Providence has assigned to us; and we will be false to our destiny if we fail to do it. Our brethren are strangers, and naked, and hungered and athirst, and woe be unto us if we fail to minister to their wants. We are bound to be foremost in this good work; not pushing others aside, nor suffering others to push us aside, but straining every nerve to do our whole duty. We know that some of us are now engaged in this good work; what we claim is that *all* should be engaged in like manner.

And as no work can be carried on efficiently without organization, so all these separate efforts should be combined under one great national organization, which shall have power and authority to do the work thoroughly. Our leading men and women should, by correspondence, or convention, immediately get up this organization. We feel jealous of this good work, jealous that our people shall do it, and thereby assert before the world the high character which is really ours. We have started so many good organizations, and suffered the other class to enjoy the fruits of them, that this effort should be guarded at all points. No nobler work could engage the labors of men or angels. Among the objects which should engage the attention of this organization should be,

1. The furnishing of clothing to the freedmen.

2. The furnishing and supporting teachers among them.

3. The furnishing and supporting physicians among them.

4. The furnishing and supporting of instructors in household labors, economics and industries.

An organization for these and kindred purposes, got up and managed by colored persons, would command the sympathies, support and pecuniary aid of the benevolent throughout this land and all christendom. Especially would it have a claim on the great Avery fund which has hitherto laid dormant so far as its American legatees are concerned.[7]

Weekly Anglo-African (New York, N.Y.), 17 January 1863.

1. On 18 June 1815, a combined force of British, Belgian, Dutch, and German troops commanded by the Duke of Wellington defeated the French army of Napoleon Bonaparte near Waterloo, Belgium. This was the final, decisive engagement of the Napoleonic Wars.

2. On 5 January 1863, Henry Highland Garnet spoke at the Cooper Institute in New York City before a large interracial audience gathered to celebrate the Emancipation Proclamation. He read the proclamation and described the events that led to its adoption. Although Garnet praised Lincoln as "the man of our choice and hope" and declared that God "had brought this thing about," he understood that the government had accepted black enlistment because "the rebels could not be subdued unless the black men were brought in to take a part." *NASS*, 10 January 1863 [14:0868]; *Lib*, 16 January 1863 [14:0694].

3. Edwin M. Stanton (1814–1869), a noted attorney, was secretary of war in the administrations of Abraham Lincoln and Andrew Johnson. He enforced the unpopular draft laws and restricted the freedom of the press during the Civil War. Although he was an early supporter of black enlistment, he angered black soldiers by ruling that they were only eligible for the rate of pay given contraband laborers. Stanton served from January 1862 until May 1868, when he resigned at Johnson's request because of disagreements over Reconstruction policy. *HTECW*, 712–13.

4. On 29 November 1862, Attorney General Edward Bates issued an official

advisement to the secretary of the treasury that "free men of color, if born in the United States, are citizens of the United States." This was the first time that the federal government had explicitly acknowledged black citizenship. Litwack, *North of Slavery*, 63.

5. There were several ill-fated and unauthorized attempts to enlist freedmen as Union soldiers in Kansas and South Carolina during 1862. During the year, the Lincoln administration hesitantly moved toward acceptance of black enlistment. In April Secretary of War Edwin M. Stanton suggested using blacks for garrison duty in the malarial regions of the South. The first authorized unit of freedmen, the First South Carolina Volunteers, was mustered in during January 1863. The first free black unit from the North, the Fifty-fourth Massachusetts Regiment, was organized one month later. Eventually, some 180,000 blacks served in the Union army during the Civil War, about 147,000 of them from the South. Another 9,600 enlisted in the Union navy. Afro-Americans comprised roughly 10 percent of the Union forces. Berlin et al., *Freedom*, 2:14; Cornish, *Sable Arm*, 31, 66–67, 79–80, 92–93, 288.

6. William J. Wilson.

7. The Avery Fund was named for Charles Avery, a wealthy Pittsburgh cotton merchant and philanthropist. In 1849 he founded the local Allegheny Institute (later Avery College), the first institution of higher learning for blacks in the United States. Upon his death in 1858, he bequeathed $150,000 to a trust fund for Christian missions in Africa and "the education and elevation of the colored people of the United States." In 1878 the Avery Fund financed the establishment of the Avery Normal Institute for blacks in Charleston. Victor Ullman, *Martin R. Delany: The Beginnings of Black Nationalism* (Boston, Mass., 1971), 69–71.

36.
H. Ford Douglas to Owen Lovejoy
3 February 1863

After the Civil War became a battle against slavery, northern blacks embraced the cause and flooded recruitment offices. Some 70 percent of all northern black males of military age joined the Union army, three times the rate for whites. Many viewed enlistment as an antislavery obligation. Black leaders argued that military service would bolster claims to American citizenship, discredit racial stereotypes, and, most important, free the oppressed. "It is our work," they announced, "and always has been." In this 3 February 1863 letter to antislavery congressman Owen Lovejoy, H. Ford Douglas reveals his deep commitment to the fight for freedom. Although whites in his regiment treated him as an equal, Douglas requested a transfer to an all-black South Carolina unit. Out of a profound sense of obligation to the slave, he wanted to use his military experience to train new recruits and better "show my faith by my works." Berlin et al., *Freedom*, 2:11–15; *WAA*, 17 January, 14, 28 February, 14 March, 4, 11, 18 April 1863.

Providence, Louisiana
February 3d, 1863

My Dear Sir:[1]

In my desire to serve the great cause of freedom whose success is now made certain by the madness of Slaveholders I have enlisted as a soldier in order to show my faith by my works. I belong to Company G 95th Reg—Ill Vol.[2]

My mistake was in not waiting until the government called colored men into the service and then I could have occupied something like an equal position among my comrades. But as it is now[,] although I am respected by my own Regiment and treated kindly by those who know me and the motives that induced me to enlist[,] still there are those in the other Regiments with whom I have to come in contact who have no regard for my feelings simply because I have the hated blood coursing in my veins. My position therefore which might be to me very pleasant and especially so when I have the conscientiousness of fighting in a cause so holy is anything but agreable. Under these circumstances I wish you to interest yourself in my behalf. I would like to get a transfere to South Carolina where there are Colored Regiments in the course of formation[3] or else a Commission in recruit for one to which I could be attached after it was formed. There could be no legal objection on this point for I am already a U.S. soldier regularly enlisted and mustered into the United States service with county and government bounties respect.[4]

I have now been six months in the service with the advantages of drill in many of its most important details, so that I think I could render more efficient service with those that I have been identified in the moral conflicts of the past than I can in my present position. You will agree with me that the Negro ought to have an intelligent idea of what he is fighting for—in this I think I could be useful.

I have written to the Hon. Hen[r]y Wilson who is a personal friend of mine[5] but have not yet recieved a reply but doubt not that he would do all he could for me if he knew my situation. I will be under many obligations if you will see him and get his influence in my behalf. Our Brigade (Deitzlers)[6] is engaged here in cutting a canal into Lake Providence in order to get into the Red River. Pardon me for this intrusion. I will indeed be happy to recieve from you a reply. I am yours very truly,
H. Ford Douglas

Applications for Appointments, RG 94, Adjutant General's Office, U.S. Colored Troops, National Archives, Washington, D.C. Published by permission.

1. Owen Lovejoy (1811–1864), the brother of abolitionist martyr Elijah P. Lovejoy, was an antislavery congressman from Illinois. In 1854, after pastoring a Congregational church in Princeton, Illinois, for seventeen years, he was elected to the state legislature. Lovejoy helped found the Illinois Republican party and served in the U.S. Congress from 1857 until his death. Although his antislavery convictions were sometimes tempered by the demands of political expediency, he remained a committed abolitionist and introduced legislation to abolish slavery in the territories. Merrill and Ruchames, *Letters of William Lloyd Garrison,* 5:34.

2. The Ninety-fifth Illinois Regiment of Infantry Volunteers was organized at Rockford, Illinois, in September 1862. From January to May 1863, it served in the XVII Corps of the Army of the Tennessee; it was stationed near Lake Providence, Louisiana, during this time. The unit participated in the third Vicksburg campaign, the siege of Atlanta, and other battles throughout the deep South. Dyer, *Compendium,* 1:520, 3:1086–87.

3. As a result of General David Hunter's efforts to form a contraband regiment in South Carolina during May 1862, that state took the lead in recruiting black troops. While Hunter was in command, the U.S. Army refused to accept the First South Carolina Volunteers into military service; his replacement, Brigadier General Rufus Saxton, maintained the unit without authorization and sent it into a skirmish against Confederate troops in Georgia that November. He then placed it under the command of Thomas Wentworth Higginson, a Massachusetts abolitionist. When the federal government changed its policy concerning black troops, the unit was formally mustered in at Beaufort, South Carolina, in January 1863. The First South Carolina Volunteers participated in engagements along the South Carolina coast and in two expeditions against Jacksonville, Florida. It was redesignated the Thirty-third U.S. Colored Troops in February 1864 and mustered out of service in January 1866. Dyer, *Compendium,* 3:1636, 1729; Cornish, *Sable Arm,* 32–55, 80–93.

4. In order to meet military enlistment quotas, local officials often offered bounties (or cash payments) to volunteers. The use of bounties was widespread, especially in the North, and often accompanied by fraud and corruption. *HTECW*, 72–73.

5. Senator Henry Wilson of Massachusetts was a strong supporter of black enlistment. Douglas had made his acquaintance during a lecture tour in 1860. Merrill and Ruchames, *Letters of William Lloyd Garrison*, 5:192–93; Harris, "H. Ford Douglas," 226.

6. Brigadier General George Washington Deitzler (1826–1884) commanded the XVII Corps of the Army of the Tennessee at this time. A farmer and real estate agent from Kansas, he had fought with the free-state forces there in the 1850s and became speaker of the territorial house of representatives. Deitzler resigned his commission in August 1863 because of declining health and returned to Kansas, where he led the state militia. Warner, *Generals in Blue*, 116–17.

37.
Editorial by Peter Anderson
14 February 1863

Black abolitionists recognized that racial progress depended on the transformation of former slaves into full citizens. Convinced that the Civil War would not change the racial attitudes of white southerners, some black leaders urged the freedmen to leave the South and settle on the vast lands in the West. Peter Anderson, the editor and proprietor of the *Pacific Appeal*, championed this view in the paper's 14 February 1863 issue. His editorial called on black leaders to work with freedmen's associations and to redirect their efforts toward acquiring western tracts. Anderson envisioned black homesteaders sharing in the anticipated growth and prosperity of the trans-Mississippi frontier. Black leaders continued to back similar programs throughout the 1870s, viewing an independent black yeomanry as crucial to a meaningful Reconstruction. Rudolph M. Lapp, *Blacks in Gold Rush California* (New Haven, Conn., 1977), 161, 241–42, 259; *PA*, 5 April, 28 June, 2 August 1862, 16 January 1864, 28 June 1879; Foner, *Reconstruction*, 600.

The Freedmen

While the free colored people in the eastern States, as also those who are on this coast, are jubilant over the Emancipation Proclamation, it must not be forgotten that there will be a vast number of freedmen that will not be enrolled in the army or placed in the navy—that outside of the Government protection, their characters, their future destiny, will, in a great degree, be in their own hands. It has been a favorite theme of debate, "Whether the character of a man is formed for him, or by him?" As far as this question relates to the freedmen, every mishap or weakness of theirs will be misconstrued by the enemies of freedom into vices of the deepest dye. To prevent this, our leading men in the east should start a system of land speculation west of Kansas, or in any of the Territories, and endeavor to infuse into the minds of these freedmen the importance of agriculture, that they may become producers. By this means they can come up with the expected growth of the Great West, receive some of the innumerable benefits that will accrue from the building of the Pacific Railroad,[1] and the taxes that they would be compelled to pay in common with other people, for the improvement of the new towns that will spring up, would entitle their children to the benefits of a common school education.

The freedmen's associations in the east will be but temporary and of little avail, except they adopt some practical plan to guide them in the way that they may obtain some of the waste land in the West. As a large number will be thrown on their own resources, it will be best to encourage them to do just like other men by putting up with hardships until they make themselves homes.

It will be fatal to their interest and progress for our leading men in the east to fete and encourage them to stay in the larger cities—Philadelphia, New York and Boston. The responsibilities of their failure in this sphere of freedom would be a stigma and reproach on the free colored people of the North, as also on our white friends who have been battling in the cause of human freedom.

Hence we of the Pacific States should not be hasty in connecting ourselves with any movement that has not a practical bearing upon our welfare. While the Government is disposed to aid and give encouragement, by enrolling and enlisting large numbers of our race in the army and navy, there will rest a great responsibility on the free colored people of the North in shaping their movements in a direction that will induce many of these freedmen to take up lands in the West. Our friends in the East should form these land associations forthwith.

Pacific Appeal (San Francisco, Calif.), 14 February 1863.

1. Congress passed the Pacific Railway Act in 1862 to authorize the building of the nation's first transcontinental railroad. Two years later, with generous federal subsidies, the two companies involved began construction. The Union Pacific Railroad laid track westward from Omaha, Nebraska, and the Central Pacific Railroad worked eastward from Sacramento, California; the two lines joined in 1869 near Ogden, Utah.

38.
James H. Hudson to Peter Anderson
25 February 1863

Black abolitionists hailed the Emancipation Proclamation as the beginning of freedom. But they recognized that President Abraham Lincoln
had adopted it as a military necessity, not a humanitarian measure; they
understood that it was a blow struck at the Confederacy, not on behalf
of the slave. Black leaders pointed out that the proclamation came two
years after the start of the Civil War and exempted slaves in the border
states and those owned by "loyal" masters. Lincoln's decision to do the
least he could against slavery, rather than the very most, left them anxious and disappointed. James H. Hudson voiced the black abolitionist
appraisal of the Emancipation Proclamation. Hudson, an agent for the
Pacific Appeal in Suisun City, California, initially welcomed Lincoln's
declaration. He urged blacks to enlist in the Union army to "liberate
our brethren in bonds" and criticized blacks who opposed involvement
in the conflict. But his original enthusiasm for the proclamation quickly
faded. Hudson's 25 February 1863 letter to the *Pacific Appeal* labeled
the proclamation a "halfway measure" and chided Lincoln for failing to
emancipate all slaves—"every chain should have been broken." Foner,
Reconstruction, 7; *WAA*, 3, 10 January, 26 September 1863, 16 July
1864; *Lib*, 16 January 1863, 3 June 1864 [14:0697, 15:0387].

SUISUN CITY, [California]
Feb[ruary] 25, 1863

MR. EDITOR:[1]

I object. I think our view of the Freedom Proclamation, its significance
and its consequences, is incorrect, not to say wrong, and I will state,
in brief, my opinions on the subject, without venturing to intrude a
lengthy argument upon your space. I am one of those who think the
President has been too dilatory in seizing, for the use of the public, such
potent means of oppressive warfare as a declaration of emancipation
would have been 12 months ago, and even now, so far from perceiving
the full requirements of the occasion—as, for instance, the necessity
for complete and decisive measures for reducing the strength of the
rebellion—our honest but incompetent President adopts a halfway measure, which purports to give freedom to the bulk of the slave population
beyond the reach of our arms, while it ignores or defies justice, by
clinching the rivets of the chain which binds those whom alone we have
present power to redeem. The proclamation should have been made
to include every bondsman on the soil of America; every chain should
have been broken, and the oppressed bidden to go free. Then, indeed,

believing we were obeying the divine law, we might have invoked God's blessing upon our arms, and we could then have boldly claimed the services of every loyal man, white or black, in suppressing this hell-born and heaven-defying rebellion. The proclamation has been brought forth by timid and heaven-doubting midwives, and proved an incompetent and abominable abortion. "Put not your trust in princes,"[2] says the inspired writer, and he might have added with truth, acknowledged by the wrongs of a long-suffering people, "nor in the rule of republics—their strength is nought, and burnt-offerings are offensive in my sight." Oh that the scales might drop from their eyes, and that they could pray, and work, and rule and fight with the fervor, the steadfastness, the wisdom and the righteousness that have characterized God's chosen people in olden times.

J. H. H.

Pacific Appeal (San Francisco, Calif.), 7 March 1863.

1. Peter Anderson (ca. 1819–1879), one of the leading black journalists in San Francisco, was a native of Philadelphia. He moved to California about 1850 and established his leadership credentials through a wide range of activities in the city's black community. Anderson participated in organized efforts to improve black education, was an officer of a black literary society called the Livingstone Institute, founded local black Masonic and Odd Fellows lodges, and played a prominent role in California's black state conventions during the 1850s and after the Civil War. He promoted black settlement in the state through a joint-stock land association. Although he rejected African colonization programs, he proposed the establishment of an independent black republic in either Mexico's Sonora province or the American West. He continued to encourage black migration to the West during and after the war.

Anderson's involvement with the black press began in 1856, when he helped found California's first black newspaper, the *Mirror of the Times*. He also served as an agent for several eastern journals and frequently corresponded with the *Weekly Anglo-African* under the pseudonym "Tall Son of Pennsylvania." Through his tailoring shop and clothing store, he accumulated sufficient capital to establish his own newspaper, the *Pacific Appeal*, in April 1862. Anderson initially acted as owner and publisher of the paper, while Philip Bell served as editor. By late summer, he assumed total control of the enterprise. The journal's content reflected Anderson's lifelong involvement in black fraternal organizations, his commitment to civil rights, and his interest in emigration. Under his proprietorship, the *Pacific Appeal* became the longest-running black newspaper of its time. Bell and other black leaders accused Anderson of ignoring the slavery issue and criticized his accommodationist tone. A personal feud with Bell became particularly bitter after the latter founded the *Elevator*, a rival local newspaper, in 1865. Anderson temporarily suspended publication of the *Pacific Appeal* in 1869 and undertook a statewide tour to personally promote ratification of the Fifteenth Amendment. His publishing career ended in July 1879 when he contracted pneumonia and died. U.S. Census, 1850; *PA*, 5 April, 28 June, 2, 9, 16,

30 August 1862, 23 August, 8 November 1873, 7 August 1875, 4, 11 November 1876; *WAA*, 22 October 1859, 15 December 1860, 20 April 1861; *ESF*, 7 April 1865 [15:0800–803]; Lapp, *Blacks in Gold Rush California*, 174–76, 212–21, 241–42, 255, 258–59, 262, 265–66.

   2. Hudson quotes from Psalms 146:3.

39.
Meunomennie L. Maimi to T. A. Maimi
March 1863

Blacks of every class and background—from racial spokesmen to common soldiers—interpreted the Civil War as a momentous struggle between the forces of slavery and freedom. The following letter by Meunomennie L. Maimi of the Twentieth Connecticut Regiment offers a compelling example. Maimi's dispatch from the front lines to his wife is deeply personal but intensely analytical. He reflected blacks' belief that the war would decide whether they would be truly free or forever enslaved, and he pledged to return from the battlefield "a free man, of a free country" or to die "with my face to the slaveholders." Like other black soldiers, he recognized that he received unequal treatment in the Union army, yet he and other black troops fought for "God, liberty and country," believing that the war represented their only opportunity to destroy slavery. *WAA*, 11 July 1863, 6 May 1865; John W. Storrs, *The Twentieth Connecticut: A Regimental History* (Ansonia, Conn., 1886), appendix 4.

> Buckingham Legion, Co. I, 20th
> Reg[imen]t., C.V.[1]
> Camp near Stafford C[ourt]
> H[ouse], [Virginia]
> March, 1863

My Dear Wife:

When I wrote you the last letter I was quite sick, and did not know as I should ever be able to write to you again; but I am better now and write to relieve your mind, in case you might worry too much about me. When I wrote my last letter, I did not expect to be able to write another; but some good news which I received and the kind usage of a few friends, who came to my hut and did what was needed for me, have saved you your husband, and I am enabled to write again. There is one thing which your selfish love for your husband has made you forget, and that is, that he is naturally a soldier, and in time of war, and particularly in times like the present, a good soldier has something else to do besides enjoying himself at home with his family. I shall come, if permitted to go home, but as soon as my health will admit, will return to duty.

Do you know or think what the end of this war is to decide? It is to decide whether we are to have freedom to all or slavery to all. If the Southern Confederacy succeeds, then you may bid farewell to all liberty thereafter and either be driven to a foreign land or held in slavery here. If our government succeeds, then your and our race will be free. The government has torn down the only barrier that existed against us as a people. When slavery passes away, the prejudices that belonged to it must follow. The government calls for the colored man's help and, if he is not a fool, he will give it.

The present is different from the Revolutionary war, for that was to decide between a king and a part of his subjects, who had fled from religious persecution in his land to a new land. He claimed even there to still hold them and sought by cruel and unjust taxation to subdue these people. They then rebelled; and after a long and bloody war won their independence and established a free government of their own. It was intended to be free to all, even to the few slaves who were in the land, brought there by the English government. The Constitution of the United States was such that it allowed each State to make its own laws, as long as they did not infringe upon the laws of the general government. Some of the Northern States in a few years set their slaves free. The other States would have followed their example, but they were in a warmer climate and, unfortunately for us, foreigners came from France and Spain, who were slaveholders, and soon found out that some parts of this country would grow cotton, rice, sugar and indigo. They then had to decide who should cultivate those plants that would produce so much wealth. They considered the climate and came to the decision that the white man could not stand it and the attendant fevers, and so they must have some other race of people beside the paleface, for he was only fit to rule in that line of business. They cast their eyes on the red men, the natives of the country and natural kings of the land. Why did they not take them? they were used to the climate—the reason was, the Indians, of whom I am in part a descendant, as well as yourself, were warriors or soldiers whose savage natures, when they found out the white man's intentions, would not submit to be chained down to them and their system of labor. They looked upon them as robbers, who came to deprive them of their natural rights and liberties; and became bitter enemies, fighting them by night and by day, surprising them at all times and everywhere, at labor or at prayer, in sunshine or storm. The white man was not safe at all; they scorned his paper treaties of peace and broke them as fast as they were made. But their bravery could not prevail; their weapons were inferior to those of the palefaces, and the want of union among them gave the victory to the white man.

The white man thought again how to get his money without his own dear self having to broil beneath a hot sun or see his wife or delicate child stoop to the labor of picking the cotton from the field or gathering rice from its damp bed. The Indian had failed him; the few captives they took died when they came to force labor upon them, thus proving the red man unable to do the labor in those climes. His fiend-like eyes fell upon the black man.[2] Thought he, "I have it. We will get some of the States that cannot grow these plants, and do not need as many hands to help them as we do, to raise blacks for us, and we will purchase these of them, and they will keep their mouths shut about this liberty that was only meant for us and our children." They denied that God made the black man a man at all, and brought their most learned judges and doctors of the gospel and laws to attempt to prove by them that the sons of Africa were not even human. They tried to convince the world that the black man sprang from the brute creation; that the kings and princes and noble sons of the sunny land sprang from the loins of monkeys and apes, who made war with each other and slaves of each other in their mother country, and it was but right to buy and steal the children of apes or monkeys and to enslave them.[3]

How do you fancy, wife, the idea of being part ape or monkey? I have often heard our grandmother tell what a noble man your great-grandfather was, how much he knew and was respected by his neighbors and the white man that owned him, and how her own father, who followed the condition of his father, who died a slave, suffered before he bought his freedom; how she and her little sisters and brothers were robbed of her hard-earned property by one who cared not for the rights of the black child. Tell grandmother that Maimi will strike for her wrongs as well as for those of others.

You will say that you are not part ape if you are part black; the slaveholders say that you are and all those who have the least drop of African blood in their veins are the same. So my wife is part baboon, and her husband is a gorilla of the masculine gender, a kind of monkey nearly as large as a man, a black man, of course. It is said that his hand, which is the foot of him, as the Irishman said, is very powerful. He hides in trees and reaches down from his perch with his hind legs, of which the foot is formed like the human hand, except the thumb, which is longer and stronger than his fingers, and seizes a man by his throat and lifts him from the ground, chokes him to death, throws his body down and afterwards stamps upon it. They travel in company and use clubs to fight with, and can drive the wild beasts before them. Such is the history of one part of our ancestors, according to the learned slaveholding traitors. They had better look sharp after that long stout thumb, for I assure them, that if once it clasps their lying throats, it shall never unclasp until their bodies are beneath its feet. What better can they expect of the monkey? They are now about being caught in their own trap; the monkeys are on the way to their doors, not with gold, as in days gone by, when they wanted their freedom, but are going with loudmouthed cannons, &c., sending forth fire, smoke, and death.

They shall see these gentle monkeys, that they thought they had so fast in chains and fetters, coming on a long visit to them, with rifle, saber, and all the terrible trappings of war. Not one at a time, cringing like whipped hounds as we were, but by thousands, and if that doesn't suffice, by millions. Like Pharaoh's lice,[4] we shall be found in all his palaces, will be his terror and his torment; he shall yet wish he had never heard of us. We will never forsake him, until he repents in sackcloth and ashes his crime of taking from us our manhood and reducing us to the brute creation. We will accept nothing but, without any mental or other reservation, our rights and liberties. He shall give up his monkeyizing, his demoniac, infernal plan of ruining our country and destroying our race. The black man shall yet hold up his head and be a man; not a poor, despised brute. But his own good hands must help strike the blows and gain the victory through blood, before the American slavery-taught white man can believe that the poor, oppressed slave and the downtrodden black man is his true friend and brother-man. With all his books and the vast amount of learning and the light of civilization shining on his path, he is still in the dark. In spite of his suffering at the hands of the slave power, the loss of his sons, who have fallen in the defense of his insulted flag, his loss of treasures and the threatened loss of his country, he is yet blind. He still bows down to these murdering slaveholders and is willing to kiss their feet, if they will but return to the Union as it was and kindly rule over him.

This is what the blind copperheads ask of them, but the slaveholder despises them and their offers, because they do it in the name of Democracy, which they hate, as there are yet some few sparks of freedom in that, and they hate everything which is free or points towards justice for any but themselves and their institutions. They ask, with arms in their hands, the right to buy and sell, to rob and murder all that are poor enough to labor for their daily bread, without respect to color or blood. They are selfish and care for no one but themselves.

These are my enemies, my flag's enemies, the flag I was born under, have suffered so much under—the enemies to God and our government. It is they who have struck down the flag which so long has defended their institutions before they left our Union. It has by them been cast to the earth and trampled under foot, because it professed to be the flag of liberty and freedom, although it was only liberty for the white man, but it included the poor white man as well the rich and noble sons of the South, the monkey-raisers and drivers. They tore that flag from its staff and in its place put their rebel rag, and swore by it that freedom should die. But they shall find that it cannot die, that its black sons as well as its loyal white sons are faithful, and will shed the last drop of blood in defense of the starry banner that is to be the emblem of freedom to all, whether black or white.

Now, wife, although I love you and would grant anything in reason to one who has been so kind and so faithful and true to her husband, yet there is something which the true man should hold dear and for which he should be willing to die, besides the wife of his bosom or the children of his loins: first, his God; then his country or his government, when it is a just one; and if he cannot do that he is no man, but a useless piece of machinery. If I did not know why you spoke those words, I would be very angry indeed. I know that it was your wifely anger at the mean treatment which your dearly beloved husband has suffered at the hands of some of his fellow soldiers that made you speak so quick and without forethought, bidding me desert my flag and leave my country to fall into the hands of its worst enemies. You did not speak such words as those on the day when I stood before you with the uniform of a volunteer, the uniform of a free man on. You told me at the door, with a smile on your face, but a tear in your eye, that if I thought it was my duty to go to what was then a white man's war, to "go, and may God bless you!" I was prouder of you that day than the day the minister bid me salute my wife.

You have never doubted my true and faithful love for you; it is still the same, or else I would come running home like a little cur that some large dog had badly frightened, and leave you to become a slave to those wretches who hate us. For if these Southern demons conquer, then you, with your Indian and Negro blood mixed in your veins, must bow down to them and become their slave or perhaps some white man's mistress, not an honored wife, loved and respected by her husband, but a mere plaything, to be cast aside as soon as he discovers a fresh victim to administer to his beastly lusts, and bear more monkeys for him to sell to others, to be used in the same way. This he has been doing for years, and the only cure that can or will relieve this disease is the present war, which he in his foolish and wicked plan began.

I do not blame you altogether for what you said about returning home, as it was cowardly in me to complain to you of the fools' bad usage. I forgive you, as it was prompted by your too-selfish love for your husband. But I want you to remember hereafter that you are a soldier's wife, a warrior's bride—one who has not a single drop of cowardly blood in his veins, and who will not desert his flag, or country, or his brother in bonds, not even for his dearly beloved wife, the friend of his bosom. Ponder this well; take the right sense of it and be proud that you have such a man for a husband. What is money but trash? and is trash to be compared to a country's and my own liberty? If the government gets so poor, before the war ends, that it cannot pay but $40 per month and no bounties, I will take that and fight on. That will buy bread for you and my poor old grandmother. If I return at all, let me come back to your arms a free man, of a free country and a free flag, and my brothers free, or else let me rest in death on the battlefield, with my face to the slaveholders, a continual reproach and curse unto him, as long as the world shall stand or a slaveholder breathe. This from your soldier-husband,

M. L. MAIMI[5]

Weekly Anglo-African (New York, N.Y.), 18 April 1863.

1. The Twentieth Connecticut Regiment was formed at New Haven in September 1862. For the next eight months, it was attached to the XII Corps of the Army of the Potomac. The regiment was stationed at Stafford Court House, Virginia, from January to April 1863, when it took part in the Chancellorsville campaign. The Twentieth later fought in the battles of Gettysburg, Atlanta, and Savannah. Dyer, *Compendium*, 3 : 1014.

2. Maimi alludes to the early development of the South Carolina coast. French and Spanish explorers first visited the region in the 1520s. When England established the colony of South Carolina in 1663 it was settled by sugar planters from Barbados, who soon made rice, indigo, and sea island cotton into profitable exports. In order to establish a labor force, they conducted slaving raids against local Native American tribes. Women and children were viewed as tractable and kept as slaves; men were killed or shipped to the Caribbean. In time, declining Native American population, runaways, and proprietary opposition led to the importation of African slaves. But as late as 1708, one-third of the slaves in the colony were Native Americans. Robert M. Weir, *Colonial South Carolina: A History* (Millwood, N.Y., 1983), 3–8, 26–27, 49, 142–53.

3. As early as the seventeenth century, Western racial theorists speculated that blacks were biologically linked to African apes and lesser primates. Many argued that blacks were a distinct species from whites. In the 1830s, ethnologists such as Josiah Nott and George Gliddon made a belief in "polygenesis," or the separate origins of the races, into an accepted tenet of anthropological thought. This theory was increasingly used to support the proslavery argument during the decades that followed. Winthrop D. Jordan, *White over Black: American Attitudes toward the Negro, 1550–1812* (Chapel Hill, N.C., 1968), 29–32, 235–39, 490–97; George M. Fredrickson, *The Black Image in the White Mind: The Debate on Afro-American Character and Destiny, 1817–1914* (New York, N.Y., 1971), 73–90.

4. Maimi refers to an account in Exodus 8 : 16–19, in which God sent a plague of lice to infest the Egyptian people because the Pharaoh of Egypt refused to emancipate his Jewish slaves.

5. Meunomennie L. Maimi (1835–?), a Philadelphia-born mulatto, was, according to the U.S. Census, a "quack doctor" in Middletown, Connecticut, before the Civil War. T. A. Maimi, his wife, was a local woman of combined black–Native American ancestry. They were married about 1860. Elizabeth Narry, an elderly black woman who also lived in their household, may have been the grandmother to whom Maimi refers. Maimi enlisted in the Twentieth Connecticut Regiment in September 1862. He later transferred to the Fifty-fourth Massachusetts Regiment, but was discharged in May 1863 due to a disability. Maimi returned to Middletown and participated in the activities of the local black community. U.S. Census, 1860; Storrs, *Twentieth Connecticut*, appendix 15; Compiled Military Service Records, RG 94, Adjutant General's Office, U.S. Colored Troops, DNA; *WAA*, 6 May 1865.

40.
Harriet A. Jacobs to Lydia Maria Child
18 March 1863

The growing number of former slaves behind Union lines aroused the anxiety of northern whites, who envisioned a flood of four million destitute freedmen moving North to compete with white workers or become an intolerable social burden. The northern press aggravated these apprehensions by describing the condition of the freedmen in disparaging terms. Even newspapers sympathetic to the former slaves often reported their plight in pitiful detail to encourage relief efforts. Black abolitionists recognized that public portraits of needy blacks reinforced popular stereotypes of a degraded and dependent race. Harriet A. Jacobs, who directed a freedmen's school in Alexandria, Virginia, disputed these reports in an 18 March 1863 letter to Lydia Maria Child. She offered a candid, firsthand assessment of the freedmen, acknowledging their poverty and misery, but defending their moral character and desire to learn. Jacobs, a former slave, lamented that so few white Americans really knew "the hearts of my . . . people." *NASS*, 16 April 1864 [15:0309]; *DM*, January, November 1862, June 1863; McPherson, *Struggle for Equality*, 148–53, 162–77; Fredrickson, *Black Image in the White Mind*, 159, 165–71; Foner, *Reconstruction*, 67–70; Sterling, *We Are Your Sisters*, 245–48.

ALEXANDRIA, [Virginia]
March 18, 1863

Since I last wrote to you, the condition of the poor refugees has improved. During the winter months, the smallpox carried them off by hundreds; but now it has somewhat abated. At present, we have one hundred and forty patients in the hospital. The misery I have witnessed must be seen to be believed. The Quakers of Philadelphia, who sent me here, have done nobly for my people.[1] They have indeed proved themselves a Society of Friends. Had it not been for their timely relief, many more must have died. They have sent thousands and tens of thousands of dollars to different sections of the country, wherever these poor sufferers came within our lines. But, notwithstanding all that has been done, very many have died from destitution. It is impossible to reach them all. Government has erected here barracks for the accommodations of five hundred. We have fifteen hundred on the list.

Many have found employment, and are supporting themselves and their families. It would do your heart good to talk with some of these people. They are quick, intelligent, and full of the spirit of freedom. Some of them say to me, "The white men of the North have helped us thus far, and we want to help *them*. We would like to fight for them, if they would only treat us like men."

The colored people could not do enough for the first regiments that came here. They had entire faith in them as the deliverers of their race. The sight of the U.S. uniform took all fear out of their hearts, and inspired them with hope and confidence. Many of them freely fed the soldiers at their own tables, and lodged them as comfortably as possible in their humble dwellings. The change is very sad. In return for their kindness and ever-ready service, they often receive insults, and sometimes beatings, and so they have learned to distrust those who wear the uniform of the U.S. You know how warmly I have sympathized with the Northern army; all the more does it grieve me to see so many of them false to the principles of freedom. But I am proud and happy to know that the black man is to strike a blow for liberty. I am rejoiced that Col. Shaw heads the Massachusetts regiment,[2] for I know he has a noble heart.

How pitiful it is that members of any religious sect should come here, and return home to report their observations, without one word of sympathy for God's suffering poor! This is suggested to me by reading the New York *Evangelist*.[3] These poor refugees undoubtedly have faults, as all human beings would have, under similar circumstances. I agree with that noble man, Gen. Saxton,[4] who says they appear to him to be "extremely human." As to drunkenness, I have seen but one case. As to stealing, I wish the writer in the New York *Evangelist* had made himself acquainted with the old slave pen here, now used for a prison.[5] When I last went there, I found seventy whites and one colored man. The marriage law has been disregarded, from old habits formed in slavery, and from want of true friends to encourage them in the observance of it now. I wish the writer of that article could have been where I was last night, in our rough, little, poorly-built church.

It was densely crowded; and although some alarm was excited by the rafters giving way overhead, quiet was soon restored, and the people were deeply attentive. Eight couples were married on this occasion.[6] We have a day school of eighty scholars, and a large number attend our evening school—mostly adults.[7] A large sewing circle,[8] composed of young and old, meet every Saturday afternoon. Three colored men teach a school in this city for those who can afford to pay somewhat for instruction. They have a large number of pupils, mostly children of colored citizens, but a few of the "little contrabands" attend their school.[9]

We are now collecting together the orphan children, of whom there are a great number, owing to the many deaths that have occurred of late. In justice to the refugee women, I am bound to testify that I have never known them, in any one instance, [to] refuse to shelter an orphan. In many cases, mothers who have five or six children of their own, without enough to feed and cover them, will readily receive these helpless little ones into their own poor hovels.

O, when will the white man learn to know the hearts of my abused and suffering people!

HARRIET JACOBS

Liberator (Boston, Mass.), 10 April 1863.

1. In the spring of 1862, Quaker women in Philadelphia organized two relief societies to collect and distribute money, clothing, and supplies to the contrabands in the South. Part of this aid went to the contraband camps at Alexandria, Virginia. Philip S. Benjamin, *The Philadelphia Quakers in the Industrial Age, 1865–1920* (Philadelphia, Pa., 1976), 128–29.

2. Robert Gould Shaw (1837–1863) of Boston commanded the Fifty-fourth Massachusetts Regiment, the first regular black troops to serve in the Civil War. Before accepting command of the unit in February 1863, he served with the Seventh New York and the Second Massachusetts regiments and saw action at the battle of Antietam. Shaw led the Fifty-fourth until his dramatic death on the parapets of Fort Wagner (in Charleston harbor) on 18 July. Peter Bruchard, *One Gallant Rush: Robert Gould Shaw and His Brave Black Regiment* (New York, N.Y., 1965).

3. Jacobs probably refers to private correspondence signed "M. H.," which was reprinted in the 6 November 1862 issue of the *New York Evangelist*. The letter was addressed to a Union army soldier in Virginia, who had written to "M. H." complaining of the "worthless contrabands" and asserting that his fellow soldiers were suffering while "ignorant, stupid, deceitful negroes were furnished with all they needed." "M. H." chastised the soldier for his racial prejudice and unchristian sentiment.

4. Brigadier General Rufus Saxton (1824–1908), a West Point graduate and career army officer, held various Union commands between 1862 and 1865 in the Department of the South. A moderate opponent of slavery, he was ordered to Port Royal, South Carolina, in April 1862 to supervise the contrabands and abandoned lands. Saxton recruited former slaves for the First South Carolina Volunteers, pressed the federal government to give them fair treatment, and distributed confiscated plantations among the contrabands. After being transferred to the Freedmen's Bureau in 1865, he resisted President Andrew Johnson's order to dispossess the freedmen and restore the land to its former owners. Although removed from this post in 1866, Saxton served in the quartermaster corps until his retirement from the army in 1888. *HTECW*, 659; Rose, *Rehearsal for Reconstruction*, 152–53.

5. Jacobs refers to the Alexandria, Virginia, slave pen used by the slave trading firm of Price, Birch & Co. during the 1850s. In 1862 the three-story brick enclosure became a temporary prison camp for deserters from the Union army. Later in the Civil War, it served as a military hospital for black soldiers. Despite the building's varied uses, the Price, Birch & Co. sign hung over the entrance as late as 1870. "History of Schools for the Colored Population," *AJE* 19:291 (1870); William B. Hesseltine, *Civil War Prisons: A Study in War Psychology* (Columbus, Ohio, 1930), 82.

6. Some black couples, especially those forcibly separated and remarried while in slavery, hesitated to formalize a marriage to one spouse before settling matters with the other. Yet contrary to Jacobs's assessment, most freedmen were anxious to legitimize slave marriages, both to symbolize their newly won freedom and to obtain the legal documentation necessary for government pensions, inheritance claims, and other family matters. Clergymen often organized mass weddings at contraband camps to encourage legal marriages among the freedmen. The ceremony to which Jacobs refers was performed by Rev. William Evans on 17 March 1863 at the First Colored Baptist Church in Alexandria. At the beginning of the service, a thunderous crash caused everyone in attendance to flee the building; order was soon restored and the wedding proceeded. Four couples were married on this occasion. Litwack, *Been in the Storm So Long*, 240–42; *CR*, 4 April 1863.

7. In February 1863, a day school for contraband children was opened at the government barracks in Alexandria. At first the teaching was done by convalescent soldiers, who volunteered their services until healthy enough to rejoin their regiments. Attendance grew quickly, and by April there were 125 scholars enrolled. Early the next year, classes moved into a new schoolhouse built by the freedmen. It was named the Jacobs Free School in honor of Harriet A. Jacobs, who helped raise funds for it in the North. By the end of 1864, the day school had 170 scholars and two teachers—Louisa Jacobs and S. V. Lawton, a black woman from Cambridge, Massachusetts. An evening school taught by three white missionaries met in the same building and instructed some 150 adult freedmen. With the support of the New England Freedmen's Aid Society, both schools continued to operate into the 1870s. *Comm*, 13 March 1863; Harriet A. Jacobs to J. Sella Martin, 13 April 1863, British Empire MSS, UkOxU-Rh [14:0799]; *NASS*, 16 April 1864 [15:0309–10]; "History of Schools for the Colored Population," 288–89.

8. Jacobs probably refers to the First Female Contraband Aid Society of Alexandria, a sewing circle formed by local black women in late 1862. The association's object was to "furnish aid and comfort" to the sick, aged, and needy among the contrabands. *CR*, 21 March 1863.

9. Jacobs refers to the First Select School, a pay school for Alexandria's contraband children founded by Rev. Clement Robinson in January 1862. From the beginning, it operated primary, normal, and theological departments in a room at Robinson's Second (or Beulah) Baptist Church. The school was supported by the American Baptist Free Mission Society and the American Baptist Home Missionary Society. In 1863 three black teachers—Robinson, Rev. G. W. Parker, and George H. Steemer—taught more than seven hundred students. The First Select School became a free school in 1866. "History of Schools for the Colored Population," 286, 290–91.

41.
George E. Stephens to Robert Hamilton
2 April 1863

After the federal government adopted emancipation as a war aim, black abolitionists renewed their campaign for black service in the Union army. Yet some blacks, still smarting from the Lincoln administration's earlier rejection of black volunteers, were suspicious of this new initiative. In early 1863, mass meetings were held across the North to assure skeptical blacks that their interests and those of the federal government were now joined—they could soldier for the Union and fight against slavery in the same stroke. In this 2 April 1863 letter to the *Weekly Anglo-African*, George E. Stephens warned that Peace Democrats (or Copperheads) hoped to restrict black involvement in the conflict. These northern opponents of the Civil War, he counseled, planned to incite racial animosity by discouraging black enlistment and then announcing that "niggers won't fight." Stephens urged blacks to support the Fifty-fourth Massachusetts Regiment, the first regular black army unit raised in the North, as a means of securing their freedom. "We have more to gain, if victorious," he declared, "or more to lose, if defeated, than any other class of men." Stephens joined the regiment later that month. *WAA*, 3 January, 9 May, 4 July, 29 August 1863.

Philadelphia, [Pennsylvania]
April 2, 1863

Mr. Editor:

One of the most impudent assumptions of authority and a long string of the basest misrepresentations have been perpetuated by a number of white men under the leadership of one Frishmuth, an illiterate German, on the people of the State of Pennsylvania; men who possess no record on the question of anti-slavery, and have not the shadow of a claim to the confidence and support of the colored men of this State, and are regarded by every intelligent colored man in the city as irresponsible militarily, pecuniarily, politically, and socially. Many of these men claim to have held quite recently commissions in either the regular or volunteer service of the United States, and rumor, which seems to be well founded, says that at least three of these men were cashiered or dismissed from the service.[1]

It will be remembered that just as soon as Gov. Andrew had obtained authority from the War Department at Washington to raise colored regiments,[2] a simultaneous response of the colored men of every State in the North was made to the call of the noble old Bay State. Every one of us felt it to be a high and holy duty to organize the first regiment of the

6. Recruiting poster for black troops
Courtesy of Chicago Historical Society

North at once, so that the irresistible argument of a first-class regiment of Northern colored men *en route* for the seat of war might overwhelm or, if possible, scatter to the four winds the prejudice against enlisting colored men in the army, and at the same time giving cheer to the hearts of good and loyal men everywhere. But no sooner did that hateful political reptile, the copperhead, discover the generous response and patriotism which this call elicited, than the insidious and guilty work of counteracting or neutralizing these pure and earnest manifestations, commenced. Every influence has been applied to dishearten us; mobbed, as at Detroit and elsewhere,[3] and in every town and village kicked, spit upon and insulted. The wily enemy knows full well that if they can impress on the minds of the masses the notion that the whites of the North are as bitter enemies as those of the South, it would be impossible to get a regiment of Northern colored men; then they would deride Massachusetts and the colored men, as they do Gen. Jim Lane of Kansas, for failing to realize certain promises and expectations regarding the promptness of our people to enlist, and yell like madmen, "niggers won't fight!"[4]

I am right glad that the black brigade is rolling up so bright a record. May they continue to drive before them the buzzard foe! You meet these copperheads at every step, and when violence is not resorted to, they come [with] the friendship and counsellor dodge. They ask, "Are you going to enlist in the army?" Of course, you answer "Yes!" They continue, "Any colored gentleman who will go down South to fight is a fool. Every one of them that the rebels catch will be hanged, or sent into the Indigo mines, or cut up into mincemeat, or quartered and pickled, or spitted,[5] or—or— What good is it going to do the colored people to go fight and lose their lives? Better stay home and keep out of harm's way."

These are the arguments that the copperheads insinuate into the ears of the credulous, the ignorant, and the timid. They do not tell you that the measure of the slaveholder's iniquity is completed; that the accumulated wrongs of two centuries are a thousand-fold more horrible than two centuries of war and massacre. They do not tell you that it were "better to die free, than live slaves"—that your wronged and outraged sisters and brethren are calling on you to take up arms and place your interests and your lives in the balance against their oppressors—that "your dead fathers speak to you from their graves," or "Heaven, as with a voice of thunder, calls on you to arise from the dust," and smite with an avenging hand the obdurate, cruel, and relentless enemy and traitor, who has trampled in the dust the flag of his country and whose life and sacred honor are pledged to wage an interminable war against your race.

Oh no, to tell us these truths would be to nerve our arms and fire our hearts for the noble struggle for country and liberty. Men and brethren! for the sake of honor, manhood and courage—in the name of God, of country, and of race, spit upon the base sycophants who thus dare to insult you. But these are silent influences which are at work. The open, tangible, bolder ones are now at work in Pennsylvania. She presents a wide theater for operations. Her colored population is more numerous than that of any other Northern State; and if the copperheads can neutralize this State, half of the object has been accomplished and the system has been thoroughly organized. Ever since Frederick Douglass's address appeared in the daily journals,[6] these men have been holding meetings and stuffing the Philadelphia papers with false accounts of their glowing success and influence over the colored people.

A few weeks ago they caused an article to appear in the *Evening Bulletin* which stated that sixty thousand dollars had been promised to them by colored men in this city.[7] At a meeting of colored men held at Philadelphia Institute on last Wednesday, two weeks ago, and upon which meeting Frishmuth and his associates introduced themselves, Mr. Rob't Jones,[8] the secretary of the meeting, read this article and demanded who the parties were that had subscribed this money. The whole gang were confounded. Not a name could be offered and not one colored man said that he reposed any confidence in those men. They forced themselves upon us, and spoke of the inadvisibility of colored men enlisting in the Massachusetts regiment; that there would be authority given to them the next day to organize a colored brigade in Pennsylvania; that President Lincoln and Gov. Curtin[9] were only arranging the preliminaries.

Frishmuth said he loved the colored man and wanted to be "de Moses ob de cullerd population"—forgetting that Moses belonged to the race which he led out of the house of Egyptian bondage. There were many colored ladies present at the meeting, yet one of those unprincipled men used the most profane and disgusting language. They belong to that ignorant class of white men who, knowing nothing of the sentiments and intelligence of colored men, labor under the hallucination that they can lead where they will we should go, and that if a white man should say to us, "You are a good nigger," we will be immediately overwhelmed with gratitude for the gracious condescension.

They have printed circulars, scattered among the colored people in Philadelphia and adjoining counties, calling on them to join the 1st Colored Penn. Brigade.[10] They hold "officers' meetings" and report their proceedings to the daily papers. They told a friend this morning that they had not yet received authority to enlist colored men. Of course not. By what authority do they thus call upon the men of color of Pennsylvania to take up arms and thus mislead them and deceive the public? By these misrepresentations all through the State, the efforts of our people, in a military point of view, have been neutralized. Even so far west as Pittsburgh, the copperhead bait has been successful. Even Geo. B. Vashon has been gulled into participating in a war meeting in Pittsburgh,[11] in response to what they were led to believe by the Philadelphia press, was a genuine call of Pennsylvania. We shall tear the curtain away, and expose to the people these gross frauds, and base attempts to deceive and mislead them.

Many men were disposed to regard these men favorably, but all sympathy was lost when they placed themselves in opposition to Massachusetts, the cradle in which the sickly puling infancy of American liberty was nursed; who has made colored men equal before her laws; who has been the protectress and benefactress of the race; who in the darkest hour of adversity, when every other State seemed bound, hand and foot, at the feet of slavery, proclaimed the right of petition against slavery; whose representatives have been insulted, abused, and their persons violated, in the halls of Congress for thundering against the citadel of Human Wrong the burnished shafts of truth and eloquence, and for her unswerving devotion to liberty, the rebel-sympathizing democracy, conscious of the irresistibility of truth and justice, and that this noble old State will never furl her banner of right while a single vestige of human wrong shall disgrace the country, are now striving to reconstruct the Union, leaving her and her sister States of New England out in the cold.

Now, these men can see no potency in these claims of Massachusetts. When these facts are presented to them, they claim that we should have "State pride." I would to God that they could have heard Isaiah C. Wears's and Prof. Green's[12] scathing rebukes to even the presumption of State pride for Pennsylvania in the breasts of colored men—a State which, instead of restoring our stolen rights, stripped us of the elective franchise, and even within the last two weeks, passed in one branch of the legislature a law excluding colored men from the State.[13] There is no meaner State in the Union than this. She has treated the families of her soldiers worse than any other State, and with her confirmed negrophobia could we expect the treatment of dogs at her hands? But in spite of all this, if such men as J. Miller McKim, Judge Kelley,[14] or Col. Wm. F. Small[15] should obtain authority to raise a regiment or brigade in Pennsylvania, I would give my heart and hand to it; but knowing, as I do, that no other colored regiment will be raised in the North until the Massachusetts one is placed in the field, I say, let every man lend his influence to Massachusetts. If, by any means, the 54th should fail, it will be a blow from which we Northern men would never recover. We would be ranked with the most depraved and cowardly of men. Our enemies, infuriated as they are beyond measure, would hunt us down like so many wild beasts, while our friends, shamed and humiliated by our criminal cowardice and imbecility, would be compelled to become passive witnesses of their unbridled violence.

Look at our brethren in the South! Those who have endured all of the horrors of the Southern prisonhouse, defying the menaces of the besotted tyranny, taking up arms to achieve with their valor those rights which

Providence has designed that all men should enjoy. Has freedom stultified our sterner aspirations, and made us forget our duty? Has the copperhead obtained an influence over us? If we thought that of what little freedom, we of the North enjoy, has had a tendency to nourish a disregard for our own and the rights of our fellow men, it were better that the mob-fiend drive us from off the face of the earth, to give place to those noble freedmen who are now bravely and victoriously fighting the battles of their country and liberty. We have more to gain, if victorious, or more to lose, if defeated, than any other class of men. Not abstract political rights, or religious and civil liberty, but with all these our personal liberties are to be secured. Many of us are insensible to the stern realities of the present hour, but they are here thundering at our very doors, and the sooner we awaken to their inexorable demands upon us, the better for the race, the better for the country, the better for our families, and the better for ourselves.

G. E. STEPHENS

Weekly Anglo-African (New York, N.Y.), 11 April 1863.

1. Several individuals and groups claimed to hold official authorization to organize black regiments in Philadelphia. One group of white officers, led by Colonel William Frishmuth, took the initiative in March 1863 and attempted to form a black brigade. Frishmuth, a native of the city who had previously commanded the 113th Pennsylvania Regiment, announced in the 24 March issue of the Philadelphia *Evening Bulletin* that he had the support of the local black community and that several "wealthy colored men" had pledged $60,000 to help outfit the brigade once it was organized. Frank H. Taylor, *Philadelphia in the Civil War, 1861–1865* (Philadelphia, Pa., 1913), 170, 187; *PEB*, 21 March 1863.

2. Governor John A. Andrew of Massachusetts lobbied the War Department in early January 1863 for permission to enlist black troops. On 26 January, he received authorization to raise "such corps of infantry for the volunteer military service as he may find convenient . . . and may include persons of African descent, organized into separate corps." Hoping to establish "a model for all future Colored Regiments," he organized the Fifty-fourth Massachusetts—the first black unit in the North—and insisted on equal pay for black soldiers. Andrew (1818–1866), a committed abolitionist and close friend of Boston's black leaders, had raised funds for John Brown's defense after the Harpers Ferry raid. He joined the Free Soil party in 1848 and won a seat in the state legislature as a Republican (1857), before serving as governor of Massachusetts (1860–66). Cornish, *Sable Arm*, 105–6; *HTECW*, 17; *WAA*, 18 April 1863.

3. Several northern cities experienced race riots during the Civil War. Provoked by wartime economic disruption and the enactment of military conscription, and fueled by Copperhead propaganda and the racist press, working-class whites directed their anger at the black community. On the evening of 6 March 1863, a mob of two hundred whites attacked a black neighborhood in Detroit, killing two blacks, maiming twenty more, burning over thirty buildings, and leaving some two hundred blacks homeless. Although police attempted to quell the riot,

soldiers from nearby cities were needed to restore order. Foner, *History of Black Americans*, 3:392–402; John C. Schneider, "Detroit and the Problem of Disorder: The Riot of 1863," *MH* 58:5–23 (Spring 1974).

4. James H. Lane (1814–1866), a Republican, represented Kansas in the U.S. Senate during the Civil War. Commissioned a brigadier general in 1861, he commanded fifteen hundred Union irregulars against Missouri Confederates in the bloodiest guerrilla fighting of the conflict. Lane favored the use of black troops and began recruiting in the contraband camps in eastern Kansas. Although the Lincoln administration refused to authorize his labors, the First Kansas Regiment of Colored Volunteers was organized in September 1862. When this unit engaged Confederate forces near Butler, Missouri, in October, it was the first time black troops had fought in the war. Lane's efforts enraged many of his constituents, some of whom doubted the military value of black soldiers. Although Lane retained his Senate seat, he destroyed his career by endorsing President Andrew Johnson's veto of the 1866 civil rights bill. Politically unpopular and accused of graft, he committed suicide. *HTECW*, 424–25; Cornish, *Sable Arm*, 69–78.

5. Stephens alludes to the Confederate policy of subjecting black Union soldiers captured in the war to execution or enslavement.

6. Stephens refers to an editorial by Frederick Douglass that appeared under the blazing headline "MEN OF COLOR TO ARMS!" in the March 1863 issue of *Douglass' Monthly*. Douglass called on black men to enlist in the Fifty-fourth Massachusetts Regiment, the only regular unit organizing among northern blacks, insisting that it offered a chance to strike a fatal blow against slavery and prejudice. "The Iron gate of our prison stands half open," he instructed. "One gallant rush from the North will fling it wide open, while four millions of our brothers and sisters, shall march out into Liberty!" This piece was widely reprinted in the northern press.

7. Stephens refers to William Frishmuth's announcement in the 24 March 1863 issue of the Philadelphia *Evening Bulletin*. Founded in 1847, the *Bulletin* became the city's first successful evening paper. Editor Gibson Peacock made it a staunch advocate of Republican politics during the Civil War. *A Checklist of Pennsylvania Newspapers: Philadelphia County* (Harrisburg, Pa., 1944), 57–58; Mott, *American Journalism*, 350n.

8. Robert Jones (1817–ca. 1890), a black Philadelphia barber, was born in Pennsylvania. He considered immigrating to Liberia, but instead settled in Hamilton, Canada West, in 1856. There he assisted fugitive slaves and organized and served as an officer of Queen Victoria's Rifle Guards, a black militia company. Jones returned to Philadelphia at the beginning of the Civil War and reestablished himself in the barbering trade. A strong advocate of black enlistment, in July 1863, he joined with fifty-four other members of the local black elite to issue a public call to arms. He also persuaded his son, C. W. Jones, to enlist in the Sixth U.S. Colored Troops. Jones remained in Philadelphia until his death. U.S. Census, 1850; William Still, *The Underground Railroad* (Philadelphia, Pa., 1872; reprint, Chicago, Ill., 1970), 272; Education and Employment Statistics of the Colored People of Philadelphia (1856), 2 vols., Pennsylvania Abolition Society Papers, "Men of Color, to Arms! Now or Never" (broadside), Leon Gardiner Collection, PHi [14:0945]; *Philadelphia City Directory*, 1866–90.

9. Andrew Gregg Curtin (1817–1894), a leading Pennsylvania Republican,

filled several state posts before serving as governor from 1861 to 1867. He proved an important ally of the federal government during the Civil War and was responsible for raising and equipping 270 regiments for the Union army. When Confederate forces threatened to invade Pennsylvania in mid-1863, he lifted the state's ban on black enlistment. Curtin was appointed minister to Russia after the war, and he later served in the U.S. Congress (1881–87). *BDAC*, 814.

10. Pennsylvania's first official black unit, the Third U.S. Colored Troops, was organized in August 1863 at Camp William Penn and ordered to the Department of the South where it participated in the siege of Fort Wagner and other operations along the South Carolina coast. Later stationed in north Florida, the regiment was mustered out of service in October 1865. The state raised ten more black units by the war's end. Dyer, *Compendium*, 3:1723; Frederick M. Binder, "Pennsylvania Negro Regiments in the Civil War," *JNH* 37:385–86, 395, 404n (October 1952).

11. Stephens probably refers to a 15 January 1863 meeting at Pittsburgh's Wiley Street African Methodist Episcopal Church. George B. Vashon delivered a lengthy address describing his views on presidential war powers. He argued, based on the views of John Quincy Adams, that the president possessed the power to emancipate slaves as a war measure. *WAA*, 31 January 1863.

12. Alfred M. Green.

13. In early 1863, the Pennsylvania state legislature considered several proposals to prevent blacks from settling in the state. One exclusion bill was voted down by a senate committee on 6 March. The Democratically controlled house of representatives approved the same bill by a fifty-two to forty vote on 25 March, but it was again rejected by the senate. Thomas Anthony Sanelli, "The Struggle for Black Suffrage in Pennsylvania, 1838–1870" (Ph.D. diss., Temple University, 1978), 137–38.

14. William Darrah Kelley (1814–1890), a Philadelphia lawyer and judge of the city's court of common pleas, was a delegate to the 1860 Republican national convention that nominated Abraham Lincoln for the presidency. He ran unsuccessfully for Congress in 1856 but won a seat in 1860 and served there until his death. Although Kelley appealed to racial prejudice in his unsuccessful 1856 campaign, he later became a Radical Republican and supported black suffrage. *BDAC*, 1218; Hans L. Trefousse, *The Radical Republicans: Lincoln's Vanguard for Racial Justice* (Baton Rouge, La., 1968), 32, 302, 314, 327–28.

15. William F. Small, a Philadelphia attorney, organized and became colonel of the Twenty-sixth Pennsylvania Regiment at the outbreak of the Civil War. He was court-martialed in April 1862 for insubordination and other offenses, but his conviction was overturned by Major General George B. McClellan. Small resumed charge of the Twenty-sixth for two months, then left the army after being wounded at the battle of Yorktown. He returned to Philadelphia and later commanded the Sixtieth Pennsylvania Regiment, a ninety-day militia unit, until mustered out in June 1863. *Philadelphia City Directory*, 1850–68; Taylor, *Philadelphia in the Civil War*, 27, 28, 52, 251; General Court Martial Case Files, RG 153, Office of the Judge Advocate General (Army), DNA.

42.
Alexander T. Augusta to Editor,
Washington *National Republican*
15 May 1863

The sight of a black man wearing a Union army uniform was a potent sign of the changing relationship between Afro-Americans and the federal government. The administration that had promised to protect slavery on the eve of the war was by 1863 bound to defend the rights of black soldiers. The experience of Alexander T. Augusta, a Union army surgeon commissioned a major in April 1863, illustrates the new alliance. On 1 May, he was assaulted twice in Baltimore by whites, who tore the oak leaf straps from his uniform; Augusta received unequivocal assistance from the Union provost marshals to whom he reported the episode. Two weeks later, writing to the Washington *National Republican* in response to malicious commentary in the Baltimore press, he recounted these events. Mocking the language of the Dred Scott decision, Augusta concluded that the response of the provost marshals proved that "even in *rowdy Baltimore* colored men have rights that white men are bound to respect." Cornish, *Sable Arm*, 94–99, 132–33; *WAA*, 9 May 1863, 13, 20 February 1864; *CR*, 30 May 1863 [14:0883–84]; *PA*, 11 July 1863 [14:0955–56]; *Lib*, 8 May 1863 [14:0841].

WASHINGTON, [D.C.]
May 15, 1863

Sir: [1]

Inasmuch as many misstatements relative to the assault upon me in Baltimore have been made, I deem it necessary, in justice to myself, as well as to all parties concerned, to give to the public a true statement of the facts as they occurred.

I started from my lodgings in Mulberry Street, near Pine, about a quarter past nine o'clock, on the morning of 1st inst., in order to take the 10 a.m. train for Philadelphia. I went down Mulberry Street to Howard, Howard to Baltimore, Baltimore to Gay, Gay to Pratt, Pratt to President, and thence to the depot. No one interfered with me during the whole route. I obtained my ticket from the agent, without the usual bond required of colored persons wishing to proceed North,[2] and took my seat in the car—little expecting anyone would make an attack upon me then.

After remaining in my seat about five minutes, I heard someone conversing behind me, but paid no attention to what they were talking about, when of a sudden a boy about fifteen years of age, who appeared to be employed about the depot, came up behind me, and, swearing at me, caught hold of my right shoulder-strap, and pulled it off. I jumped

7. Alexander T. Augusta in uniform

up, and, turning towards him, found a man standing by his side who had directed me which car to get in, and while I was remonstrating with the boy for what he had done, he pulled the other one off; while at the same time the boy threatened to strike me with a club he held in his hand. I then turned towards the door of the car near where I was standing, and found I was surrounded by about eight or ten roughs; and knowing that should I touch one of them all the rest would pounce upon me, I thought it best to take my seat and await what further issue might take place.

Shortly after I had taken my seat, the parties who had assaulted me left the car, and a policeman came in and stood near me. A person standing by asked him if he intended to interfere. He answered by saying it depended upon circumstances. I then turned towards him, and said to him, "If you are a policeman, I claim your protection as a United States officer, who has been assaulted without a cause." Just about that time, I was informed that the provost guards were in the car, and that I had better apply to them for protection. I called to the guards and told them I was a United States officer; that I had been assaulted and my shoulder-straps torn off by employees of the road, and that I claimed their protection. Having satisfied them of my connection with the service, they assured me of their protection. I might have gone on in that train, but I was determined to stop back, so as to have the parties punished, knowing full well that the same thing might occur again, unless a stop was put to it at once. I therefore went up to the provost marshal's office with one of the guard, and reported the facts to Lieut. Col. Fish, the provost marshal.

He examined my commission, and finding it was all right, said he did not care who it was, so he was a United States officer, and claimed his protection, he should have it to the fullest extent. He then deputed Lieut. Morris to accompany me to the depot and arrest the parties. The lieutenant told me I was as much authorized as an officer to arrest them as he was; and that I had better go ahead of him and the guard, fearing that if the parties saw them they would get out of the way. He directed me, at the same time, that when I saw any one of the parties to go up to him and place my hand upon his shoulder and claim him as my prisoner, and he would be on hand to take him in charge. I knew this was an extraordinary step for me to take in Baltimore, but I told him I would do it. I accordingly went down to the depot, and when near it I recognised one of the parties crossing the street; I went up to him, and, while accusing him of taking off my straps, put my hand upon his shoulder and claimed him as my prisoner. I then ordered the guard to take him into custody, which he did. I then hunted around the depot for the boy, but could not find him.

The lieutenant having come up by this time, we started for the provost marshal's office, and when opposite Marsh market on Baltimore street,

Lieut. Morris, the guard, and the prisoner, being on the opposite side of the street, a man, whom I learned afterwards to be named Hancock, emerged from the market and assaulted me. I called the guard across and had him taken into custody. We then proceeded to the office unmolested, where I remained until about half past twelve o'clock, when Lieut. Morris told me it was time to start for the depot, to take the one o'clock train. I got ready and we proceeded together, and every step we took after leaving the office, the crowd which was standing around the door increased. No one, however, interfered with me until we arrived at the corner of Pratt and President streets, when a man, whose name I since learned to be Dunn, was standing in our way, and as soon as I reached him, he dealt me a severe blow on the face, which stunned me for a moment and caused the blood to flow from my nose very freely. In an instant, Lieut. Morris seized him by the collar and held him fast;[3] and I not knowing that there was anyone else in the crowd to protect me, made for the first door I saw open. When I reached it, a woman was standing there and pushed me back to prevent me from entering. In the meantime I looked back and saw a person with my cap and a revolver in his hand. He told me to stand still, that I was protected. I came down the steps, and proceeded between two guards with revolvers drawn until we reached the depot.

Upon our arrival, Lieut. Morris put the prisoner upon a settee, and placed a guard over him, with orders to shoot him if he dared to stir from the spot. A short time after we arrived, two other persons were identified as having been engaged in the last assault upon me, and were arrested. I washed the blood from my face and prepared to take my seat in the cars, when an officer, whom I subsequently learned to be Major Robertson,[4] of Maj. Gen. Hooker's staff, having learned the facts of the case from Lieut. Morris, came up to me and told me he was going to Philadelphia, and offered to protect me at the risk of his own life. The guard surrounded me with drawn revolvers, conducted me to the cars, and remained with me until the train started. During the time we were waiting for the train to start, I learned from the guard that when I was struck by Dunn, they were in the crowd dressed in citizens' clothes, and were just about to shoot him when Lieut. Morris ordered them not to shoot, as he had the prisoner safe.

When the train was about to start, Lieut. Morris, in addition to Maj. Robertson, who had volunteered to protect me, sent on two armed cavalry to guard me to Philadelphia, or as long as I might want them. I, however, did not consider it necessary to detain them after we arrived, and accordingly discharged them from any further attendance upon me. Since my return to Washington, I have learned that some of the parties have been tried, and sent to Fort McHenry.[5]

These, Mr. Editor, are the facts of the case, and I deny, in toto, the profane language attributed to me by the Baltimore *Clipper*.[6]

Now it seems that, in this transaction, I have been blamed by two classes of persons. The first say that I should not have passed through Baltimore in uniform, because, say they, the people of Baltimore are opposed to it, and even Union men do not wish to see colored men wearing the United States uniform.

Well, in answer to this class, I will say that the people of Baltimore were opposed to the Massachusetts troops passing through there two years ago, and mobbed them, but the Government of the United States was strong enough to put down that spirit then, and I apprehend it is strong enough now to protect colored troops under similar circumstances. And furthermore, while I have always known Baltimore as a place where it is considered a virtue to mob colored people, still, I had a right to expect a safe transit through there after the resolutions passed only two weeks before at the National Union League, on the anniversary of the attack upon the Massachusetts troops, calling on the President of the United States to place not only spades but muskets in the hands of black men to put down the rebellion.[7] And more especially, as I had only volunteered to bind up the wounds of those colored men who should volunteer, as well as those rebels and Copperheads whom the fortune of war might throw into my hands. But, sir, I may take still higher grounds than these to justify my course. For I hold that my position as an officer of the United States entitles me to wear the insignia of my office, and if I am either afraid or ashamed to wear them anywhere, I am not fit to hold my commission, and should resign it at once.

The other class that blame me are those who say I acted wrongly in not shooting down anyone who dared to interfere with me. Well, in answer to this class, I can only say that while I am aware that I had the authority as an officer of the United States to defend myself to that extremity, I do not think, had I have done so, I would have accomplished so much for liberty as I did by allowing those whose special duty it was to protect me.

The question has no doubt been frequently asked, "What has been gained by this transaction?" I will answer. It has proved that even in *rowdy Baltimore* colored men have rights that white men are bound to respect. For I was told by a gentleman since I returned, whom I saw in the crowd at Baltimore, that when Dunn was taken to the provost marshal's office, the marshal reprimanded the officer who had him in charge for not shooting him when he struck me, and told him if a case of the kind occurs again, and the officer in charge does not shoot the aggressor, his commission shall be broken.

In conclusion, Mr. Editor, I desire to return my sincere thanks to Lieut.

Col. Fish for his prompt protection, to Lieut. Morris for the alacrity with which he carried out Col. Fish's orders, to Major Robertson for his kindness in volunteering his services, and the brave men of the guard for risking their lives in my defence. I remain, sir, Yours, very respectfully,

A. T. Augusta[8]
Bachelor of Medicine,
Surgeon U.S.V.

Christian Recorder (Philadelphia, Pa.), 30 May 1863.

1. William J. Murtagh, a local printer, edited and published the Washington (D.C.) *National Republican*, a party daily, from 1860 to 1888. During the 1860s, the paper reported favorably on the local black community and backed Radical Reconstruction. Murtagh became entangled in Washington politics and openly complained of corruption in the police department. In 1865 he was named to the district board of police commissioners and later served as board president (1870–77), but charges that he abused his authority led to the abolition of the board in 1878. *Washington City Directory*, 1860–71; Whyte, *Uncivil War*, 23; *RCHS*, 37/38:62–63 (1937), n.s. 48:375 (1971–72); Kenneth G. Alfers, *Law and Order in the Capital City: A History of the Washington Police, 1800–1886* (Washington, D.C., 1976), 38–42n, 53.

2. Southern state legislatures enacted a variety of restrictions to control the movement of free blacks within their borders. Some required that free blacks entering their jurisdiction, even for a brief period, had to post a security bond to guarantee their conduct; those traveling North had to present papers certifying their free status. In 1805 Maryland adopted a similar system of restrictions. Berlin, *Slaves without Masters*, 93–94, 165, 349.

3. Three Baltimore whites—Charles W. Hancock, James Dunn, and Harrison Wilson—were arrested for assaulting Augusta. Hancock had been a conductor on the city's streetcars. Dunn is described as "a young man." *DM*, June 1863; *Lib*, 8 May 1863; *Baltimore City Directory*, 1860.

4. Augusta refers to Major George H. Roberts, Jr., who served under Brigadier General Joseph Hooker in the Army of the Potomac. He worked at his father's hardware business in Philadelphia before and after the Civil War. *HTECW*, 370; *DM*, June 1863; *Philadelphia City Directory*, 1850–68.

5. Situated on Whetstone Point in the Chesapeake, Fort McHenry played a key role in Baltimore's defense during the War of 1812. The fort served as a military fortification during the Civil War and regularly housed civilians arrested as Confederate sympathizers. Charles Lewis Wagandt, *The Mighty Revolution: Negro Emancipation in Maryland, 1862–1864* (Baltimore, Md., 1964), 173–75, 213.

6. The attacks on Augusta were reported in the 2 May 1863 issue of the *Baltimore Clipper*, a daily and weekly paper published from 1839 to 1865. The *Clipper* charged that Augusta had engaged in a verbal confrontation with the conductor of the train. *Lib*, 8 May 1863; Gregory, *American Newspapers*, 258.

7. Augusta refers to a 20 April 1863 meeting of the Union League of Maryland at the Maryland Institute in Baltimore. The gathering, which was called to demonstrate support for the Union war effort, resolved that the Lincoln administration "should use all men, white or black, in the way they can be most useful, and

to the extent they can be used, whether it be to handle a spade or shoulder a musket." This session commemorated an attack two years earlier on the Sixth Massachusetts Regiment, the first fully equipped unit to respond to Lincoln's call to arms, as it entered Baltimore on the way to Washington, D.C. Assailed by a prosecessionist mob, the regiment opened fire, fought its way to the local railway station, and boarded a train for the district. Four soldiers and twelve citizens of Baltimore were killed in the incident and dozens more were wounded. Maryland authorities responded by cutting railroad and telegraph lines between D.C. and the North, jeopardizing the security of the nation's capital for nearly a week. *BACA*, 21 April 1863; McPherson, *Battle Cry of Freedom*, 285–86.

8. Alexander Thomas Augusta (1825–1890) was born to free black parents in Norfolk, Virginia. As a young man, he journeyed to Baltimore and worked there as a barber, while obtaining an elementary knowledge of medicine. In 1847 he married Mary O. Burgoin, a local woman of Huguenot descent. About that time, he moved to Philadelphia, hoping to study medicine at the University of Pennsylvania; denied entry because of his race, however, he took private instruction from a sympathetic member of the faculty. Committed to a career as a physician, Augusta traveled to California and earned the funds necessary to pursue that goal. After failing to gain admission to an American medical school, he enrolled at Trinity Medical College of the University of Toronto in 1850; six years later he received the long-sought degree in medicine.

Augusta remained in Toronto, Canada West, and established a successful medical practice, while supervising staff at the city hospital and directing an industrial school. He also participated in local antislavery activities and founded the Provincial Association for the Education and Elevation of the Colored People of Canada, a literary society devoted to black uplift. Augusta briefly immigrated to the West Indies about 1860, but he returned to Baltimore after the outbreak of the Civil War. He offered his medical services to the Union army in October 1862. The following April, he received a major's commission as a surgeon for black troops, becoming the army's first black physician and its highest-ranking black officer at the time. This antagonized some whites and he was mobbed in Baltimore and Washington for publicly wearing his officer's uniform. In March 1865, he was promoted to the rank of lieutenant colonel. After the war, Augusta accepted an assignment with the Freedmen's Bureau, heading the agency's Lincoln Hospital in Savannah, Georgia. While there, he encouraged black self-help, urged the freedmen to support separate institutions, and won the respect of the city's white physicians.

After being discharged from military service in October 1866, Augusta returned to private practice in Washington, D.C. Between 1868 and 1877, he also served on the staff of the local Freedmen's Hospital and taught anatomy in the recently organized medical department at Howard University, becoming the first black appointed to the faculty of an American medical college. Despite his accomplishments, he was repeatedly refused entry to the local society of physicians, an affront that he feared would impede the progress of younger black physicians in the city. *DANB*, 19–20; *PFW*, 20 June 1857 [10:0733]; *Lib*, 7 August 1857 [10:0777]; *TG*, 3 March 1860 [12:0542]; *WAA*, 5 May 1860, 16 February, 30 November 1861 [12:0684, 13:0326, 0943]; *DM*, June 1863; Todd L. Savitt, "Politics in Medicine: The Georgia Freedmen's Bureau and the Organization of Health Care," *CWH* 28:49, 52, 58 (March 1982).

43.
Sattira A. Douglas to Robert Hamilton
9 June 1863

Recruitment became a central feature of black abolitionism. Black leaders advocated service in the Union army, confident that valor on the battlefield would affirm decades of antislavery agitation, refute allegations of black inferiority, and win emancipation and full American citizenship. The war represented the first genuine opportunity to obtain "indemnity for the past, and security for the future." Sattira A. Douglas of Chicago, whose husband—H. Ford Douglas—was serving in the Ninety-fifth Illinois Regiment of Infantry Volunteers, expressed this view in a 9 June 1863 letter to the *Weekly Anglo-African*. Arguing that the war offered an unprecedented occasion to advance equal rights, she urged black men to enlist. If they failed to respond to the call, she warned, "it will only prove the correctness of the aspersion indulged in by our enemies, that we are unworthy of those rights which they have so long withheld from us." *WAA*, 17, 31 January, 18 April, 23 May, 5 December 1863, 5 November, 3 December 1864.

                                                    Chicago, Ill[inois]
                                                    June 9th, 1863

Mr. Editor:

I occasionally get a glimpse of your lively, wide-awake sheet, and this week, through the kindness of a friend, being favored with a copy and noticing in it one or two communications and an editorial upon the all-absorbing topic of colored men participating in this great American rebellion, I thought that, although many good things had already been said, it would not be amiss for me to request permission to communicate, through its columns, a few thoughts entertained by one who feels the deepest interest in and is watching with the most intense anxiety the transpiring events of this struggle, particularly those that relate to colored men. I was much interested in the letter from Geo. L. Stearns, and fully indorse the sentiments it contains.[1] It is true that now is offered the only opportunity that will be extended, during the present generation, for colored men to strike the blow that will at once relieve them of northern prejudice and southern slavery. If they do not now enroll themselves among those other noble men who have gone forth to do battle for the true and right, it will only prove the correctness of the aspersion indulged in by our enemies, that we are unworthy of those rights which they have so long withheld from us, and that freedom would not be appreciated by us, if possessed.

It is no less true of nations than of individuals, that that which is the most dearly bought is the most highly prized, and the liberty, which we sacrifice our all to obtain, will be proportionately appreciated. This revolution, like all others, is to act as a national purifier. We are now undergoing a process of fermentation, and all those false and unwholesome theories which have and do possess the American mind in regard to the relation which the colored race is to sustain towards the other nations of the world, are to work to the surface and pass off. This war is also to act as an educator, not only national, but individual. It is to teach us, regardless of sex or complexion, hard lessons of sacrifice, of courage, and of fortitude. We are to stand forth in our own individual light, either as cringing, cowering creatures, shielding ourselves from the duties and responsibilities of the hour beneath every shadow of a subterfuge, or, uncovering our brows and breasts to the tempest, stand fearless and undaunted, firm in our convictions of right, knowing that the storm, though violent, will have an end, and the sun of peace will shine through the overshadowing cloud. Colored men have everything to gain in this conflict: liberty, honor, social and political position are now placed within their grasp. They have these on the one and on the other slavery, prejudice of caste, and all other attendant evils.

The men who have been freed by the Proclamation seem generally to understand what is required of them, from their willingness to enlist. It is gratifying to see the efficient work of the recruiting agent for Massachusetts, not only in this section, but wherever they are laboring. Mr. C. H. Langston,[2] the agent in this State, has posted himself at Quincy, where he has easy access to the freedmen as they are making their way from Missouri to this State; and by his efforts a goodly number of these pass weekly through our city, going to swell the ranks of dark-hued but determined avengers, whose destination is the far South. I have unbounded faith in an unseen Providence, and I know He will protect them and lead them on to victory.

SATTIE A. DOUGLAS

Weekly Anglo-African (New York, N.Y.), 20 June 1863.

1. Douglas refers to a 9 May 1863 letter by George Luther Stearns, which appeared a week later in the *Weekly Anglo-African*. Stearns criticized New York City blacks who objected to black military service. Stearns labeled as childish their call for federal guarantees to protect black soldiers captured by Confederate forces and advised blacks to enlist because "this is the time God has given your race to conquer its freedom from northern prejudice and southern pride and avarice." Stearns (1809–1867), a Boston businessman and abolitionist, had supplied rifles to free-state forces in Kansas during the 1850s and was one of the so-called "Secret Six" who funded John Brown's raid at Harpers Ferry. He helped

organize the Republican party in Massachusetts. Commissioned a major in 1863 and placed in charge of black recruitment by the War Department, Stearns directed a recruiting network that employed more than twenty agents throughout the North and upper South. He resigned early the next year after a policy dispute with Secretary of War Edwin M. Stanton. Stearns later helped found the *Nation*, a liberal journal devoted to black suffrage and other Radical Reconstruction policies. *WAA*, 16 May 1863; *DAB*, 17:543–44.

2. Charles Henry Langston (1817–1892), the brother of black abolitionist John Mercer Langston, was born in Louisa County, Virginia, to Ralph Quarles, a planter, and Quarles's manumitted slave, Lucy Langston. After the death of his parents in 1834, he moved to Ohio and became one of the first blacks enrolled in the preparatory department at Oberlin College. While teaching at black schools in Chillicothe and Columbus during the 1840s and 1850s, Langston emerged as a leader among Ohio blacks. He championed the black press, led the statewide black Masonic organization, presided at black state conventions, attended the 1848 and 1853 black national conventions, and stridently opposed Ohio's black laws. He served as the western agent for the Sons of Temperance after 1848.

Langston was best known for his contributions to the abolitionist crusade. In 1853 he became recording secretary and business agent for the Ohio Anti-Slavery Society. Five years later, he helped create the Ohio State Anti-Slavery Society, an ambitious black civil rights organization; working out of a central office in Cleveland, he served as the society's executive secretary until the Civil War. He participated in underground railroad activities in both Columbus and Cleveland, achieving notoriety for his role in the 1858 Oberlin-Wellington rescue of fugitive slave John Price. Langston was fined $100 and sentenced to twenty days in jail, but his impassioned defense of the rescuers' actions made him an antislavery hero across the North. He also aided John Brown and publicly endorsed slave violence, justifying it on the basis of the "pure and righteous principles" expressed by the Bible and the Founding Fathers.

A supporter of the Union cause from the beginning of the Civil War, Langston recruited for the Fifty-fourth and Fifty-fifth Massachusetts regiments in Ohio, Indiana, and Illinois. He moved to Kansas during the war and emerged as one of the state's foremost black educators and political activists. He founded a school for contraband children at Leavenworth, served as principal of a black normal school at Quindaro, led a statewide campaign for black suffrage, and dominated Kansas's black state conventions through the 1880s. One of the leading black Republicans in Kansas during Reconstruction, he abandoned the party and ran as the Prohibition candidate for state auditor in 1886. In 1869 he married Mary S. Leary, the widow of Harpers Ferry raider Lewis S. Leary. They settled on a farm near Lawrence and had two sons—Dessalines and Nathaniel Turner Langston. Langston urged other blacks to settle in rural Kansas, supported the Exoduster movement of 1879–80, and formed a Colored State Emigration Board to aid needy migrants. He moved to Lawrence in 1888, opened a grocery, and helped edit a local journal called the *Historic Times* during his last years. *DANB*, 381–82; Cheek and Cheek, *John Mercer Langston*, 14, 17–22, 85, 88–90, 97–98, 111–13, 136–39, 145–47, 170–76, 180, 185–97, 215, 218, 320–32,

352–69, 380–84, 393–95, 426; Brandt, *Town That Started the Civil War*, 250–51; Eugene H. Berwanger, "Hardin and Langston: Western Black Spokesmen of the Reconstruction Era," *JNH* 64:105–13 (Spring 1979); Arnold Rampersad, *The Life of Langston Hughes*, 2 vols. (New York, N.Y., 1986–88), 1:7–8; Thomas C. Cox, *Blacks in Topeka, Kansas, 1865–1915: A Social History* (Baton Rouge, La., 1982), 77.

44.
Editorial by Robert Hamilton
20 June 1863

Once the recruitment table was opened to black volunteers, the call
for black officers quickly followed. Although black soldiers displayed
uncommon courage, ability, and commitment during the Civil War,
scarcely one hundred received commissions, primarily as surgeons,
chaplains, or members of the Louisiana Native Guard, and only one
became an officer in a regular combat role. As black troops proved
themselves in battle, pressure for promotions increased. Black leaders
understood the enormous importance of wearing officers' epaulets and
denounced official refusals to grant them as an "insulting endorsement
of the old dogma of negro inferiority." Robert Hamilton's 20 June 1863
editorial in the *Weekly Anglo-African*, written less than two weeks after
black troops had fought fiercely to blunt a Confederate attack at the
battle of Milliken's Bend, acknowledged the difficulty of obtaining commissions for worthy blacks. But responding to a report that white officers had fled in the face of the enemy, he maintained that black bravery
deserved to be rewarded by the appointment of officers who could
stand the test of battle. Berlin et al., *Freedom*, 2:303–12; McPherson,
Negro's Civil War, 237–39.

None but brave Officers for Black Troops
We have been anxiously waiting for the official account of the battle at
Milliken's Bend, but thus far have waited in vain. The newspapers' ac-
count of the affair is as follows:

The fight at Milliken's Bend on Saturday was of more importance than
at first related. The Rebels were 1,800 strong, under Henry McCulloch.[1]

Our forces were less than 1,000, over 600 of whom were negroes.

The Rebels at first drove our forces, nearly surrounding them.

The fight was conducted with energy and desperation by our forces,
and the Rebels were held at bay until a gunboat came to our assistance.

Eyewitnesses report our loss in killed at 134, 100 of whom were
negroes.

The wounded were about the same number. The list of the killed is
very large, in consequence of many of the wounded being killed under
the "no quarter" cry.

The Rebels left over 100 dead on the field, and took away several
wagon loads of their wounded.

The negroes, it is reported, fought better than their white officers,
many of whom, it is said, skulked.

Whether this cowardice of the officers accounts for the delay of a
report, we cannot say, but suppose such must be the case.

8. Black troops at the battle of Milliken's Bend

From Langston Hughes, Milton Meltzer, and C. Eric Lincoln, eds., *A Pictorial History of Blackamericans*, 5th rev. ed. (New York, 1973)

The splendid fighting done by the colored troops at Jacksonville, Port Hudson and Milliken's Bend has forever settled the question in reference to their fighting qualities, and has in our opinion shown the absolute necessity of massing these troops to make them effectual for great purposes. From what we know of the fighting at Port Hudson, there can be but little doubt that if General Banks's army had been composed entirely of black troops they would have captured that place.[2]

In saying this we do not detract from the merits of other troops, but they have not the same incentives to fight. Our life, our liberty, our country, our religious privileges, our family, OUR ALL is at stake; and we know that, if successful, the blessings attendant upon an enlightened christian civilization will be ours; but if we fail—if the Union is overthrown—then a night of darkness and horror comes upon us, the like of which no people ever saw.

These things are well understood by every black man in the army; and this knowledge and the determination to be free will carry him over entrenchments and into the very jaws of death itself.

This truth must be thoroughly understood by the government, so that its appointment of officers for colored regiments may be from the bravest of the brave, or many such scenes will be witnessed as took place at Milliken's Bend.

We suppose that it is asking too much *at this time* to request the promotion of those brave fellows who actually led on that memorable occasion, but we believe the day is rapidly approaching when full justice will be done them by the government.

We know that colored men are not prepared to lead upon the battlefield scientifically, they never having had the opportunity to study the art of war; but when our 100,000 are put in the field under the command of the gallant Fremont, with Hunter, Sigel, Higginson, Birney, Montgomery, Fairman,[3] and others whom we might name as his aides, our young men will soon be made sufficiently proficient for all work.

Weekly Anglo-African (New York, N.Y.), 20 June 1863.

1. Brigadier General Henry E. McCulloch (1816–1895), a Mexican War veteran and Texas legislator, commanded Confederate forces in Texas during the Civil War. He fought outside of the state once, when he was temporarily sent to relieve the 1863 Union siege of Vicksburg, Mississippi. During that campaign, McCulloch led the Confederate assault at the 7 June battle of Milliken's Bend. *HTECW*, 458–59.

2. The performance of black troops during the first half of 1863 proved to skeptical politicians and military leaders that blacks possessed the courage and ability to fight. In March the First South Carolina Volunteers, a regiment of former slaves, occupied Jacksonville, Florida, seized supplies, and disrupted Confederate operations. Acting on orders from Nathaniel P. Banks (1816–1894), the commander of the Department of the Gulf, blacks joined in a controversial as-

sault upon fortified positions guarding the remaining stretch of the Mississippi River under Confederate control. These units included four regiments of the Corps d'Afrique—comprised of recently freed slaves—and the Louisiana Native Guard—made up of free blacks from New Orleans. The battle of Port Hudson, Louisiana, on 27 May marked the first large-scale use of black troops in the war and proved to doubters such as Banks that they would make effective soldiers. He reported that their valor in the face of heavy fighting settled "the question that the negro race can fight with great prowess." On 7 June, two other black Louisiana regiments engaged a larger force of 1,500 to 3,000 Confederates at Milliken's Bend, Louisiana, in one of the bloodiest engagements of the war. One Union commander reported that it was "impossible for men to show greater gallantry than the negro troops in this fight." *HTECW*, 38, 596–97; Cornish, *Sable Arm*, 137–40, 142–45.

3. Hamilton refers to several Union officers with antislavery leanings. Major General John C. Frémont (1813–1880) commanded the Western Department in Missouri at the beginning of the Civil War. His July 1861 order to free the slaves of Confederate sympathizers in his department was reversed by President Abraham Lincoln, but attracted considerable support from blacks who hoped that Frémont would lead a black regiment. Major General David Hunter (1802–1886) also attempted to emancipate slaves under his jurisdiction in May 1862, only to have his actions reversed by Lincoln. As commander of the Department of the South, he authorized the formation of the First South Carolina Volunteers. Brigadier General Franz Sigel (1824–1902), a German immigrant, commanded the XI Corps of the Army of the Potomac until February 1863, when he temporarily left active duty because of illness. He opposed slavery and the policy of denying officer's commissions to blacks. Colonel Thomas Wentworth Higginson (1823–1911) of the First South Carolina Volunteers was a well-known radical abolitionist, Unitarian clergyman, and supporter of John Brown. Brigadier General William Birney (1819–1907), one of two sons of abolitionist James G. Birney to serve in the Union army, commanded the Twenty-second U.S. Colored Troops. He raised seven black regiments and while assigned to Baltimore, helped hasten emancipation in Maryland. Birney later commanded a division of black troops in the X Corps of the Army of the Potomac. Colonel James Montgomery of the Second South Carolina Volunteers ardently defended the reputation of black troops against charges by white leaders in the North. A petition to Governor Horatio Seymour of New York state in mid-1863 recommended James Fairman (1826–1904) to command a proposed regiment of black troops. Fairman, a Scottish-born landscape painter, served two years in the Union army. After the war, he studied art in Europe, then taught at Olivet College in Michigan. *CWD*, 314–15, 418–19, 761; *HTECW*, 688; Berlin et al., *Freedom*, 2:105–8, 341; Tilden G. Edelstein, *Strange Enthusiasm: A Life of Thomas Wentworth Higginson* (New York, N.Y., 1970); George C. Groce and David H. Wallace, eds., *The New-York Historical Society's Dictionary of Artists in America, 1564–1860* (New Haven, Conn., 1957), 219–20.

45.
Harriet Tubman to "Boston Friends"
30 June 1863

The Civil War brought new responsibilities and new roles for black
women in the antislavery movement. They used their fund-raising skills
to assist contraband relief and soldiers' aid efforts in dozens of communities across the North. Mary Ann Shadd Cary recruited black troops
for Indiana and Connecticut regiments. Harriet Jacobs, Charlotte L.
Forten, and Sojourner Truth, among others, went South as teachers,
missionaries, and relief workers. Already renowned for her underground railroad "expeditions" into the upper slave states, Harriet
Tubman expanded her activities during the war. Arriving in South
Carolina in May 1862, she used her knowledge of regional customs and
terrain to serve the Union army as a scout and spy. She also guided hundreds of slaves away from their masters and provided for their needs
once they reached Union lines. Tubman described these activities in a
30 June 1863 letter to friends in Boston. Sterling, *We Are Your Sisters*,
245–305; *Comm*, 17 July 1863.

BEAUFORT, S[outh] C[arolina]
June 30, 1863

* * *[1] Last fall, when the people here became very much alarmed for
fear of an invasion from the rebels, all my clothes were packed and sent
with others to Hilton Head, and lost; and I have never been able to get
any trace of them since. I was sick at the time, and unable to look after
them myself. I want, among the rest, a *bloomer* dress,[2] made of some
coarse, strong material, to wear on *expeditions*. In our late expedition up
the Combahee river, in coming on board the boat, I was carrying *two
pigs* for a sick woman, who had a child to carry, and the order "double
quick" was given, and I started to run, stepped on my dress, it being
rather long, and fell and tore it almost off, so that when I got on board
the boat there was hardly anything left of it but shreds. I made up my
mind then, I would never wear a long dress on another expedition of the
kind, but would have a *bloomer* as soon as I could get it. So please make
this known to the ladies, if you will, for I expect to have use for it very
soon, probably before they can get it to me.

You have, without doubt, seen a full account of the expedition I refer
to. Don't you think we colored people are entitled to some credit for that
exploit, under the lead of the brave Colonel Montgomery? We weakened
the rebels somewhat on the Combahee river by taking and bringing away
seven hundred and fifty-six head of their most valuable livestock, known
up in your region as "contrabands,"[3] and this, too, without the loss of a

single life on our part, though we have good reason to believe that a number of rebels bit the dust. Of these seven hundred and fifty-six contrabands, nearly or quite all the able-bodied men have joined the colored regiments here.

I have now been absent two years almost, and have just got letters from my friends in Auburn, urging me to come home. My father and mother are old and in feeble health, and need my care and attention. I hope the good people there will not allow them to suffer, and I do not believe they will. But I do not see how I am to leave at present the very important work to be done here. Among other duties which I have is that of looking after the hospital here for contrabands.⁴ Most of those coming from the mainland are very destitute, almost naked. I am trying to find places for those able to work, and provide for them as best I can, so as to lighten the burden on the Government as much as possible, while at the same time they learn to respect themselves by earning their own living.

Remember me very kindly to Mrs.—— and her daughters; also, if you will, to my Boston friends, Mrs. C., Miss H., and especially to Mr. and Mrs. George L. Stearns,⁵ to whom I am under great obligations for their many kindnesses. I shall be sure to come and see you all if I live to go North. If you write me, please direct your letter to the care of E. G. Dudley,⁶ Beaufort, S.C. Faithfully and sincerely your friend,

HARRIET TUBMAN⁷

Commonwealth (Boston, Mass.), 17 July 1863.

1. These asterisks appear in the original printed version of the document. Tubman's letter was excerpted in the Boston *Commonwealth*.

2. The Bloomer costume was introduced by Elizabeth Smith, a daughter of abolitionist Gerrit Smith, and consisted of a long loose-fitting coat and pantaloonlike trousers gathered at the ankles. Named after American feminist Amelia Bloomer, this clothing style attracted widespread criticism and ridicule, but many nineteenth-century women's rights advocates wore it as a badge of their radicalism. Alice Felt Tyler, *Freedom's Ferment: Phases of American Social History from the Colonial Period to the Outbreak of the Civil War* (New York, N.Y., 1962), 441–42.

3. In early June 1863, acting on information gathered by Tubman and her fellow scouts, Colonel James Montgomery led the Second South Carolina Volunteers in a raid up the Combahee River in South Carolina. The expedition destroyed Confederate supplies and carried away thousands of dollars worth of valuable rebel property, including nearly eight hundred slaves. No Union lives were lost. Montgomery (1814–1871) had worked with free-state forces in Kansas during the 1850s and along with James Lane, was one of the earliest advocates of black enlistment. He commanded a brigade, which included the Fifty-fourth Massachusetts Regiment, that conducted military operations along the South Carolina coast in mid-1863. Although he styled himself "a friend of the negro" and vigorously defended the ability of black soldiers, he held many racist beliefs;

contrary to military law, he summarily shot black deserters. *Comm*, 10 July 1863; Emilio, *History of the Fifty-Fourth Regiment*, 36–37, 40–48, 114, 130; Cornish, *Sable Arm*, 149–50, 191; Quarles, *Negro in the Civil War*, 226–27.

4. From mid-1862 to 1864, Tubman worked as a nurse and matron at a hospital for contrabands and black soldiers in Beaufort, South Carolina. Her duties included bathing patients, changing their bandages, and using her knowledge of folk medicine to treat cases of dysentery and malaria. She served under the direction of Henry K. Durant, the hospital's acting assistant surgeon. Leslie A. Falk, "Black Abolitionist Doctors and Healers, 1810–1885," *BHM* 54:268–69 (Summer 1980).

5. Tubman's Boston friends included Lydia Maria Child, George L. Stearns, and his wife, Mary Elizabeth Stearns. The latter, the daughter of a Maine judge who became a planter in Puerto Rico, married Stearns in 1843. She was an active member of Boston's Transcendentalist circles. A devoted abolitionist, she helped raise funds for the movement, assisted fugitive slaves, and endorsed her husband's financial backing of John Brown's raid. She later supported Radical Reconstruction and advocated that "those who till the soil come to own the soil." The Stearnses provided Tubman with financial assistance. *DAB*, 17:543–44; Frank Preston Stearns, *The Life and Public Services of George Luther Stearns* (Philadelphia, Pa., 1907), 44–45, 88–89, 95, 159, 176, 194, 354; Hinton, *John Brown and His Men*, 140; *ASA*, 1 November 1860 [12:1066]; *Lib*, 27 December 1861 [13:1002].

6. E. G. Dudley came to Beaufort, South Carolina, as an agent of the federal government during the Civil War. He was a delegate to the July 1867 Republican state convention in Charleston. John S. Reynolds, *Reconstruction in South Carolina, 1865–1877* (Columbia, S.C., 1905), 59.

7. Harriet Tubman (1821–1913), a legendary figure in the underground railroad, was born to slave parents Benjamin Ross and Harriet Greene near Cambridge on Maryland's eastern shore. Although called Araminta as a child, she later chose her mother's name. Laboring as a field slave through her teenage years, she developed the muscular build, physical endurance, and deep religious faith that became her trademarks. An accident left her prone to chronic narcoleptic seizures for the remainder of her life. When she escaped from slavery in 1848, her free black husband of four years, John Tubman, stayed in Maryland and took another wife. Having reached freedom, Harriet resolved to help other slaves do the same. By working as a cook, laundress, and scrubwoman in Philadelphia and Cape May, New Jersey, she financed the first of her famous expeditions into the South—a journey to Baltimore to rescue her sister and two children. She made at least nine trips during the 1850s to lead some 180 slaves to freedom—most were relatives and friends from plantations near Cambridge. Tubman carefully planned each escape and boasted of having never lost a "passenger." These trips remain shrouded in mystery because of Tubman's illiteracy and the secret nature of underground railroad activity. But her work so alarmed Maryland planters that they announced a $40,000 reward for her capture.

As sectional controversy increased, Tubman redirected her efforts, viewing the conflict as the climax of the struggle for freedom. She met with John Brown a half dozen times during 1858–59 and raised money for his Harpers Ferry raid. After going to Beaufort, South Carolina, in May 1862, she spent three years working as a nurse and cook among the contrabands there. She also became a scout and spy for the Second South Carolina Volunteers. Able to travel without suspicion in rebel territory, she located cotton storehouses, ammunition depots, and slaves awaiting liberation and informed Union military officials. During the latter months of the Civil War, Tubman was employed in freedmen's hospitals in Virginia.

After the war, Tubman returned to Auburn, New York, where she had settled with her parents in 1858. She raised money for freedmen's schools, collected clothing for destitute children, and aided the sick and disabled. In 1903 she turned her house into the Harriet Tubman Home for Aged and Indigent People. She also lectured throughout the East, worked with black women's groups and the African Methodist Episcopal Zion church, advocated women's suffrage, and served as a delegate to the first annual convention of the National Association of Colored Women (1896). Although widely celebrated in her later years, Tubman lived in meager personal circumstances. White friends and benefactors attempted to provide for her welfare by financing the publication of two biographies by Auburn teacher Sarah H. Bradford—*Scenes in the Life Of Harriet Tubman* (1868) and *Harriet Tubman: The Moses of Her People* (1886). They also tried to secure her a government pension; she finally received one in 1890 as the widow of Nelson Davis, a war veteran who in 1869 became her second husband. Benjamin Quarles, "Harriet Tubman's Unlikely Leadership," in *Black Leaders of the Nineteenth Century*, ed. Leon Litwack and August Meier (Urbana, Ill., 1988), 43–57; *NAW*, 3:481–83; Sterling, *We Are Your Sisters*, 67, 222–23, 258–61, 397–99, 411; *NASS*, 18 July 1863; *WAA*, 29 August 1863.

46.
Manifesto of the Colored Citizens of
the State of New York
16 July 1863

Many black abolitionists viewed the Civil War in apocalyptic terms—
an epic confrontation between the forces of liberty and slavery, with the
fate of humanity in the balance. This vision of the war as a conflict tran-
scending national boundaries became more pronounced after the Emancipation Proclamation. Robert Purvis regarded it as "a war between
freedom and despotism the world over." Frederick Douglass asserted
that the federal government fought to free "the whole world from
slavery" and spoke of Union troops "writing statutes of eternal justice
and liberty." The delegates who gathered at a black state convention in
Poughkeepsie, New York, during 15–16 July 1863 shared this grand vision. Reacting to Governor Horatio Seymour's reluctance to enlist black
troops in New York state, they issued a manifesto on the meaning of the
war. The document—which was drafted by a committee consisting of
P. B. Randolph, Jonas H. Townsend, N. B. Thompson, Peyton Harris,
Benjamin F. Randolph, and Isaac Deyo—rejected the notion of the
war as a narrow "fratricidal conflict" and portrayed it as a cataclys-
mic struggle to determine the fate of civilization and human progress.
It warned that failure to end slavery would inaugurate "a reign of
horror as never yet has been known on earth." *NASS*, 16 May 1863
[14:0863–64]; David W. Blight, *Frederick Douglass' Civil War: Keeping Faith in Jubilee* (Baton Rouge, La., 1989), 101–21; Philip S. Foner,
The Life and Writings of Frederick Douglass, 5 vols. (New York, N.Y.,
1975), 3:390; *WAA*, 1 August 1863; Quarles, *Negro in the Civil War*,
188–89.

MANIFESTO
OF THE COLORED CITIZENS OF THE STATE OF NEW YORK,
IN CONVENTION ASSEMBLED

The war now raging so fiercely over the broad and fertile acres of this,
the best heritage ever enjoyed by man, is not a "fratricidal conflict," as
many deem it, but, on the contrary, by reason of the momentous issues
at stake and involved therein, is one of the most justifiable wars that was
ever inaugurated beneath the smiling, radiant dome of all the broad heavens. It is one of the most sacred which the earth has ever groaned under
or mankind ever witnessed, for the reason that it is a combat for the
sacred rights of Man against the myrmidons of Hell itself. It is a battle
for the right of self-government, true democracy, just republicanism, and
righteous principles, against anarchy, misrule, barbarism, human slavery,

despotism, and wrong. On the one side is arrayed the hosts of Belial,[1] backed by willfulness, injustice, usurpation, anger and passion; on the other, in serried ranks, stand honor, human liberty, justice, truth, and honesty. This is not a battle of boys but [a] struggle of giants. Let the North be conquered, and the salt tears of the oppressed will water the ground for many a long decade of years, and many a hecatomb will uprear its head, and many a sod be nurtured by the blood of liberty-loving human beings. The strife now waging is not between North and South—is not only in behalf of the Negro; but the greatest principles the world has ever known constitute the two halves of the *casus belli*[2]— barbarism and freedom—civilization and slavery; it is a death struggle between the feudal ages and the nineteenth century; and every drop of blood shed from Northern veins is a sacrifice on the holy altars of human freedom, and those forever consecrate to the ever-blessed Redeemer of Mankind! The impending issues are such that if the representatives of human liberty yield the battle, and retire ingloriously beaten, the age will recede a century, and the hands upon the clock of Progress will cease to move across the face of Time. Let the cohorts of freedom be beaten and disgraced, and not only all true lovers of the race will suffer, but every lover and true worshipper of the living God will mourn over the desolation.

This contest is one in which every son and daughter of the land is and of necessity must be interested. It is the bounden duty of us all—all who are not craven cowards—all in whom the warm blood leaps, and all who feel what a terrible thing is HUMAN SLAVERY—to up and struggle for God and the Right.

Defeat in this momentous epoch of human history means more than a rout upon the battlefield, inasmuch as such defeat will not only rivet our chains still firmer than of yore, but will forever stand as the synonym of American disgrace and will be the record of our perpetual disfranchisement, and be the bouleversement of human society, civilization and democratic republican institutions, from progress and health to anarchy, decay and final ruin—a ruin utter, total and complete; for the common sense of mankind cannot fail to see that if the cause of freedom fails now, human advancement will be something read about in books, instead of being a living, ever-present fact; and in the reign of tyranny thence ensuing, the human heart must of necessity become chilled and frozen; art, science and religion must go out like oilless lamps; darkness must eclipse the light; the garden of the mind run to waste and weeds; human genius be vagabond, stifled and dumb as of old, and the spirit of misrule will sweep the fair green earth with the besom of destruction, scattering desolation far and wide, and inaugurating such a reign of horror as never yet has been known on earth. Let the cohorts of freedom now yield an inch, and the blood of Jesus will almost have been shed in vain; for in their defeat, Christianity itself must suffer; the sacrifice of Calvary prove a failure, the spontaneity of the human soul be chilled and frozen; human genius be stifled, talent be warped, and eloquence be dumb, as in the dead years of the far off past. Great God! What a spectacle in this nineteenth century! A million of men arraying themselves in arms against liberty! and in favor of their own degradation!

Quos Deus vult perdere, prius dementat.[3]

That the movers of this rebellion are mad, utterly insane, no reasonable man can doubt, else whence the horrible blasphemy—not in words, but in bloody deeds, and still more bloody intent, now expressed by millions? else whence the spirit which has prompted rational men to the suicidal policy of shattering to pieces the fairest fabric of human liberty ever erected on the soil of earth? else whence the perfect frenzy which sets men on, in the face of the age, and before high Heaven, to trail the banner of this proud nation, this hope of the world, this blessed refuge of the oppressed of all lands, in the dust? Aye, truly, the devil is the masterly engineer of this awful work of spoliation, ruin and disaster, else deluded men would never have dared to hurl an iron rain against the flag of the free as it floated over Sumter's stony ramparts.[4] Lone flag of liberty! whose folds offered a shelter to all whose limbs have ever felt the gyves of European tyranny. Father of Mercy, what a spectacle! Men in arms, battling for what mankind have ever fought against since the world began! Tyranny, despotism, and human slavery! The banner whose blazonry is the stars of heaven, to fall tattered to the dust before the sulphurous hail of treason's cannonry!—a treason, too, more foul and despicable than aught ever before witnessed by His starry eyes, looking down from the deep blue sky!

Such being the case, and their disease having proved to be incurable by ordinary means, such as reason, justice, patriotism; therefore

1. *Resolved*, That more effective remedies ought now to be *thoroughly* tried, in the shape of warm lead and cold steel, duly administered by 200,000 black doctors, more or less under the direction of Surgeon General John Charles Fremont, or such other person fit for the office, as might be selected.

2. *Resolved*, That we, the colored citizens of this State, are LOYAL and TRUE to the Government; that our fortunes rise or fall with it; that we are ready, anxious and willing to demonstrate that truth and loyalty on the field of battle, or wherever else we can aid in restoring the nation to its integrity and prosperity; that we firmly and confidently rely on the Government for the protection and treatment due to civilized men, and believe we shall receive it.

3. *Resolved*, That in this perilous crisis of our country, whoever is not for her is against her, and ought to be attended to in such a manner as to

prove that the Government has not yet exhausted all her strength, but has abundant power left, not only to protect its children, but to punish treason and traitors wherever they may be found.

4. *Resolved*, That in the success of the Union arms, we, the colored citizens of the United States, behold the first bright, unmistakable gleam of hope for ourselves and our kindred the wide world over. But, on the contrary, with the success of Southern despotism, our rising sun will forever set in a night and gloom that may never know an ending. In it we see the certainty of a still further riveting of the chains and gyves of slavery on the limbs of us who, by every law of God and man, ought to be free. With the success of the rebellion will inevitably come the loss to us of all that man holds dear; the perpetual degradation of labor, of our race and order, and of those who shall inherit our places. With the success of that bad cause will come the perpetuation of ignorance among us, and the total disfranchisement of all of us, who, in the face of obstacles greater and more formidable than men of any race on earth have ever yet confronted and surmounted, have achieved education, property, and some little consideration in community.

5. *Resolved*, That the twaddle about the "unconstitutionality of the means" resorted to, and depended on to wipe out this rebellion and the rebels, is on a par with that of the footpad, who, when worsted by his intended victim, exclaimed, "Oh! you've kicked in a tender spot, hit below the belt, knocking the wind clean out of me, which you know isn't fair!"

6. *Resolved*, That no man is fit for liberty who is unwilling or afraid to fight for it, if need be, to the bitter end; and that colored men, as well as others, have by nature certain inalienable rights, among which is that of fighting for the land that gave them birth, for the banner that floats over us, for our wives and little ones, and for the freedom of the generations that shall succeed us.

7. *Resolved*, That we stand in the door of the dawn; that the spirit of liberty is abroad in the land; that her benignant eye is fixed upon the four million blacks of this country, and that her flight is towards them!

8. *Resolved*, That the soldiers of the Union armies are not contending for a party, not for the spoils of war, but for Empire—for universal Human Right and Liberty—to maintain intact the heritage bequeathed to the ages by the men of '76; to make this continent in very truth the same refuge for the oppressed of all lands in spite of caste, complexional differences, wealth, poverty, sect, or creed. And as the nation, in this perilous hour of her existence, calls for our aid, it is our duty to grandly give it, and that immediately.

9. *Resolved*, That liberty is more than the golden vision of the poet; more than the creed of scholastics and dogmatists; more than the dream of the enthusiasts; more than the plaything of tyrants and knaves; and

our charter to its possession, Time has not annulled, Force has not abrogated, Usurpation has not falsified, Heaven has not revoked it, Earth has not erased, Hell has not filched, and if we do our duty, the time is not far distant, when the world will gladly concede it!

10. *Resolved*, That recent events have demonstrated that men of negro lineage hold the balance of power in this contest, and that we should prove recreant to all that constitutes manhood did we fail instantly to throw our weight for the Government, not alone in words, but by sturdy blows. We should strike, and strike hard, to win a place in history, not as vassals, but as men and heroes, never forgetting that God, as ever, strikes for the right, ever helping those most who help themselves. Let us do this, and posterity, reading of our achievements in centuries yet to be, shall say, while pointing to the record we shall have left behind us:

> These were the great old masters,
> These were the men sublime
> Whose distant footsteps echo
> Down the corridors of Time.[5]

Weekly Anglo-African (New York, N.Y.), 1 August 1863.

1. Belial is the personification of lawlessness in the Bible. The term is used in 2 Corinthians 6:15 as another name for Satan.

2. *Casus belli* is a Latin phrase meaning "the cause of war."

3. *Quos deus vult perdere, prius dementat* is a Latin phrase meaning "those whom God wishes to destroy, he first makes mad."

4. The committee refers to the Confederate bombardment of Fort Sumter in Charleston harbor, which signaled the beginning of the Civil War.

5. The committee quotes stanza 5 of *The Day is Done* (1845) by American poet Henry Wadsworth Longfellow.

47.
The New York City Draft Riots

William P. Powell to William Lloyd Garrison
18 July 1863

Essay by J. W. C. Pennington
20 July 1863

During the summer of 1863, federal efforts to implement a military conscription act provoked a wave of racial violence. Reluctant to join in a war for black freedom and resentful of economic competition, white workers attacked black neighborhoods in several northern cities. The most devastating riots occurred in New York City during 13–17 July. For five days, white mobs laid siege to the black community, looting and burning homes, businesses, and social institutions. Several blacks were killed, dozens were brutally beaten, and hundreds fled the city. This unprecedented level of racial violence terrorized local blacks. The following letters by two black abolitionists, composed just hours after the riot was quelled, invoke the community's temperament. Writing to the *Liberator*, William P. Powell recounted his family's dramatic escape from the Colored Seamen's Home. A devoted Garrisonian, he reaffirmed his pacifist principles despite the harrowing experience. His moving lament, "What more could I do?," reflects the despair of those blacks whose loyalty and civic-mindedness were rewarded with the savagery of a mob. J. W. C. Pennington's account of the riots appeared in an essay in the *National Principia*. While unsuccessfully searching for his family, Pennington had risked several encounters with the mob. He demanded an official investigation into the origin of the outbreak, convinced that the violence against blacks was part of a larger pro-Confederate conspiracy. Iver Bernstein, *New York City Draft Riots* (New York, N.Y., 1990); *Report of the Committee of Merchants for the Relief of Colored People, Suffering from the Late Riots in the City of New York* (New York, N.Y., 1863), 7–31 [14:0656–68]; *WAA*, 25 July, 1, 8, 14 August 1863.

New Bedford, [Massachusetts]
July 18, 1863

FRIEND GARRISON:

   With a sorrowful heart, I write you a narrative of the outrages perpetrated upon myself and defenceless family[1] by a lawless, infuriated New York mob.[2] On the afternoon of the 18th inst., the Colored Sailors'

9. Black victim of the New York City draft riots
Illustrated London News, 8 August 1863

Home, No. 2 Dover street, was invaded by a mob of half-grown boys. At this Home, established under the direction of the American Seamen's Friend Society,[3] boarded the last eleven months four hundred and fifty colored seamen. Founded on the strict principles of temperance, and the moral and religious elevation of my brethren of the sea, it was the only refuge where *they* could rest secure, when in port, from the snares and temptations which unhappily beset them on shore.

More than thirteen years ago, the anniversary meeting of the American Anti-Slavery Society was mobbed, and driven out of the Broadway Tabernacle and other public buildings by the notorious Capt. Rynders and his hellish crew.[4] That was an outrage for which it was hoped New York had condoned for by confession, contrition and satisfaction, and had received absolution and remission of their sins, from the ghastly hands of our downtrodden humanity.

Dear Garrison, throughout the course of your eventful life, as the unflinching advocate of the suffering dumb of our enslaved race, in which you have never faltered, and have, from time to time, been mobbed, imprisoned, bruised, beaten, and dragged through the streets of Puritan Boston as a malefactor,[5] you can well enter into my feelings. As a man of peace, I have religiously, and upon principles eternal as the heavens, never armed myself with deadly weapons of defence, and thus have been at the mercy of the bloodthirsty Vandals.[6] It was the wisdom of one insignificant man that once saved a besieged city. I thank God who has given me the victory—to rely wholly upon His all-protecting arm. It was better that all my property should be destroyed, as it has been, and my family stripped of everything except the clothing in which they escaped with their lives, than that one drop of blood should be shed in defence of their lives. Let us thank God that He still reigns, and that He will yet make the wrath of man to praise him.

From 2 P.M. till 8 P.M. myself and family were prisoners in my own house to *king mob*, from which there was no way to escape but over the roofs of adjoining houses. About 4 P.M., I sent a note to Superintendent Kennedy for protection, but received none, from the fact that he had been seriously injured by the mob in another part of the city.[7] Well, the mob commenced throwing stones at the lower windows until they had succeeded in making an opening. I was determined not to leave until driven from the premises. My family, including my invalid daughter (who is entirely helpless), took refuge on the roof of the next house. I remained till the mob broke in, and then narrowly escaped the same way. This was about 8½ P.M. We remained on the roof for an hour; still I hoped relief would come. The neighbors, anticipating the mob would fire my house, were removing their effects on the roof—all was excitement. But as the object of the mob was plunder, they were too busily engaged in carrying off all my effects to apply the torch. Add to this, it began to rain as if the very heavens were shedding tears over the dreadful calamity. "Hung be the heavens with black!"[8]

How to escape from the roof of a five-story building with four females—and one a cripple—besides eight men, without a ladder, or any assistance from outside, was beyond my *not* excited imagination. But the God that succored Hagar in her flight[9] came to my relief in the person of a little, deformed, despised Israelite—who, Samaritan-like, took my poor helpless daughter under his protection in his house;[10] there I presume she now is, until friends send her to me. He also supplied me with a long rope. I then took a survey of the premises, and fortunately found a way to escape; and though pitchy dark, I took *soundings* with the rope, to see if it would touch the next roof, after which I took a clovehitch around the clothesline which was fastened to the wall by pulleys, and which led from one roof to the other over a space of about one hundred feet. In this manner I managed to lower my family down to the next roof, and from one roof to another, until I landed them in a neighbor's yard. We were secreted in our friend's cellar till 11 P.M., when we were taken in charge by the police, and locked up in the Station house for safety. In this dismal place, we found upwards of *seventy* men, women and children—some with broken limbs—bruised and beaten from head to foot. We stayed in this place for twenty-four hours, when the police escorted us to the New Haven boat, at 11 P.M. Thus we escaped from an infuriated mob, leaving our invalid daughter in New York in the hands of kind friends.

All my personal property, to the amount of $3000, has been scattered to the four winds, which, "like the baseless fabric of a vision, leaves not a wreck behind,"[11] except our lives; and so the Lord be praised.

As a devoted loyal Unionist, I have done all I could do to perpetuate and uphold the integrity of this free government. As an evidence of this devotedness, my oldest son is now serving my country as a surgeon in the United States army,[12] and myself had just received a commission in the naval service. What more could I do? What further evidence was wanting to prove my allegiance in the exigencies of our unfortunate country? I am now an old man, stripped of everything which I once possessed, of all the comforts of life; but I thank God that He has yet spared my life, which I am ready to yield in the defence of my country. I am, Sir, yours, &c.,

WM. P. POWELL

Liberator (Boston, Mass.), 24 July 1863.

POUGHKEEPSIE, [New York]
July 20, 1863

I left New York city, about the middle of June, and came to this city, to enter upon my duties as an educator, under the employment of the Board of Education, here.[13] I left my family at 312 West 26th street, near

10th avenue, in the 16th Ward, where we have resided, with seven other colored families, for several years.[14] After closing my school for vacation, and presiding over the deliberation of the Colored State Convention, held here on the 15th and 16th,[15] I took the evening boat on Friday for New York city, arriving there on Saturday morning, at the foot of Harrison street. I went, cautiously and peaceably, to my residence, on foot. When I got to the corner of 26th street and 10th avenue, within four doors of my home, I was at once attacked with stones and brickbats, from different quarters, with the shout, "*kill the d—d nigger.*" When I reached the door, and placed my hand on the knob, I found the mob had preceded me, and such was the state of feeling in the neighborhood that I did not deem it prudent to enter a single store to make any inquiry about my family, and others whom I left in my house. On the same block, opposite side, near the 11th avenue, were four tenant houses occupied by colored families. At the risk of my life, I passed down that way, and so along the North river, on the line of the 11th avenue, up to the depot of the Hudson river road. Here, for the first time during my tour, I met a friendly white man—a German—God bless him—who said to me, "Why, Doctor, is it not too soon for you to be in the city? Do be careful which way you go!" This was at the corner of 31st street and 10th avenue. My German friend advised me to take 30th street, as I wanted to go toward the 7th avenue, and he acted as my lifeguard a part of the way. I passed through many streets and districts where I knew colored people have had their residences and business places; and at every step death and desolation stared me in the face. I had a number of narrow escapes. I believe that had I showed any signs of fear or cowardice, I should have been set upon, and killed. At some other time I will give incidents that will prove the truth of what I say. I will only add now, that I failed to find my family. I do not know, while writing this, where my wife is. I, therefore, returned to Poughkeepsie by the *Mary Powell*, on Saturday evening the 18th inst.

I have facts in my possession, which I will not state now, to prove that the recent onslaught upon the colored people in New York, and other cities, is the result of a deliberate arrangement. And in view of this fact, it is due to humanity, and to the Union cause, to the reputation of New York city, and every other city, that a *commission should be at once instituted, with full power to ferret out the whole scheme in New York city.* I tell you, sir, that the leaders in the late bloody mob have their eyes upon your *Wall street banks!* The negro is only the black herring. Those who will drag black herring are expected to feed the hounds that run on the track. The American people have been dragging black herring long enough. You had better stop. *I speak as unto wise men, judge ye what I say.*[16] The idea of expatriating or exterminating black men from this land of their birth is obsolete and barbarous. The thing cannot be done. We are resolved, at all hazards, to maintain our position here.

While walking on the bloodstained sidewalks, in New York, I could but recur to the lines of my favorite author, Robert Pollok, the Scotch poet. Book IV, at the beginning.

> One passion prominent appears! the lust
> Of power, which oftimes took the fairer name
> Of liberty, and hung the popular flag
> Of freedom out. Many, indeed, its names.
> When on the throne it sat, and round the neck
> Of millions rivetted its iron chain,
> And on the shoulders of the people laid
> Burdens unmerciful—its title took,
> Of tyranny, oppression, despotism;
> And every tongue was weary cursing it.
> *When in the multitude it gathered strength,*
> And, like an ocean bursting from its bounds,
> Long beat in vain, went forth resistlessly,
> It bore the stamp and designation then,
> *Of popular fury,* ANARCHY, REBELLION—
> And honest men bewailed all order void;
> All laws annulled; all property destroyed;
> The venerable, murdered in the streets;
> The wise despised; streams, red with human blood;
> Harvests, beneath the frantic foot trode down;
> Lands, desolate; and famine at the door. * * *
> Conflicting cruelty against itself,
> By its own hand it fell; part slaying part,
> And men who noticed not the suicide,
> Stood wondering much, why earth from age to age,
> Was still enslaved, and erring causes gave.
> This was earth's liberty—its nature this—
> However named, in whomsoever found,
> And found it was, in all of woman born,
> Each man to make all subject to his will;
> To make them do, undo, eat, drink, stand, move,
> Talk, think, and feel, exactly as he chose,
> Hence, the eternal strife of brotherhoods,
> Of individuals, families, commonwealths.
> The root from which it grew was pride; bad root,
> And bad the fruit it bore. Then wonder not,
> That long the nations from it richly reaped
> Oppression, slavery, tyranny, AND WAR;
> Confusion, desolation, trouble, shame.
> And, marvellous though it seem, this monster,

> When it took the name of slavery, as oft it did,
> Had advocates to plead its cause; * * * *
> Unchristian thought! on what pretence soe'er
> Of right inherited, or else acquired;
> Of loss, or profit, or what plea you name,
> To buy and sell, to barter, whip, and hold
> In chains, a being of celestial make,
> Of kindred form, of kindred faculties,
> Of kindred feelings, passions, thoughts, desires,
> Born free, and heir of an immortal hope!
> Thought villainous, absurd, detestable!
> Unworthy to be harbored in a fiend![17]

My copy of Pollok, with my other valuable books, notes, and manuscripts, are now in the possession of his majesty the mob, if not destroyed; but I think I have quoted correctly, and, I know, also, that that graphic author describes what I saw.

There is one point which must be made and insisted upon. The city and State of New York must pay us for every dollar's worth of property destroyed, and they must be made to feel responsible for the lives lost, the limbs broken, the families broken up, &c. The season is advancing, stern winter will soon be at our doors again; and what, in the name of Divinity and Humanity, is to become of our poor scattered families? Let us then have no false or side issues. The rebel mob has been allowed to do its work, not on the banks of the Potomac, but of the Hudson. Let those who are true to the Union cause show it by aiding in the relief of those who have suffered.[18]

J. W. C. PENNINGTON

National Principia (New York, N.Y.), 30 July 1863.

1. Powell married Mercy O. Haskins (1814–?), a woman of Native American descent, in 1832, while living in New Bedford, Massachusetts. She helped him operate the Colored Seamen's Home and later ran the Globe Hotel at the same address. The couple had five sons—William P., Jr. (b. 1836), Edward B. (b. 1836), Sylvester H. (b. 1838), Isaiah (b. 1842), and Samuel (b. 1849)—and two daughters—Nancy O. (b. 1840) and Sarah A. (b. 1845). The four oldest sons were educated in England and served in the Union army at the time of the New York City draft riots. Sarah, an invalid, contributed to the family's income by making wax flowers, designing bridal and funeral wreaths, and teaching needlework lessons. Several black seamen also lived in the Powell home at the time of the riots. U.S. Census, 1850; Foner, *Essays in Afro-American History*, 89; George W. Forbes, Biographical Sketch of William P. Powell, Antislavery Collection, MB; *WAA*, 12 August 1865.

2. The most severe draft riots of the Civil War occurred in New York City during 13–17 July 1863. Military conscription sparked the violence, but other conditions—economic rivalry between blacks and working-class whites, strong

anti-Republican sentiment, and an influential Copperhead and racist press—contributed to the intensity of the protest. Over a five-day period, white mobs clashed with police, destroyed public and private property, and vented their rage on the city's black community. Blacks were assaulted in the streets and driven from their homes. The Colored Orphan Asylum was burned and the Colored Seamen's Home ransacked. The rioting terrorized black residents, many of whom fled the city or sought sanctuary in police custody. At least eleven blacks were killed and hundreds were injured or suffered property losses. Union army regiments were eventually brought in to restore order. The casualties, which included more than one hundred deaths, made this rioting the most violent urban insurrection in American history. Bernstein, *New York City Draft Riots*, 3–42, 288–89n.

3. Powell established the Colored Seamen's Home in 1839 in New York City. It operated under the auspices and with the financial support of the American Seamen's Friend Society, a Protestant benevolent organization devoted to mission work among those in the maritime trades. Powell used a great deal of his own income to sustain the home, which provided lodging, clothing, and meals to many of the two thousand black stewards, cooks, and sailors who stayed in the city between voyages. He required lodgers to adhere to temperance principles, urged them to deposit a portion of their earnings in the Seamen's Bank for Savings, and encouraged an activist atmosphere—he hung a portrait of Crispus Attucks, pointed proudly to the role of black sailors in distributing David Walker's *Appeal* in the South, led frequent discussions of slavery and black rights, and made available a large library of reform books and tracts. He involved black seamen in the work of the Manhattan Anti-Slavery Society and in local efforts to aid and protect fugitive slaves. The facility closed its doors from 1851 to 1861, when Powell lived in England, but reopened at 2 Dover Street upon his return. In 1862 he joined several lodgers in founding the American Seamen's Protective Union Association to advocate sailors' rights and headquartered it in the home. Such visibility made the building a target for white mobs during the July 1863 draft riots. Although operations had to be suspended for three months while it was refurbished and repaired, it continued to operate into the immediate postwar period. Foner, *Essays in Afro-American History*, 89–106.

4. On 7 May 1850, the annual meeting of the American Anti-Slavery Society was threatened by a New York City antiabolitionist mob led by Isaiah Rynders (1804–1884), a boatman, gambler, and Tammany Hall politician. Rynders, whose "Empire Club" was a watering hole for ruffians and party hacks, was often hired by the local Democratic organization to disrupt rival political meetings and antislavery conventions. On this occasion, the mob muscled its way to the speaker's platform to harass William Lloyd Garrison, Frederick Douglass, and Samuel Ringgold Ward. Rynders seized the podium, haranguing the crowd and hurling racial epithets at Douglass and Ward. But at this critical moment in the antislavery movement, their verbal rejoinders offered eloquent evidence to refute Rynders's racist characterizations. Merrill and Ruchames, *Letters of William Lloyd Garrison*, 4:10; Garrison and Garrison, *William Lloyd Garrison*, 3:291–99.

5. William Lloyd Garrison was attacked on several occasions by antiabolitionist mobs. The most dramatic of these episodes occurred on 21 October 1835 at a meeting of the Boston Female Anti-Slavery Society. Garrison was seized by a mob,

bound with a rope, and led through the streets. The police intervened and placed Garrison in jail to prevent further violence. Garrison and Garrison, *William Lloyd Garrison*, 2:9–37.

6. Powell compares the mob to the Vandals, a small but aggressive Germanic tribe that invaded Rome in 455. Their name became synonymous with looting and destroying.

7. John A. Kennedy (1803–1873) was superintendent of police and provost marshal for New York City during the Civil War. He had been appointed commissioner of emigration in 1849 and later gained a seat on the city's common council. The Lincoln administration called on Kennedy in 1861 to investigate rumors of an assassination plot against the president; because he worked so closely with the federal government over the next few years, he was severely criticized for politicizing the police. Kennedy was savagely beaten by the mob during the New York City draft riots. *ACAB*, 3:516–17; *Lib*, 16 January 1863 [14:0694]; Bernstein, *New York City Draft Riots*, 18, 37, 45, 300.

8. Powell quotes from part 1, act 1, of *Henry VI* (1591) by William Shakespeare.

9. Hagar's flight is described in Genesis 21:9–21. Hagar, an Egyptian woman, was a servant to the Jewish patriarch, Abraham, and his wife, Sarah. She bore a son by Abraham named Ishmael, but because of Sarah's jealousy, she and the boy were forced to flee into the desert. According to legend, Hagar was the progenitor of the Arab people.

10. Powell compares the action of his unidentified Jewish neighbor, who hid Powell's invalid daughter, Sarah, to that of the Samaritan in Luke 10:29–37. In this parable of Jesus, a Samaritan—an outcast—aids the victim of a robbery along a heavily traveled road, after his bleeding, battered body has been ignored by members of the social elite who pass by.

11. Powell joins two lines excerpted from act 4, scene 1, of *The Tempest* (1611–12) by William Shakespeare.

12. William P. Powell, Jr. (1836–?), the eldest son of William P. Powell, was born in New Bedford, Massachusetts, and grew up in New York City. He obtained a medical education in England during the 1850s and was inducted into the Royal College of Surgeons. In 1861 the younger Powell returned to the United States and established a private medical practice in New Bedford. He served as a surgeon in the Union army during the last two years of the Civil War, supervising the staff at the Freedmen's Hospital in Washington, D.C., for a time. After the war, he remained in Washington and established a successful medical practice. U.S. Census, 1860; *WAA*, 1 July 1865; Berlin et al., *Freedom*, 2:331n.

13. Pennington taught at a black public school in Poughkeepsie in 1863. Blackett, *Beating against the Barriers*, 80.

14. Pennington married his second wife, Elmira Way (1814–?), in 1848. She had been the domestic servant of Edward Godwin, the editor of the Hartford *Connecticut Courant*. In 1863 the couple lived with Pennington's son, Thomas (b. 1844), in a four-story brick home at 312 West Twenty-sixth Street in New York City, which they operated as a boardinghouse after buying it three years before. Blackett, *Beating against the Barriers*, 36, 39; U.S. Census, 1860; *WAA*, 21 April 1860.

15. Pennington chaired the black state convention that met in Poughkeepsie,

New York, during 15–16 July 1863. Eighteen delegates attended, most of whom were from Dutchess County. They adopted several resolutions denouncing the white view of the war as a "fratricidal conflict." Rather, they declared, it was "one of the most justifiable wars that we ever imagined . . . a combat for the sacred rights of Man." The convention pledged the loyalty of New York blacks to the Union cause, called for 200,000 black volunteers, and appointed a central committee to encourage black recruitment. *WAA*, 1 August 1863.

16. Pennington quotes 1 Corinthians 10:15.

17. Pennington recites at length from book 4 of *The Course of Time* (1827) by Scottish poet Robert Pollok (1798–1827). The asterisks in this poem appear in Pennington's original document.

18. New York City merchants and religious groups responded to the draft riots with an organized attempt to assist black victims. Over $40,000 was collected by a "Committee of Merchants for the Relief of Colored People Suffering from the Late Riots." The committee also helped blacks file damage claims for compensation from the municipal government. Bernstein, *New York City Draft Riots*, 55–56.

48.
The Fifty-fourth Massachusetts Regiment

Lewis H. Douglass to Frederick Douglass
and Anna Murray Douglass
20 July 1863

George E. Stephens to William Still
19 September 1863

Blacks rallied behind the Fifty-fourth Massachusetts Regiment—the
first black unit recruited in the North—as the standard-bearer of their
abolitionist commitment. Mustered into service in February 1863, the
Fifty-fourth represented an opportunity to simultaneously free the slave,
secure equal rights, and affirm black worth to a skeptical nation. Black
communities encouraged recruitment efforts, collected money and supplies for the troops, and followed reports of the unit's every move. Black
leaders Frederick Douglass and Peter Vogelsang, Sr., sent their sons to
enlist. The *Weekly Anglo-African* observed that "every black man and
woman feels a special interest in the success of this regiment." Organized by Massachusetts governor John A. Andrew and led by Robert
Gould Shaw, a Boston abolitionist, the Fifty-fourth attracted enlistees
from nearly every Northern state and included several former slaves.
On 28 May, an enormous Boston crowd hailed its departure for South
Carolina. The men of the regiment proved their bravery in battle when
they led an 18 July charge against Fort Wagner, a key to the Union siege
of Charleston. Confederate defenders caught the Fifty-fourth in a furi-
ous cross fire and drove the Union army from the field. Shaw died leading his men; the regiment suffered some 256 killed or wounded, including most of the officers. Although the attack failed, the extraordinary
valor of the Fifty-fourth dissolved doubts about black soldiers and fa-
cilitated the enlistment of nearly 180,000 more—some 10 percent of all
Union troops. The following letters from two members of the regiment
were written in the aftermath of the Wagner assault; they describe the
battle, note its impact on the unit, and reveal what black soldiers believed their efforts would accomplish. Led by Colonel Edward N. Hallowell throughout the remainder of the war, the Fifty-fourth saw further
action along the South Carolina–Georgia coast and fought valiantly
at the battle of Olustee in Florida in early 1864. *WAA*, 4, 11 April, 30
May, 6, 13 June 1863, 20 February 1864; Emilio, *History of the Fifty-
Fourth Regiment.*

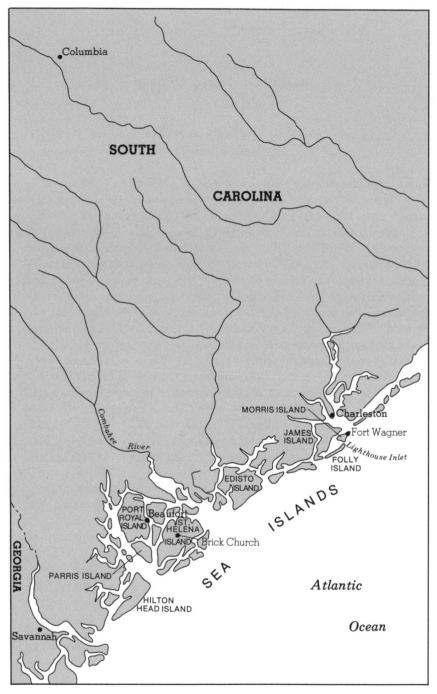

Fig. 2. Coastal South Carolina

MORRIS ISLAND,
S[outh] C[arolina]
July 20th, 1863

My Dear Father and Mother: [1]

Wednesday July 8th, our regiment left St. Helena Island for Folly Island, arriving there the next day, and were then ordered to land on James Island, which we did. On the upper end of James Island is a large rebel battery with 18 guns. After landing we threw out pickets to within two miles of the rebel fortification. We were permitted to do this in peace until last Thursday, 16th inst., when at four o'clock in the morning the rebels made an attack on our pickets, who were about 200 strong. We were attacked by a force of about 900. Our men fought like tigers; one sergeant killed five men by shooting and bayoneting. The rebels were held in check by our few men long enough to allow the 10th Conn. to escape being surrounded and captured,[2] for which we received the highest praise from all parties who knew of it. This performance on our part earned for us the reputation of a fighting regiment.

Our loss in killed, wounded and missing was forty-five. That night we took, according to our officers, one of the hardest marches on record, through woods and marsh. The rebels we defeated and drove back in the morning. They, however, were reinforced by 14,000 men, we having only half a dozen regiments. So it was necessary for us to escape.

I cannot write in full, expecting every moment to be called into another fight. Suffice it to say we are now on Morris Island. Saturday night we made the most desperate charge of the war on Fort Wagner, losing in killed, wounded and missing in the assault, three hundred of our men. The splendid 54th is cut to pieces. All our officers, with the exception of eight, were either killed or wounded. Col. Shaw is a prisoner and wounded. Major Hallowell[3] is wounded in three places, Adj't James[4] in two places. Serg't Simmons is killed,[5] Nat. Hurley[6] (from Rochester) is missing, and a host of others.

I had my sword sheath blown away while on the parapet of the Fort. The grape and cannister, shell and minnies swept us down like chaff, still our men went on and on, and if we had been properly supported, we would have held the Fort, but the white troops could not be made to come up. The consequence was we had to fall back, dodging shells and other missiles.

If I have another opportunity, I will write more fully. Goodbye to all. If I die tonight I will not die a coward. Goodbye.

LEWIS [7]

Douglass' Monthly (Rochester, N.Y.), August 1863.

Morris Island, [South Carolina]
Sept[ember] 19, 1863

Dear Sir:

I have learned through the daily papers that there is an extensive movement in progress, for the enlistment of Colored troops in the north & west, and, that the sum of Fifty thousand dollars has already bene subscribed by Patriotic parties to aid such enlistments. All movements of this Character you certainly know, have my hearty concurence and, I wish to do all in my power to aid them[.] In fact I believe as you do that the arming of every available Cold man north & south the speediest method which could be devised to eradicate that semblance of inferiority of our race, which cruel slavery has created[.] If there is one spark of manhood remaining in the bosom of the slave that has resisted the surging waves of oppression ~~the school of the soldier~~ the school of the soldier will fan it into a glowing flame and it is the means—only means by which the collective power of the negro race can be brought to bear on the civil and political affairs of the country. The purpose of this note is to ask your kind offices in my behalf in a matter which I think is of the greatest importance and, interest to me. I propose to associate with my own the name of Mr. Frederick Johnson,[8] one of the most accomplished soldiers in the 54th Mass. vol. Infantry. He is a Sergeant of Co (C) and acting Sergeant Major (Sergeant Lewis Douglass being absent on leave). We desire to apply to Major Stearns[9] or who ever else may be the proper authorities, for the positions of "drill Sergeants." We can obtain from the officers of our Regiment satisfactory testimonials of our qualifications for the position. Sergeant Johnson is a member of Rev. Mr. Grimes Church Boston,[10] is personally acquainted with Gov. Andrew. The most important letter Gov. Andrew, has addressed to our Regt. was directed to Segt. Johnson. I cannot speak in terms too glowing of Sergeant J. when I say that he is a Christian and a soldier. I think it not an uncreditable ambition nor an over-reaching one, to ask a position of this ~~Character~~ kind. The recommendation of the officers might be sufficient to secure us this. But I am a Philadelphian in a Massachusetts Regt. In making my application I wish to indicate, if nessesary, my social character with Mr. Still, Mr. Jacob C. White Jr., and Rev. J. Gibbs[11] and Mr. S. I expect to be in Phila, Providence willing sometime about the first or fifteenth of Oct. on thirty days Furlough.

Now in explanation I will say, that evidences teach us that Cold men have nothing to Hope for here in the way of promotion. Since the disasters of the 18th July, vacancies among the commissioned officers of the Regiment have been steadily filled up by whites from other Regiments. Only a few days ago a white Sergt. major and, a Sergeant of the 26th Mass. vols. were honored with commisions as 2nd Of's in the 54th and, more than one officer here has expressed himself as opposed to commisioning Col̲d men.[12] The matter of commisioning Col̲d men says Gov. Andrews, "Lays in the hands of Company and Regimental command- ers." In more than one case the Sergeants have bene compelled to take command of Companies, the commissioned officers were so few. The Ser- geants (myself among the number[)] came out on "dress parade" and took ~~my~~ their posts as if they had bene a̶ commisioned officers (whose duty they were compelled to do, ~~as I was~~ while in command of theyir companies) but to my indignation an order, was read commanding Ser- geants, not to take the place of commissioned officers in line. The order was signed by Col̲. Littlefield.[13] The 54th is not a Regiment of soldiers, but, ditchers, and, the spade and shovel is their only implement of war- fare. We have not had a company drill since the death of Col̲. Shaw, when he lived predudice and self-sufficintcy hid their mean and spiteful heads. The Regiment is in a state of demoralization. The men are compelled to perform the heaviest kind of Fatigue duty with no pay and impressed with the idea that the officers care nothing for their welfare. They (the offi[cers]) even desire to curtail the number of men allowed by Genl̲ Gil- more,[14] per month "on leave of absence." When we left Readville, my company had 94 men we have now total 71 men left. We are entitled to 2 men according to the apportionment. But, we have such but one, these are some of the reasons which has led us to desire this new field of service, and made us lose heart with the 54th[.] Trusting you will favor us with an early reply, I remain very truly yours for the Liberty and progress of our Race,

> G. E. Stephens
> Sergeant Co. B 54th Regt. Mass.
> Infantry

Leon Gardiner Collection, Historical Society of Pennsylvania, Philadelphia, Penn- sylvania. Published by permission.

1. Anna Murray Douglass (1813–1882), the first wife of Frederick Douglass, was born in freedom near Denton, Maryland. At age seventeen, she moved to Baltimore and worked as a domestic servant for a wealthy white family. She met Douglass there while attending meetings of the East Baltimore Improvement So- ciety, a moral reform association for free blacks. She encouraged and assisted his escape from slavery, and they were married in New York City by J. W. C. Pen- nington in September 1838. The Douglasses had five children—Rosetta, Charles, Lewis, Frederick, Jr., and Annie (d. 1860). After resettling in Massachusetts, Anna Douglass briefly became involved in female antislavery societies in both Lynn and Boston and participated in the Boston antislavery fairs. She also sup- plemented her husband's antislavery income by working as a shoe binder. In later years, she devoted herself to family concerns and to supporting Douglass's abo- litionist work. Sterling, *We Are Your Sisters*, 133–34; William S. McFeely, *Fred- erick Douglass* (New York, N.Y., 1991), 65–70, 73, 81, 92, 103, 136, 142, 145, 154–55, 207, 218–19, 248, 297–98, 312.

2. The Tenth Connecticut Regiment was organized in October 1861 at Hartford. It was attached to the X Corps of the Department of the South at the time of the battle of Secessionville on James Island, South Carolina, where it was saved from certain annihilation by the Fifty-fourth's quick response during the fighting. The Tenth also participated in the siege of Charleston, including the July 1863 assault on Fort Wagner, and later saw action in the campaigns against Petersburg and Richmond, Virginia. It was present for General Robert E. Lee's surrender at Appomattox. Dyer, *Compendium*, 3:1011; Emilio, *History of the Fifty-Fourth Regiment*, 59–61.

3. Edward N. Hallowell (1836–1871), a Philadelphia merchant, was a lieutenant colonel in the Fifty-fourth Massachusetts Regiment at the time of the attack on Fort Wagner. He began his military career on the staff of General John C. Frémont and served in the Twentieth Massachusetts before joining the black regiment. Although seriously wounded in the Wagner assault, he recovered and commanded the unit for the remainder of the war. Close to his troops, Hallowell joined in their protest of the federal government's refusal to pay black and white troops the same wages. Emilio, *History of the Fifty-Fourth Regiment*, 9, 81, 89, 136, 163–64, 190–91, 328.

4. Garth W. James (1845–1883) was an abolitionist and the younger brother of American novelist Henry James. He enlisted in the Forty-fourth Massachusetts Regiment in 1862, then in March 1863, became captain of Company C in the Fifty-fourth Massachusetts. He was wounded twice in the July 1863 assault on Fort Wagner. James resigned his commission in January 1864. He helped manage a Florida plantation after the war and sought to prove that "the freed Negro under decent and just treatment can be worked to profit of employer and employee." He eventually drifted to Milwaukee, Wisconsin, and died there after a prolonged illness. Leon Edel, *Henry James: A Life* (New York, N.Y., 1985), 17, 61–63, 286, 291; Emilio, *History of the Fifty-Fourth Regiment*, 333–34; Lawrence N. Powell, *New Masters: Northern Planters during the Civil War and Reconstruction* (New Haven, Conn., 1980), 29.

5. Douglass was mistaken. First Sergeant Robert J. Simmons, who enlisted in Company B of the Fifty-fourth Massachusetts Regiment in March 1863, was wounded and captured during the Wagner assault. Simmons (1839–1865), a Bermuda-born black, worked as a clerk in New York City before the Civil War. His mother's home was destroyed and a nephew killed in the city's July 1863 draft riots. Simmons was imprisoned in Charleston and died there in August, following the amputation of an arm. Emilio, *History of the Fifty-Fourth Regiment*, 93, 348; Bruchard, *One Gallant Rush*, 130–31, 144.

6. Nathaniel Hurley (1846–1865), a laborer from Rochester, New York, joined the Fifty-fourth Massachusetts Regiment in March 1863. A private in Company C, he was captured during the Fort Wagner assault and died two years later in a Confederate prison camp at Florence, South Carolina. Emilio, *History of the Fifty-Fourth Regiment*, 361.

7. Lewis Henry Douglass (1840–1908), the eldest son of Frederick Douglass, was born in New Bedford, Massachusetts. He learned the printer's trade and became involved in the antislavery movement by helping his father publish the *North Star, Frederick Douglass' Paper*, and *Douglass' Monthly*. He accompanied his father on several speaking tours and participated in antislavery gatherings

during the early 1860s. In 1862 he married Amelia Loguen, the daughter of black abolitionist Jermain Wesley Loguen of Syracuse. Douglass enlisted in the Fifty-fourth Massachusetts Regiment in March 1863 and received the noncommissioned rank of sergeant major. Although he survived the assault on Fort Wagner, he was stricken with typhoid fever and discharged from active service in May 1864 due to lingering illness.

Douglass settled in Washington, D.C., after leaving the Union army. He attended the National Convention of Colored Men, which met in the city in February 1866, and was named to a delegation to carry black grievances to President Andrew Johnson and the Congress. Later that year, he went West to seek his fortune and became secretary of the Red, White, and Blue Mining Company in Colorado. He soon settled in Denver, taught evening classes for blacks in politics and government, and helped lead a movement to integrate local schools.

Douglass returned to Washington in 1868 and obtained employment at the Government Printing Office. But he found his opportunities limited by the refusal of the local typographers' union to open its membership to blacks. Angered by this injustice, he soon joined and became secretary of the Colored National Labor Union. Douglass was also a delegate to the 1869 black national convention in Baltimore. He worked with his father and J. Sella Martin to establish the *New National Era* in 1870. Although he initially managed the paper's printing office, he eventually became one of its editors. Later in the decade, he was appointed a deputy U.S. marshal and served under his father in the district.

Douglass established himself in the real estate business in the early 1890s. He remained a forceful voice for black labor and civil rights issues throughout the remainder of his life. In later years, he criticized American colonial policy in the Philippines, asserting that it sought "the extension of race hate and cruelty, barbarous lynching and gross injustice" to the dark-skinned peoples of the Orient. McFeely, *Frederick Douglass*, 81, 222–26, 234–36, 247–49, 258, 271, 313–14, 372; Blackett, *Beating against the Barriers*, 255, 258, 276; Benjamin Quarles, *Frederick Douglass* (Washington, D.C., 1948), 205, 226, 281; *WAA*, 7 January 1860, 2 May, 15 December 1863; *Lib*, 11 July 1862 [14:0390]; *DM*, September 1862 [14:0470]; Eugene H. Berwanger, "Reconstruction on the Frontier: The Equal Rights Struggle in Colorado, 1865–67," *PHR* 44:325–27 (August 1975); Foner and Walker, *Black National and State Conventions*, 349, 354, 391, 394–95; *NEW*, 20 January, 7 April 1870; Willard B. Gatewood, *Black Americans and the White Man's Burden* (Urbana, Ill., 1975), 211–12; *AlexM*, 15 November 1908.

8. Frederick Johnson (1838–?) was a black hairdresser in Boston before the Civil War. He enlisted in March 1863, becoming a sergeant and clerk of Company C in the Fifty-fourth Massachusetts Regiment. A black women's organization in Boston regularly sent him copies of the *Weekly Anglo-African*, which he distributed to his fellow soldiers. In August 1865, Johnson was mustered out of service with the regiment. Emilio, *History of the Fifty-Fourth Regiment*, 351; *WAA*, 9 May 1863, 11 February 1865; *Boston City Directory*, 1851, 1857.

9. George L. Stearns.

10. Stephens refers to Leonard A. Grimes and his Twelfth Baptist Church.

11. Jonathan Clarkson Gibbs (ca. 1827–1874), a leading Presbyterian clergyman and Reconstruction politician, was the brother of black abolitionist Mifflin

W. Gibbs. Although born into Philadelphia's black elite, he learned carpentry as a youth and followed that trade until adulthood. After studying at Dartmouth College and Princeton Theological Seminary, he was ordained a Presbyterian pastor. From 1854 to 1859, Gibbs served the Liberty Street Presbyterian Church in Troy, New York, often with the support of the American Home Missionary Society. He was involved in the campaign to expand black suffrage in New York state during this time. After accepting a call to Philadelphia's First African Presbyterian Church in 1859, he became a key figure in the local underground railroad and contributed articles to the *Anglo-African Magazine*. During the Civil War, Gibbs urged black enlistment in the Union army, joined freedmen's relief efforts as a member of the Pennsylvania Social, Civil, and Statistical Association, took part in the campaign to end segregated streetcars in the city, and served as a vice-president of the Pennsylvania State Equal Rights League. An active participant in the black convention movement throughout the 1850s, he represented Philadelphia at the 1864 black national convention in Syracuse.

Gibbs went to Wilmington, North Carolina, in April 1865 to do missionary work among the freedmen. He established and directed a black school and took charge of the local Second Presbyterian Church. Troubled by the racism and paternalism he witnessed from northern white teachers, he wrote concerned letters to Presbyterian officials in the North. Gibbs worked with the freedmen in the Carolinas until 1867, when he was transferred to Florida, where he entered politics, believing that there was an "obvious necessity for ability in secular" as well as religious matters. As a delegate to Florida's 1868 constitutional convention, he so impressed Republican leaders that they appointed him secretary of state, a position he held until 1873, often serving as acting governor during the governor's absences from Tallahassee. Later, as state superintendent of public instruction (1873–74), he oversaw the establishment and rapid expansion of an orderly system of public schools in Florida. Despite white opposition, he enlarged opportunities for black education, pushed for integrated schools, and secured the adoption of uniform textbooks and a standardized curriculum regardless of race. Death threats and harassment from the Ku Klux Klan became commonplace for Gibbs, who slept armed in the attic of his house each night. Gibbs died on 14 August 1874 in the midst of a spirited campaign for the Republican nomination to Congress. Although apoplexy was the official cause of death, mystery surrounds his demise. *DANB*, 257–58; Joe M. Richardson, "Jonathan C. Gibbs: Florida's Only Negro Cabinet Member," *FHQ* 42:363–68 (April 1984); Liberty Street Presbyterian Church Session Minutes, 20 May 1854, PPP [8:0788]; *FDP*, 14 September 1855 [9:0826–27]; *Lib*, 1 October 1858 [11:0379]; *WAA*, 23 July, 10 September 1859, 25 February 1860 [11:0869, 12:0510]; *CR*, 5 April 1862, 14 January, 6 May, 25 November 1865 [14:0212, 15:0671, 0874–75, 16:0468]; *NASS*, 17 December 1864 [15:0616].

12. Stephens apparently misidentified the two white officers who joined the Fifty-fourth Massachusetts Regiment. He probably refers to William L. Whitney, Jr., of the Forty-fourth Massachusetts and Daniel G. Spear of the Twenty-fourth Massachusetts, who became officers in the Fifty-fourth, along with four other whites, after the July 1863 assault on Fort Wagner. Although black recruits were accepted into the Union army in 1863, military leaders refused to promote black veterans and continued to place white officers in charge of black regiments. Black

soldiers such as Stephens believed in their capacity to lead and pressured white officials to commission them. But even with the help of sympathetic regimental commanders and such politicians as Vice-President Hannibal Hamlin, Henry Wilson, and James A. Garfield, qualified blacks made painfully slow progress. Of the one hundred blacks commissioned by the end of 1865, nearly two-thirds were chaplains, surgeons, or members of the Louisiana Native Guard. Only Lieutenant Stephen A. Swails of the Fifty-fourth Massachusetts Regiment received a regular commission during the war; two other members of the unit, Peter Vogelsang, Jr., and Frank M. Welch, obtained promotions several months after Appomattox. The highest-ranking black officer, Major Martin R. Delany, never saw active field service. Stephens received a commission in July 1865, but it was denied by the War Department. Emilio, *History of the Fifty-Fourth Regiment*, 335–38; Berlin et al., *Freedom*, 2:303–11.

13. Colonel Milton S. Littlefield (1832–1899), an Illinois lawyer, served in the Fourteenth Illinois Regiment during the first two years of the Civil War. In April 1863, he was given charge of the Fourth South Carolina Volunteers (later the Twenty-first U.S. Colored Troops). Following the ill-fated attack on Fort Wagner, he was temporarily assigned to command the Fifty-fourth Massachusetts, provoking considerable criticism within the regiment. In early 1864, the Fifty-fourth again served under his command after the battle of Olustee, Florida. Littlefield later served as superintendent of black recruitment in the Department of the South and was promoted to brigadier general before the end of the war. *CWD*, 485; Emilio, *History of the Fifty-Fourth Regiment*, 107, 176; Berlin et al., *Freedom*, 2:394–95.

14. Major General Quincy A. Gillmore (1825–1888), a West Point graduate and civil engineer, was given command of the Department of the South in July 1863. He planned and coordinated the siege of Charleston and ordered the failed attack on Fort Wagner. In May 1864, he was reassigned to the Army of the James. Injuries sustained in the defense of Washington, D.C., that July kept him out of action for the remainder of the war. Gillmore remained in the U.S. Army Corps of Engineers until his death. *HTECW*, 310–11.

49.
First Annual Report of
the Contraband Relief Association
Presented at the Fifteenth Street Presbyterian Church
Washington, D.C.
9 August 1863

Black women labored for more than three decades to support the
American antislavery movement. They organized fund-raising projects
to subsidize abolitionist journals, to finance lecturers in the field, and to
aid fugitive slaves at stations along the underground railroad. During
the Civil War, black women in communities across the North and in
Canada West redirected their fund-raising efforts to meet the needs of
black soldiers and newly freed slaves in the South. One principal organization, the Contraband Relief Association of Washington, D.C., assisted
slaves who escaped to the Union lines. It was founded in August 1862
by forty local black women, including Elizabeth Keckley, a personal servant to Mary Todd Lincoln. Under Keckley's guidance, the organization
solicited supplies from dozens of black churches and women's organizations from Baltimore to Boston, then distributed them to the freedmen.
The CRA celebrated its first anniversary on 9 August 1863 with a
crowded public gathering at the Fifteenth Street Presbyterian Church.
After opening remarks, Keckley read the association's annual report,
which suggests the extensive relief network developed by Washington's
black women. Ripley et al., *Black Abolitionist Papers*, 2:510–11n,
3:62, 201–4; Sterling, *We Are Your Sisters*, 245–50; Elizabeth Keckley, *Behind the Scenes: Thirty Years a Slave and Four Years in the White
House* (1868; reprint, New York, N.Y., 1968), 112–16; CR, 22 August 1863.

FIRST ANNUAL REPORT OF THE CONTRABAND
RELIEF ASSOCIATION

This Association had its origin in sympathy with destitute and suffering freedmen. One year has passed away since the ladies of Washington,
being deeply impressed with their deplorable condition, which was made
known to us by their appeals to our sympathies, at the suggestion of our
President, met at the house of a friend on the evening of the 9th of August, 1862, to devise some plan to ameliorate their condition. It was then
agreed to form themselves into an association. Officers were elected, consisting of a president, two vice presidents, two secretaries, a treasurer, a
board of directors, and a visiting committee.[1]

10. Elizabeth Keckley
From Elizabeth Keckley, *Behind the Scenes* (New York, 1868)

The address of the constitution adopted, briefly sets forth its objects in the following words:

As the fluctuations incident to human life subject all to changes in their conditions, so the present state of affairs existing in this country, having caused many of the hitherto oppressed people of a portion of God's race to be cast among us in a most deplorable condition, our hearts have been made to sympathize with them, and we have pledged ourselves to do all we can to alleviate their sufferings. We propose to visit them, to inquire into their wants, and relieve them as far as we are able, to advise with and counsel them, feeling it to be our duty to assist them toward a higher plane of civilization.

We meet on this, the anniversary of our Association, to lay before those who have kindly sustained us in our labour of love and mercy, the manner in which we have disposed of the various contributions placed in our hands, adding that we have not by any extraordinary method solicited donations, yet every appeal made by us to a generous and humane public has been responded to. We have, also, by our own exertions greatly added to our treasury, and we are happy to say that every effort made by us to obtain funds to alleviate in any way the distresses of our afflicted brethren has been crowned with success, and a widely-extended sympathy has been manifested toward us by our friends at home and abroad, resulting in donations of money and clothing from the following quarters:

From Freedmen's Relief Association of District of Columbia, $5; Baptist Church of Boston, $24; Fugitive Aid Society of Boston, $25; Presbyterian Church, Brooklyn, $24; Waiters of Metropolitan Hotel, New York, $23; Young Misses of Baltimore, $23; Union Progressive Association of Boston, $65; Mrs. President Lincoln, $200; Concerts given by the Association in Presbyterian Church, $249; Festivals given, $108.64; monthly contributions from members and individual donations, $66. Total, $885.64.

Of this amount we have expended for clothing, fuel, freight on donations of clothing received from the North, for bedclothes, nourishment for the sick, &c., $663; leaving a balance of $172.

In addition to the clothing purchased by us, we have received from friends at the North, and from individuals, the following:

Received of Mrs. President Lincoln, 15 boxes of clothing and $10 worth of groceries; Fugitive Aid Society of Boston, 13 barrels of clothing; Rev. Mr. Grimes' church, of Boston, 12 barrels of clothing; Ladies' Relief Association of Boston, 9 barrels and one box of clothing; Israel Church, of Washington, 2 boxes of clothing; Mr. Seedham, of Washington, 1 box of goods; Mr. Beman, of New Haven, 6 barrels of clothing; Mr. J. Bowers, of Philadelphia, 1 box of clothing; American Freedman's Society, of New York, 1 barrel of clothing, besides very many articles from individuals of this city,[2] all of which have been faithfully distributed by the visiting committee, Mrs. Slade, President, who has been untiring in her efforts to do her utmost for the welfare of this people, and who has rendered to the Association most faithful and efficient service.[3] We have not accomplished as much during the last year as we had desired, yet there is satisfaction in knowing that, as we have fed the hungry, clothed the naked, and ministered to the wants of the suffering, we have been instrumental in doing some good.

Thus far our work, owing to our limited means, has been chiefly relieving their more immediate wants, and which, of course, claimed our first attention. Next year we hope to accomplish much more, and trust that our friends at home and abroad, who have so generously reposed confidence in us and in our plans during the past year, will continue to assist us, thus enabling us to carry on the good work in which we are engaged, and aid us in extending the field of our labours for the benefit of all who shall come within our reach.

Christian Recorder (Philadelphia, Pa.), 22 August 1863.

1. On 9 August 1862, Elizabeth Keckley and thirty-nine other black women of Washington, D.C., met at the home of Jane Le Count Cook, the widow of prominent Presbyterian clergyman John F. Cook, to form the Contraband Relief Association. Keckley was named president, Annie E. Washington and Mary L. Cook became secretaries, and Louisa Slade was chosen to head the visiting committee. Keckley, a personal servant to Mary Todd Lincoln, developed the idea for the association after viewing a fund-raising festival for wounded white soldiers and determining that "well-to-do colored people [could] go to work to do something for the benefit of the suffering blacks." In September 1862, Keckley undertook a tour to interest northern blacks in the CRA's work. The association became a conduit for black relief efforts, receiving money and supplies donated by black communities in the border states and the North, then providing aid to contraband camps and freedmen's hospitals in Washington and northern Virginia. In early 1864, the CRA also began assisting needy families of soldiers in black regiments. That July it changed its name to the Ladies' Freedmen and Soldiers' Relief Association to reflect its expanded role. *CR*, 1 November 1862; Keckley, *Behind the Scenes*, 111–16; *WAA*, 24 January, 4 April 1863, 9 January, 30 July 1864.

2. Dozens of black churches, relief organizations, and individuals collected money, food, and clothing for the Contraband Relief Association. Among the most active congregations were Rev. Leonard A. Grimes's Twelfth Baptist Church in Boston, the Israel African Methodist Episcopal Church of Washington, D.C., and the Siloam Presbyterian Church of Brooklyn. Both Israel AME and Washington's Fifteenth Street Presbyterian Church allowed the association to use their sanctuaries for fund-raising concerts. The CRA organized several auxiliaries, including Young Ladies' Contraband Relief Associations in Baltimore and Wash-

ington, and two branches in Boston—the Fugitive Aid Society headed by Sarah Martin, the wife of black abolitionist J. Sella Martin, and the Colored Ladies' Relief Association, headed by Octavia Grimes, the wife of Leonard A. Grimes. It worked closely with unaffiliated organizations such as the National Freedmen's Relief Association of Washington, the Brooklyn-based American Freedmen's Friend Society, and the Union Progressive Association of Boston. G. F. Needham of Washington, Rev. Amos G. Beman of New Haven, and John C. Bowers of Philadelphia also collected goods for the CRA. When Elizabeth Keckley visited New York City on a fund-raising tour in September 1862, she was given a donation by chief steward Robert Thompson, who had solicited contributions from the black waiters at the city's Metropolitan Hotel. The CRA received regular subsidies from President Abraham and Mary Todd Lincoln. Keckley, *Behind the Scenes*, 114–15; *WAA*, 3, 10, 17, 24, 31 January, 4 April 1863.

3. Louisa Slade, the wife of black Washington businessman William Slade, headed the visiting committee of the Contraband Relief Association. From 1862 through 1865, she distributed food, fuel, and clothing to needy freedmen in the District of Columbia and northern Virginia. Although this impaired her health, she undertook a lengthy fund-raising tour of the North in late 1865. *WAA*, 10 January, 25 October 1863, 19 August, 3 September 1865.

50.
Report by the Anti-Slavery Committee of the Genesee Conference of the African Methodist Episcopal Zion Church Presented at Binghamton, New York
5 September 1863

The Civil War opened a "grand field for missionary labor" in the South. Many northern clergymen and reformers believed that providing Christian education to some four million freed slaves was an essential element of Reconstruction. Much of the responsibility for this missionary venture fell to the major black denominations—the Baptist, African Methodist Episcopal, and African Methodist Episcopal Zion. Working independently or in concert with the American Missionary Association, these bodies sent ministers and lay workers South to establish schools and churches. The new opportunities that the war presented to black churches were discussed at the AMEZ's Genesee Conference, which convened in Binghamton, New York, during 5–13 September 1863. The session attracted eighteen delegates from western New York and northeastern Pennsylvania. An antislavery committee headed by Rev. George Bosley and Rev. Jermain Wesley Loguen drafted a report portraying the conflict as a "holy war"—a "righteous visitation" of God's retributive justice. Invoking the spirit of Christian Reconstruction, it called on black church members to become "willing instruments" of God and prepare themselves to preach and teach among the freedmen. Washington, *Frustrated Fellowship*, 49–81; Walker, *Rock in a Weary Land*, 46–81; John J. Moore, *History of the A.M.E.Z. Church in America* (York, Pa., 1884), 158; J. W. Hood, *One Hundred Years of the African Methodist Episcopal Zion Church* (New York, N.Y., 1895), 276; Richardson, *Christian Reconstruction*, 3–14, 143–59.

ANTI-SLAVERY REPORT

Whereas, In one short year so unlooked for, and far beyond human agency, have been the results of this war. That in spite of the bones that whiten beneath Southern skies, or the tides made crimson by the life-blood fresh from thousands of America's noblest sons, we feel to silently rejoice in the fullness of our gratitude to him, "Who holdeth the destinies of nations in the hollow of His hand."

And whereas, Notwithstanding the dishonesty, and even treachery, which have characterized some contractors in this war, yet the Omnipotent arm of a justly retributive God is uplifted against the iniquity in high and low places; and he is educating the American nation to know truly the law of liberty that they so long have professed.

Resolved, That we may rightly regard this as a holy war, because it is God's war; for it is really a righteous visitation of the provoked wrath of Him who has said, "I will remember their iniquities against them," [1] and who has promised that Ethiopia should stretch forth her hands, as we believe, without the galling yoke of slavery, but free to act and worship God according to the dictates of an enlightened conscience.

Resolved, That in the passing history of this country, its progress is making strides unparalleled in rapidity, for, whereas one year ago the President's proclamation had not been issued, but by the enforcement of the same, not only two million of our brethren have been made free, but are engaged in national services as United States soldiers.

Resolved, That our colored troops, through the wisdom of the ruler of battles, have proved themselves heroes, not only at Port Hudson, Milliken's Bend, Fort Wagner and the department of the Cumberland,[2] but every time they have had an engagement with the enemy, thereby refuting the charge of those who have said, in the face of evidences to the contrary, that colored men were unfit to be soldiers or freemen.

Resolved, That we give those brave soldiers who have enlisted in our respective charges, not only our heartfelt prayers, but whenever opportunity is offered, our substantial remembrance to their needy families who may be in our midst.

Resolved, That we give our united influence in sustaining the President and government in bringing about justice to our long outraged and neglected people, at all times giving God the glory for bringing them to see the expediency of such an equitable movement.

Resolved, That it is no longer our duty simply to stand still and see the salvation of the Lord, but we must be willing instruments in bringing about the ultimate glory of the end. Therefore we must hold ourselves in readiness to go to any of the many freed portions of the South at the first call to preach the Gospel to the poor, and to educate our war-freed brethren to respectable citizenship, and a manhood perfect in the beauty of holiness.

GEORGE BOSLEY, Chairman[3]
J. W. LOGUEN, Secretary

Weekly Anglo-African (New York, N.Y.), 7 November 1863.

1. The report paraphrases a statement repeated in Jeremiah 14:10, Ezekiel 21:23, and Hosea 8:13 and 9:9.
2. The Department of the Cumberland was organized in October 1862 and headquartered in Nashville, Tennessee, under the command of Major General William S. Rosecrans. Although the department's first black combat regiment was not mustered in until October 1863, Rosecrans and military governor Andrew Johnson had earlier impressed blacks into work gangs to help construct the city's

fortifications. *HTECW*, 196; Berlin et al., *Freedom*, 2:122–23; Cornish, *Sable Arm*, 237.

3. George Bosley, an African Methodist Episcopal Zion clergyman, was ordained in the 1840s. Bosley's ministerial career spanned five decades and included several years as an itinerant in western New York state and pastorates in the AMEZ's Baltimore, Allegheny, and Philadelphia conferences. He served a congregation in Schoharie, New York, at the time of the 1863 Genesee Conference. Moore, *History of the A.M.E.Z.*, 232, 273, 293; Hood, *One Hundred Years*, 226; *WAA*, 24 October 1863.

51.
Editorial by Robert Hamilton
26 September 1863

The Civil War offered black abolitionists a new occasion to secure old objectives. With fresh enthusiasm and revived hope, they carried their antebellum goals into the war years. Although many white abolitionists concluded that with the coming of emancipation their work was finished, black leaders understood that only the context of the struggle had changed. Enfranchisement, civil and political equality, and economic opportunity remained key elements of the black abolitionist agenda. As early as 1862, black leaders began discussing the terms of freedom, repudiating schemes for gradual or compensated emancipation and demanding equal rights for the slaves. Robert Hamilton criticized limited views of emancipation in a 26 September 1863 editorial in the *Weekly Anglo-African*. He warned readers that freedom without the vote was merely "a partial emancipation unworthy of the name." Arguing that white abolitionists were unprepared for the new tasks that the end of slavery had brought, he urged blacks to organize in pursuit of their full rights as American citizens. Failure to do so, he cautioned, would doom the race to a long and incomplete process of emancipation—a "mockery of freedom." Ripley et al., *Black Abolitionist Papers*, 3:63–66; *Lib*, 15 August 1862 [14:0441].

THE PERILS BY THE WAY

The first and greatest difficulty in the way of emancipation is that there are no settled principles, no adequate organization, arranged to compass it. The very discussions on the matter are desultory and do not seem to reach the pith of the question. By that strange pertinacity with which old ideas cling to the public mind, it is what to do with the whites, in the reconstruction of the rebel States, that principally occupies the attention of writers, the disposition of their black fellow-citizens seeming a matter of secondary, if of any, importance.

It would naturally be supposed that the Abolitionists, pure and simple, were the proper parties to lay out, at least in principles, the method of emancipation and affranchisement, for we include both these ideas in the kind of emancipation now under discussion, emancipation without affranchisement being a partial emancipation unworthy of the name. But for this thing the Abolitionists are not prepared, and it is no blame to them that are not. Their mission was aggressive, destructive, mighty to tear down the strongholds of slavery and overwhelm its abettors with the debris of their ruined structures. That was a special mission, requiring its especial gifts of reckless daring and fiery energy such as has illustrated their pathway during the last generation of men. A very different mission, requiring also peculiar gifts, gifts of construction, tempered with calm thought, and sweetened with a deep love of all mankind, and a profound faith in humanity, is required to consummate emancipation at the South. It was, doubtless, a profound view of these truths which led J. M. McKim of Philadelphia to offer his resignation of office in the Abolition organization—his work as such *was done*.[1] President Lincoln would seem to hold the same views, in appointing distinguished humanitarians rather than distinguished Abolitionists to form a commission to report well-known facts in regard to modern emancipation.[2]

If it be true then that emancipation is perilled for the want of settled principles and adequate organizations to bring it about, this peril may be easily overcome. Organizations should be immediately formed, and the principles widely and continuously published to enlighten and convince the public mind. The duty of such organizations falls especially upon the free blacks (so called) of the free States; they know more on these subjects than all the world besides. To show how little the ablest and most philanthropic white men know on this matter, we need only quote the reiterated opinion of Horace Greeley, that "by enlisting in the army *now*, black men can save their race in this country, and the opportunity is rapidly passing away," etc., etc.[3] Why, dear old *Tribune*! we enlisted freely, fought determinedly, not to say heroically, in '76 and '12, and you gave us chains and slavery, fugitive slave laws, and would have dehumanized us entirely if God had let you! There are our Irish brethren, have they not crimsoned every British battlefield with their blood, and have they not for their reward the scornful slur they "are aliens in blood, aliens in religion?" Nay, further, did not New York and Connecticut and Pennsylvania and Virginia and North Carolina grant citizenship to the extent of voting at the polls to black men for their soldierly deeds in the Revolutionary war, and then gradually took back the well-earned right?[4] And why? Because of the second great peril in the way of emancipation today; to wit:

Gradual Emancipation. It cannot be expected that the condition which shall be fixed on the freedmen in the rebel States will be in advance of the general public sentiment of the land. And the highest point which such sentiment has attained is to grant gradual emancipation; by gradual emancipation, we do not mean the farcical programme recently gone through with in Missouri;[5] we mean the process which the blacks have been undergoing in the so-called free States for the last fifty years. Until this war's necessities knocked the last vestige of prejudice—the military caste—from the usages of old Massachusetts, God bless her! there was not a free black man in all these United States. With the name, and some of the privileges of freemen, we have been, and are still undergoing, the oscillating process of gradual emancipation—today decked with laurels for the well-won victory, and tomorrow, hung at the lamppost because we are not white. Today we are "citizens of the United States," with Secretary Seward who needs us to conquer back the South—tomorrow, when Jeff. Davis *et genus omne*[6] accept Mr. Seward's cordial invitation to return to their vacant seats in Congress, what will we be, with that serene, bland, euphuistic Secretary Seward?[7] Let us hear what a foreign black gentleman says of this gradual emancipation, as partially experienced by him in the noble State of New York ten years ago:

> You perhaps have read the narratives of African (African American) sufferings, but painfully intense as they are, they are only the outside—they are only the visible. There are a thousand little evils which can never be expressed. There is a sorrow of the heart, with which the stranger cannot intermeddle. There are secret agonies known only to God, which are far more acute than any external tortures. Oh! it is not the smiting of the back, until the earth is crimsoned with streams of blood; it is not the amputation of the limbs; it is not even the killing of the body; it is not these that are the keenest sufferings that a people can undergo. Oh! no; these affect only the outward man, and may leave untouched the majestic mind. But those inflictions which tend to contract and destroy the mind, those cruelties which benumb the sensibilities of the soul, these influences which chill and arrest the currency of the heart's affections—these are the awful instruments of suffering and degredation, and these have been made to operate upon the Afric-American.— *Rev. Edward Blyden in "Africa's Offering."*[8]

Now we affirm that the highest grade of emancipation which the public mind assigns to the slaves in the rebel States, is this gradual emancipation, such as they see *enjoyed* by the free black of the free States, and which they think quite good enough for the colored man. Is there a man among us who is not shocked at the possibility of our brethren being obliged to pass through this process of gradual emancipation? this mockery of freedom? How then is this great peril of gradual emancipation to be overcome? By forming organizations and spreading the doctrines of IMMEDIATE EMANCIPATION with affranchisement. We who know and have felt the pain, the penalties, the soul-cutting degradations of gradual emancipation; we who have for years yearned for and struggled for the rights and privileges of free citizens, are of all men the first called upon to form these organizations and to preach these doctrines. It is here that we can serve our people and save our country; here that the Lord has mercifully appointed us to labor; here that we can labor with the greatest hope of success. Immediate emancipation is the New Evangel which alone can save our land and its glorious institutions; one period, one lustrum of our national history has gone down in darkness and fire and blood; if we would give a different and more glorious character to the new period on which we are about entering, then we must save the nation from the curse of gradual emancipation, or any other experiment for the indefinite perpetuation of slavery. "All free, or all slave," said Abraham Lincoln.[9] Free now, liberty now, liberty henceforth, liberty forever! Could there be, will there be in all time a more glorious cause to struggle for? Would that we could convey to others a portion of what we feel on this subject; would that we could touch the hearts and the lips of our young men with the holy flame which this theme inspires, for this is OUR WORK, brethren! There is no use in our standing by marvelling at the doings of Providence, rejoicing over the noble sayings of our noble President, or expecting that emancipation is coming somehow or other—Providence has done all it can do, Abraham Lincoln has done much more than we ever dreamed he would do—it is our turn now to wheel into the ranks and shout the glad chorus of Immediate and Universal Emancipation!

Weekly Anglo-African (New York, N.Y.), 26 September 1863.

1. J. Miller McKim resigned as corresponding secretary of the Pennsylvania Anti-Slavery Society in May 1862. He had concluded that slavery would soon be abolished and that many of the society's functions were no longer needed. *Lib*, 9 May 1862.

2. Hamilton refers to the establishment of the American Freedmen's Inquiry Commission. After intensive lobbying by Massachusetts abolitionists, the War Department created the commission in March 1863 and instructed it to investigate the condition of the freedmen "and to report what measures will best contribute to their protection and improvement, so that they may defend and support themselves." The members of the commission—Robert Dale Owen, Samuel Gridley Howe, and Colonel James McKaye—were philanthropists and anti-slavery advocates, but not of the radical sort that Hamilton sought. The findings and recommendations in their reports expanded opportunities for black military service, sparked the creation of the Freedmen's Bureau, and laid the foundation for Radical Reconstruction. John G. Sproat, "Blueprint for Radical Reconstruction," *JSH* 23:33–41 (February 1957).

3. Horace Greeley, the editor of the *New York Tribune*, was an early supporter of black enlistment. In July 1862, he urged the federal government to recruit 100,000 former bondsmen for the Union army. On 19 August, he published his famous "Prayer of Twenty Millions," which advised President Abraham Lincoln to abolish slavery and enlist black troops. In May 1863, Greeley joined a committee of thirteen prominent New Yorkers in pressing the Lincoln administration to raise black regiments in the state. Allan Nevins, *The War for the Union*, 4 vols. (New York, N.Y., 1960–71), 2:301n; Quarles, *Negro in the Civil War*, 30, 34, 159, 188.

4. Few of the state constitutions adopted in the wake of the American Revolution expressly restricted suffrage on the basis of race. But between 1807 and 1838, six states—New Jersey, Maryland, Connecticut, Tennessee, North Carolina, and Pennsylvania—disfranchised black voters. In 1821 New York enacted a $250 property requirement for black suffrage. Despite Hamilton's assertion, free

blacks were not allowed to vote in Virginia prior to the Fifteenth Amendment (1870). John Hope Franklin and Alfred A. Moss, Jr., *From Slavery to Freedom: A History of Negro Americans*, 6th ed. (New York, N.Y., 1988), 141; Litwack, *North of Slavery*, 74–92.

5. On 1 July 1863, Missouri's Unionist state convention approved a gradual emancipation ordinance. The measure would not take effect until 1870 and stipulated that "all persons emancipated by this ordinance shall remain under . . . the authority of their late owners . . . as servants" until 1876. Slaves older than forty in 1870 were exempted and would remain slaves for life. Slaves younger than twelve would remain in bondage until twenty-three years of age. Although the ordinance was a political victory for slaveholding loyalists, it had little meaning in a state disrupted by political chaos, Union military occupation, and guerrilla warfare. Berlin et al., *Freedom*, 1(1):405–6.

6. *Et hoc genus omne* is a Latin phrase meaning "and all others of the kind."

7. Hamilton refers to Secretary of State William H. Seward's conciliatory attitude toward the South. Seward hoped for a harmonious reconciliation of the warring sections, conducted peace negotiations with Confederate officials, and opposed Radical Republican calls for a punishing Reconstruction. He championed Lincoln's plan to fully restore the seceded states when 10 percent of their electorate took an oath of allegiance to the federal government, leaving the southern white elite in positions of political authority, including the U.S. Congress. Nevins, *War for the Union*, 3:457, 461–65; Van Deusen, *William Henry Seward*, 378–88.

8. Hamilton excerpts a passage from "Hope for Africa: A Discourse," an essay in *Liberia's Offering: Being Addresses, Sermons, etc.* (1862) by Edward Wilmot Blyden. It was originally delivered as a lecture on 21 July 1861 at the Seventh Avenue Presbyterian Church in New York City. Blyden (1832–1912), who was born in the West Indies, settled in Liberia in 1851 and became a leading spokesman for African colonization. His multifaceted career included work as a Presbyterian clergyman, the editor of the *Liberia Herald*, and a president of Liberia College. He also held several key political posts in Liberia, including secretary of state, minister of the interior, and ambassador to Britain. After an unsuccessful campaign for the Liberian presidency (1885), he moved to Sierra Leone to become director of Islamic education. His intellectual contributions are summed up in two influential books—*Christianity, Islam, and the Negro Race* (1887), which demonstrated the appeal of Islam for African blacks, and *African Customs* (1908), an early sociological analysis of West African society. Lynch, *Edward Wilmot Blyden*.

9. Hamilton paraphrases a line from Abraham Lincoln's famous "House Divided" speech, which was delivered on 16 June 1858 at the close of a Republican state convention in Springfield, Illinois. Lincoln asserted that "this government cannot endure, permanently half slave and half free." Abraham Lincoln, *Speeches and Writings, 1832–1858*, ed. Don E. Fehrenbacher (New York, N.Y., 1989), 426.

52.
Martin R. Delany to Edwin M. Stanton
15 December 1863

Black abolitionists played a central role in the recruitment of black troops. Frederick Douglass, William Wells Brown, John Mercer Langston, Henry Highland Garnet, Mary Ann Shadd Cary, and other prominent blacks traveled throughout the North and Canada West, addressing mass rallies to convince blacks that the war was now their fight. They directed enlistees to regiments with sympathetic white officers, warned blacks of fraudulent enlistment schemes, and served as liaisons between government officials and recruits. Martin R. Delany was one of the most successful black recruiters. In early 1863, he generated enlistments for the Fifty-fourth Massachusetts Regiment. Later that year, as the first black to receive a state recruiting contract, he supervised a network of black agents that helped fill other regiments in Massachusetts, Ohio, Rhode Island, and Connecticut. On 15 December 1863, Delany wrote to Secretary of War Edwin M. Stanton requesting federal authority to enlist black soldiers in Union-occupied areas of the South. He maintained that men who had the respect of the black community, such as himself and John Jones, would prove the "most effective means of obtaining Black Troops." Stanton failed to respond to Delany's request. But two years later, at President Abraham Lincoln's insistence, Delany was commissioned a major and sent to South Carolina to enroll volunteers among the freedmen. *WAA*, 7 March, 4 April 1863; Ripley et al., *Black Abolitionist Papers*, 2:520–22, 3:59–60; McPherson, *Negro's Civil War*, 173; Ullman, *Martin R. Delany*, 282–90, 294–313.

> Box 764, P.O.
> 172 Clark St[reet]
> Chicago, Ill[inois]
> Dec[ember] 15th, 1863

Sir:

The Subject and policy of Black Troops have become of much intrest in our Country, and the effective means and method of raising them, is a matter of much importance.

In consideration of this Sir, I embrace the earliest opportunity of asking the privilege of calling the attention of your Department to the fact, that as a policy in perfect harmony with the course of the President and your own enlightened views,[1] that the Agency of intelligent competent black men adapted to the work must be the most effective means of obtaining Black Troops; because knowing and being of that people as a race, they can command such influence as is required to accomplish the object.

I have been successfully engaged as a Recruiting Agent of Black Troops, first as a Recruiting Agent for Massachusetts 54th Regt. and from the commencement as the Managing Agent in the West and South-West for Rhode Island Heavy Artillery,[2] which is now nearly full; and now have the Contract from the State Authorities of Connecticut, for the entire West and South-West, in raising Colored Troops to fill her quota.[3]

During these engagements, I have had associated with me, Mr. John Jones,[4] a very respectable and responsible business colored man of this city, and we have associated ourselves permanently together, in an Agency for raising Black Troops for all parts of the Country.

We are able sir, to command all of the effective black men as Agents in the United States, and in the event of an order from your Department giving us the Authority to recruit Colored Troops in any of the Southern or seceded states, we will be ready and able to raise a Regiment, or Brigade if required, in a shorter time than can be otherwise effected.

With the belief sir, that this is one of the measures in which the claims of the Black Man may be officially recognised, without seemingly infringing upon those of other citizens, I confidently ask sir, that this humble request, may engage your early notice.

All satisfactory References will be given by both of us.

I have the honor to be sir, Your most obt. Very humble servt.,

M. R. Delany

M. M. Wagoner, Secry.[5]

Letters Received, RG 94, Adjutant General's Office, U.S. Colored Troops, National Archives, Washington, D.C. Published by permission.

1. As early as 1862, Secretary of War Edwin M. Stanton openly advocated the recruitment of black troops for the Union army. Shortly before Delany wrote this letter, Stanton announced that, after being tested in battle, "the slave has proved his manhood, and his capacity as an infantry soldier." Cornish, *Sable Arm*, 31–33, 132.

2. Delany helped fill the Fourteenth Rhode Island Heavy Artillery Regiment, which was organized in August 1863. The unit served in Texas, saw limited action in Louisiana, and performed garrison duty at New Orleans. For a brief time, the members of the Fourteenth published a newspaper called the *Black Warrior*. The regiment's designation was later changed to the Eighth and then to the Eleventh U.S. Colored Heavy Artillery. It was mustered out of service in October 1865. Dyer, *Compendium*, 3:1630; *WAA*, 7 January 1865.

3. Delany contracted to recruit black troops for the Twenty-ninth Connecticut Regiment. The unit was mustered in during March 1864, performed distinguished duty in South Carolina and Texas, and was actively engaged in the 1864–65 Virginia campaigns against Petersburg and Richmond. In April 1865, two companies of the Twenty-ninth were the first Union infantry to enter the fallen Confederate capital. The regiment was discharged in November after suffering 198 deaths due to battle casualties and disease. Ullman, *Martin R. Delany,*

283–87; Isaac J. Hill, *A Sketch of the 29th Regiment of Connecticut Colored Troops* (Baltimore, Md., 1867).

4. John Jones, a black businessman, worked with Delany in 1863 to enlist black troops at their Chicago recruiting office. Jones (1816–1879) was born to a free mulatto mother and a German immigrant in Greene County, North Carolina. As a youth, he was apprenticed to a tailor in Somerville, Tennessee, where he met Mary Ann Richardson, a local free black; they married in 1844 and settled in Alton, Illinois. One year later, they moved to Chicago, drawn by the city's business opportunities and more relaxed application of the state's black laws. Jones opened a small tailoring shop there and turned it into a thriving business.

After arriving in Chicago, Jones joined the antislavery movement. His home was a gathering place for local abolitionists, he frequently hosted visiting lecturers such as Frederick Douglass, and he accompanied Douglass on one speaking tour through the West. Following the passage of the Fugitive Slave Law, he urged Chicagoans to defend fugitives in their midst "at all hazards, even should it be to the shedding of human blood." He organized a black vigilance committee to patrol the streets for slave catchers and persuaded the city's common council to ignore requests for police assistance in recapturing fugitives. Jones's house became the "local headquarters of the underground railroad," and he and his wife sheltered hundreds of runaway slaves in its basement, before forwarding them to safety in Canada West. He attended the 1848 and 1853 black national conventions, headed the Illinois State Council for the Colored People, and participated in Illinois's first two state black conventions, presiding at one and convincing delegates to reject the emigration movement as "fatal to our hopes and aspirations."

Beginning in 1847, Jones devoted much of his energy to the abolition of the state's black laws. He helped organize a repeal effort and petition drive in Illinois's fourth congressional district. In 1864 he published and circulated a pamphlet entitled *The Black Laws of Illinois and a Few Reasons Why They Should be Repealed* at his own expense. About that same time, he formed the Chicago Repeal Association to spearhead a second petition drive, coordinated the campaign, and lobbied against the black laws in the legislature. After the legislature struck down a black exclusion law in 1865, he directed other successful campaigns for equal suffrage and an end to segregated schools in the state. He also helped secure ratification of the Reconstruction amendments in the Illinois legislature.

Jones personally achieved many firsts—he was the first Illinois black to serve on a grand jury (1870), the first to become a notary public (1871), and the first elected to public office (1872). While serving as Cook County commissioner for three years, he established himself as a powerful figure in the local Republican party. Although Jones lost part of his fortune in the famous 1871 Chicago fire, he remained one of the city's most prominent citizens until his death. Ullman, *Martin R. Delany*, 282–88; Charles A. Gliozzo, "John Jones: A Study of a Black Chicagoan," *IHJ* 80:177–88 (Autumn 1987); Charles A. Gliozzo, "John Jones and the Black Convention Movement," *JBS* 3:227–36 (December 1972); *DANB*, 366–67; Robert L. McCaul, *The Black Struggle for Public Schooling in Nineteenth-Century Illinois* (Carbondale, Ill., 1987), 17–19, 22, 41–43, 69, 72, 74, 79–86, 94, 100.

5. Marcellina M. Wagoner, the daughter of black Chicago barber and abolitionist Henry O. Wagoner, served as Delany's secretary in his efforts to recruit black troops for the Union army during 1863–64. By 1870 she had moved to Denver, Colorado, and married black painter Robert L. Moss; together they produced at least one child, Robert, Jr. Although her husband died a few years later, Marcellina Moss continued to reside in Denver well into the 1880s, apparently supporting herself as a seamstress. Martin R. Delany to Mary Ann Shadd Cary, 7 December 1863, Mary Ann Shadd Cary Papers, DHU [15:0108]; U.S. Census, 1870; *Denver City Directory*, 1871–81.

53.
"Rhode Island" to Robert Hamilton
10 January 1864

The Lincoln administration's failure to protect black prisoners of war called into question its commitment to equal treatment for all Union troops. When Confederates threatened to execute or enslave captured black soldiers, black leaders urged the War Department to respond in kind. In July 1863, President Abraham Lincoln ordered that "for every soldier of the United States killed in violation of the laws of war a rebel soldier shall be executed, and for every one enslaved by the enemy or sold into slavery a rebel soldier shall be placed at hard labor." But his policy was never fully implemented, and it failed to substantially affect battlefield conditions. Although the Confederacy softened its official statements, as the war progressed and Southern losses mounted, growing numbers of black soldiers were executed, enslaved, or consigned to harsh military labor. This 10 January 1864 letter from an anonymous black seaman to the *Weekly Anglo-African* sought to awaken the North to the perils faced by black troops. It praised their bravery and advised the federal government to give them the protection they deserved by enforcing its policy of retaliation. Cornish, *Sable Arm*, 168–70; Berlin et al., *Freedom*, 2:567–70, 578–93.

> U.S. GUNBOAT,
> *South Carolina*[1]
> LIGHT HOUSE INLET,
> [South Carolina]
> Jan[uary] 10th, 1864

MR. EDITOR:

Allow me through the columns of your valuable paper to call the attention of the authorities and their representatives to a grave neglect of their duties. It is well known that from the time the first gun was fired at Sumter and the Nation was alarmed, and when the President called for troops, although the services of black men were not included at that time, yet they too responded to the call, and in our Army and Navy they are well represented, although no protection was guaranteed in case they were captured as prisoners of war.

Since the 10th of June, 1862, I have been serving my country in her Navy, and during the whole of that time have been engaged in the blockading duty off Charleston and its vicinity. Early last year, the rebels captured the U.S. Gunboat *Isaac Smith*, engaged in blockading duty here.[2] Among those captured with her were two colored men. I have not yet been able to find out where they belonged, but suffice it to say that they were free men from the North; and to this day it has been impossible to find out or to get information from the rebels what they have done with them.

Again last month, while the U.S. Brig of War *Perry* was engaged in blockading duty at Murrell's Inlet, they had a boat captured. There was a colored man among those captured, belonging to Newburyport, Massachusetts, a free man. Last week Admiral Dahlgren[3] sent an expedition there to capture some Salt Works. It proved unsuccessful, whilst there two contrabands came off to the Flag Ship and reported that the rebels had hung the colored man.[4] They also reported that they had shot down two of their number who were endeavoring to escape. I have heard it expressed by officers high in command here, that it is a shame, a burning shame, that the government does not take some action in this matter. If protection is not guaranteed, if the authorities do not intend taking any notice of these acts committed by these ruffian murderers as they are in every sense of the word, why then they cannot expect us to fight for the flag.

I love this cause and I will never cease lending my efforts, feeble though they are, in maintaining the glorious cause of freedom. I have always intended that if ever it became so that I could face a rebel, I would never give him quarters, and before they take me or rather than surrender, I would blow out my brains.

In this department there are a great many young men from New York and Massachusetts. They have left home, its comforts and pleasures, friends and relatives, to help subdue the rebellion, and can the government be so regardless of them? I trust immediate inquiry will be made in regard to these men, and if the rebels do not give prompt and ample satisfaction, then enforce the Retaliatory Proclamation.

I should not have written you to insert this in your columns were it not for the indignant feeling that is felt by the colored men in the fleet generally. I am happy to inform our people that Admiral Dahlgren is much loved and respected by the colored men in the fleet, and they believe that he uses his best efforts in their behalf. I have it from good authority that an expedition will leave here soon for Savannah. The health of the colored troops on Morris Island is excellent.

RHODE ISLAND

Weekly Anglo-African (New York, N.Y.), 23 January 1864.

1. The iron-hulled *U.S.S. South Carolina* was built in 1860 and saw action with the Gulf and South Atlantic Blockading Squadrons during the Civil War. It was responsible for the capture of some twenty-two Confederate vessels. Paul H. Silverstone, *Warships of the Civil War Navies* (Annapolis, Md., 1989), 80–81.

2. The *U.S.S. Isaac Smith* was attached to the U.S. Navy's South Atlantic Blockading Squadron and performed blockade duty and artillery bombardment

along the South Carolina–Georgia coast. On 30 January 1863, it was disabled by Confederate batteries in the Stono River and captured. Renamed the *C.S.S. Stono*, it was wrecked on a breakwater in Charleston harbor that June while attempting to run the Union blockade. Silverstone, *Warships of the Civil War Navies*, 92, 238.

3. Rear Admiral John A. B. Dahlgren (1809–1870) commanded the U.S. Navy's South Atlantic Blockading Squadron from July 1863 until the end of the Civil War. He commanded the Washington Navy Yard at the outbreak of the war, coordinated the Union effort to blockade Charleston harbor, and established and directed the Navy's ordnance department. He also invented a rifled cannon—the Dahlgren gun—that saw widespread use during the conflict. *HTECW*, 202–3.

4. The *U.S.S. Perry* was attached to the U.S. Navy's South Atlantic Blockading Squadron from November 1863 through the end of the Civil War. In December 1863, a black sailor from the *Perry* was captured while on shore and hung by Confederate troops. Two months later, an expedition sent out by Admiral John A. B. Dahlgren captured the Confederate officer who had ordered the execution. Dahlgren placed the officer in irons and forwarded a request to the Department of the Navy to implement the policy of retaliation in the case. Silverstone, *Warships of the Civil War Navies*, 134; *WAA*, 19 March 1864.

54.
Anonymous Washington, D.C., Correspondent
to Robert Hamilton
17 January 1864

Blacks throughout the nation shared a common vision of racial progress through moral reform, economic independence, and political
enfranchisement. But northern black leaders who went South during
the Civil War often brought a patronizing attitude toward the freedmen that turned their earnest moralizing into unwelcome criticism.
These new arrivals were frequently rebuffed by southern blacks who
wished to retain their distinct folk religion and their local preachers,
viewing them as "bone of their bone, flesh of their flesh." This 17
January 1864 letter by an anonymous Washington, D.C., correspondent of the *Weekly Anglo-African* provides a southern perspective on
northern black attitudes. Commenting on recent speeches by northern
racial spokesmen Charles Lenox Remond, John Mercer Langston, and
Henry Highland Garnet to Washington's black community, it singled
out Remond's remarks as insensitive and condescending. In defending
the modest progress made by southern blacks, the correspondent reminded readers of cultural differences between blacks in the two regions
and called on northern black leaders to leave their stereotypes at home
and to bring to the South "light, example, wisdom, and not so much
fault finding." Foner, *Reconstruction*, 100–102, 113; Walker, *Rock
in a Weary Land*, 64–65, 74–76; Richardson, *Christian Reconstruction*, 143–45; *PA*, 27 February 1864; *WAA*, 30 January, 19 November,
24 December 1864.

Washington, D.C.
Jan[uary] 17, 1864

The great number of strangers now in Washington makes it very
lively. Several of our great men from North, East, and West have been
with us. Among them are Rev. H. H. Garnet, C. L. Remond, and J. M.
Langston, Esq. Each of these gentlemen lectured for us: 1st, Mr. Garnet
before the Ladies' Contraband Relief Association; 2d, Mr. Remond
before Israel Lyceum on Friday evening, Jan. 15, at Union League Rooms
before an audience of an equal number of white and colored persons,
and at the 19th Street Baptist Church. At each of these places, Mr.
Remond's remarks were well received, but we feel sorry to say that
our learned friend showed a degree of unkindness in his remarks at the
close of Mr. Garnet's lecture at the 15th Street Church, which created
some hard feeling on the part of our citizens who were so unfortunate as

to hear him.[1] The remarks which gave offense were in substance as follows:

> I am truly sorry to learn that among your people here there exists such a degree of prejudice one to another. You speak of the white man's prejudice, but you need not expect the white man to be true to you unless you first learn to be true to your own people. I know you do not like for me thus to expose your wrongs in this particular before the white portion of your audience, but a wrong is a wrong, and these wrongs the white men know. And I am also told that if one among you should by his industry or energy rise in position a little above another, he only lives in this degree to gain your prejudice. This indeed is a miserable state of things which should not be. First be true to yourselves then, etc.

These remarks were thought by many to be unkind, addressed as they were to a social Southern people by one coming, as did Mr. Remond, from the cold, reserved, and ceremonious East; whose people have all the while shown this very prejudice to a great degree to us from the South whom chance might have thrown among them, more especially in days gone by. On many occasions our people have been made objects of scorn, and have been set aside as fools and as those "from behind the sun," and on other occasions we have seen demonstrations of this prejudice in the East and North that would startle us here in the hospitable South. Then for this gentleman, who indeed was honored by being called to speak after this great man, Rev. H. H. Garnet, to get up with no more befitting subject than a slanderous falsehood, and making it worse by saying it had been told to him, is beyond endurance. By whom had he been told? By some humbug who no doubt had come here expecting to have people here gather him up, fill his lean pockets, and worship him as a god.

No such uncalled for, out of place remarks were needed by that intelligent audience. It would have been better for that gentleman to have remained silent than to have chilled this audience who had been so friendly and kindly entertained by the Rev. Mr. Garnet. We are a peculiar people—we have our peculiar customs which are very agreeable to us as a people. It is true these customs and ways may not please a Yankee at first sight. So it may be with us when we go in *Yankeedom*. They have their "H-o-w-s," and we have our "Whats." But we should not fall out about this. It may be true that we are not as fast as some of our Northern or Eastern Cities in building up our great institutions for particular classes, but we are laboring day and night to bring all our forsaken people here to the surface at one time. I rather think that more prejudice is shown by our Northern and Eastern brethren than we show one to another. We are slandered in all our efforts put forth for the good of our people. For instance, your people circulated such base reports as that our ladies here, whose characters are unimpeachable, had deprived those poor contrabands of the goods sent to them, and sold the same.[2] What people but a prejudiced one would have circulated such reports? Remond and Smith, who accompanies him,[3] made some few side hits at us here for our slow-coachism in not having free schools, the right of franchise, etc., etc. As a matter of course, we have been free here so long, it is a wonder that we have not got beside ourselves and rebelled against the United States. Men in big meetings, when before smiling anti-slavery audiences, can make use of big words, but bring these men here and put them to work and they will be found wanting.

We are sorry to be called on to speak so plain, but we can't help it. Our remarks may be received unkindly by these gentlemen, but we are a sensitive people, who have been unjustly treated and criticized by persons who think when coming to Washington that they are coming South among a lot of slow ninnyheads. But do not mistake yourselves, gentlemen, though we may seem slow to you—yet we can assure you we are wide awake and filling our places with as much credit as any other people placed in like situations. Do not come among us with your hastily-formed opinions, backed up by hearsay, but bring us light, example, and wisdom, and not so much faultfinding.

We have had already enough of politics and of slavery—of the latter we are nearly tired to death. We read it, we sing it, we pray it, we talk it, we speak it, we lecture it, and the whole United States is in arms against it. You come to tell us it is dead. Well, if that is so, I thank God. Don't bother its carcass. Let us improve the living who have been under slavery. You, who come from your grand school districts and boast of your equal collegiate privileges at the East, do give us some token of your refined and cultivated talents in lectures on Literature, Science, and Art. Don't come anymore riding that old weather-beaten horse, anti-slavery.

The smallpox is on the increase in this city.[4] The police reported for the week ending Jan. 16, one thousand six hundred cases other than in the hospital for contagious diseases.

The city is very gay at this season. Many marriages are taking place. Among the number is that of Rev. Sandy Alexander to Miss Smith of Fredericksburg, Va. He was married at his own church by Rev. S. A. Madden.[5] We wish this couple much happiness.

The Ladies' Contraband Relief Association received from New York Colored Grammar School No. 1 the sum of $88, which was brought on by the Rev. Mr. Garnet.[6] This present was gladly received, and will be hailed with great joy by the little motherless contraband children and the poor old decrepit. What makes this more valued is that it is from the children of the male and female department of a grammar school of colored children. We hope other schools will follow their example.

Weekly Anglo-African (New York, N.Y.), 30 January 1864.

1. Henry Highland Garnet spoke before the Contraband Relief Association on 4 January 1864 and gave a second lecture at the Fifteenth Street Presbyterian Church four days later. Charles L. Remond was one of several speakers who addressed a "freedom jubilee" at the Israel African Methodist Episcopal Church on New Year's Eve. The next day, he spoke at a meeting of the Israel Lyceum at the same church. On 6 January, Remond addressed a large interracial audience in the meeting room of the Union League of Washington, receiving "thunders of applause" for his remarks. He remained in the capital until at least 16 January, unable to leave the city because he had not obtained the military pass required of blacks. *WAA*, 9, 23 January 1864; *CR*, 16, 23 January 1864.

2. In late 1863, two black clergymen from Baltimore and Philadelphia reported to a freedmen's aid society in New York City that members of the Contraband Relief Association sold donated items and pocketed the funds, rather than distributing them among needy freedmen. These allegations circulated in the *Weekly Anglo-African* and prompted many New York City blacks to withhold further contributions. The rumors were probably sparked by "slanderous remarks" made by Rev. Thomas H. C. Hinton, an African Methodist Episcopal minister in the district. *WAA*, 9 January, 13 February, 12 March 1864.

3. Remond was accompanied by John J. Smith (1821–?), a Boston barber and antislavery activist. A free black from Richmond, Virginia, Smith settled in Boston in 1843 and participated in a wide range of activities in the black community there. He presided at planning sessions, protest meetings, and civic celebrations; served as an officer of the African Lodge No. 1; and worked with other local blacks to aid and protect fugitive slaves. His barbershop was a gathering place for local black abolitionists and sympathetic whites such as Charles Sumner. Smith represented Boston at the 1858 Massachusetts black state convention and the 1859 New England Colored Citizens Convention.

He became pessimistic about black prospects in the United States during the late 1850s, but remained skeptical of emigration movements. With the coming of the Civil War, he encouraged local blacks to rally behind the Union cause and persuaded many who frequented his shop to enlist. After the war, Smith became a leading black spokesman for the Republican party in Massachusetts. He was elected to the state legislature in 1868, 1869, and 1872 and served on Boston's common council in the 1880s. *CR*, 23 January 1864; John Daniels, *In Freedom's Birthplace: A Study of the Boston Negroes* (Boston, Mass., 1914), 57, 101–2n; *Boston City Directory*, 1843–49; *Lib*, 4 October 1850, 5 September 1856, 3 August 1857, 19, 26 February, 13 August 1858, 15 July 1859, 29 June 1860, 26 April 1861 [6:0598, 10:0286, 0768, 11:0149, 0160, 0321–22, 0858, 12:0841, 13:0479]; *WAA*, 16 November 1861, 3 January 1863 [13:0907]; Horton and Horton, *Black Bostonians*, 37, 60, 142n.

4. Washington, D.C., suffered from chronic outbreaks of smallpox during the Civil War, largely due to the influx of uninoculated contrabands, Union recruits, and destitute whites fleeing the Confederacy. A smallpox epidemic during the winter of 1863–64 created widespread panic when it reached into the city's

social and political elite. Margaret Leech, *Reveille in Washington, 1860–1865* (New York, N.Y., 1941), 215, 249, 251.

5. Sandy Alexander began his ministry in 1856 as pastor of the Second African Baptist Church in Washington, D.C. He founded two other local Baptist congregations but had returned to his first parish by the date of this letter. His new wife was probably one of a large number of black refugees from Fredericksburg, Virginia, who had settled in Washington in 1862. The couple was married by Samuel A. Madden, the pastor of the Nineteenth Street Baptist Church. John W. Cromwell, "The First Negro Churches in the District of Columbia," *JNH* 7:87–90 (January 1922); Sobel, *Trabelin' On*, 288–90; *WAA*, 13 February 1864.

6. Henry Highland Garnet delivered a donation from Colored Ward School No. 1, one of the oldest and largest black public schools in New York City. Freeman, "Free Negro in New York City," 343, 345.

55.
John S. Rock to the Soldiers
of the Fifth United States Colored
Heavy Artillery Regiment
30 May 1864

Although separated from the freedmen by distance, class, and cultural style, northern black leaders felt a sense of kinship with them. Heartfelt expressions of racial solidarity with the former slaves reflected their conviction that the war would determine the fate of all Afro-Americans. Throughout the Civil War, they committed themselves to improving the condition of southern blacks and subduing the Confederacy. Black abolitionists such as John S. Rock fulfilled their antislavery obligations by helping to recruit some 147,000 black soldiers in areas of the South occupied by federal forces. Rock and others like him recognized that the contributions of southern blacks would be critical to winning the war for freedom. Rock's 30 May 1864 letter to members of the newly organized Fifth U.S. Colored Heavy Artillery Regiment, a unit largely made up of former Mississippi slaves, expresses gratitude for the sacrifices southern blacks were making in the conflict. And it reveals Rock's understanding that shared wartime experiences would determine their common destiny—"When you suffer we shall suffer and when you triumph we shall triumph." Rock asked them to "remember that the colored soldier has the destiny of the colored race in his hands." Berlin et al., *Freedom*, 2:11–15.

Boston, [Massachusetts]
May 30th, 1864

Men, Brethren and Soldiers:[1]

I have learned with great great satisfaction that you are soldiers in the United States Army. That you have volunteered to fight not only for your own liberties but also for the liberty of your wives and children, and for the land of your birth. That you have willingly and cheerfully th[r]own yourselves as living sacrifices on the altar of your country and have resolved come what may never to become false to it or to liberty.

In consideration of these facts I have taken the liberty to write to you and to thank you for your loyalty and patriotism which have prompted you to enter upon such a high and holy mission. ł

I assure you brethren that you are right that not only the loyal portion of the North but the whole civilized world sympathizes with you and what is more than all, the god of Justice and of Liberty is on your side and He evidently means now to show to the people of this country that who have so long and so cruelly outraged and oppressed our people that this is the time he has chosen for Ethiopia to stretch forth her hands unto God!

Brethren I beg you to remember that the colored soldier has the destiny of the colored race in his hands. We look forward with hope for your brave deeds, and we are in constant expectation of hearing great things from you. Our prospects and happiness are identical with your prospects and happiness. When you suffer we shall suffer and when you triumph we shall triumph. Our prayers are constantly ascending the throne of grace for you, that you may never falter but always stand fast in the liberty wherewith Christ has made you free. Go forth bravely as I know you will and when you have vanquished the enemies of your country and of liberty come home to the bosoms of your families to enjoy the rights and privileges of freemen. Then we shall expect you to educate and prepare yourselves and your families to become useful and respected members of society.

Your friends have heard of Massachusetts and the love its people have for liberty and to show your appreciation of these sentiments they have sent here to have a flag painted for your regiment. They have done well to trust it to our Most Excellent Governor[2] who will see to it that their wishes are complied with, and I think you will be pleased with what he has sent you. May you always remember that your flag comes from a state that does not recognise slavery but gives to the humblest of her citizens—equal rights. You can well afford to be proud of your flag, and of the sentiments of the people of this state. May it assist you through the blessing of God to extend these ~~blessings~~ principles. I need not caution you for I know you have already resolved that it shall never fall into the hands of the enemy. We at the North are contending for and shall not be satisfied until we get equal rights for all. We may not get them at once, but it is our duty to ask for them[,] work for them and to fight for them, ~~and~~ until we get them. We look to you to do your part and we shall do ours.

Brethren I have confidence in you and know that you are valiant and patriotic. Go forth to the help of the Lord against the mighty and with the impetuosity of the patriots, and in contempt of all danger, putting your trust in the living future and the god of armies, deal rapid and deadly blows on the enemies of your liberty.

The barbarities inflicted upon you—the outrages committed upon your families[,] two centuries of outrage and oppression and the hope of a glorious future are so many summons for battle. God gives men their liberty who can and dare defend them and the thought quickens the blood in our veins when we remember that the God of Justice and Liberty is on your side. With great respect, I am, Gentlemen & Soldiers, Your Obedient Servant,

John S. Rock

George Ruffin Papers, Moorland-Spingarn Research Center, Howard University, Washington, D.C. Published by permission.

1. This unit was designated the Fifth U.S. Colored Heavy Artillery Regiment during March and April 1864, then became the Sixth U.S. Colored Heavy Artillery. Originally organized as the Second Mississippi Heavy Artillery in September 1863, the regiment performed garrison duty at Natchez and Vicksburg, participated in several minor engagements in the Departments of the Mississippi, Tennessee, and the Gulf, and was mustered out of service in May 1866. Dyer, *Compendium*, 3:1344, 1721.
2. John A. Andrew.

56.
The 1864 Presidential Election

J. W. C. Pennington to Robert Hamilton
9 June 1864

"Africano" to Robert Hamilton
18 July 1864

In spite of Lincoln's growing reputation as "the emancipator," northern blacks remained divided in their opinion of him. This disagreement surfaced during the 1864 presidential election. The *Weekly Anglo-African* spoke for more pragmatic types who viewed Lincoln as their best hope to sustain the war against slavery. The New York City paper justified Lincoln's election by pointing to the way the war had changed his views on racial matters. But sterner, less compromising spokesmen enumerated Lincoln's failings: his enforcement of the Fugitive Slave Law, his endorsement of colonization, limitations in the Emancipation Proclamation, and the unequal treatment of black troops. The following letters by black abolitionist J. W. C. Pennington and "Africano," an anonymous soldier in the Fifth Massachusetts Cavalry Regiment, address these divisions among northern blacks. Pennington stressed Lincoln's integrity and judged his value to blacks by the actions of his political enemies. "Africano," who had suffered the inequities of administration policy toward black soldiers, looked to General John C. Frémont—"one of liberty's most radical sons"—as blacks' best hope. *WAA*, 25 June, 30 July, 24 September, 5 November 1864; McPherson, *Struggle for Equality*, 260–86.

New York, [New York]
June 9th, 1864

MR. EDITOR:

The prospect of having HIS EXCELLENCY ABRAHAM LINCOLN for our next President should awaken in the inmost soul of every American of African descent emotions of the most profound and patriotic enthusiasm. There was a kind and wise Providence in bringing Mr. Lincoln into the Presidential chair, and I believe that the same all-wise Providence has directed him in everything he has done as our President. I say OUR President, because he is the only American President who has ever given any attention to colored men as citizens. I believe that his renomination by the Convention is not only sound policy, but that it is equivalent to re-election, and especially if colored men will do their duty at the ballot box next November.

It lies with colored men now to decide this great issue. The wisest, the safest, and the soundest policy for colored Americans is to exert all our influence to keep our present Chief Magistrate where he is for four years from next March.

There are many reasons why we, as colored men, should prefer Mr. Lincoln for our next President. Among the many I may say: 1. He is an honest President. 2. He is faithful to the whole nation. 3. He commands the respect of the world. 4. He is more cordially hated by the Copperheads of the North and the rebels of the South than any other living man. 5. His reelection will be the best security that the present well-begun work of negro freedom and African redemption will be fully completed. May God grant us four long years more of the judicious administration of that excellent man, ABRAHAM LINCOLN, and when I speak thus I believe I speak the sentiments of nine-tenths of my colored fellow-citizens. What say you, Mr. Editor?

J. W. C. PENNINGTON

Weekly Anglo-African (New York, N.Y.), 25 June 1864.

Point Lookout, M[arylan]d
July 18, 1864

MR. EDITOR:

Coinciding with my brother soldier of the 54th Mass.,[1] I would say a few words as to the necessity of colored men, soldiers particularly, voting, if such is allowed, for the creator of the Emancipation proclamation. Many of our intelligent colored men believe in Mr. Lincoln; but *we*, who have studied him thoroughly, know him better, and as *we* desire to conglomerate in the land of our nativity, and not be severed from the ties we hold most dear, we hail the nomination of one of liberty's most radical sons—John C. Fremont. Mr. Lincoln's policy in regard to the elevation and inseparability of the negro race has always been one of a fickle-minded man—one who, holding anti-slavery principles in one hand and colonization in the other, always gave concessions to slavery when the *Union* could be preserved without touching the peculiar institution. Such a man is not again worthy the votes of the voting portion of the colored race, when the intrepid Fremont, explorer of the Mariposa Valley,[2] the well-known freedom-cherishing, negro-equalizing patriot, is the competitor. The press, like Mr. Lincoln, has always been, and will ever be, in favor of negro colonization; for, like him, they fear competition, and it is not extraordinary if the press should now uphold Mr. Lincoln, though dissatisfied with his vacillating administration, to keep John C. Fremont from occupying the presidential chair. The loyal and truehearted people of the North will, no doubt, weigh the two men now before the public, and choose the one not found wanting. We are within ourselves satisfied that the Cleveland Convention will carry its object—that of electing Freedom's son—while the Baltimore Convention, with its nominee for reelection, will return to the plowshare.[3]

While we thank Mr. Lincoln for what the exigencies of the times forced him to do, we also censure him for the non-accomplishment of the real good this accursed rebellion gave him the power to do, and which if he had done, instead of bartering human sinews and human rights with slaveholding Kentucky,[4] the world would have looked upon him as the magnanimous regenerator of American institutions, and the benevolent protector of human freedom.

AFRICANO [5]

Weekly Anglo-African (New York, N.Y.), 6 August 1864.

1. "Africano" probably refers to a letter by an anonymous member of the Fifty-fourth Massachusetts Regiment, which appeared in the 16 July 1864 issue of the *Weekly Anglo-African*. Bearing the pseudonym "Seporello," it predicted that Abraham Lincoln's reelection would mean the triumph of colonization. The author indicated his preference for John C. Frémont, or even George B. McClellan, and urged black soldiers to vote where permitted.

2. In 1845–46 John C. Frémont explored the Sacramento and upper San Joaquin valleys of central California for the U.S. Army. He visited the region near the village of Mariposa during this time. Ray Allen Billington, *Westward Expansion: A History of the American Frontier*, 3d ed. (New York, N.Y., 1967), 571–72.

3. Four hundred delegates gathered at Cleveland on 31 May 1864 to select John C. Frémont as the presidential candidate of an insurgent Radical Democratic party. Support for the nomination came from abolitionists, German-American radicals, and disgruntled War Democrats; not a single prominent Republican attended the convention. Delegates approved a platform that called for a constitutional amendment prohibiting slavery and guaranteeing equal rights to all citizens, urged Congressional control of Reconstruction, demanded the redistribution of confiscated rebel lands, and denounced Lincoln's suspension of civil liberties during wartime. Republicans (now calling themselves the National Union party) met in Baltimore during 7–8 June and unanimously renominated Lincoln. The choice of George B. McClellan by the Democrats undermined backing for Frémont's third-party movement. When Atlanta fell to Union troops in September, it revitalized popular support for the Lincoln administration. He won 212 of 233 electoral votes, capturing majorities in all but three states. McPherson, *Struggle for Equality*, 269–86.

4. The Emancipation Proclamation applied only to those slaves in Confederate-held territory. Lincoln hoped the measure would punish the seceded states, without destroying support for the Union in those slave states and portions of slave states under federal control. The more than 200,000 slaves in Kentucky did not officially gain their freedom until the ratification of the Thirteenth Amendment (1865). Berlin et al., *Freedom*, 1(1):493–518.

5. "Africano," an anonymous member of the Fifth Massachusetts Cavalry Regiment, corresponded with the *Weekly Anglo-African* on five occasions during

the last half of 1864. His 25 June letter, which described fighting by black troops in Virginia, sparked a lively and lengthy exchange with Christian Fleetwood—a black officer of the Fourth U.S. Colored Troops—in subsequent issues of the *Anglo-African.* "Africano" wrote several other pieces on the 1864 presidential election, describing Lincoln as a "fickle minded man" and criticizing his administration for its colonization schemes, limited emancipation policy, and inequitable treatment of black soldiers. *WAA,* 25 June, 9, 23 July, 6, 13 August, 17, 24 September, 5 November 1864.

57.
William D. Forten to Charles Sumner
18 June 1864

In spite of the achievements and sacrifices of black soldiers on the battlefield, Afro-Americans continued to endure the injury and indignity of
racial discrimination. A poignant 18 June 1864 letter from William D.
Forten to Senator Charles Sumner told of the personal costs of the war
for blacks—a burden made all the more insufferable by white prejudice.
Forten, a member of one of Philadelphia's most distinguished black
families, acknowledged that a recent family tragedy had deepened his
despair over racial injustice. His elder brother, Robert Bridges Forten,
had returned from England in March to enlist in the Union army, but
contracted typhoid fever while recruiting black soldiers in Baltimore
and died within a few weeks. This letter, written to Sumner on behalf of
a young man seeking an officer's commission in a black regiment, offered William Forten an opportunity to contrast his brother's sacrifice
with the obstacles still faced by his race—unequal pay for military service, exclusion from officers' training, the persistence of discrimination
in the North. Unaware that the U.S. Congress had enacted legislation
three days earlier guaranteeing equal pay for black soldiers, he lamented
that "the black man, disowned—dishonored—disgraced and dehumanized . . . now lifts his head and proudly walks into the front ranks of
certain death unprotected[,] unregarded." William D. Forten to Charles
Sumner, 7 June 1862, Charles Sumner Papers, MH [14:0335]; Janice
Sumler Lewis, "The Fortens of Philadelphia: An Afro-American Family
and Nineteenth-Century Reform" (Ph.D. diss., Georgetown University,
1978), 102, 179–84.

Phila[delphia], [Pennsylvania]
June 18th, 1864

Sir:
    'Tis no easy matter to resist the spirit which prompts an acknowledge-
ment of favors received, especialy when they proceed from a source
claiming our warmest respect and <u>love</u>.
    Therefore in performing this agreable duty I give the spirit of thank-
fulness its fulest scope and bid you rest assured of my warmest gratitude
for your kind rememberance.
    The War with all its attendant horrors almost obscure my vision and
the fate of the intrepid black-man whose body is in the breach is truly
appalling. Oh my God! my God! Where, Oh where is thy justice?
    Who Sir will give the true history of this war? Whose hand dare
paint this hell-black picture? Whose tongue will be loosened to tell the

startled Nations this tale of horror cruelty & crime? The black-man, disowned—dishonored—disgraced and dehumanized—trampled in the dust for a long century[,] now lifts his head and proudly walks into the front ranks of certain death unprotected unregarded, in order that the country may have a Constitution, and his oppressors <u>liberty</u> & <u>law</u> who in return for this exhibition of disinterested patriotism and bravery, hurl him out from its benefits, and brand him a felon. Sir, very keen are my feelings on this subject at present as but a short time has elapsed since my hand was laid for the last time on the cold brow of my brother who came from the enjoyment of liberty—equality & citizenship in England to do battle for their recognition in this, his own Native land. He has gon, without one glimse at their day dawn, and we who are left to mourn beheld the sun of truth gradually darkened by the clouds of treachery & conservatism.

Judge Kelly in a speach delivered in the House of Representatives Apl 30th—on equalizing the pay of our Soldiers, kindly alluded to my brother's breif career;[1] they were play mates in youth. [Line illegible.] I would most respectfully solicit your advice as to the course to be persued by a young man desirous of obtaining a position as an officer in the Army. He comes well recommended, has served out his time and been honorably discharged, his papers accredit him as lieutenant commanding company in 2d Louisiana regiment.[2] He waas at the ever memorable storming of Port Hudsons heightes and was there placed in command of a company, also at New Orleans in command of one of Col. Plumly's companys.[3] He desires a lieutenancy in a colored regiment. The School for training officers for colored troops excludes applicants other than white[4] (it shames me to be compelled to write thus of my native city, and those who profess so much in behalf of the outr[a]ged Negro). But nevertheless tis so, this young man tried the experiment and his failure only inspires him to renewed exertions, In his behalf I venture to solicit your advice, Very respectfully Yours,

W. D. Forten[5]

Charles Sumner Papers, Houghton Library, Harvard University, Cambridge, Massachusetts. Published by permission.

1. Congressman William D. Kelley of Pennsylvania made a compelling speech in the U.S. House of Representatives on 30 April 1864. He praised black contributions to the war and indicted American racial attitudes, declaring that the federal government's refusal to grant equal pay to black troops was "pregnant evidence of the terrible weight of prejudice which has clouded the judgment and conscience of the American people." Kelley pointed to the death five days earlier of his boyhood friend, Sergeant Robert Bridges Forten (1814–1864), as evidence of the sacrifices blacks were making for the Union cause. Forten was the son of Philadelphia abolitionist James Forten, Sr., and the father of well-known diarist Charlotte Forten Grimké. He had worked in his father's sail-making business and

been active in the Vigilant Committee of Philadelphia. Disillusioned over the future of blacks in the United States, Forten moved his wife and family to Canada West in 1855, then settled three years later in England, where he worked as a commercial agent.

The Emancipation Proclamation altered his view of the United States and prompted him to return home. On 2 March 1864, although fifty-one years old, Forten joined the Forty-third U.S. Colored Troops. He was quickly promoted to sergeant and transferred to Maryland to help recruit black troops, but he contracted typhoid fever and died on 25 April. His military funeral was the first ever granted to a black in Philadelphia. Prominent reformers such as J. Miller McKim and Lucretia Mott and scores of the city's black and white residents turned out for the ceremonies at Camp William Penn and escorted Forten's remains through the city to St. Thomas's African Episcopal Church for burial. *Congressional Record*, 2 May 1864, 1996–98; Lewis, "The Fortens of Philadelphia," 42–43, 112, 128–29, 179–81.

2. Forten refers to the Second Regiment of Louisiana Native Guards, which was organized at New Orleans in October 1862. Unlike the First Regiment, whose members were largely drawn from the city's mulatto elite, the Second was primarily comprised of laborers. Although it participated in minor engagements in southern Louisiana and Mississippi, the unit spent most of the war performing garrison duty. It became the Second Regiment of Corps d'Afrique in June 1863, was designated the Seventy-fourth U.S. Colored Troops in April 1864, and was mustered out of service in October 1865. John W. Blassingame, *Black New Orleans, 1860–1880* (Chicago, Ill., 1973), 39; Dyer, *Compendium*, 3:1214, 1718, 1735.

3. Colonel John S. Plumly of Philadelphia, the son of Garrisonian abolitionist B. Rush Plumly, commanded the Sixth Louisiana Infantry, a home guard regiment that only served during the summer of 1863 in New Orleans. Plumly later saw action in another black unit that was part of a brigade raised by his father, a major in the Union army. Peyton McCrary, *Abraham Lincoln and Reconstruction: The Louisiana Experiment* (Princeton, N.J., 1978), 145, 147; Dyer, *Compendium*, 3:1214; *WAA*, 29 August 1863.

4. Forten refers to the Free Military School founded in December 1863 by the Philadelphia Supervisory Committee for Recruiting Colored Regiments. Located in downtown Philadelphia, it offered a two-week officer training course for whites who volunteered to serve in black regiments. Candidates were screened by a supervisory board. Upon completion of the course, they were eligible to take an examination in Washington, D.C., to determine if they would receive a commission in a black regiment. Although the school refused such training to blacks, it offered classes to black applicants from Maryland who wished to become noncommissioned officers in black units. Before it closed in late 1864, the school instructed 1,031 white candidates—most of whom passed their examinations—and some 21 blacks. Binder, "Pennsylvania Negro Regiments," 401–4.

5. William Deas Forten (1823–ca. 1900), the son of abolitionists James E. and Charlotte Forten, was a member of one of the most prominent black families in nineteenth-century Philadelphia. The younger Forten became involved in local antislavery activities at an early age and helped revive the Vigilant Committee of Philadelphia following the passage of the Fugitive Slave Law. He also contributed

to the black voting rights campaign as a coauthor of the *Memorial of Thirty-thousand Disfranchised Citizens of Philadelphia* (1855). During the Civil War, he encouraged black enlistment in the Union army, participated in soldiers' aid organizations, and continued to advance black enfranchisement through the National Equal Rights League and its Pennsylvania auxiliary. Forten belonged to several black civic and literary organizations, including the Banneker Institute. He managed his father's sail-making business for several decades and maintained the family residence until 1899, when he entered the local Stephen Smith Rest Home for the Aged. Lewis, "The Fortens of Philadelphia," 47–48, 77, 138, 141–43, 177–84, 203–25, 243; Foner and Walker, *Proceedings of the Black State Conventions*, 1:148; *FDP*, 13 November 1851 [7:0177]; *VF*, 15 January 1852 [7:0350]; *PF*, 9 December 1852 [7:0851].

58.
Sattira A. Douglas to Robert Hamilton
4 July 1864

Black denominations, the American Missionary Association, and other male-controlled organizations sponsored much of the schooling and refugee work among the freedmen. But northern women cooperated across racial lines to support such efforts. Dozens of teachers and relief workers—black and white—labored under the auspices of female re-form alliances, church groups, and contraband relief associations. Phila-delphia Quaker women funded Harriet Jacobs's labors in the contra-band camps at Alexandria, Virginia. The Woman's National Loyal League, a feminist-abolitionist society led by Susan B. Anthony and Elizabeth Cady Stanton, sponsored Sojourner Truth's lecture tours on behalf of freedmen's rights. Sattira Douglas taught at a freedmen's school in Leavenworth, Kansas, with support from the league's Chicago auxiliary. She also distributed supplies forwarded by the Colored Ladies Freedmen's Aid Society of Chicago, a federation of black women that provided the essentials of life—food, fuel, and clothing—to residents of the contraband camps on the Kansas frontier. Douglas's 4 July 1864 letter to the *Weekly Anglo-African* suggests how she and other black women tapped a well-developed network of interracial women's organi-zations to assist those struggling to make the transition from slavery to freedom. Benjamin, *Philadelphia Quakers*, 128–29; Sterling, *We Are Your Sisters*, 251–52; *WAA*, 12 December 1863, 4 June, 30 July 1864; *CR*, 24 October 1863, 12 March 1864.

Leavenworth, Kansas
July 4, 1864

MR. EDITOR:

It has been a long, long time since I looked into your sanctum, but I imagine I shall be none the less welcome; and if there should rest upon your contenance the shadow of a frown on my entrance, I know it will be dissipated when you hear what I have to say.

You will perceive by the postmark of this letter that I am away out in "Bleeding Kansas," and well I may say bleeding, for never since the days when the glorious Old Martyr stood here face to face with border ruffi-anism and bid defiance to the minions of slavery has quiet and order been permanently established. The city of Leavenworth is now under military restrictions, owing to the fact that Quantrill, the dread guerilla chief, has entered this State and with his band of marauders threatens us with a reenaction of the heart-rending scenes of Lawrence.[1]

But all this time I have been running on, and have not told you what I intended to from the outset, viz., what I am doing and also what my co-laborers are and have been doing for the past six or eight months. In doing this, I hope to give you an inkling of the condition and prospects of our people in this the first city of the far west. Learning that there were a great many freed people here, and an insufficiency of teachers, I accepted an appointment tendered me by the Women's Loyal League, of Chicago,[2] to come and assist in the school already established and taught by Mr. C. H. Langston.

On arriving here, I found Mr. Langston in a school having an enrollment of 346 pupils with a regular attendance of from 180 to 200. He informed me that in the attendance there had been a very great decrease in consequence of the appearance in the school of the smallpox and measles, together with the fact that many families as the Spring approaches had moved off into the country, there better to secure employment and live independent of charity. I also ascertained that many other children were prevented from attending school for want of proper clothing. Learning this, I immediately wrote to the Colored Ladies Freedmen's Aid Society of Chicago,[3] stating the fact, and they kindly and promptly responded by shipping a lot of goods to us forthwith, which we are daily expecting to receive. The noble-hearted men and women, who, far removed from the camps and communities of freedmen and who are constantly remembering them by sending clothing and in other respects ministering to their wants, are not aware what a great amount of good they are doing. They are not only sending physical comfort, but are also aiding in their intellectual advancement. Too much praise cannot be awarded Mr. Langston for the self-sacrificing perseverance with which he has labored for the welfare of his people here. He has, by nobly acting the part of the good Samaritan toward them, secured their undying confidence and esteem and is regarded by them as a beloved benefactor. So assiduously has he labored that his health has become greatly impaired, and after my arrival, he left school to recuperate, and myself with two others have since conducted it. Last Winter the destitution was so great and demands for help so urgent that Mr. Langston was compelled to give the school into other hands and devote his time exclusively to collecting money, buying fuel and provisions to distribute among the sufferers.

The excessive hot weather has rendered it necessary for us to close school for a two months' vacation, at the end of which time public schools for colored children will be established. These, according to a provision made by the Legislature at its last session, will be supported by the city and be under the supervision of the city school board, the same as other schools.[4] The passage of this act I regard as a gain of considerable importance to our people here, for which we are indebted to the united efforts of Captain William D. Matthews[5] and Mr. C. H. Langston. More anon.

SATTIE A. DOUGLAS

Weekly Anglo-African (New York, N.Y.), 23 July 1864.

1. Fighting between free-state and proslavery settlers in Kansas during the 1850s earned the territory the sobriquet "Bleeding Kansas." Douglas compares those hostilities to the guerrilla raids conducted in the region by William Clarke Quantrill and his band during the Civil War. Quantrill (1837–1865), a gambler and petty thief, exploited wartime circumstances to rob and ransack Unionist settlements along the Kansas-Missouri border. Although romanticized as avenging angels by postwar exponents of the "Lost Cause," Quantrill and his nearly four hundred raiders were little more than outlaws. After Confederate officials promoted Quantrill to colonel, he acted with some official sanction, but most Confederate military leaders opposed his actions. On the morning of 21 August 1863, Quantrill's raiders sacked the undefended village of Lawrence, Kansas, killing more than 150 men, women, and children. A year later, they attacked Centralia, Missouri, and killed, mutilated, and scalped an equal number of Union soldiers, many of whom were unarmed. Quantrill was fatally wounded by Union troops in May 1865 while attempting to extend his activities into Kentucky. *HTECW*, 606; Michael Fellman, *Inside War: The Guerrilla Conflict in Missouri during the American Civil War* (New York, N.Y., 1989), 25–26, 97–100, 103–7, 135, 249–52, 259.

2. Douglas refers to the interracial Chicago auxiliary of the Woman's National Loyal League. Organized in May 1863 by Elizabeth Cady Stanton and Susan B. Anthony, the WNLL was feminist in tone, but dedicated to a single goal—the complete end of slavery. Members hoped to collect one million signatures on petitions calling for a constitutional amendment to abolish the institution. They established state and local auxiliaries throughout the North to conduct the campaign. The Chicago chapter, which was formed during the fall of 1863 by league agent Josephine Griffing of Ohio, gathered hundreds of signatures but also reflected her personal interest in freedmen's aid. In early 1864, Senator Charles Sumner of Massachusetts presented WNLL petitions bearing 400,000 signatures to Congress, hastening legislative ratification of the Thirteenth Amendment. The WNLL disbanded in 1865 after the amendment was passed. *CR*, 21 November 1863; Wendy F. Hammond, "The Woman's National Loyal League: Feminist Abolitionists and the Civil War," *CWH* 35:39–58 (March 1989).

3. The Colored Ladies Freedmen's Aid Society of Chicago was formed in September 1863 and became one of the most active organizations of its type in the West. Members met twice a week to make and mend garments and to bundle food, clothing, cooking utensils, and other items for shipment to suffering former slaves. Most of this aid went to contraband camps in the Mississippi Valley and on the Kansas frontier. To support its relief work, the society sponsored benefit lectures in the Chicago black community and hired Mary Ann Shadd Cary as a traveling fund-raising agent. Mary R. Jones, the wife of black abolitionist John Jones, acted as the organization's president; Sattira Douglas served as treasurer

until she left for Kansas in mid-1864. *CR*, 24 October, 21 November 1863, 12 March 1864; *WAA*, 12 December 1863, 4 June 1864.

4. In March 1864, the Kansas legislature passed an educational reform act making local school boards responsible for the support and supervision of public schools for blacks. *AM*, April 1864.

5. William D. Matthews (1828–?), a free black farmer from Caroline County, Maryland, moved to Kansas in 1858. The outbreak of the Civil War caused a flood of former slaves into the state from Missouri, swelling Kansas's black population from one to six thousand. Matthews dedicated himself to their assistance and traveled throughout the East to raise funds for contraband relief. Because of these labors, he was named superintendent of contrabands for the Kansas Emancipation League; in this role, he directed relief and education efforts in the contraband camps and organized freedmen's savings clubs and land associations. In 1862 Matthews joined the First Kansas Volunteers and was appointed captain of Company D. Two years later, he lobbied the state legislature for legislation to support black schools. He promoted equal suffrage for Kansas blacks during the latter part of the war. Compiled Military Service Records, RG 94, Adjutant General's Office, U.S. Colored Troops, DNA; *WAA*, 31 January 1863, 23, 30 July 1864, 11 February 1865; *PP*, 7 December 1861, 27 March 1862; Quarles, *Negro in the Civil War*, 126.

59.
The Mission to the Freedmen

Edward Scott to George Whipple
22 July 1864

John N. Mars to George Whipple
29 July 1864

Many of the northern blacks who went South as preachers, teachers, and relief workers had little previous contact with slave culture. They were surprised, bewildered, and often dismayed by what they encountered. Initial contact with the freedmen revealed vast cultural differences and brought unexpected problems. The racist attitudes of some white coworkers further complicated their task. Two July 1864 letters by Edward Scott and John N. Mars to George Whipple, the corresponding secretary of the American Missionary Association, dramatize the trials of the missionary experience. Scott, a Baptist clergyman from Rhode Island, was pessimistic about the prospect of elevating the adult freedmen on Parris Island, South Carolina. Frustrated by their preference for folk religion and the Gullah language, he judged them to be uneducable "he[a]thens." His letter also depicted the exhausting work, harsh conditions, and unhealthy climate endured by missionaries and their families; in Scott's case, this proved prophetic, for he died a few months after his arrival in the South. John N. Mars, a Methodist pastor from Massachusetts, worked among the freedmen in Portsmouth, Virginia. The following report was one of several he sent to the AMA in 1864 on the racism that he found among both northern and southern whites. Mars urged AMA administrators to carefully screen their missionaries in order to insure a teaching staff free from racial prejudice and wholly committed to the task of Christian education. He asked them not to send those who sought "to make money or dominear over Gods poor." Richardson, *Christian Reconstruction*, 189–209; De Boer, "Afro-Americans in American Missionary Association," 223, 247–53, 297, 304–8; John N. Mars to George Whipple, 1, 15 March, 6, 25 April, 27 May, 18 June, 29 August 1864, AMA-ARC [15:0264–66, 0283, 0300, 0319–20, 0358–59, 0404, 0512–14].

Parris Island, [South Carolina]
July 22, 1864

Dear Sir:

These few lines will inform you that we are still in this department trying to due what littele good we can to the freedmen of S.C. I would just say that all the hope that I can see as regards them is the saving of

11. Freedmen's school

From *Harper's Weekly*, 15 December 1866

the rising generation, by giving th~~at~~em all the good instruction we posibel
can, and we may see the ~~froot~~ fruit of the laber spent here in times to
come. The old pe[o]pel some of them seme to have a great disposan to
learn, to read the Bibel, and some are willing to compose in their A B and
C. But there is verey littel hop[e] of them ever becoming good readers,
yet I can see some imporvment in boath old and younge. Slavery has left
them more lick he[a]thens, in some respect, than anny thing els[e]. It is
very hard for me to understand their language, you must almost larn a
new Tung here,[1] for such jabeling I never hurd in my life. We have Tou
good schools ~~th~~ here on the Fuller plantasan so call, one Class by Mrs.
Foursight and one by my wife, Mrs. Scott, Mrs. Armstrong being removed to taek the place of one of the Taechers that di[e]d on another
plantasan.[2] The schools are doing as well as can be expected for the time
of year, an sesan of the year. We have also a good Sabbath School co-
nected with the school wich maek it quit[e] interesting, and the children
seme to lick it boath old and young[,] which is all so doing its part in
laing a fondaison as a gied for [o]thers in the morn of life. But we lack
very much some small Books for the Children to read to their Parent and
others[.] All that we have had to distr[i]but is a few papers, some good
letters. Book[s] with good [morals] atacht to them might due much good.
As to my laber, I have Tried to preach every Sunday sence I have been
here, sometimes twice but for the most part once. I fele that I shold be
glad to traill all over this Island but I cannot stand it to go on foot. It
would use me up in one month, in this hot climent and if I stay here I
shall have to have a Horse from Oncell Sam or some one Else. Brother
Riecherson[3] [due] my wife to taek charge of the family here as [house]
~~ceep~~ Ceeper, and also to spend a few hour in Taeching witch has made it
quit[e] hard for her, yet between us we have made it work [midling well].
As To Trials we will not say a word, for God has been good to me and
my family, and we have resan to praes him for his wondefull goodness to
the Children of men. God has a work for me and mine to due here, and
I hop[e] I shell lern to due it if it is his will.

Notes

The Stove that was sent to me I ded not [receive] and we cannot here
anny thing payment as yet. I wish you had sent that Larg[e] Box on eveny
if I had to pay the frait for it for the very thing that we needed most are
in that Box and if I stay here I must have them. For there is nothing here
in Thess [House] and if I had not sent for anny, we all here wood have
been in a poor packell as to cooking now.

When ~~I~~ we came to thess [House] all that we found to Ceep [house]
One Stor[e] Bed and a stan[d], not a banch not a cheir and hardly anny
thing to eat out of and if we had not had a few things in her Trunk, we
should have been in a [hard] fixt. But I went right back to [Bufurd][4] and

bought me some ~~bord~~ lomber, and whent to work and bilt me a [back-stool] and Tabel and some banches to set on and it has taek me a good part of the time to maek The Taechers and my family [Comfertebl],

N. B.

My Dear Brother:

I due not want to find fault, but I must say to you in confidence that there is a rong here, somewere—for it seme to be the aim of about all to maek money and they due not chere if they maek it off of the ~~Rason~~ rason that belong to the Taecher or Minester, and therefore [hard] to farm here, sometimes, and come short by the Connivery of them that does the rason for us. We have it on thess plantasan, and I have had to work hard to ceep [Sisters] [two illegible marks] and my wife here. I have fish & bought chickens and anny thing that would ceep them comferteble. All that [I] wish to say is that we ought to have all that O[n]cell Sam allows us. You may here from some one else[,] therefore I will say [no] more at Present. There is a good herd of youn[g] game here ~~cept on the land~~. They tell us sometimes that they have been right to find us [shellters, should] all such tawk these things. I hear from you and others too littele. I shall atend to my duty. You will pray for us. Yours with respect,

E. Scott

Please to forgive for my bad speling.

American Missionary Association Archives, Amistad Research Center, Tulane University, New Orleans, Louisiana. Published by permission.

Portsmouth, V[irgini]a
July the 29, [18]64

Dear Sir:

In obediance to the requirement of the Missionary rule,[5] I feal it a pleasure as well as a duty to address a few lines to the Missionary board,[6] not all-togather a report, but with it, a few facks, thoughts, and Surgestions. First, I have continued my labours, in Gosport Teaching, and Preaching, in the same manner, and place that I did last month. The School at Gosport under the Charge of Mr Harris,[7] is in a very flourishing Condition, and numbers regular about 145, and is on the increas, also the Sabbath School there in Gosport is fulley attended, and some of the Children have been led to give their hearts to God. Our new preaching place, and Sabbath School on the Whitehead farm,[8] is a Success; we commenced first, under a large birch Tree, and after the first two meetings, and Schools, the people went to work and put up what they call a meetinghouse, that will hold some 250, or 300, persons whare we preach, and have a fine, and flourishing Sabbath School. There is quit a religious intrest in this part of the work, and I think quite a number have recentley been hopefuley led to the Saviour, and give good evidence that God for

Christ sake hav forgiven them, there Sins, and to God, be all the Glorey for ever Amen. The two last weekes, Mr. Bell, has desired me to take Charge of the Monitor Class, and hear there lessons, and I have done so. Some of the monitors, are quite a help in School, but cant fill the place of a Teacher, but are helps, and this may be the best way and quickest to rais up for this people Teachers amoungst them selves, who will impart instruction to them rising rising generations. But the monitors need much instruction to prepare them for this work, and I think it would be a good moove, if some of these monitors could be sent North to School, six months or a year, if no lounger it would be a great help to them, and a good investment for some benevolent Society. Who will respond to the above and say send them to us for one year. Mr. Harris is doing a good work hear, and is mutch loved by all his Schollars. Mr. Bells, School was in a very flurshing condition, when it closed, and the Sabbath School also, and much improved to what it was, when Mr. Bell took the Charge. The Change has been, I think, boath in the School, and in the house, for the Glorey of God, and the good of the Mission. Since Mr. and Mrs. Bell[9] has kept the house, they have boath shown a Christian Spirit and Example, and by there Conduct have said, that God was not a resp[ec]tor of persons, but had maid of one blood all Nations that dwell on the face of the hole Earth.[10] I cant for my life see what moat motive a man or a woman can have to come here to Teach as a Christian Missionary to these freedmen, with there hearts full of prejudice, against identifying them selves with those they go to teach. Jesus Christ, receved Sinners, and eat with them, and he says learn of me &c. I feal that it is my duty, here to say that Mr. and Mrs. Bell give Complete satisfaction boath, in the School, and in the house, to all that are not Copper heads at heart, and that have the cause of Christ and humanity at heart. Mr. and Mrs. Bell, have maid no distinction betwene the Colord and white Teachers, but have treated them all alike, so far as I know, and that is, as it should be. While Mr. Eastman[11] kept the house, there was some unpleasent fealings manefested, that if there had not been a change, that this portion of the Mission, would suffered greate loss, if not entirely broken up. All the foul seed Sown by Mr. E[,] Mr. Bell, had to Contend with when he came in as Superintendant of the Mission house. But thankes be to God, who gave to Mr. Bell, and his good Lady the right Spirit and they have wed out those obnoxous, and bitter weeds, that was growing from the foul seed that had been sown. Now what is needed to give Success in this greate Mission work, is men, and women, white and Colord, whoes hearts are in the right place, and have a firm Christian principal, and have come here to do good, and not to make money, or to dominear over Gods poor. It is to be regretted that after such anxiety has been felt, and pains taken, by the Missionary board, to get suitable persons for the work, that the Mission should be imposed uppon by any one, who feals that God has Created him, or her, so much better than he has others. But it is evident that God is now working out this greate problem of mans Equality, and rights, as given to man by his Creator. But I have said more then I desired, when I commenced, and not as much as I could say in truth on this matter, and which I hope some others will say. For how is the Missionary board to know unless it is by those that are in the field, and their fruit. I have not been induced to write this by any one, for no one new of it untill I had written, but I felt promted, by a sence of duty, and love of humanity, and pure Christianity, to speak out plainley. If I am wroung, pleas tell me, and give me any advice you think I need, I want to be right. There has been two deaths, of Teachers in the Mission family[12] of which you have been informed by others. Mr. Harris, well will give you a full report about his Schools, day, and Sabbath Schools. I went up to Peetersburge, but it was to Shelley there to make any stand at present. We are rather unsettled at present about a house, the Mission house whare wee now live, is to be given up to the owner, and we may have to breake up for a time. The most of our family have gone North on a vacation, a few remain, and will not go. I should like to go to Baltamore, and spend for or five days to Confernce,[13] if I can get some one to Teach my Class while I am gone, for when the Schools commence, they will be needed. But I close by hoping that this may find you all well in body, and happy in God. Yours with much respect,

J. N. Mars

P.S. The weather is very hot here 88.

American Missionary Association Archives, Amistad Research Center, Tulane University, New Orleans, Louisiana. Published by permission.

1. Most blacks along the South Carolina–Georgia coast spoke Gullah, a creole or pidgin language created by the first slaves brought to the region. Although its vocabulary was largely English, it employed rules of grammar, gestures, and intonation patterns derived from African roots. *DAAS*, 305–6.

2. Scott operated his American Missionary Association school on a five hundred–acre farm that had been owned by planter Robert Fuller before the Civil War. In July 1864, classes were taught by his wife, Mary A. Scott, and Martha A. Forsaith of Manchester, New Hampshire. Forsaith had come South in May and remained on Parris Island until late the following year. Although working for the AMA, Mary Scott was supported by the Freewill Baptist Home Missionary Society. Mary J. Armstrong (1843–1868), a New York City native, left Scott's school earlier in the month to fill a vacancy created by the 21 June death of Georgianna M. Warren, who had taught at an AMA school in the vicinity of Beaufort. Armstrong had come to Parris Island in early 1864 and continued to teach for the AMA in Hampton (Va.), Charleston, and Savannah after the war. Edward Scott to George Whipple, 22 July 1864, AMA-ARC [15:0461]; Theodore Rosengarten, *Tombee: Portrait of a Cotton Planter* (New York, N.Y., 1986), 224–25; *Eighteenth Annual Report of the American Missionary Asso-*

ciation (New York, N.Y., 1864), 26; *AM*, August 1864, August 1868; *Nineteenth Annual Report of the American Missionary Association* (New York, N.Y., 1865), 23.

3. Scott refers to Rev. William T. Richardson of New York, who served as superintendent of education for the American Missionary Association in Beaufort. Between June 1863 and the end of the Civil War, Richardson supervised twenty-six schools, thirty-four teachers, and more than two thousand pupils along the South Carolina–Georgia coast. In 1865 he organized AMA schools in Savannah, hiring local blacks as teachers and allowing the black community a role in their governance. Richardson filled AMA posts in Virginia and Alabama after the war. Richardson, *Christian Reconstruction*, 28–29, 57–58, 200, 237; De Boer, "Afro-Americans in American Missionary Association," 297; *Twentieth Annual Report of the American Missionary Association* (New York, N.Y., 1866), 22; *Twenty-first Annual Report of the American Missionary Association* (New York, N.Y., 1867), 48–50.

4. Scott refers to the village of Beaufort, which was located about seven miles from Parris Island.

5. Mars refers to the command of Jesus in Matthew 28:19 to "go ye therefore, and teach all nations, baptizing them in the name of the Father, and of the Son, and of the Holy Ghost."

6. Between November 1863 and November 1864, the executive committee of the American Missionary Association consisted of AMA officials Simeon S. Jocelyn, Charles B. Wilder, William E. Whiting, and nine clergymen and physicians from the New York City area. *AM*, December 1863.

7. William D. Harris (1827–1873), a free black from North Carolina, was working as a plasterer in Cleveland when he heard American Missionary Association agent William Davis speak at Oberlin about the plight of the contrabands at Fortress Monroe. This awakened a desire to go to Virginia and "labor with my people." Harris, who had several years of teaching experience, was sent to Portsmouth in February 1864 to assist white teachers in the AMA schools there. One month later, he was placed in charge of a recently established AMA school at Gosport on the southeastern edge of Portsmouth. Through his "visiting and vigilant efforts," Harris increased the enrollment from 56 to 122 by the end of March; it grew to 238 pupils in April. He operated this thriving school in the basement of a local Methodist church with the assistance of teachers Edmonia Highgate, John N. Mars, H. R. Arnold, and two contrabands.

Harris also aided the local black community—he started a night school for adult freedmen, opened three Sunday schools, set up classes for wounded black soldiers convalescing in the military hospital at Portsmouth, visited the needy in nearby contraband camps, and helped them fill out government forms to obtain fuel, clothing, and rations. Bishop John Mifflin Brown of the African Methodist Episcopal denomination said he wished there were "a dozen William Harrises in Virginia." In September 1865, Brown appointed Harris to the pulpit of the Third Street AME Church in Richmond. Harris soon founded seven other AME mission congregations in Richmond and surrounding towns. He later served AME parishes in Washington, D.C., and Charleston and Columbia, South Carolina. In late 1868, he married Elizabeth P. Worthington, a white AMA teacher from Virginia. De Boer, "Afro-Americans in American Missionary Association," 276, 281–87, 418–24; Mansfield, "That Fateful Class," 124–36, 149–50, 170–72.

8. About one hundred contraband families settled on the Whitehead farm near Portsmouth. They constructed cabins and subdivided the land, allowing each family up to one acre to cultivate. William D. Harris and John N. Mars visited the settlement and worked with the residents to build a church and schoolhouse. In June 1864, the first worship service and Sunday school classes met in the new structure. Mansfield, "That Fateful Class," 145.

9. William S. Bell, a Massachusetts clergyman, served as the American Missionary Association's superintendent of education at Norfolk and Portsmouth, Virginia. He built a residence for AMA teachers and expanded the number of schools operated by the association at Portsmouth. His wife, Lucie L. Bell, was also an AMA teacher. Richardson, *Christian Reconstruction*, 60; De Boer, "Afro-Americans in American Missionary Association," 421; Fen, "Notes on the Education of Negroes," 206–7; *WAA*, 29 April 1865.

10. Scott combines portions of Acts 10:34 and 17:26.

11. Addison W. Eastman, a Methodist exhorter from Newbury, Vermont, served in 1863 as a clerk and hospital steward with the Union army in Virginia. In March 1864, he assumed a teaching post with the American Missionary Association at Portsmouth, where he cooperated with black activists at the North Street African Methodist Episcopal Church. By August 1864, he had moved to another AMA school at the Wise farm near Norfolk. H. N. Burton to Simeon S. Jocelyn, 26 January 1864, Testimonials by D. Packer, William H. Hill, and B. F. Ketchum, AMA-ARC; *WAA*, 9 April 1864.

12. Louise Smith and H. R. Arnold, teachers employed by the American Missionary Association, died at Portsmouth in July 1864. *AM*, September 1864.

13. Mars refers to the first Washington Conference of the Methodist denomination, which met in Baltimore during 27–31 October 1864. He attended and was named pastor of the city's Sharp Street Methodist Episcopal Church. *WAA*, 12 November 1864; John N. Mars to George Whipple, 3 November 1864, AMA-ARC [15:0589].

60.
George E. Stephens to Robert Hamilton
1 August 1864

Secretary of War Edwin M. Stanton promised black recruits the same treatment and pay as white troops, yet the highest-ranking black soldier received less military scrip than the lowest-ranking white. Cheated out of bounties, issued inferior weapons and insufficient rations, relegated to relentless fatigue duty, brutalized for minor breaches of discipline, and executed with alarming frequency for infractions of the military code, black enlistees believed that they suffered "under a tyranny inexorable as slavery itself." For blacks the military pay issue mirrored their long-standing struggle for racial equality and full citizenship. Although they assured the Lincoln administration that they would "fight for God, liberty and country, not money," they worked hard to expose the demoralizing injustice of unequal pay. Black leaders such as William Wells Brown and John S. Rock quit their recruitment work in protest. Members of the Fifty-fourth and Fifty-fifth Massachusetts Regiments refused their pay for eighteen months, subjecting themselves to charges of mutiny and their families to poverty and want. As one soldier declared, "To accept our pay in this way would degrade us, and mark us as inferior soldiers, and would be a complete annihilation of every vestige of our manhood." The following letter by George E. Stephens to the *Weekly Anglo-African*, one of many he wrote from the battlefield, conveys the full significance of the pay issue for black troops. *WAA*, 11 July 1863, 30 January, 26 March, 23, 30 April, 3, 22 October 1864; Berlin et al., *Freedom*, 2:17–22.

Morris Island, S[outh] C[arolina]
Aug[ust] 1, 1864

Mr. Editor:

Two or three months ago, it was announced that Congress had passed a law equalizing the pay of colored troops. This was at the closing period of the session. The colored troops, which had been enlisted under the law of 1862, were unpaid. This was known, of course, at Washington. The noble Major Stearns was compelled to resign, because the pledges he had been authorized by Sec. Stanton to make to the colored man were broken by the War Department, who refused to pay soldiers who had black skins more than seven dollars per month.[1]

Thus free men were reduced to servitude. No matter what services he might render—no matter how nobly he might acquit himself—he must carry with him the degradation of not being considered a man, but a thing. The foreigner, the alien, of whatever color, or race, or country, are enrolled and paid like native Americans; but the latest refinement of cruelty has been brought to bear on us.

In the Revolutionary War, and in the War of 1812, colored men fought, and were enrolled, and paid, the same as the whites; and not only this, were drilled and enlisted indiscriminately in the same companies and regiments. Little did our forefathers think that they were forging chains for the limbs of their own race. Look how nobly Forten, Bowers, and Cassey, and those colored patriots of the last war, rallied to the defence of Philadelphia; yet how were the colored people repaid? By stripping them in '38 of their right of franchise.[2] Now the plan is to inveigle the black man into the service by false pretences, and then make him take half pay. If he doesn't take half pay and behave himself, as a vender of religious tracts down here said, "Shoot 'em." Why, sir, the rebels have not reached the daring extreme of reducing free men to slaves. Does the Lincoln despotism think it can succeed? There are those who say, you should not talk so—"you hurt yourself." Let me say to those men, we cannot be injured more. There is no insult—there is no cruelty—there is no wrong, which we have not suffered. Torture, massacre, mobs and slavery. Do you think that we will tamely submit like spaniels to every indignity?

I shall speak hereafter my wrongs, and nothing shall prevent me but double irons or a pistol ball that shall take me out of the hell I am now suffering: nearly eighteen months of service—of labor—of humiliation—of danger, and not one dollar. An estimable wife reduced to beggary, and dependent upon another man—what can wipe out the wrong and insult this Lincoln despotism has put upon us? Loyal men everywhere hurl it from power—dismember it—grind it to atoms! Who would have believed that all the newspaper talk of the pay of colored soldiers having been settled by Congress was a base falsehood? There is not the least sign of pay, and there are hints from those in authority that we will not get paid, and will be held to service by the terrors of our own bullets. Seventeen months and upwards! Suppose we had been white? Massachusetts would have inaugurated a rebellion in the East, and we would have been paid. But—Oh, how insulting!—because I am black, they tamper with my rights. How dare I be offered half the pay of any man, be he white or red.

This matter of pay seems to some of those having slaveholding tendencies a small thing, but it belongs to that system which has stripped the country of the flower of its youth. It has rendered every hamlet and fireside in this wide country desolate, and brought the country itself to bankruptcy and shame. It is a concomitant of the system. Like as the foaming waves point the mariner to the hidden rocks on which his storm-driven ship will soon be lost, this gross injustice reveals to us the hidden insidious principles on which the best hopes of the true patriot will be dashed.

G. E. S.

Weekly Anglo-African (New York, N.Y.), 27 August 1864.

1. On 15 June 1864, Congress passed a military appropriations act that established an equal rate of pay for black and white troops. Prior to that enactment, black enlistees were paid under the provisions of the Militia Act of 1862, which had authorized the Lincoln administration to employ blacks in military service. The 1862 law mandated that all black soldiers, regardless of rank, would receive $7 per month, plus a $3 clothing allowance, about half the amount paid to the lowest-ranking white recruit. This conflicted with the pledge of Secretary of War Edwin M. Stanton that black recruits would receive equal pay. When the War Department adopted the lesser pay rate in June 1863, black soldiers and white recruiters such as George L. Stearns felt betrayed. Stearns resigned in disgust; many black recruits, especially those in the Fifty-fourth and Fifty-fifth Massachusetts Regiments, refused to accept unequal pay or the state's offer to compensate them for the difference. For eighteen months, the two regiments rejected repeated attempts by paymasters to dispense military scrip. They enlisted the support of sympathetic white officers, abolitionists, and politicians and lobbied Congress to reverse the policy. Some black regiments verged on mutiny over the issue, and several soldiers were shot for refusing orders, asserting that their enlistments were fraudulent because the government had reneged on its promise. Berlin et al., *Freedom*, 2:362–68, 400; Emilio, *History of the Fifty-Fourth Regiment*, 47–48, 109, 130, 135, 142, 179–81, 190–91, 220, 227–28.

2. In September 1814, as British forces threatened to attack Philadelphia, black leaders urged the local black community to improve the fortifications along the Schuylkill River south of the city. A Committee of Defence headed by James Forten, John C. Bowers, Joseph Cassey, Absalom Jones, Richard Allen, and Russell Parrott persuaded more than 360 blacks to volunteer for the task. Despite such actions, Pennsylvania blacks were disfranchised in 1838. Julie Winch, *Philadelphia's Black Elite: Activism, Accommodation, and the Struggle for Autonomy, 1787–1848* (Philadelphia, Pa., 1988), 20–21, 38.

61.
James McCune Smith to Robert Hamilton
August 1864

The Emancipation Proclamation was the first step in the long process of freeing some four million slaves. With formidable political and economic obstacles remaining, black abolitionists focused on "land and the ballot." Frederick Douglass feared that without political rights, the freedmen would become "slaves to the community." Other black leaders stressed the need for radical land reform to create economic opportunities for the freedmen. James McCune Smith assessed the prospects for Reconstruction in a two-part series entitled "The War—Its Issues," which was published under the pseudonym "S." in the *Weekly Anglo-African*. The first essay appeared in the 20 August 1864 issue and expressed Smith's skepticism that the war would destroy slavery. He argued that limitations in the Emancipation Proclamation, the indecision of the federal government, and indifference on the part of antislavery societies would preserve "all the wrongs of slavery without its name." One week later, Smith's second article emphasized the economic issues involved in ending slavery. He explained how land and labor policies might keep blacks in virtual bondage. Smith's insights into the dynamics of American capitalism surpassed conventional antislavery thought. His discussion of the tensions between economic classes echoed contemporary socialist critiques of capitalism, and he anticipated the penetration of northern money into the South. Smith warned that only when the government assured blacks of land ownership and fair labor contracts would the task of emancipation be complete. *WAA*, 20 August 1864, 26 August 1865 [16:0124]; *DM*, November 1862, June 1863; Foner, *Reconstruction*, 60–76; McPherson, *Struggle for Equality*, 238–59.

MR. EDITOR:

We have endeavored to show that there is neither in the political, nor religious, nor philanthropic worlds of the American people, any agency at work which can compass the entire abolishment of slavery. In spite of such proof, there are many who will persist in prophesying the certain downfall of slavery, as an outgrowth of this war. The reasons for this belief are too numerous to be examined in detail. They may be classified under two general statements: 1st. The Providence of God. 2d. The destruction of slavery by the removal of its support—by a sort of natural death.

In regard to the first ground of belief, we have nothing to say, for we believe that the age of "miracles is past." And, we fail to see in the history or character of the American people any special attraction for a special providence.

Hence we confine our examination to those influences, which, as an outgrowth of this war, will tend to abolish or maintain slavery. We have failed, in a former article, to discover any adequate force for the abolishment of slavery. In confirmation of this view, we call attention to a letter copied into another column from the Norfolk, Va., correspondent of the *Independent*.[1]

The main support of slavery before the war, a support which will be strengthened rather than weakened at the end of the war, is that it is a condition of society in which *"capital owns labor."* The thousands of colossal fortunes which this war has already created will find no better investment than buying up the lands of the rebel States. And, owning the land, the ownership of labor also will speedily accrue to them. What defence can the landless, penniless, outlawed *emancipado*[2] make against the land-monopolizing, monied, lawmaking capitalist—who says to him, work for this pittance or get you gone and starve! In free society, there is a perpetual conflict between labor and capital; the more nearly they are balanced, the more free the state of society, but when either gets the upper hand there is more or less of slave society introduced. Generally, capital is predominant, because capital can wait, while labor cannot. It is only in the instance where labor is scarce, and society exigent, that labor is in the ascendant—as today, in the north. It is amusing, in this instance, to see labor put on lordly airs; as in such advertisements as the following:

TO BOSS COBBLERS—Take notice that in and after Monday, 29th inst., journeymen cobblers will require four dollars a day, and in addition beer and tobacco; besides half pay for blue Monday.[3]

IZZY BOTCH, Chairman

Capital, of course, succumbs for the moment, but it goes to Congress and gets a law passed, it sends its agents to Europe, and within six months there will be so many cobblers and laborers and mechanics of all kinds imported that Mr. I. B. and his trade union will become applicants at the soup houses, and for outdoor relief for the poor. In slave society, there is *no conflict* between capital and labor; labor lies prostrate, and capital dictates its own terms, which are perpetual subjugation; in other words, perpetual slavery. So far from this war diminishing the wish or the power of capital to own labor, it will increase both. Colossal monopolies are parceling out even the free States for their ownership. The slave in the South will have namesakes in fact, if not in title, North of Mason and Dixon's line. Capital invested in a single article, alcohol, actually bought up a working majority of last Congress; how much more easily could it subsidize any of the one-horse legislatures of a reconstructed rebel State, so as to make things right about the freedmen. The word *slavery* will, of course, be wiped from the statute book—by the bye, slavery is a *legal* institution in none of the slave States, being nowhere ordained by statute—but the "ancient relation" can be just as well maintained by cunningly devised laws. In fact, the word "slave" was already dying out of the Southern vocabulary; it was "my servant" and "my people."

The special manner in which capital will seize upon and own labor in the reconstructed States requires no foretelling. The white man, owning the land, the capital and the lawmaking, already owns labor. In deference to the world's opinion, capital may for a few years, after the war ends, deck its victim with the garlands of freedom—only to make the sacrifice more complete in the end. We need not even wait until the end of the war to see things drifting in this direction.

At Arlington Heights, we are called upon to witness a blessed instance of what philanthropy and thrift are doing for the freedman. It is a scene of almost Arcadian beauty and simplicity, in which neat-looking cottages, well-cultivated land, and a happy peasantry are rejoicing under the rule of a master who generously allows able-bodied men eight dollars a month, without any chance of ownership in the soil, while the same men, by crossing the Potomac, would command thirty or forty dollars per month, as many of them as can be had![4]

On the coast of South Carolina, after a year of experimenting on the willingness of the freedmen to work and their ability to support themselves, a plan was begun of cutting up the large estates into twenty and forty acre plots, to be sold to the freedmen at government prices for government lands, and government terms of payment. This plan was eminently fair and just; it was also a radical abolishment of slavery. It made the freedman owner of his own labor, and also an owner of a fair share of the land. It promised success also; for at the first sale of these lands, the freedmen came up promptly and bought largely, showing the thrift and shrewdness of men worthy of citizenship. Capital, however, took the alarm. Capital went to Washington; capital hocus-pocuss'd and bought up the rest of the land, or at least placed it beyond the reach of the freedmen.[5]

In 1860 we fell in with a youth about twenty years old, five feet four in height, of great energy of character, who was clerking in one of our large wholesale houses, at eight hundred or a thousand dollars a year. In 1862, we heard of him as married, and putting up at the ——— Hotel (the most expensive in the city). "How so?" said we to a mutual acquaintance. "Cotton," was the reply. In the Spring of this year, we again fell in with our acquaintance of 1860. He had just returned from New Orleans, near which he had hired one or more plantations of a thousand acres, also about eight hundred and fifty freedmen, whom he paid eight dollars a month; and they were so fond of him, it was really painful for him to tear himself away. He had been always a violent hater of Abolitionists, but now they might set him down as a thoroughgoing Abolitionist; and he expected to clear about a million and a half dollars by his first year's operation. Wasn't he a first-rate Abolitionist?

And so capital, aided by the government (which is, in wartime, the minion of capital), pursues its ownership of labor, and whatever the condition of the freedman today under the biting necessities of war, that condition will not be bettered after peace; under the harrow, a nation is nearest to doing justice by its own downtrodden. It is no reply to these statements that government has recently raised the wages of all able-bodied freedmen to eighteen dollars a month. An able-bodied freedman on a cotton plantation today earns four thousand dollars per year when government raises his wages to $216 a year, add for his support another hundred, and there is a fair profit to capital of one hundred and eighty four dollars. And government will aid capital to cheat the freedman out of three thousand five hundred dollars per year!

It may be objected to all this that free labor will go down South, in the shape of emigrants from abroad or disbanded soldiers from our armies. Capital will outstrip the first in getting possession of the most fertile lands. As to our soldiers, how many able-bodied men will be left of them when this "cruel war" is over? "Our losses were only four thousand," is the weekly, and our "losses are small, only a thousand," the daily report of the newspapers. A thousand! one-fourth killed, one-fourth maimed for life, and one-fourth taken to Libby Prison or Belle Isle to be starved to death.[6] How many soldiers will we have left from a war which costs us a thousand men per diem?

For these reasons, we do not see that American slavery will go out of existence as an issue or result of the present war.

S.

Weekly Anglo-African (New York, N.Y.), 27 August 1864.

1. Smith refers to a letter signed "A Missionary to the Freedmen," which appeared in the 11 August 1864 issue of the New York–based *Independent*. Written from Norfolk, it recounted recent incidents of discrimination under Union military occupation and urged immediate action to grant full citizenship to blacks. It was reprinted in the 27 August issue of the *Weekly Anglo-African*.

2. *Emancipado* is a Spanish term referring to Africans imported into Cuba and bound as servants for five to seven years before being freed. Smith uses it to denote all freedmen. Howard Jones, *Mutiny on the Amistad* (New York, N.Y., 1987), 18–19.

3. Nineteenth-century artisans often used Mondays—traditionally called "Blue Monday"—to repair and sharpen their tools, carry in supplies, discuss current events, and ready the shop for the work week ahead. Herbert G. Gutman, *Work, Culture, and Society in Industrializing America* (New York, N.Y., 1976), 37–39.

4. Smith refers to Freedmen's Village, a contraband camp established in 1863 on General Robert E. Lee's Arlington, Virginia, estate. Former slaves worked the estate and created a model community. Although Smith implies that this arrange-

ment was exploitative of free black labor, conditions on the estate were considerably better than the crowded, disease-ridden encampments in nearby Washington, D.C. The success of Freedmen's Village led to the establishment of similar camps on other confiscated lands across the Potomac River from Washington. Allan J. Johnston, "Surviving Freedom: The Black Community of Washington, D.C., 1860–1880" (Ph.D. diss., Duke University, 1980), 186–87.

5. Smith refers to the Port Royal experiment on the South Carolina Sea Islands, the earliest and best publicized of the efforts to prepare the former slaves for the transition to freedom. When the Union navy occupied Port Royal in November 1861, virtually all the white inhabitants fled to the mainland, leaving some ten thousand blacks in control of the plantations. Sea Island blacks abandoned cotton production and began planting corn and potatoes for their own subsistence. But scores of northern missionaries, teachers, government officials, and businessmen soon descended on the region, establishing schools and churches for the freedmen and assuming nearly total control of the local economy. They quickly forced Sea Island blacks back into cotton production, believing that it would better prepare them for the change to a free labor economy. Although the federal government auctioned off confiscated rebel plantations during 1863–64, only a small portion went to groups of freedmen, who pooled their meager resources to complete the purchase. Most plantations ended up in the hands of Union army officers, government officials, and northern speculators and cotton companies. Despite their desire to become landowners, a majority of Sea Island blacks were forced to work as wage laborers for these northern investors. Rose, *Rehearsal for Reconstruction*.

6. Libby Prison and Belle Isle were Confederate military prisons in Richmond, Virginia. Notorious Libby Prison, a former factory, housed some one thousand Union officers. The prison camp on Belle Isle, located in the rapids of the James River, held more than seven thousand Union enlisted men. Because of makeshift conditions at both locations, inmates suffered from overcrowding, starvation, exposure, and disease. *HTECW*, 54, 437–38.

62.
Speech by John S. Rock
Delivered at the Wesleyan Methodist Church
Syracuse, New York
6 October 1864

Black abolitionists quickly grasped the watershed quality of the Civil War. A hard-won but unmistakable expansion of black freedom and the nation's emerging commitment to destroying slavery signaled the beginning of a new era. To prepare to meet these fresh opportunities, black leaders gathered during 4–7 October 1864 at the Wesleyan Methodist Church in Syracuse, New York. Delegates attended from eighteen states in both the North and the South, making this the most representative black national convention prior to Reconstruction. They united to form the National Equal Rights League, the first nationwide organization devoted solely to promoting black equality. Through its extensive network of state and local auxiliaries, the NERL offered blacks a platform to debate strategy and an independent vehicle to champion social change. Many blacks invested their hopes for suffrage, civil rights, and a just Reconstruction in the league. In this eloquent speech delivered on the convention's third day, John S. Rock captured the meaning of the war for blacks and the new expectations that they shared. "We ask the same for the black man that is asked for the white man," he noted, "nothing more and nothing less." *Proceedings of the National Convention of Colored Men, Held in the City of Syracuse, N.Y., October 4, 5, 6, and 7, 1864* (Boston, Mass., 1864), 36–52 [15:0554–61]; *WAA*, 5, 12, 19 November 1864, 18 February, 1 April, 6 May 1865; *Lib*, 23 December 1864; Sanelli, "Struggle for Black Suffrage in Pennsylvania," 149, 164–68, 173, 188–94.

I come from Massachusetts, where we are jealous of every right. I received information a few days ago that a sergeant in the Fifty-fourth Massachusetts Regiment, who is a splendid penman, had been detailed by his captain as a clerk in his department; and that, when the officer in command learned this, he immediately ordered the sergeant back to his regiment, saying in his order, that "no negro will be allowed to hold any position in this department except that of a cook or a laborer." A copy of this order was forwarded to me; and I immediately presented the case to our most excellent Governor, who was going to Washington that evening. The result is, the sergeant is restored back to his position as clerk, and the officer who made the order has suddenly left for the North. (Applause.) This result was at once forwarded to me; and I immediately communicated it to his Excellency the Governor, when he sent me this noble reply:

COMMONWEALTH OF MASSACHUSETTS,
EXECUTIVE DEPARTMENT,
BOSTON, [Massachusetts]
Oct[ober] 4, 1864
JOHN S. ROCK, ESQ.
DEAR SIR:

I am glad to hear of the favorable result in the case referred to. I had no doubt what the result would be; but it is through you that I first learn it definitely. I thank you for your kind expressions of acknowledgment to me personally; and with a constant willingness to do my part, always, to insure equal opportunities for usefulness and success in all the occupations and duties of life to men of equal intelligence, industry, and integrity, whether they be white or black, I am, very truly, yours,

JOHN A. ANDREW

(Great applause.)

All we ask is equal opportunities and equal rights. This is what our brave men are fighting for. They have not gone to the battlefield for the sake of killing and being killed; but they are fighting for liberty and equality. (Applause.) We ask the same for the black man that is asked for the white man; nothing more and nothing less. When our men fight bravely, as they always do, they don't like to be cheated out of the glory and the positions they so dearly earn. Many of our grandfathers fought in the Revolution, and they thought they were fighting for liberty; but they made a sad mistake, and we are now obliged to fight those battles over again, and I hope, this time, to a better purpose. We are all loyal. Why are we not treated as friends? This nation spurned our offers to rally around it for two long years, and then, without any guarantees, called upon us at a time when the loyal white men of the North hesitated. We buried the terrible outrages of the past, and came magnanimously and gallantly forward. In the heroism displayed at Milliken's Bend, Port Hudson, Fort Wagner, Olustee, in the battles now going on before Richmond,[1] and everywhere where our men have faced the foe, they have covered themselves all over with glory. (Applause.) They have nobly written with their blood the declaration of their right to have their names recorded on the pages of history among the true patriots of this American Revolution for Liberty. (Applause.) Witness, if you please, the moral heroism of the Massachusetts soldiers, spurning the offers of seven dollars a month, which the Government insultingly tempted them with for eighteen months, when it was known that they were without means, and that many of them had wives at home and children crying to them for bread when there was none to give them. But they bore it manfully, and have lived to see the right triumph. (Applause.) My friends, we owe much to the colored soldiers; not only to the Massachusetts men, but to every brave man who has taken up the musket in defence of liberty. (Applause.) They have done wonders for the race. Let us stand by them and their families, and be ready at any and at all times to assist them, and to give them a word of cheer.

Though we are unfortunately situated, I am not discouraged. Our cause is flying onward with the swiftness of Mercury.[2] Every day seems almost to be an era in the history of our country. We have at last reached the dividing line. There are but two parties in the country today. The one headed by Lincoln is for Freedom and the Republic; and the other, by McClellan,[3] is for Despotism and Slavery. There can be no middle ground in war. The friends and the enemies of the country are defined, and the one or the other must triumph. We are to have but one government throughout the broad territory of the United States. Two systems of government so innately hostile to each other as that of the North is to that of the South could not exist on the same soil. We should be like the Romans and Carthaginians; among whom, says Paterculus, "there always existed either a war, preparations for a war, or a deceitful peace."[4] The fate of this Republic will be settled in this contest; and its enemies must either be subdued or annihilated, and it is of but little consequence which. (Applause.)

Proceedings of the National Convention of Colored Men, Held in the City of Syracuse, N.Y., October 4, 5, 6, and 7, 1864 (Boston, Mass., 1864), 23–25.

1. Rock refers to major Civil War battles involving black troops. The battle of Olustee on 20 February 1864 was the largest combat engagement in Florida during the war. The Fifty-fourth Massachusetts Regiment, the Eighth U.S. Colored Troops, and the First North Carolina Volunteers accompanied Union forces under the command of Brigadier General Truman Seymour. Confederates halted Seymour's advance toward Tallahassee and destroyed about one-third of his invading force. As Union troops fled the field under withering fire, the Fifty-fourth Massachusetts advanced and prevented a general rout. At the time of Rock's speech in October, Union and Confederate forces were maneuvering in Virginia in some of the bloodiest fighting of the war. From May 1864 to April 1865, the Army of the Potomac and the Army of the James—both with thousands of black soldiers—pursued General Robert E. Lee's Army of Northern Virginia in an attempt to end the conflict by crushing his forces and capturing the Confederate capital at Richmond. Emilio, *History of the Fifty-Fourth Regiment*, 148–73; *HTECW*, 545; Cornish, *Sable Arm*, 266–83.

2. In ancient Roman mythology, Mercury was the wing-footed messenger of the gods.

3. George B. McClellan.

4. Rock draws from an obscure chronicle of Rome written in 30 A.D. by Gaius Velleius Paterculus (b. 19 B.C.), a soldier and historian. Paterculus's quote refers to the Punic Wars—a series of conflicts between Rome and Carthage in the second and third centuries B.C. Harry T. Peck, ed., *Harper's Dictionary of Classical Literature and Antiquities* (New York, N.Y., 1897), 1183.

63.
John S. Rock to Charles Sumner
17 December 1864

As black leaders tested the changes brought by the Civil War, their personal victories evoked a sense of optimism throughout the black community. When Secretary of State William H. Seward granted Henry Highland Garnet an American passport, blacks viewed it as an affirmation of their citizenship claims. When the Union army commissioned Martin R. Delany as its first black field officer, they regarded it as an acknowledgment of their abilities. Similarly, when John S. Rock became the first black admitted to argue cases before the U.S. Supreme Court, they understood that the nation's highest judicial body had tacitly repudiated the Dred Scott decision. Rock had written to Charles Sumner in December 1863, seeking the senator's assistance in gaining permission to practice before the court. Sumner, who was well acquainted with the black Boston attorney, advised against the attempt while Roger B. Taney sat as chief justice. But Taney died in October 1864 and was replaced by antislavery politician Salmon P. Chase. On 17 December, Rock again wrote Sumner, repeating his request, and the senator successfully lobbied Chase on his behalf. Rock's swearing in ceremony before the Supreme Court on 1 February 1865 was a remarkable moment in Afro-American history. Blacks recognized the symbolic importance of a black lawyer standing before the court and being treated with respect, dignity, and equality. Reflecting on the significance of Rock's accomplishment, the *Weekly Anglo-African* reminded its readers that "only a few months ago a black man could not enter the sanctum sanctorum of American justice without a broom . . . in hand." Schor, *Henry Highland Garnet*, 179–80; Ullman, *Martin R. Delany*, 296–302; Levesque, "Boston's Black Brahmin," 332–36; *WAA*, 11 February 1865; *NASS*, 4 March 1865 [15:0771]; *Lib*, 24 March 1865 [15:0790].

Boston, [Massachusetts]
Dec[ember] 17th, 1864

Hon. Sir & Friend:

Again permit me to ask the favour of your influence in my behalf. I believe it will be a matter of great benefit to me to be admitted to the bar of the S.C.U.S. We now have a <u>great</u> and <u>good</u> man for our Chief Justice,[1] and with him I think my color will not be a bar to my admission. As you are acquainted with him and coming from this Commonwealth I take the liberty to ask you to consult with him. I will see to getting someone to make a motion if that is necessary, for I understand very well that it might be considered as compromising your position as a Senator to go out of

12. John S. Rock admitted to practice before the U.S. Supreme Court
Courtesy of Library of Congress

your way to make a motion of this kind—and yet I want to have the satisfaction of knowing that through your influence the matter was brought before the Court.

If you will do me the favor to consult with the proper persons and let me hear from you at your earliest convenience you will greatly oblige me. I shall be in Philadelphia by the last of this week. Please let me hear from you by that time if convenient to you.

Please direct 858 Lombard St., Phil.

Hoping to hear from you soon, I have the Honor to be, Dear Sir, Your obt. servant

John S. Rock

Charles Sumner Papers, Houghton Library, Harvard University, Cambridge, Massachusetts. Published by permission.

1. Salmon P. Chase (1808–1873) was appointed chief justice of the U.S. Supreme Court in December 1864. As a young Ohio lawyer, his energetic defense of black runaways earned him the sobriquet "Attorney General for Fugitive Slaves." Chase entered politics in the 1840s, became a leading figure in the Liberty and Free Soil parties, and served in the U.S. Senate (1849–55) and as governor of Ohio (1856–60). After failing to secure the Republican presidential nomination in 1860, he became secretary of the treasury in Abraham Lincoln's administration. As chief justice, he presided over the impeachment trial of President Andrew Johnson and arbitrated the critical legal issues of Reconstruction. *DAB*, 4:27–34.

64.
Joseph E. Sampson to Robert Hamilton
23 January 1865

Black contributions to the Union war effort extended well beyond the enlistment of some 180,000 soldiers. Throughout the North and Canada West, black communities mobilized in response to humanitarian needs created by the conflict. They assisted refugee slaves through relief associations and provided for black recruits and their families through soldiers' aid societies and auxiliaries of the U.S. Sanitary Commission. Many antebellum black organizations—churches, antislavery societies, vigilance committees, and benevolent associations—joined the wartime relief movement. African Methodist Episcopal congregations in the North channeled goods to the Union Relief Association (a society within Washington's Union AME Church), as part of a nationwide network of black organizations that forwarded money and supplies to groups in Union-occupied areas of the South. The Colored Ladies Auxiliary of the Soldiers' Aid Society of Northern Ohio carried on this charitable work. The society's corresponding secretary, Joseph E. Sampson, reported on its activities in the following letter to the *Weekly Anglo-African*. He noted that the members sewed clothes, collected items for fund-raising fairs in the East, attended the wounded in hospitals, and even provided soldiers in the field with subscriptions to the *Anglo-African*. *WAA*, 20 February, 9, 30 July, 6 August, 17 September 1864, 26 August 1865; *CR*, 4, 11 October 1862, 27 August 1864; Ripley et al., *Black Abolitionist Papers*, 2:510–11.

> CLEVELAND, O[hio]
> Jan[uary] 23, 1865

MR. EDITOR:

In behalf of the Colored Ladies Auxiliary Soldiers' Aid Society, organized in this city since June '63, I am moved, in justice to their patriotic efforts to promote the cause of our sick and wounded braves, to lay before the public a synoptical report of their labors from time to time.

This Society, through the unceasing energy of its President, Mrs. Mary E. Parker, and other officers, especially its very efficient Secretary, Mrs. Lavinia Sabb, has done much to raise it to its present standard,[1] and I am proud to say its paramount end is to minister to the wants of our soldiers in the field and hospitals. The ladies assemble every Thursday to make up articles of wear for the soldiers, and could you but peep into their business department and see their activity, witness the rapid movements of needle and scissors—I am sure that in making your exit you would do so with the best impression of female organizations and would feel in favor of ladies' rights generally. The first Thursday evening in the month they have their monthly meetings for the collection of dues, the reception of members, and to devise methods of advancing their noble cause, and in many instances to vote every dollar out of the treasury for some humane purpose, and trust in God and the philanthropy of a generous people to replenish it. One very important feature connected with their monthly exercises is an address by some one of our colored minds which tends to add interest to the meetings as well as give stimulus to the non-aspirant. It was the second Soldiers' Aid Society (of color) organized in the West,[2] and since their organization, they have aided the families of soldiers in our midst, and have sent garments and nourishments to our 5th United States Regiment[3] while sick in the hospital at Camp Delaware, as well as visiting them in person and like ministering angels bathed their feverish brows and moistened their parched lips.

From the proceeds of their great fair they contributed two hundred and twenty-five dollars to aid the Sanitary Commission,[4] and the residue of a hundred dollars was expended for other humane purposes. I will further add, that they contributed eighteen dollars toward sending your valuable paper to our soldiers in the army. At a monthly meeting not long since, I saw exhibited a beautiful and valuable set of vases which was sent as a present to the Colored Soldiers' Sanitary Fair held in Philadelphia.[5] Thus you see that the patriotism of our ladies actuates them to cooperate with any enterprise tending to the promotion of a good and noble end.

In sending you this imperfect report of the Ladies Soldiers' Aid Society, I do so of my own accord, for if a thing is not told it is never known to any but the receivers, and I am free to confess my jealousy when I read from time to time of the great work that is being performed by the good ladies in almost every city in the East, while so far as newspaper mention goes, apparently we of the far West, occupy the humble seat of do-nothing. But proud am I that I can turn darkness into light—by telling you that the ladies of Cleveland are alive to the events of the day, or in other words, are up and doing.

J. E. SAMPSON[6]
Cor. Secretary

Weekly Anglo-African (New York, N.Y.), 4 February 1865.

1. The Colored Ladies Auxiliary was one of 525 chapters of the Soldiers' Aid Society of Northern Ohio, itself a branch of the U.S. Sanitary Commission. Formed in June 1863 to assist Union soldiers and their families, this black association was led by Mary E. Parker, Lavinia Sabb, and Lucie Stanton Day and received liberal support from Cleveland's black community. It initially forwarded supplies to the Sanitary Commission, but later worked independently, sending donations to black soldiers' aid societies in Washington, D.C., and Norfolk, Virginia. Members also cared for members of the Fifth U.S. Colored Troops in the

hospital at nearby Camp Delaware. When Abraham Lincoln's funeral train passed through the city in April 1865, these women honored the fallen president by placing a wreath on his open casket. They decided not to disband at the end of the Civil War and were led by Parker into the postwar years. *WAA*, 14 November 1863, 21 January, 13 May, 3 September 1865; W. A. Ingham, *Women of Cleveland and Their Work* (Cleveland, Ohio, 1893), 124–38; Kenneth L. Kusmer, *A Ghetto Takes Shape: Black Cleveland, 1870–1930* (Urbana, Ill., 1976), 26.

2. The first such organization, the Colored Soldiers' Aid Society of Chicago, had been formed in April 1863. *WAA*, 2 May 1863.

3. The Fifth U.S. Colored Troops, Ohio's first black regiment, was officially organized in November 1863 at Camp Delaware. Most of its recruits were young free blacks from Cleveland and the southern part of the state. Created to meet federal draft quotas and protect white Ohioans from military service, it became a proud symbol for the state's blacks. Within days of its first assignment, the Fifth liberated hundreds of Virginia slaves, gained seventy new recruits, and captured several rebel prisoners. Between December 1864 and April 1865, the unit participated in battles at Richmond, Petersburg, New Market Heights (where it suffered 236 casualties), and Fair Oaks, Virginia, and in several engagements in North Carolina. It was mustered out of service in September 1865. Cheek and Cheek, *John Mercer Langston*, 406–8; Dyer, *Compendium*, 3:1724; Berlin et al., *Freedom*, 2:346–47, 772–73; Cornish, *Sable Arm*, 279.

4. The U.S. Sanitary Commission was organized by civilians in June 1861 to care for sick and wounded soldiers and provide relief for their families. Rev. Henry W. Bellows of New York City headed the commission's extensive organization, which attracted the voluntary assistance of northern intellectuals, reformers, and business leaders such as Frederick Law Olmsted, Samuel Gridley Howe, and George Templeton Strong. Its Washington, D.C., headquarters and its seven thousand auxiliaries solicited donations and sponsored hundreds of fund-raising fairs; by the end of the war, they had raised over $7,000,000 and collected and distributed some $12,000,000 worth of supplies. At its height, the commission employed more than five hundred nurses, medical assistants, and other workers. *HTECW*, 656–67; George Fredrickson, *The Inner Civil War: Northern Intellectuals and the Crisis of the Union* (New York, N.Y., 1965), 98–102.

5. Sampson refers to a fair held at Philadelphia's Concert Hall on 19 December 1864 by the Ladies Sanitary Commission of St. Thomas's African Episcopal Church. The gathering raised more than $1,200 for the work of the society, which had been organized as an auxiliary of the U.S. Sanitary Commission in April 1863 by members of the local black elite. It met weekly and regularly forwarded clothing and other supplies to black soldiers and to the contrabands at Port Royal, South Carolina. After 19 December, the fair was moved to St. Thomas's Church. Foner and Walker, *Proceedings of the Black State Conventions*, 1:148 [15:0712]; Foner, *Essays in Afro-American History*, 30; *WAA*, 8 October 1864, 7 January 1865.

6. Joseph E. Sampson (?–1897), the brother of noted black journalist John P. Sampson, was born in Wilmington, North Carolina. He worked as a carpenter in Cleveland during the Civil War, served as corresponding secretary for the Colored Ladies Auxiliary of the Soldiers' Aid Society of Northern Ohio, and repre-

sented local blacks at the 1865 annual meeting of the National Equal Rights League. Sampson returned to Wilmington about 1871 and participated in local civic affairs, including terms as the city's mayor and registrar of deeds. *Cleveland City Directory*, 1861–71; *WAA*, 21 January, 18 March 1865; Foner and Walker, *Black National and State Conventions*, 45; *CR*, 26 August 1897; *RG*, 21 August 1897.

65.
Editorial by S. W. Rogers
22 April 1865

The resentment that many black abolitionists felt toward Abraham
Lincoln dissolved after his 14 April 1865 assassination. Most blacks
mourned his death as a catastrophe. For all his shortcomings, Lincoln
had proven more sympathetic to their aspirations than any previous
president. While the bondsmen lost their liberator, black leaders believed that Lincoln's death lessened chances for a meaningful Reconstruction. The *Weekly Anglo-African*, once one of Lincoln's sharpest
critics, now ruefully noted that the unreconstructed South was "dancing
the scalp dance over the remains of our murdered President." The shock
that blacks felt at Lincoln's death and their attempts to mythologize him
in its wake found expression in this 22 April editorial from the New
Orleans *Black Republican*. The paper, which had been founded on the
day Lincoln died, was edited by former slave Rev. S. W. Rogers and
proclaimed itself "the true organ of the American colored people of
Louisiana." It hoped to guide black opinion and ally all classes of
Louisiana blacks with the national government. Rogers's editorial expresses the profound sense of loss blacks felt over the assassination and
reveals how rapidly blacks deified "the name of 'Abraham, the Martyr.'" WAA, 22, 29 April, 6, 13, 18 May, 24 June 1865; Henry Lewis
Suggs, ed., *The Black Press in the South, 1865–1979* (Westport, Conn.,
1983), 157–59, 172n; Ripley, *Slaves and Freedmen in Civil War Louisiana*, 85.

ASSASSINATION OF PRESIDENT LINCOLN
The 13th of April will be a day forever memorable in history by an act
of atrocity that has no parallel in the annals of men. On the evening of
that day, the President of the United States of America, while sitting quietly in his box at the theater—almost his only relaxation—in the capital
of the country, in the company of his wife, in the very midst of his friends,
at the zenith of his power, was shot to death by an assassin, who, after
the deed of blood, leaped from the box to the stage, and exclaimed:
"Now the South is avenged—be it so to all tyrants," and succeeded in
escaping. At the same hour, the Hon. William H. Seward, Secretary of
State, while lying hopelessly ill in his bed, in his own house, in the same
city, is assaulted by a desperate accomplice of the murderer of Mr. Lincoln, and cut nearly to death, in the midst of his family and attendants,
several of whom were seriously if not fatally wounded.[1]
    In the face of crimes so appalling, men are stunned. "Who next?" is
the whispered inquiry.
    These dreadful deeds are a fitting finale of this brutal and bloody re-

bellion. They are the natural results of it. By the rebellion, these men were instigated to the perpetration of crimes that are but the *great* crime compressed into individual acts. They are the fell spirit of slavery breaking from the knife of the assassin—slavery, that for two hundred years has educated whole generations in cruelty and the spirit of murder; that, in the end, drove half a nation to a rebellion to destroy liberty, now whets the knife of the assassin to murder, in cold blood, the most illustrious exemplar of freedom.

Rebels may condemn these horrible acts; they may seek to run down the responsibility to some individual insanity, but they can never clear the skirts of the rebellion of the responsibility for the madness of the murderers. The assassins are the natural outcrop of that vast stratum of cruelty and of crime which slavery has been so long depositing below the surface of society. The greatest earthly friend of the colored race has fallen by the same spirit that has so long oppressed and destroyed us. In giving us our liberty, he has lost his own life. Following the rule of the great and glorious in the world, he has paid the penalty of Apostleship. He has sealed with his blood his Divine commission to be the liberator of a people. Hereafter, through all time, wherever the Black Race may be known in the world; whenever and wherever it shall lay the foundations of its power; build its cities and rear its temples, it will sacredly preserve if not deify the name of "*Abraham, the Martyr.*"

Black Republican (New Orleans, La.), 22 April 1865.

1. On the evening of 14 April 1865, while watching a performance of *Our American Cousin* from his private box at Ford's Theater in Washington, D.C., Abraham Lincoln was shot by actor John Wilkes Booth. While making his escape, Booth leaped to the stage and reputedly shouted, "*Sic semper tyrannus!*"—Latin for "thus be it ever to tyrants"—the Virginia state motto. Booth and a small group of conspirators intended to assassinate several prominent officials, including Vice-President Andrew Johnson and Secretary of State William Seward. While Booth was carrying out his part in the plot, a former Confederate guerrilla named Lewis Paine forced his way into Seward's Washington residence, assaulted his family, and wounded Seward—then convalescing from a carriage accident—with a bowie knife. Lincoln died the next morning, but Seward recovered. *HTECW*, 440–41; Van Deusen, *William Henry Seward*, 413–14.

66.
J. Sella Martin to Editor, *New York Evening Post*
24 April 1865

On 21 April 1865, Abraham Lincoln's funeral train pulled out of the nation's capital, carrying the slain president's body home to Springfield, Illinois. Blacks in Washington, Baltimore, and Philadelphia honored the "Emancipator" by participating in observances along the route. New York City's black leaders were outraged on 22 April when the common council denied them permission to march in the funeral procession as it passed through the city. The council explained that their request had come too late and that Irish and white Masonic marchers had threatened to withdraw if blacks were allowed to participate. Local black leaders denounced the decision with cries of "Shame! Shame!" The city's influential Union League supported their protest and rebuked the council's decision as an insult to the state's gallant black troops, "to the rights and feelings of the living," and "to the memory of the honored dead." When the War Department telegraphed a request "that no discrimination respecting color should be exercised in admitting persons to the funeral procession," the council relented. But black marchers were placed so far back in line that Lincoln's coffin had left the city by the time they joined the procession. Scores of blacks met at J. Sella Martin's First Colored Presbyterian Church to condemn the council's actions. In this 24 April letter, which the *New York Evening Post* refused to print, Martin denounced the council's racist behavior and revealed how blacks viewed their participation in the ceremonies. Dorothy Meserve Kunhardt and Philip B. Kunhardt, Jr., *Twenty Days* (New York, N.Y., 1965), 140–54; *WAA*, 29 April, 6, 13 May 1865.

> 132 Thompson Street
> New York, [New York]
> April 24, 1865

To the Editors of the Evening Post:[1]

A committee, consisting of some of the most respectable colored citizens, was appointed to wait on the Committee of Arrangements of the Common Council, to have a place assigned the body which they represented; and after two visits they were compelled to leave the Common Council Committee without an answer, and therefore without any assignment of a place in the procession. Supposing that the Citizens' Committee was an associate, and not a subordinate committee, another committee on behalf of the colored citizens waited on Mr. Moses Taylor this morning to see if arrangements could not be made for us to join the procession from Union Square, but the Committee was informed by Mr.

13. J. Sella Martin
Courtesy of Moorland-Spingarn Research Center, Howard University

Taylor that the committee which he represented did not wish to come in conflict with the Common Council, and he gave it as his opinion that the Citizens' Committee was subordinate to that of the Common Council.[2] Mr. Taylor, however, referred the committee waiting on him to a gentleman whom they were unable to see.

The prospect, therefore, is that every man with a colored face will be refused the much-coveted though melancholy satisfaction of following the corpse of the best public benefactor the country had ever given them. In the lowest forms of civilized life, the most puerile wishes and most insignificant directions of the dead are carried out. Great disrespect to the dead, and sometimes great injury to the feelings of the living, is done when interest or wilfulness stands in the way. And shall the most highly civilized people do what the most barbarous would scorn to be guilty of doing? The last public words of Mr. Lincoln leave no doubt that had he been consulted, he would have urged, as a dying request, that the representatives of the race which had come to the nation's rescue in the hour of peril, and which he had lifted by the most solemn official acts to the dignity of citizens and defenders of the Union, should be allowed the honor of following his remains to the grave.[3]

But, besides this disrespect to what everyone knows would have been the wishes of Mr. Lincoln, a great injustice is done the living by this unjust exclusion of us from participating in a sacred duty and high privilege.

It would be an overwhelming thought if we did not believe that great injustice is done to the sentiments and feelings of the better class of our white fellow-citizens, and certainly great injustice is done to a people who are excluded on account of a complexion which they did not give themselves.

Sella Martin

Liberator (Boston, Mass.), 5 May 1865.

1. William Cullen Bryant (1794–1878), a popular poet best remembered for *Thanatopsis* (1817), became the editor of the *New York Evening Post* in 1829. He remained in that capacity for nearly half a century, becoming one of the three most influential American journalists of his time. Bryant opposed slavery, condemned the Compromise of 1850 and the Kansas-Nebraska Act, supported the Republican party, backed the arming of free-state settlers in Kansas, and lionized John Brown as a hero and a martyr. But after the Civil War, he turned against Radical Reconstruction and supported the conservative policies of President Andrew Johnson. *DAB*, 3:200–205.

2. At least three committees representing local blacks asked that their organizations be allowed to march in New York City's 25 April 1865 funeral procession honoring Abraham Lincoln. But the common council, the city's governing board, announced that it wanted "positively no black people in our procession." Blacks then approached a citizens' committee established by the New York Chamber of

Commerce to help coordinate the Lincoln observances. It was chaired by Moses Taylor and included several dozen local businessmen. Taylor (1806–1882), a member of one of the city's wealthiest families, had made a fortune in the Mediterranean and West Indian trades and in real estate, then headed several banks, coal businesses, and railroad companies. During the Civil War, he chaired the Loan Committee of Associated Banks of New York City, which provided money to the federal government and to the committee overseeing arrangements for Lincoln's funeral train. Although not a member of the common council, Taylor wished to avoid conflict with that body and informed local blacks that the citizens' committee lacked the authority to alter the council's decision. Blacks were permitted to join the procession only after a telegram requesting their inclusion arrived from the War Department. *WAA*, 29 April, 6, 13 May 1865; Kunhardt and Kunhardt, *Twenty Days*, 153–54; *NYEP*, 22, 24 April 1865; *NYTi*, 24 May 1882; Daniel Hodas, *The Business Career of Moses Taylor: Merchant, Finance Capitalist, and Industrialist* (New York, N.Y., 1976).

3. Martin refers to Abraham Lincoln's 11 April 1865 "Speech on Reconstruction." In this final public address, Lincoln advocated limited suffrage for Louisiana blacks. Lincoln, *Speeches and Writings, 1859–1865*, 697–701.

67.
Speech by Charles Lenox Remond
Delivered at the Union Square Congregational Church
New York, New York
9 May 1865

William Lloyd Garrison's efforts to disband the American Anti-Slavery Society during the latter years of the Civil War demonstrated how much blacks and whites disagreed over the meaning of abolitionism. Many AASS members shared Garrison's view that the Emancipation Proclamation and the Thirteenth Amendment ended the need for their good works. Although some whites remained committed to the black abolitionist agenda during Reconstruction, others considered black suffrage a secondary issue, for which the AASS bore no responsibility. Black leaders such as Henry Highland Garnet and Charles L. Remond argued that the destruction of slavery only began the hard work of securing black rights, yet many whites—more concerned with their place in history—retired to write their memoirs and "repose on the laurels already won." As late as 1874, when Reconstruction's failures were clearly defined, white abolitionists met in Chicago to celebrate their "triumph" and "period of self-sacrifice." The bitter debate among white abolitionists over the future of the AASS disappointed black abolitionists, including lifelong black Garrisonians like Remond. In the following remarks, delivered at the society's annual meeting on 9 May 1865, Remond concluded that "it is utterly impossible for any of our white friends, however much they may have tried, fully to understand the black man's case in this nation." *WAA*, 26 September 1863, 20 May, 26 August 1865 [16:0124]; Lawrence J. Friedman, *Gregarious Saints: Self and Community in American Abolitionism, 1830–1870* (Cambridge, England, 1982), 255–80.

I differ very materially from the friend who has just taken his seat. If I understand the Declaration of Sentiments and the Constitution, the object of this Society includes the very point to which our friend Mr. Keese refers,[1] for the emancipation of the slave and the elevation of the free people of color were the original objects of the American Anti-Slavery Society. The work now being done in every part of our country for the enslaved and the nominally free comes strictly and logically within the purposes of this Society.

Now, I am not among the number who would retain for a moment any one of the members or officers of the Society against his or her wish; for I hold that the man or the woman who remains reluctantly within its pale is of no service to our cause at this critical moment, and it strikes me they have but little to do but ask to be excused. I cannot understand the necessity for disbanding the Society, especially since it is doubtful in my own mind whether a new Society could be got into full play before some valuable hours, days and perhaps months shall be lost to us.

Now, while I am upon the platform, allow me to remark, once for all, that if I understand the spirit of this platform, it is, that the individual judgment shall remain inviolate upon it; and if I shall differ in my remarks from my friend Mr. Garrison,[2] or any other member of the Society, I protest against the imputation that the colored man who differs from his old and tried friends becomes an ingrate. Sir, if there is one word which I hate next to slavery, it is ingratitude; still, I hold that, as colored men or as white men, we may differ from these old friends without being liable to that charge.

Now, sir, how does the case stand in this country? It is assumed (and I do not know that I object to the assumption, only when things are brought to a very fine point, as they are sometimes here) that our white friends understand the black man's case; that they have so often put their souls in his stead, that it cannot be otherwise. To a great extent, this is true; but in many particulars it is not true. Now, while I defer to some and reverence others—and I hope no man can prove himself more grateful than I feel towards our friends—I do assume here that it is utterly impossible for any of our white friends, however much they may have tried, fully to understand the black man's case in this nation. I think I could name one or two men, perhaps a dozen here, who get very near to it, but not exactly "on the square," so to say. Our friend Mr. Garrison told us today, that anti-slavery being the order of things, there is no further necessity for anti-slavery work. Why, sir, if my friend should go out upon the highways and byways here, and put the very question which he has assumed as a foregone conclusion, he would find himself so utterly overwhelmed with opposition that he would hardly understand himself. I deny, from beginning to end, that anti-slavery, according to this platform, characterizes any State in this country. I deny, without fear of successful contradiction, that the anti-slavery which takes its color from this platform has a majority in the nation at the present time. Put the question nakedly to the American people today, whether they are prepared for the entire and full recognition of the colored man's equality in this country, and you would be voted down ten to one. This being true, I cannot sit here and hear these assertions and assumptions without raising my protest against them. While coming through in the cars last evening (I give this as an isolated case), I gave the conductor my ticket, as the other passengers did. When the others gave up their tickets, he handed them checks. He gave me no check, and I asked him if he did not intend to. He turned round, and gave me to understand that my black face was check enough. Again, I was going to a meeting of our friends in Salem last week, to consult in reference to the question of free suffrage and schools for the black man, and during my walk from my home to the Lyceum Hall, I heard the expressions, "D—d nigger on the stomach," "d—d nigger on the brain," etc., etc. Such expressions were never more rife in our country than at the present moment. And yet we are to understand that anti-slavery is the order of the day! Sir, it is not true.

But I will not occupy the time further, except to say, that standing as we do at this moment between the fires of rebellion in the South, and this hatred of the colored man in the North, I hope nothing will be done within this Society that shall look like a betrayal of our movement. I know how much our friends have been tried, how much they have sacrificed; and I do not blame those who are growing old, like myself, for their desire to retire. Still, sir, this retirement may be done in a way that shall cause great harm to our cause, and great harm to the colored people throughout the country. I hope, therefore, that this Society may be continued, and if its present officers desire to retire, we will endeavor to succeed them with others.

National Anti-Slavery Standard (New York, N.Y.), 20 May 1865.

1. Immediately before Remond made these remarks, Samuel Keese urged delegates to disband the American Anti-Slavery Society and advised them to work through equal rights associations "to secure to the colored people their rights as American citizens." Keese (1793–1880), a Quaker abolitionist from Peru, New York, joined the movement in the 1830s. He was a member of the New York State Anti-Slavery Society and served on the AASS board of managers in 1841–42. *NASS*, 20 May 1865 [15:0897]; John R. McKivigan, *The War against Proslavery Religion: Abolitionism and the Northern Churches* (Ithaca, N.Y., 1984), 212; *P*, 13 October 1837 [2:0219]; *Lib*, 25 June 1836, 29 June 1855, 16 September 1864; *FI* 37:666 (1880).

2. At the beginning of the meeting, William Lloyd Garrison offered a series of resolutions declaring that since the "year of jubilee is come . . . further antislavery agitation is uncalled for." He proposed that the American Anti-Slavery Society be dissolved and a committee appointed to liquidate the society's debts. *NASS*, 20 May 1865 [15:0896].

68.
Constitution of the Colored Men's Equal Rights League
of Richmond
9 May 1865

Northern black abolitionists and southern freedmen shared similar goals for Reconstruction. They wanted the vote, full political and civil rights, educational opportunities, disfranchisement of the former rebels, and redistribution of confiscated rebel lands. The National Equal Rights League, which had been founded at the 1864 black national convention, provided a means to unite all Afro-Americans behind these objectives. Through state and local auxiliaries, the league brought together hundreds of blacks from across the nation to fight for their rights and liberties. The league's Louisiana chapter joined free blacks and former bondsmen—"the rich and poor, the literate and the educated and the country laborer"—to promote equal suffrage, oppose the state's odious labor system, and demand land reform. On 9 May 1865, black leaders in Richmond, Virginia, met at the house of black shoemaker Robert W. Johnson, heard an address by black abolitionist and journalist T. Morris Chester of Philadelphia, organized the Colored Men's Equal Rights League of Richmond, and adopted the following constitution. This NERL auxiliary, which was established the same day that the city's notorious Confederate mayor Joseph Mayo resumed office, pledged to fight for "recognition of the rights of the colored people of the Nation as American citizens." Foner, *Reconstruction*, 64–65; Ripley, *Slaves and Freedmen in Civil War Louisiana*, 178–79; WAA, 19 November 1864, 1 April, 20 May 1865.

PREAMBLE AND CONSTITUTION OF THE COLORED MEN'S
EQUAL RIGHTS LEAGUE OF RICHMOND, VA.

WHEREAS, The purposes entertained by the callers of this meeting, and those who have responded to that call, can best be promoted by a closer union of all interested in the principles of justice and right sought to be established; therefore be it

1. Resolved, That we proceed to organize an association, to be called the Equal Rights League of Richmond, Virginia.

2. Resolved, That in the establishment of the Colored Men's Equal Rights League of Richmond, we do not seek to disorganize or in any way interfere with any existing Society or institution of a benevolent or other character; but believing that the interests of colored men generally will be best subserved and advanced by a union of all our energies and the use of our means in a given direction, we therefore invite the cooperation of such societies in the advancement of the objects of the League.

14. Black activist speaking on the steps of the Virginia State House in Richmond
From Langston Hughes, Milton Meltzer, and C. Eric Lincoln, eds.,
A Pictorial History of Blackamericans, 5th rev. ed. (New York, 1973)

ARTICLE 1ST

The objects of this League are to encourage sound morality, education, temperance, frugality, industry, and promote everything that pertains to a well-ordered and dignified life, and to obtain by appeals to the minds and consciences of the American people, or by legal process when possible, a recognition of the rights of the colored people of the Nation as American citizens.

ARTICLE 2D — ELIGIBLE TO MEMBERSHIP

Any person twenty-one years old may be permitted to become a member of this League by paying one dollar initiation fee and twenty-five cents per month thereafter, without distinction on account of color or sex.

ARTICLE 3D — OFFICERS

The officers shall consist of a President, two Vice-Presidents, Recording, Assistant Recording and Corresponding Secretaries, a Treasurer, and an Executive Committee, consisting of the officers of the League and two other persons to be elected by the League at the same time with other officers.

ARTICLE 4TH

The President shall preside at all the regular meetings of the League and of the Executive Committee, see that all decrees of the League are duly executed, and perform such other duties as may be imposed by the League.

The Vice-Presidents in the order of their election shall, in the absence of the President, perform his duties.

The Recording Secretary shall duly record the proceedings of the League and of the Executive Committee; draw all orders on the Treasurer when directed by the proper authority; receive all money paid to the League; pay the same to the Treasurer and take his receipt therefor.

The Corresponding Secretary shall, under the guidance of the League and of the Executive Committee, conduct the correspondence of the League; receive from the agents of the League or other persons all documents of historical, statistical, or general interest; and shall carefully preserve, arrange, and tabulate such documents for the use of the League.

The Treasurer may, with the consent of the Executive Committee, deposit all monies belonging to the League in some solvent bank of the city of Richmond, subject to the President and his order. The Executive Committee may require him to give security in same as may seem to them best, for the faithful performance of his duties. He shall report to the League annually, and to the Executive Committee whenever required, the condition of the treasury. He shall pay out money only upon order of the Executive Committee, and when properly signed by the President and the Recording Secretary.

ARTICLE 5TH

The Executive Committee shall establish an office in the city of Richmond, in which place they shall hold such sessions as may be necessary to promote the purposes of the League; they may hire an agent or agents who shall visit the different counties or corporations of the State accessible to them, and call the people together and urge them to take the steps necessary to secure the rights and make the improvements for the attainment of which objects this League is formed.

They shall make an annual report to the Association of their labors, and shall recommend such improvements as may be suggested by their official experience.

They shall cause orders to be drawn on the Treasurer for the payment of such expenses as may be incurred in the carrying out of the purposes of the Association. They shall have power to fill any vacancies occurring during the year in the official department of the League.

ARTICLE 6TH

The officers shall hold their offices for one year, or until their successors are elected.

The officers of the League may receive such compensation as may be determined upon by the Executive Committee.

The Executive Committee shall have power to invite speakers on special occasions to address the League, and they shall make all necessary arrangements for such purposes.

ARTICLE 7TH

The rules as laid down in Jefferson's Manual[1] shall be the standing rules of order of this Association, in all points not herein provided for.

No member shall be allowed to speak more than twice upon the same subject without permission of the President, nor shall he be allowed to speak longer than five minutes at one time.

At any annual meeting of this League the constitution may be altered or amended by a vote of the majority of the members present.

OFFICERS:[2]

President—Robert W. Johnson
1*st Vice-President*—Rev. Fields Cook
2*d Vice-President*—Alpheus Roper
Recording Secretary—James Burwell
Assistant Recording Secretary—George Forrester
Corresponding Secretary—Nathaniel H. Anderson
Treasurer—Joseph E. Farrar

Weekly Anglo-African (New York, N.Y.), 24 June 1865.

1. The Colored Men's Equal Rights League of Richmond used Thomas Jefferson's *Manual of Parliamentary Practice: Composed Originally for the Use of the Senate of the United States* (1864).

2. The officers of the Colored Men's Equal Rights League of Richmond lived in the city's free black community before the Civil War and became spokesmen for local blacks during Reconstruction. Robert W. Johnson (1825–1898), a shoemaker and political activist, was the catalyst behind the founding of the local league. A prominent figure in antebellum black Richmond, he chaired local emancipation celebrations, attended the 1865 Virginia black state convention, represented the Richmond auxiliary at that year's annual meeting of the National Equal Rights League, and presided over the local chapter of the Union League, an interracial organization devoted to the political education of the freedmen. An aggressive labor organizer, he served as an officer of the Colored National Labor Union in the early 1870s. Johnson sat on Richmond's city council from 1874 to 1878.

Fields Cook (1814–1897) was one of the most popular black political figures in postwar Virginia. Born in slavery in nearby King William County, he was hired out as a young man in Richmond, where he became a highly skilled barber and leech doctor, developed an extensive interracial clientele, accumulated considerable savings, and purchased his freedom before 1850. The self-taught Cook was a lay preacher and deacon in the city's First African Baptist Church prior to the war and helped its members throw off white control after emancipation. Beginning in 1865, he lectured on behalf of equal rights and black suffrage at political meetings throughout the state, angering whites who threatened his life on several occasions. In June 1865, he led a delegation of Richmond blacks who met with President Andrew Johnson to protest Union army misconduct against local blacks. Cook represented the city at several black state and national conventions and statewide Republican gatherings during the early years of Reconstruction and helped found and direct the Richmond and Alexandria branches of the Freedman's Savings Bank. In 1869 he ran as an Independent candidate for the U.S. Congress. Although his political influence dimmed with the rise of Jim Crow, he remained important among Virginia's black Baptists, serving Richmond and Alexandria congregations until his death.

Nathaniel H. Anderson, barber James B. Burwell, plasterer Alpheus Roper (1830–?), and carpenters Richard George Forrester (1826–?) and Joseph E. Farrar (1832–?) also resided in Richmond's free black community before the Civil War. They became minor political leaders after the war. Roper, Forrester, and Farrar served on Richmond's city council during the 1870s and 1880s. In 1886 Burwell and Farrar played leading roles in starting a local black political movement called the Workingmen's Reform party. Farrar ran again for alderman in 1890 on an all-black Independent Republican slate. Little is known about Anderson, but he commanded sufficient respect to be chosen as chair of the Richmond delegation to the 1865 Virginia black state convention. *Richmond City Directory*, 1866–76; *RP*, 23 January 1897, 14 May 1898; Rachleff, *Black Labor in the South*, 41, 45, 52, 58, 144, 154, 162; Chesson, "Richmond's Black Councilmen," 196–202; *WAA*, 19 August 1865; Foner and Walker, *Proceedings of the Black State Conventions*, 2:259–61, 267; John T. O'Brien, "From Bondage to Citizenship: The Richmond Black Community, 1865–1867" (Ph.D. diss., University of Rochester, 1974), 184, 275, 324, 426; Foner and Walker, *Black National and State Conventions*, 45–46, 57, 350–52; Osthaus, *Freedmen, Philanthropy, and Fraud*, 106, 116, 230; Taylor, *Negro in the Reconstruction of Virginia*, 188, 211–16, 254, 258; Marie Tyler McGraw and Gregg D. Kimball, *In Bondage and Freedom: Antebellum Black Life in Richmond, Virginia* (Richmond, Va., 1988), 34–36, 45.

69.
H. Ford Douglas and the Impressment of Black Troops

Soldiers of the Kansas Independent Battery of United States Colored Light Artillery to H. Ford Douglas
19 June 1865

H. Ford Douglas to John Barber
20 June 1865

Military service helped prepare the generation of black leaders that guided the struggle for equality during Reconstruction. Opportunities for advancement in the Union army were limited, but some black soldiers rose in the enlisted ranks and a select few became officers. Black commissioned and noncommissioned officers looked out for the varied interests of their men—from founding schools and churches across the South to redressing illegal acts by military authorities. An example involved members of the Kansas Independent Battery of U.S. Colored Light Artillery, who had been coerced to enlist in the Union army through beatings and death threats. Without the intercession of the unit's black commander, Captain H. Ford Douglas, the injustice might have gone unnoticed. On 19 June 1865, Private Gabriel Grays, a member of the battery, wrote to Douglas and explained the unit's plight. The other members affixed their marks. One day later, after validating their claims, Douglas wrote Lieutenant John Barber, the post adjutant at Fort Leavenworth, explaining the circumstances of the case and asking that the men be mustered out of service. Following an investigation by the post commander and the War Department, the request was granted and the members of the battery were released from further duty on 22 July. Foner, *Reconstruction*, 9–10; *WAA*, 28 January, 12 July 1865; Berlin et al., *Freedom*, 2:311n, 421–23.

Fort Leavenworth, [Kansas]
June 19th, 1865

Sir:

   We the undersigned members of Indpt Cold Battery[1] trusting in you as an officer who desires to see Justice done to all men we therefore Respectfully request you to use your Influence to have us mustered out of Service for the following Reasons.

   1st. That we were pressed into Service by force of numbers without any Law civil or millitry to Sanction it[.][2] Many of us were knocked down and beaten Like dogs[,] others were dragged from our homes in the dead hour of and forced into a Prison without Law or Justice. Others were tied and thrown into the river and held there untill forced to subscribe to the Oath. Some of us were tied up by the thumbs all night[,] we were starved[,] beaten[,] kept out all night untill we were nearly frozen and but one alternative to join the service or nearly suffer death.

2nd. The Exigencies of the war are past and as our services are no longer needed to put down the Rebellion[,] as our enlistment was Illegal and unjust[,] therefore we Respectfully request to use your influence to have us discharged from this Service that we may return to our famillies some of whom have not seen them for five or Six months and having no means to send them they are in a Suffering Condition and we therefore Request you to use your influence to have us discharged from service. We are Captain Very Respectfully Your Obt Servants,

Gabriel Grays	Henry Willison
Wilson Parker	Merrit Buckner
Robert Clayburn	Frank Forbush
William Madden	George Clark
Lonzo Eddings	Jack B[o]lton
Wm. Woods	John Taylar
Milford Mines	Simon Woodson
Jessey Hughs	Henry Hampleton
Charley Morton	Levi Seales
Archa Still	David Crocket
B̶a̶ Bialia Johnson	Scott Runels
John Ward	Ben Henderson
Henry Walker	Gus Morehead
Berry Richerson	John Foular
Charley Turner	Robert Sharp
John Yeager	Lorage Higgins
Ben Baker	Frank Gibbs
John Crump	David Hair
C. W. Belt	Willison Thatcher
George H̶a̶n̶c̶k̶ Hancock	Jessey William
Ben. F. Hancock	Archa Johnson
Lewis Buford	Calvan Fieds
Alix More	J̶a̶c̶k̶s̶ Jackson Haddox
Samul Colman	Zack Colwell
Henry Miton	Icaca Sheales
George Miters	Marchel Holingworth
Tip Dean	

Letters Received, RG 94, Adjutant General's Office, U.S. Colored Troops, National Archives, Washington, D.C. Published by permission.

Head Q[uarte]rs Independent
Col[ore]d Battery
Fort Leavenworth, Kan[sas]
June 20th, 1865

Sir:

In response to this communication from the men of this Battery I have the honor to most respectfully call the attention of the Major General Commanding the department[3] to the following statement of facts.

This Battery was raised while Major General Curtis was in command of the Department.[4] More than (75) per cent of the men who now belong to it, are the victims of a cruel and shameless conscription. Not under the ordinary forms which are usually resorted to, but in opposition to all civil and military law. Before I became connected with the company I have seen men dragged through the streets of Leavenworth from their wives and little ones who were dependent upon them for their daily bread—mid winter, and placed on the bleak knob of Fort Sully,[5] and there starved until from shere exhaustion they were compeled to swear into the service. These facts I am prepared to substantiate by more than a thousand witnesses. Now General since the necessity for their service no longer exists, I would most respectfully request that this Battery be at once mustered out of the service. I am General Very Respectfully Your Obt. Servant,

H. Ford Douglas
Capt. Independent Batt'y
U.S. Col[ore]d Art. (Light)

Letters Received, RG 94, Adjutant General's Office, U.S. Colored Troops, National Archives, Washington, D.C. Published by permission.

1. The Kansas Independent Battery of U.S. Colored Light Artillery, the only all-black military unit of the war, was organized at Leavenworth, Kansas, in December 1864 and attached to the Department of Kansas. All of its commissioned officers—Captain H. Ford Douglas, First Lieutenant William D. Matthews, and Second Lieutenant Patrick H. Minor—were black. The unit remained in Leavenworth and was mustered out of service in July 1865. Dyer, *Compendium*, 3:1723; Cornish, *Sable Arm*, 215–16.

2. Throughout much of the Civil War, blacks were plagued by impressment into military service. The practice existed in limited form before 1863, but after the Lincoln administration authorized black enlistments, many Union officers countenanced arbitrary and often brutal recruitment practices to fill black regiments. Even abolitionist Thomas W. Higginson's famed First South Carolina Volunteers rounded up recruits at bayonet point among the contrabands. When the U.S. Congress amended the Enrollment Act of 1863 in July 1864, it unwittingly systematized the abuses by authorizing the hiring of recruiters whose sole purpose was to fill regimental quotas from the Southern states. Nearly one thousand officials accompanied Union forces, often kidnapping blacks and threatening, beat-

ing, or killing those who resisted. The practice outraged some military leaders and proved a dismal failure; it was outlawed in March 1865 after producing only 5,052 recruits over eight months. Berlin et al., *Freedom*, 2:39–41, 55–57, 74–78, 115–21, 138–41, 151, 176–80.

3. Douglas refers to Major General Grenville M. Dodge (1831–1916), who commanded the Department of Missouri—which then included Kansas—from December 1864 until after the Civil War. Dodge, an engineer, obtained a commission at the beginning of the war and was soon promoted to brigadier general. He held various commands in the Army of the Tennessee from 1862 until wounded at the battle of Atlanta in August 1864. After resigning his commission in 1866, he became a railroad official and lobbyist and represented Iowa in the U.S. Congress. *HTECW*, 223.

4. Major General Samuel R. Curtis (1805–1866) commanded the Department of Kansas from January 1864 to January 1865. An engineer, lawyer, Mexican War veteran, and Iowa congressman, he rejoined the Union army at the beginning of the Civil War. He was promoted after his victory at Pea Ridge, Arkansas, in March 1862. After the war, Curtis served as a U.S. peace commissioner to the Native Americans and a commissioner of the Union Pacific Railroad. *WWWCW*, 160; *HTECW*, 198–99.

5. Fort Sully, part of the sprawling military garrison at Fort Leavenworth, Kansas, was a hastily constructed earthworks built at the western edge of Leavenworth in anticipation of a Confederate attack. Robert B. Roberts, ed., *Encyclopedia of Historic Forts: The Military, Pioneer, and Trading Posts of the United States* (New York, N.Y., 1988), 296–97.

70.
Address by a Committee of Norfolk Blacks
26 June 1865

"With the cessation of war, our anxieties begin," observed editor Robert Hamilton in the *Weekly Anglo-African*. While 1865 wore on, southern white resistance clouded prospects for racial progress, and black abolitionists became increasingly apprehensive. In February black leaders in Norfolk, Virginia, began organizing to prevent the restoration of civilian rule in the city. On 5 June, they met and appointed a committee consisting of Henry Highland Garnet and seven leading local blacks to draft an address stating their concerns about the postwar situation. Three weeks later, the committee included the address in a pamphlet bearing the title *Equal Suffrage*. It outlined the condition of southern blacks and their requirements for a meaningful Reconstruction. The committee observed that despite emancipation, many of the legal, economic, and psychological vestiges of slavery remained. Slave codes remained in force; planters conspired to resurrect slavery through a system of forced labor; and southern whites, defeated in war, harbored resentment and racial hatred toward blacks. These black leaders recommended the formation of political, land, and labor associations to promote black civil rights, land ownership, and fair employment practices. Most important of all, they called for the vote. They reminded the public that southern blacks could play an essential role in the process of national reunification—their political empowerment would not be merely an act of justice, but a practical measure allowing an interracial coalition of Union loyalists in the South. *WAA*, 15 April, 11 November 1865; Herbert Aptheker, *To Be Free: Studies in American Negro History* (New York, N.Y., 1969), 138–44; *Equal Suffrage: Address from the Colored Citizens of Norfolk, Va., to the People of the United States* (New Bedford, Mass., 1865), 10–15; Foner, *Reconstruction*, 124–75.

ADDRESS
From the Colored Citizens of Norfolk, Va.,
to the People of the United States

Fellow Citizens:

The undersigned have been appointed a committee, by a public meeting of the colored citizens of Norfolk, held June 5th, 1865, in the Catharine Street Baptist Church, Norfolk, Va., to lay before you a few considerations touching the present position of the colored population of the southern States generally, and with reference to their claim for equal suffrage in particular.

We do not come before the people of the United States asking an impossibility; we simply ask that a Christian and enlightened people shall, at once, concede to us the full enjoyment of those privileges of full citizenship which, not only, are our undoubted right, but are indispensable to that elevation and prosperity of our people which must be the desire of every patriot.

The legal recognition of these rights of the free colored population, in the past, by State legislation, or even by the Judiciary and Congress of the United States, was, as a matter of course, wholly inconsistent with the existence of slavery; but now that slavery has been crushed, with the rebellion, sprung from it, on what pretext can disabilities be perpetuated that were imposed only to protect an institution which has now, thank God, passed away forever? It is a common assertion, by our enemies, that "this is a white man's country, settled by white men, its government established by white men, and shall therefore be ruled by white men only." How far are these statements true and the conclusion reasonable? Every schoolboy knows that, within twelve years of the foundation of the first settlement at Jamestown, our fathers as well as yours were toiling in the plantations on James River for the sustenance and prosperity of the infant colony.[1] Since then, in New England, New York, and the middle Atlantic States, our race has borne its part in the development of even the free North, while throughout the sunny South, the millions upon millions of acres in its countless plantations, laden with precious crops, bear witness to the unrequited industry of our people. Even our enemies and old oppressors, themselves, used to admit, nay contend for, the urgent necessity of our presence and labor to the national prosperity, for whenever slavery was to be defended, they were always ready to prove that the negro must be the laborer in the South, because a white man's constitution could not withstand the climate.

Again, is it true that this government owes its existence entirely to white men? Why, the first blood shed in the Revolutionary war was that of a colored man, Crispus Attucks, while in every engraving of Washington's famous passage of the Delaware is to be seen, as a prominent feature, the woolly head and the dusky face of a colored soldier, Prince Whipple;[2] and let the history of those days tell of the numerous but abortive efforts made by a vindictive enemy to incite insurrection among the colored people of the country, and how faithfully they adhered to that country's cause. Who has forgotten Andrew Jackson's famous appeal to the colored "citizens" of Louisiana, and their enthusiastic response, in defence of liberty, for others, which was denied themselves? Then did the peaceful stability of the government of the United States, during the (to all but the colored race) happy years that preceded the late rebellion, owe nothing for its continuance to the colored people? Fellow citizens, was not the maintenance of that peace and order, and thereby of your prosperity, wholly owing to the submissive patience with which our race endured the galling slavery of which they were the victims, in the faith and assurance that God would yet work out their deliverance? Then what has been the behavior of our people during the past struggle? Have we in any way embarrassed the government by unnecessary outbreaks on the one hand, or thwarted it by remissness or slackness in response to its calls for volunteers on the other? Let the fact that, in the short space of nine months, from what was called the contraband camp at Hampton, near Fortress Monroe, and from other parts of this State alone, over *twenty-five thousand* colored men have become soldiers in the army of the United States, attest our devotion to our country. Over 200,000 colored men have taken up arms on behalf of the Union, and at Port Hudson, Olustee, Milliken's Bend, Fort Wagner, and in the death-haunted craters of the Petersburg mine,[3] and on a hundred well-fought fields, have fully proved their patriotism and possession of all the manly qualities that adorn the soldier.

Such, as everyone knows, have been the relations and attitude of the colored people to the nation in the past, but we believe our present position is by no means so well understood among the loyal masses of the country, otherwise there would be no delay in granting us the express relief which the nature of the case demands. It must not be forgotten that it is the general assumption in the South that the effects of the immortal Emancipation Proclamation of President Lincoln go no further than the emancipation of the negroes then in slavery, and that it is only constructively even that that Proclamation can be said, in any legal sense, to have abolished slavery, and even the late Constitutional amendment, if duly ratified, can go no further;[4] neither touch, nor can touch, the slave codes of the various southern States, and the laws respecting free people of color consequent therefrom, which, having been passed before the act of secession, are presumed to have lost none of their vitality, but exist as a convenient engine for our oppression until repealed by special acts of the State legislatures. By these laws, in many of the southern States, it is still a crime for colored men to learn or be taught to read, and their children are doomed to ignorance; there is no provision for insuring the legality of our marriages; we have no right to hold real estate; the public streets and the exercise of our ordinary occupations are forbidden us unless we can produce passes from our employers, or licenses from certain officials; in some States, the whole free negro population is legally liable to exile from the place of its birth for no crime but that of color; we have no means of legally making or enforcing contracts of any description; we have no right to testify before the courts in any case in which a white man is one of the parties to the suit; we are taxed without representation, and, in short, so far as legal safeguards of our rights are concerned, we are defenceless before our enemies. While this is our position as regards our legal status before the State laws, we are still more unfortunately situated as regards our late masters. The people of the North, owing to the greater interest excited by the war, have heard little or nothing for the past four years of the blasphemous and horrible theories formerly propounded for the defence and glorification of human slavery, in the press, the pulpit and legislatures of the southern States; but, though they may have forgotten them, let them be assured that these doctrines have by no means faded from the minds of the people of the South; they cling to these delusions still, and only hug them the closer for their recent defeat. Worse than all, they have returned to their homes, with all their old pride and contempt for the negro transformed into bitter hate for the new-made freeman, who aspires to the exercise of his new-found rights, and who has been fighting for the suppression of their rebellion. That this charge is not unfounded, the manner in which it has been recently attempted to enforce the laws above referred to proves. In Richmond, during the three days' sway of the rebel Mayor Mayo, over 800 colored people were arrested, simply for walking the streets without a pass;[5] in the neighboring city of Portsmouth, a mayor has just been elected on the avowed platform that this is a white man's government, and our enemies have been heard to boast openly that soon not a colored man shall be left in the city; in the greater number of counties in this State, county meetings have been held at which resolutions have been adopted *deploring*, while accepting, the abolition of slavery, but going on to pledge the planters composing the meeting to employ no negroes save such as were formerly owned by themselves without a written recommendation from their late employers, and threatening violence towards those who should do so, thereby keeping us in a state of serfdom, and preventing our free selection of our employers: they have also pledged themselves, in no event, to pay their late adult slaves more than $60 per year for their labor in the future, out of which, with characteristic generosity, they have decided that we are to find clothes for ourselves and families, and pay our taxes and doctors' bills, in many of the more remote districts, individual planters are to be found who still refuse to recognize their negroes as free, forcibly retaining the wives and children of their late escaped slaves; cases have occurred, not far from Richmond itself, in which an attempt to leave the plantation has been punished by shooting to death; and finally, there are numbers of cases known to ourselves in the immediate vicinity of this city in which a faithful performance, by colored men, of the duties or labor contracted for, has been met by a contemptuous and violent refusal of the stipulated compensation. These are facts, and yet the men doing these things are, in many cases, loud in their professions of attachment to the restored Union, while committing these outrages on the most faithful friends the Union can ever have. Even well known Union men have often been found among our oppressors; witness the action of the Tennessee legislature in imposing unheard of disabilities upon us, taking away from us, and giving to the County Courts, the right of disposing of our children, by apprenticing them to such occupations as the court, not their parents, may see fit to adopt for them;[6] and in this very city, and under the protection of military law, some of our white friends who have nobly distinguished themselves by their efforts in our behalf have been threatened with arrest by a Union mayor of this city[7] for their advocacy of the cause of freedom.

Fellow citizens, the performance of a simple act of justice on your part will reverse all this; we ask for no expensive aid from military forces stationed throughout the South, overbearing State action, and rendering our government republican only in name; give us the suffrage, and you may rely upon us to secure justice for ourselves, and all Union men, and to keep the State forever in the Union.

While we urge you to this act of simple justice to ourselves, there are many reasons why you should concede us this right in your own interest. It cannot be that you contemplate with satisfaction a prolonged military occupation of the southern States, and yet, without the existence of a larger loyal constituency than at present exists in these States, a military occupation will be absolutely necessary to protect the white Union men of the South, as well as ourselves,[8] and if not absolutely to keep the States in the Union, it will be necessary to prevent treasonable legislation. Even as we write, the news comes that, acting under the advice of Governor Pierpont, the legislature of this State has restored to thousands of white voters, who were but recently in arms against the national authority, the right of franchise of which they were deprived, for their crime of treason,[9] by the constitution under which that legislature sits, and it is now proposed to call a convention for the repeal of those sections of the new constitution, forbidding the assumption of any portion of the rebel State debt;[10] and at the municipal election which took place in Norfolk on the 24th inst., a mayor and council[11] supposed to favor the payment of more than $100,000 of bonds issued by the City Council during the rebel occupation, for the payment of the expenses of rebel enlistment and the support of the families of rebel soldiers, was elected by a large majority over a loyal ticket opposed to such assumption of rebel debt. Ask yourselves if it is reasonable to expect that senators and representatives from southern constituencies, lately in unanimous rebellion, will be willing to vote taxes required to pay the interest on the debt incurred in crushing that rebellion.

You have not unreasonably complained of the operation of that clause of the Constitution which has hitherto permitted the slavocracy of the South to wield the political influence which would be represented by a white population equal to three-fifths of the whole negro population; but slavery is now abolished, and henceforth the representation will be in proportion to the enumeration of the whole population of the South, *including people of color*, and it is worth your consideration if it is desirable or politic that the fomenters of this rebellion against the Union, which has been crushed at the expense of so much blood and treasure, should find themselves, after defeat, more powerful than ever, their political influence enhanced by the additional voting power of the other two-fifths of the colored population, by which means four southern votes will balance in the Congressional and Presidential elections at least seven northern ones. The honor of your country should be dear to you, as it is, but is that honor advanced in the eyes of the Christian world when America alone, of all Christian nations, sustains an unjust distinction against four millions and a half of her most loyal people, on the senseless ground of a difference in color? You are anxious that the attention of every man, of every State legislature, and of Congress, should be exclusively directed to redressing the injuries sustained by the country in the late contest; are these objects more likely to be effected amid the political distractions of an embarrassing negro agitation? You are, above all, desirous that no future intestine wars should mar the prosperity and destroy the happiness of the country; will your perfect security from such evils be promoted by the existence of a colored population of four millions and a half, placed, by your enactments, outside the pale of the Constitution, discontented by oppression, with an army of 200,000 colored soldiers whom you have drilled, disciplined, and armed, but whose attachment to the State you have failed to secure by refusing them citizenship? You are further anxious that your government should be an example to the world of true republican institutions; but how can you avoid the charge of inconsistency if you leave one-eighth of the population of the whole country without any political rights, while bestowing these rights on every immigrant who comes to these shores, perhaps from a despotism under which he could never exercise the least political right, and had no means of forming any conception of their proper use?

We have now shown you, to the best of our ability, the necessity of the recognition of the right of suffrage for our own protection, and have suggested a few of the reasons why it is expedient you should grant us that right; but while we stand before you, pleading with you for our fellows on the grounds of humanity and political expediency, we would not have you forget that our case also stands on the basis of constitutional right. No sane person will for a moment contend that color or birth are recognized by the Constitution of the United States as any bar to the acquisition or enjoyment of citizenship. Further, the Congress of the Confederation expressly refused in June 1778 to permit the insertion of the word "white" in the fourth article of Confederation, guaranteeing to the "free inhabitants" of each State the privileges and immunities of citizens in all the States.[12] Free people of color were recognized voters in every State but South Carolina at the time of the formation of the Constitution of the United States, and therefore clearly formed part of the "people" of the United States, who in the language of the preamble to the Constitution, "ordained and established" that Constitution. It follows, then, that they are entitled to a full participation in all the benefits that Constitution was ordained to confer, and, among others, to that inestimable blessing of "a republican form of government," guaranteed to the people of each State by Sec. 4th, Art. IV of the Constitution. Further, from time immemorial, before the Constitution was established, and, since its establishment, in accordance with its spirit and express provisions, our people have enjoyed all the rights of citizens, including that of suffrage, in many of the northern States; but if their right to vote is refused in other States, what becomes of their rights under Sec. 2d, Art. IV of the Constitution, which guarantees to them as citizens of such a State, "all the privileges and immunities of citizens in the several States," if the constitutional supremacy of that provision is to be set aside by State enactment? We believe this position to be impregnable, as stated in the words of counsel, in the report of the case which forms Appendix "B" to this address, that all the State laws imposing disabilities upon colored people on the ground of color, "being but a creation of slavery, and passed for its maintenance and perpetuation, are part and parcel of the system and must follow its fate." [13] If we turn to the State constitutions and bills of rights, our case is still stronger. The constitution of Georgia *now* only prescribes as the qualification that a voter must be "a citizen and inhabitant"; [14] and while in the constitutions of other of the southern States is found the word "white," when describing the necessary qualification for the right of suffrage, yet, on the other hand, in most instances, their bills of rights claim the exercise of the suffrage as the natural and legal right of every freeman, in the most unqualified manner. For instance, in Delaware, the bill of rights declares that "every freeman having sufficient evidence of permanent common interest with and attachment to the community, hath the right of suffrage." The bill of rights of the State of Virginia, adopted in 1776, and since prefacing and forming part of every constitution of Virginia, declares also in Section 6th, "that all elections ought to be free, and that *all men* having sufficient evidence of common interest with, and attachment to the community, *have* the right of suffrage, and *cannot be taxed* or deprived of their property for public uses, without their own consent, *or that of their representatives* so elected, nor bound by any law to which they have not in like manner assented for the public good"; and yet, in defiance of this provision, the present constitution goes on to confine the right of voting to white men exclusively. [15]

It is hardly necessary here to refute any of the slanders with which our enemies seek to prove our unfitness for the exercise of the right of suffrage. It is true that many of our people are ignorant, but for *that* these very men are responsible, and decency should prevent *their* use of such an argument. But if our people are ignorant, no people were ever more orderly and obedient to the laws; and no people ever displayed greater earnestness in the acquisition of knowledge. Among no other people could such a revolution have taken place without scenes of license and bloodshed; but in this case, and we say it advisedly, full information of the facts will show that no single disturbance, however slight, has occurred which has not resulted from the unprovoked aggression of white people, and, if anyone doubts how fast the ignorance which has hitherto cursed our people is disappearing 'mid the light of freedom, let him visit the colored schools of this city and neighborhood, in which between two and three thousand pupils are being taught, while, in the evening, in colored schools may be seen, after the labors of the day, hundreds of our adult population from budding manhood to hoary age toiling, with intensest eagerness, to acquire the invaluable arts of reading and writing, and the rudimentary branches of knowledge.[16] One other objection only will we notice; it is that our people are lazy and idle; and, in support of this allegation, the objectors refer to the crowds of colored people subsisting on government rations, and flocking into the towns. To the first statement, we reply that we are poor, and that thousands of our young and able-bodied men, having been enlisted in the army to fight the battles of their country, it is but reasonable that that country should contribute something to the support of those whose natural protectors that country has taken away. With reference to the crowds collected round the military posts and in the cities, we say that though some may have come there under misapprehensions as to the nature of the freedom they have just received, yet this is not the case with the majority; the colored man knows that freedom means freedom to labor and to enjoy its fruits, and in that respect evinces at least an equal appreciation of his new position with his late owners; if he is not to be found laboring for these late owners, it is because he cannot trust them, and feels safe, in his new-found freedom, nowhere out of the immediate presence of the national forces; if the planters want his labor (and they do), fair wages and fair treatment will not fail to secure it.

In conclusion, we wish to advise our colored brethren of the State and nation that the settlement of this question is to a great extent dependent on them, and that supineness on their part will do as much to delay if not defeat the full recognition of their rights as the open opposition of avowed enemies. Then be up and active, and everywhere let associations be formed having for their object the agitation, discussion, and enforcement of your claims to equality before the law, and equal rights of suffrage. Your opponents are active; be prepared, and organize to resist their efforts. We would further advise that all political associations of colored men, formed within the limits of the State of Virginia, should communicate the fact of their existence, with the names and post office addresses of their officers, to Joseph T. Wilson,[17] Norfolk, Va., in order that communication and friendly cooperation may be kept up between the different organizations, and facilities afforded for common and united State action, should occasion require it.

Second—Everywhere in Virginia, and doubtless in all other States, your late owners are forming labor associations for the purpose of fixing and maintaining, without the least reference to your wishes or wants, the prices to be paid for your labor;[18] and we say to you, "Go and do likewise." Let labor associations, be at once formed among the colored people throughout the length and breadth of the United States, having for their object the protection of the colored laborer by regulating fairly the price of labor, by affording facilities for obtaining employment by a system of registration, and last, though by no means least, by undertaking on behalf of the colored laborer to enforce legally the fulfillment of all contracts made with him. To insure uniformity of action in this matter throughout this State, it is desirable that a means of communication be afforded the different associations, and, for this purpose, Mr. Wm. Keeling,[19] of No. 96 Church street, Norfolk, Va., a member of this committee, will receive all communications giving information of such associations formed within the limits of this State.

Third—The surest guarantee for the independence and ultimate elevation of the colored people will be found in their becoming the owners of the soil on which they live and labor. To this end, let them form land associations in which, by the regular payment of small instalments, a fund may be created for the purchase at all land sales of land on behalf of any investing member, in the name of the association, the association holding a mortgage on the land until, by the continued payment of a regular subscription, the sum advanced by the association and the interest upon it are paid off, when the occupier gets a clear title. Communications from all such associations in this State, with a view to the formation of a Union of the Virginian Colored Land Associations, will be gladly received by Mr. Geo. W. Cook,[20] No. 21 Fox Lane, Norfolk, Va. Any of our white friends in this State, favorable to the views set forth in this address, would do us a great benefit by signing the pledge forming the cover of this pamphlet and forwarding it with their names and addresses to either of the Recording Secretaries of the Democratic Republican Association, described in Appendix "A," Messrs. C. E. Johnston, or T. L. R. Baker, both of Norfolk.[21]

In concluding this address, we would now make a last appeal to our fellow citizens of all classes throughout the nation. Every Christian and humane man must feel that our demands are just; we have shown you that their concession is for us necessary, and for you expedient. We are Americans, we know no other country, we love the land of our birth and our fathers, we thank God for the glorious prospect before our country, and we believe that if we do but obey His laws, He will yet enthrone her high o'er all the nations of the earth, in glory, wealth, and happiness; but this exalted state can never be reached if injustice, ingratitude, and oppression of the helpless mark the national conduct, treasuring up, as in the past, God's wrath and your misery for a day of reckoning; as the path of justice alone is ever the safe and pleasant way, and the words of Eternal Wisdom have declared that the throne (or nation) shall be established only by righteousness and upheld by mercy. With these reflections, we leave our case in the hands of God, and to the consideration of our countrymen.

Signed, on behalf of the colored people of Norfolk and vicinity, June 26th, 1865.

> Dr. THOMAS BAYNE, Norfolk Chairman of Committee[22]
> JNO. M. BROWN, Pastor of the African Methodist
>   Episcopal Church, Bute Street, Norfolk Va.[23]
> THOMAS HENSON, Pastor of the Catharine Street
>   Baptist Church, Norfolk Va.[24]
> WM. KEELING, 96 Church Street, Norfolk, Va.
> GEO. W. COOK, 21 Fox Lane, Norfolk, Va.
> JOSEPH T. WILSON, 26 Hawk Street, Norfolk, Va.
> THOS. F. PAIGE, Jr., 27 Hawk Street, Norfolk, Va.[25]
> H. HIGHLAND GARNET, Pastor 15th St. Presbyterian
>   Church, Washington, D.C., Honorary Member

Equal Suffrage: Address from the Colored Citizens of Norfolk, Va., to the People of the United States (New Bedford, Mass., 1865), 1–9.

1. The committee refers to the introduction of African slaves into the colony of Virginia in 1619.

2. Prince Whipple, a member of a wealthy African family, was sent to study in the American colonies during the 1760s. But when he arrived in Baltimore, he was sold as a slave to William Whipple, who later became an aide to George Washington during the American Revolution. Prince Whipple received his freedom and participated in the war, acting as a bodyguard for his former master. A black soldier reputed to be Prince Whipple figures prominently in two famous paintings of Washington crossing the Delaware River in December 1776. In Thomas Sully's work (1819), Whipple is one of four horsemen accompanying Washington on the river's bank. Emanuel Leutze's rendering (1851) depicts Whipple as an oarsman in the bow of Washington's boat. Kaplan and Kaplan, *Black Presence in the Era of the American Revolution*, 49–52; Nell, *Colored Patriots*, 198–99.

3. During the siege of Petersburg, Virginia, Union forces under Major General Ambrose E. Burnside attempted to break Confederate defenses by tunneling beneath enemy trenches and packing the shaft with eight thousand pounds of gunpowder. When detonated on 30 July 1864, this created a deafening explosion, hurling nine companies of Confederate infantry into the air, killing and maiming

more than three hundred men, and leaving a crater 170 feet long and 30 feet deep. Several white regiments followed with an assault on Confederate lines, but they were poorly led and failed to exploit their advantage. After three hours, two black brigades attached to IX Corps of the Army of the Potomac were sent into the fight. They temporarily gained ground, then suffered staggering losses as Confederates regrouped and counterattacked. Rebel forces rimmed the crater, subjecting Union troops to murderous fire. Many black soldiers fled in panic, while others surrendered, only to be shot by enraged rebels. Union officers and the northern press criticized the conduct of blacks at the Battle of the Crater, but a court of inquiry exonerated them and found the commanding generals, including Burnside, responsible for the fiasco. Of the nearly 4,000 Union casualties during the battle, 1,327 were blacks. *HTECW*, 190; Cornish, *Sable Arm*, 273–78.

4. The committee refers to the Thirteenth Amendment, which abolished slavery in the United States. Although adopted by the Congress in January 1865, it was not ratified by the required two-thirds of the states until December. The amendment failed to address the legal legacy of slavery—a vast array of state black laws that remained in effect throughout the South after the Civil War. Most of these enactments were eventually repealed by state legislatures and constitutional conventions, invalidated by federal court decisions, or struck down by the Fourteenth and Fifteenth amendments. Foner, *Reconstruction*, 66–67, 199–201, 208–9, 242–44.

5. Joseph Mayo (1795–1872), an attorney and outspoken secessionist, served as mayor of Richmond from 1853 through the end of the Civil War. Although he pledged not to surrender the city to Union troops, he was forcibly removed from office in April 1865 by conquering soldiers. One month later, Governor Francis H. Pierpont reinstated Mayo and his entire staff. On 7 June, Mayo reopened his mayor's court—used to enforce local black codes before the war—and ordered civilian police onto the streets. He persuaded Union military authorities to reinstate the pass system and impose curfews for blacks. Any black not carrying a pass signed by a white employer could be arrested, imprisoned, and assigned to work for local planters. Northern missionaries reported that police and Union troops were waging a "reign of terror" against the city's black population. Richmond blacks held a mass meeting on 10 June to protest the actions of Mayo and his police force. They also appealed directly to President Andrew Johnson, who forced the governor to remove Mayo from office. By mid-June, the pass and curfew regulations had been abolished and new officials appointed to administer police and military affairs in Richmond. *ACAB*, 4:277; Emory M. Thomas, *The Confederate State of Richmond: A Biography of a Capital* (Austin, Tex., 1971), 19, 29, 94; John T. O'Brien, "Reconstruction in Richmond: White Restoration and Black Protest, April–June 1865," *VMHB* 89:274–81 (July 1981).

6. Several southern states, including Tennessee, approved child apprenticeship laws at the end of the Civil War. These granted local courts the authority to bind black minors to labor without pay for white employers. Although state legislatures ostensibly created the system to provide for orphans and other children without adequate parental care, it often resulted in the forced separation of black families and the exploitation of black children as plantation workers. Foner, *Reconstruction*, 201–2; Stephen V. Ash, *Middle Tennessee Society Transformed, 1860–1870* (Baton Rouge, La., 1988), 199.

7. James L. Belote (?–1867), a Union loyalist, was the mayor of Norfolk during the final year of the Civil War. Biographical File, VNP.

8. The committee was justified in its concern about the end of Union military occupation in the South. The U.S. Army quickly withdrew its troops from many parts of the region after the Civil War. By 1867 only sixteen thousand soldiers remained, and many were stationed on the southwestern frontier to control the Native American population. Military rule ended in Virginia in 1869. Foner, *Reconstruction*, 3–4, 148, 308n, 412.

9. Francis H. Pierpont (1814–1899), a lawyer and businessman from western Virginia, was elected governor of the state's loyal counties in June 1861 and served until removed from office by General John M. Schofield in April 1868. Although Pierpont opposed slavery, he despised abolitionists, rejected black enfranchisement, and tolerated only limited rights for blacks. He supported and carried out President Johnson's amnesty policy, which enfranchised all eligible former Confederates who took a loyalty oath. Charles H. Ambler, *Francis H. Pierpont: War Governor of Virginia and Father of West Virginia* (Chapel Hill, N.C., 1937).

10. Section 27 of the 1864 Virginia state constitution repudiated debts incurred by the Confederate state government and prohibited local governments from honoring Confederate bonds or debts.

11. Thomas C. Tabb, a local attorney with Confederate sympathies, was elected mayor of Norfolk in the 25 May 1865 city elections. He served for one year, then left the office to take a judicial post. A fifteen-member common council headed by its president, John B. Whitehead, was elected at the same time. Biographical File, VNP; *NV*, 4, 16 January 1866; Tommy L. Bogger, "The Slave and Free Black Community in Norfolk, 1775–1865" (Ph.D. diss., University of Virginia, 1976), 311.

12. Article 4 of the Articles of Confederation accorded "all free inhabitants" of each state "all the privileges and immunities of free citizens in the several states." South Carolina delegates to the Continental Congress attempted to insert the word "white" into this article, but failed to muster the votes needed for the amendment. In his dissenting brief in *Dred Scott* v. *Sanford* (1857), Justice Benjamin R. Curtis cited the rejection of the South Carolina amendment as an early affirmation of black American citizenship. Merrill Jensen, *The Articles of Confederation* (Madison, Wis., 1966), 263; Litwack, *North of Slavery*, 61–62.

13. Appendix B of *Equal Suffrage* (1865), the pamphlet in which this address was originally published, reported on the question of black testimony in the civil case of *Graff* v. *Howard* (1864) in the Alexandria County (Va.) Court. Isaac Dorsey, a Massachusetts black, was called to testify on behalf of the plaintiff, but his testimony was excluded on the objection of the attorney for the defendant because the two parties to the case were white. Acting on the advice of Calvin Pepper, the attorney for the plaintiff, Dorsey filed a writ of *mandamus* to allow his testimony, citing article 4, section 2, of the U.S. Constitution as his cause. Pepper argued that the law under which Dorsey's testimony was excluded, being "a creation of slavery," had been invalidated by emancipation. *Equal Suffrage*, 17–26.

14. The committee refers to article 4, section 1, of the 1798 Georgia state constitution.

15. The committee quotes from section 6 of the Bill of Rights in the 1776 Virginia state constitution. Article 3, section 1, of the 1864 state constitution granted voting rights to "every white male citizen . . . of the age of 21 years."

16. During the summer of 1863, the American Missionary Association established freedmen's schools in two of Norfolk's black churches. By that September, the AMA employed twenty-one teachers and instructed more than three thousand students in eleven day and evening schools in the city. Engs, *Freedom's First Generation*, 52–53.

17. Joseph T. Wilson (1836–1891), a black seaman, was born in Norfolk, but eventually moved to New Bedford, Massachusetts. He traveled extensively in the South Pacific before the Civil War. When he received the news that the war had begun, he left Santiago, Chile, and sailed to New Orleans in search of his father, who had been sold there. Wilson enlisted in the Second Regiment of Louisiana Native Guards and later transferred to the Fifty-fourth Massachusetts Regiment. Released from military service after being wounded at the battle of Olustee, Florida, in February 1864, he returned to Norfolk and became involved in Republican party politics and equal rights associations. He represented Portsmouth at the 1867 Republican state convention and later held several appointed and elected offices. Wilson was an officer in the Grand Army of the Republic and compiled a historical record of black soldiers entitled *The Black Phalanx* (1890). He also wrote *Emancipation: Its Course from 1102 to 1875* (1881), *Voice of a New Race* (1882), and *Twenty-two Years of Freedom* (1882). Introductory notes by Sara Dunlap Jackson in Joseph T. Wilson, *The Black Phalanx* (Hartford, Conn., 1890; reprint, New York, N.Y., 1968).

18. Shortly after the war ended, white planters throughout the South organized to control black workers. On 1 June 1865, planters from seven central Virginia counties met at the Louisa County Courthouse to establish uniform wage rates and working conditions for black agricultural laborers. Planters in several areas of the state formed "labor regulating associations" to fix maximum wages, draw up model contracts, agree on penalties for violations of labor contracts, and pledge themselves not to sell or lease land to the freedmen. Litwack, *Been in the Storm So Long*, 414–16; *NASS*, 10, 24 June 1865, 10 February 1866.

19. William Keeling, a black restaurateur, held leadership positions in several Norfolk civic and fraternal organizations, including the Humane Aid Society and a black Masonic lodge. He encouraged local blacks to enlist in the Fifty-fourth Massachusetts Regiment during the Civil War. Keeling represented Norfolk at the 1864 black national convention in Syracuse and in the National Equal Rights League, which emerged from that gathering. After the war, he became involved in local politics as an officer of the interracial Democratic Republican Association and as vice-president of the Union Monitor Club, a voting rights league. *Norfolk City Directory*, 1869–81; *Convention of Colored Men . . . in Syracuse* (1864), 5, 7, 8 [15 : 0540]; Foner and Walker, *Black National and State Conventions*, 58, 102; *WAA*, 4 April 1863, 6 February, 2 April 1864, 16 December 1865.

20. George W. Cook, a laborer, was a member of Norfolk's free black community before the Civil War. He was appointed in September 1862 to supervise the American Missionary Association's two local freedmen's schools, but his inattentiveness and nepotism brought about his dismissal within four months. In

May 1865, Cook became secretary of the Norfolk Land Association, a black alliance organized to assist the freedmen in "becoming owners of the soil." He called for black communities throughout the state to create similar bodies, hoping to form a Union of Virginia Colored Land Associations; although several local land associations were formed, and blacks purchased some 100,000 acres in Virginia by the early 1870s, it appears that the statewide body never got beyond the planning stage. Cook was a delegate to the 1865 Virginia black state convention and later became involved with black suffrage and Freedmen's Bureau issues. *Norfolk City Directory*, 1872–81; Mansfield, "That Fateful Class," 96–98; John Oliver to Simeon S. Jocelyn, 3 November 1862, AMA-ARC [14:0571]; *WAA*, 5 December 1863, 30 April, 10 December 1864, 12 August 1865 [16:0058]; Bogger, "Slave and Free Black Community in Norfolk," 312–14; Taylor, *Negro in the Reconstruction of Virginia*, 131–33; Foner and Walker, *Black National and State Conventions*, 102.

21. Appendix A of *Equal Suffrage* (1865), the pamphlet in which this address was originally published, outlined the objectives and discussed the June 1865 founding of the Democratic Republican Association, an interracial organization of Union loyalists devoted to equal rights in Norfolk. Two local whites, Charles E. Johnston and Thomas L. R. Baker, acted as the recording secretaries for the association. Johnston was an assistant superintendent for the Freedmen's Bureau during 1865–66. Baker, a notary public, attorney, and detective, later obtained the city's paving contract. He precipitated a local race riot in 1866 when he was seen driving a carriage filled with black women to an equal suffrage parade. *Equal Suffrage*, 16–17; *WAA*, 16 December 1865; *Norfolk City Directory*, 1866–81; John Hammond Moore, "The Norfolk Riot, 16 April 1866," *VMHB* 90:161 (April 1982).

22. Thomas Bayne (1824–1889), a local dentist and civic leader, was born in slavery in North Carolina; his slave name was Samuel Nixon. After being sold several times during his youth, he was acquired in 1846 by Dr. C. L. Martin, a Norfolk dentist. He worked as an assistant in his master's medical practice and eventually became a skilled dentist. His literacy and freedom of movement allowed him to aid slaves escaping from the Norfolk area. Fearing punishment for this antislavery activity, he left his wife and daughter in the spring of 1855, traveled the underground railroad to Philadelphia, and finally settled in New Bedford, Massachusetts. Taking the name Thomas Bayne, he established a successful dental practice and became involved in local civic affairs. With support from Republican and temperance groups, he won a seat on the city council in 1860. Bayne returned to Norfolk in early 1865 and established himself as a leader of the local black community. An itinerant preacher and eloquent speaker, he carried the call for equal rights to communities of freedmen throughout eastern Virginia, winning praise as "the most spectacular, the most radical, and one of the most hated of the Negroes in politics." He served as a delegate to the state constitutional convention in 1868 and brought the issues of integrated education and tax relief for the poor to Virginia's Reconstruction debate. Aptheker, *To Be Free*, 233n; Still, *Underground Railroad*, 258–59 [9:0712, 12:0408, 13:0414]; *WAA*, 28 April 1860, 16 February 1861 [12:0660, 13:0327]; William Still, "Journal C. of Station No. 2 of the Underground Railroad, 1852–1859," Pennsylvania Abolition Society Papers, PHi [7:0961–62]; Foner and Walker, *Black*

National and State Conventions, 81, 89–103; Foner, *Reconstruction*, 87, 111, 319, 322, 327.

23. John Mifflin Brown (1817–1893), a bishop of the African Methodist Episcopal church, was born in Delaware, but went to Philadelphia as a youth to pursue an education. He studied with Rev. James N. Gloucester and learned the barber's trade from Frederick A. Hinton, members of the local black elite. Brown continued his studies while plying his trade in Amherst, Massachusetts, and Poughkeepsie, New York. In 1841 he entered Oberlin College. Brown became a pastor in the AME church in 1844. Over the next decade, he served congregations in Detroit, Columbus (Ohio), and Pittsburgh and helped establish the denomination's Union Seminary. He also participated in black state conventions in Indiana and Ohio and defended the AME's antislavery commitment against black critics.

Brown spent most of his ministry in the South. In 1853 he was assigned to St. James AME Church in New Orleans. Local authorities, suspicious of his preaching and contact with slaves, imprisoned him on several occasions. After serving Louisville and Baltimore congregations before the Civil War, he took charge in 1863 of the newly organized Bute Street AME Church in Norfolk. Brown assumed a prominent role in the city's black community, participated in the local voting rights campaign, represented blacks in their relations with the federal government, and encouraged the establishment of a branch of the Freedman's Savings Bank. As the corresponding secretary of the denomination's missionary society, he also raised $10,000 to build southern black schools and churches during this time.

In 1868 Brown was elected an AME bishop and given the task of organizing congregations, conferences, and colleges throughout the South. Widely regarded as a religious scholar, he was formal in his demeanor and methodical in his work. His accomplishments included the founding of Paul Quinn College in Waco, Texas, and the Payne Institute in South Carolina. *DANB*, 68–69; Smith, *African Methodist Episcopal Church*, 190–93; William J. Simmons, *Men of Mark: Eminent, Progressive and Rising* (Cleveland, Ohio, 1887; reprint, New York, N.Y., 1968), 1113–18; Wayman, *Cyclopaedia of African Methodism*, 9; *CR*, 9 July 1864; Cheek and Cheek, *John Mercer Langston*, 126–27, 144, 192; Foner and Walker, *Proceedings of the Black State Conventions*, 1:176–77, 224–25, 245; Israel L. Butt, *History of African Methodism in Virginia* (Hampton, Va., 1908), 32–33; Osthaus, *Freedmen, Philanthropy, and Fraud*, 16, 31.

24. Thomas Henson, a black Baptist clergyman, was reared in New Bedford, Massachusetts. After working in Boston as a clothier during the 1840s, he decided to enter the ministry. Henson pastored the Zion Baptist Church in New York City (1851–55), the First Independent Baptist Church in Boston (1855–58), and the Meeting Street Baptist Church in Providence (1860). While living in New York City, he officiated at the controversial interracial marriage of William G. Allen and Mary E. King. But Henson's community leadership extended well beyond his clerical role. He joined with other Boston blacks to support William Lloyd Garrison and the *Liberator*, encouraged the black press, and helped organize the Rhode Island Committee of Vigilance in Providence. Attracted by the opportunity to work among the freedmen, Henson became the pastor of Norfolk's Catharine Street Baptist Church (later the Bank Street Church) in Decem-

ber 1862. He was the first black minister of the congregation, which had been formed in 1840. Under his leadership, the church regularly hosted black political gatherings during Reconstruction. Henson remained at the church for a decade. *Lib*, 1 November 1839, 3 April 1840, 8 July 1842 [3:0248, 0374, 4:0451]; *CA*, 4 December 1841 [4:0319]; Sobel, *Trabelin' On*, 240, 258, 262, 267; George A. Levesque, "Black Boston: Negro Life in Garrison's Boston" (Ph.D. diss., State University of New York at Binghamton, 1976), 377; William G. Allen, *The American Prejudice Against Color: An Authentic Narrative, Showing How Easily the Nation Got into an Uproar* (London, 1853), 87 [8:0023]; Handbill of the Rhode Island Vigilance Committee, Newspaper Clipping File, RHi [9:0780]; *Boston City Directory*, 1840–41; *WAA*, 21 February 1863, 1 July 1865; Biographical File, VNP; Reuben Jones, *A History of the Virginia Portsmouth Baptist Association* (Raleigh, N.C., 1881), 224–25.

25. Thomas F. Paige, Jr., a black grocer, was the secretary of the Union Monitor Club, a voting rights association in Norfolk. He also served as president of the Atheneum Club, a black literary society, and worked as a local correspondent for the *Weekly Anglo-African*. Paige operated a hotel and billiard parlor in Norfolk during the 1880s. *Norfolk City Directory*, 1874–81; *WAA*, 11 June, 9 July 1864, 1 July 1865.

71.
Speech by Martin R. Delany

Delivered at the Brick Church
St. Helena Island, South Carolina
23 July 1865

Black abolitionists represented a third voice in the debate over Reconstruction. Frustrated by southern white resistance and northern indifference, black leaders concluded that they best represented the freedmen's interests. Major Martin R. Delany, a Freedmen's Bureau agent on the South Carolina Sea Islands after the war, nourished an assertiveness and a sense of independence among the former slaves and used his position to challenge the pass system and protect black workers from white exploitation. Local whites complained to government officials that he had "stirred up trouble." On 23 July 1865, when more than five hundred freedmen crowded into the Brick Church on St. Helena Island to hear Delany speak, the Union army asked lieutenants Alex Whyte, Jr., and Edward R. Stoeber to attend, to take extensive notes on Delany's remarks, and to submit an official account of the proceedings. Whyte reported that "the general tone of the speech was such as to produce <u>discontent</u> among the Freedmen." Delany warned his listeners to beware of racism and exploitation on the part of northern carpetbaggers as well as southern planters. The following memorandum by Whyte conveys the spirit of Delany's address. Ullman, *Martin R. Delany*, 324–52; *WAA*, 13 May, 9 September, 7 October 1865 [16:0181, 0187–88]; Martin R. Delany to Major O. D. Kinsman, 20 October, 11 November 1865, Registered Letters Received, South Carolina Assistant Commissioner, RG 105, Bureau of Refugees, Freedmen, and Abandoned Lands, DNA [16:0314, 0413].

I came to talk to you in plain words so as you can understand how to throw open the gates of oppression and let the captive free. ***[1] In this state there 200,000 able, intelligent, honorable negroes, <u>not an inferior race</u>, mind you, who are ready to protect their liberty. *** The matter is in your own hands. Yes I will fight them and take them man by man. *** I want to tell you one thing, do you know that if it was not for the black man this war never would have been brought to a close with success to the Union, and the liberty of your race if it had not been for the negro? I want you to understand that. Do you know it, do you know it, do you know it? (Cries of yes, yes, yes.) They can't get along without you. *** Yankees from the North who come down here to drive you as much as ever it was before the war.[2] Its slavery over again, northern, universal U.S. Slavery. *** But they must keep their clamps off. *** If I were a slave

I would be the most worthless one on the plantation. I would not do anything. *** They (i.e. before the war) have often told you, "Sam, you lazy nigger, you don't earn your salt. If you dont do better I'll sell you to the first trader that comes along," at the same time they were making their thousands annually on every one of you. *** And so it is with these Yankees from the North[,] they don't pay you enough. I see too many of you dressed in rags, and shoeless. *** These Yankees talk smooth to you, o, yes; their tung rolls just like a drum (laughter), but its slavery over again as much as ever it was. *** I expect Gen. Saxton back very soon, he is working with me, when this matter will be settled, I mean about lands—when you can plant and work your own farms.[3] Don't be anxious for large places[,] 40 acres is enough[4][—]cotton will bring 30¢ for two years to come[,] that is putting it at a low estimate (Here he explained a mathematical calculation showing that they could make $900 per year on this staple) and then your little cabins will be floored, barns built, and carpet will take the place of bare floors. *** (The last paragraph is well, A.W.Jr.) But you must only deal with the Govt. accredited agents, recognize none but authorized cotton agents.[5] I know that Cotton has been raised by you, these fellows have told you they would send it north and sell it for you—months pass, and when you ask for money they will tell you the Cotton is not yet sold. *** There are good Yankees and when you come across a good Yankee he is smart. *** The figure is yellow trowsers and claw hammer coat, dealing in wooden hams and nutmeg's (and calculated to impress the negro with feelings of indignation towards the white people from the north now residing here—engaged in the products of this climate). But what I don't like, and what won't have is these fellows from the north, who were nothing at home, and ape the southerner with a big broad brim hat—he has his overseer too, a chuckle headed slave driver on the fence or in the crotch of a tree, and say "Sam or Jim do this, do that, light my pipe," as lazy as any southerner or overseer was. They promise you 30¢ task, you are to get ⅓ crop and I will see that you get it. *** You must not think you are Yankees, you are negroes the same as I am. *** (He gave the idea that the real Yankee is smart—but those here were not conscientious).

"There is something rotton in Denmark."[6]

Sgd, Alex Whyte Jr.
2nd Lt 128th U.S.C. Troops

Letters Received, RG 94, Adjutant General's Office, U.S. Colored Troops, National Archives, Washington, D.C. Published by permission.

1. The asterisks in this document appear in the original memorandum.

2. Reconstruction provided opportunities for northern businessmen and investors in the South. Most were Union army veterans who liked the culture and climate of the region and came to buy cotton lands or build factories and busi-

nesses. Northerners who came South were often called "carpetbaggers" and depicted as corrupt political opportunists by southern whites. *HTECW*, 115.

3. Delany's work was supervised by Rufus B. Saxton, the assistant commissioner of the Freedmen's Bureau for South Carolina, Georgia, and Florida. Saxton encouraged the confiscation and redistribution of former rebel lands among the freedmen. He was removed from his post in January 1866 after obstructing efforts to remove blacks already working these lands. Ullman, *Martin R. Delany*, 333.

4. On 12 January 1865, General William T. Sherman issued Field Order No. 15, setting aside for black settlement some 400,000 acres of confiscated rebel lands along the South Carolina coast. Each black family was promised forty acres and the loan of an army mule. The phrase "forty acres and a mule" soon became synonymous with radical land reform in the South, but the federal government declined to make it part of its Reconstruction program. Foner, *Reconstruction*, 70–71.

5. Delany refers to agents authorized by the U.S. Department of the Treasury to purchase cotton grown on confiscated lands.

6. Delany quotes from act 1, scene 4, of the play *Hamlet* by William Shakespeare.

72.
Jermain Wesley Loguen to Robert Hamilton
25 July 1865

For some black abolitionists, the end of the Civil War meant the opportunity to return to the South. These men and women, many of them
former slaves, approached the journey with nostalgia for the past and a
deep concern about the freedmen's future. In the summer of 1865, Jermain W. Loguen, an African Methodist Episcopal Zion clergyman and
underground railroad activist from Syracuse, traveled to Tennessee to
assess the condition of the former slaves. He visited the plantation from
which he had escaped thirty-two years before, located his mother and
acquaintances from his early life in slavery, and organized dozens of
churches. His presence in Tennessee attracted broad public attention,
particularly in Nashville, where he addressed a crowd of over three
thousand at a Fourth of July celebration. Loguen reported on these activities in a 25 July letter to the *Weekly Anglo-African*. After viewing
the freedmen's situation, he sounded an urgent call for black political
empowerment and predicted a "dark day for the friends of freedom" if
Union troops withdrew from the South before blacks gained full political equality. He urged northern black teachers and clergymen to go
South, if only for a brief period, and educate the freedmen. Loguen's
earnest counsel to "get acquainted with the freedmen" suggested that
northern blacks could learn from their experience in the South. *WAA*,
8, 22 July 1865; *CR*, 12 August 1865.

Syracuse, [New York]
July 25th, 1865

MR. EDITOR:

I am once more at my "Salt City" home,[1] after an absence of nearly
two months. I have been away down in my fatherland, where in days
gone by I have often seen the slaveholder's merciless whip fall upon the
backs of my poor brothers and sisters until the warm blood would flow
therefrom and drop to the ground. I visited Columbia and while there
looked in vain for the whipping-post and auction-block; those silent pro-
claimers of barbarism in man were removed from sight.[2] The slave-pens,
thank God, have changed their inmates. In place of the poor, innocent
and almost heartbroken slaves, who have year after weary year been
placed there to wait for the negro trader to make up his gang, and then
driven in chains to the sugar or cotton fields, there to drag out a miserable existence away from friends and all that is dear; in place of the
young slave mother begging for her only babe, with no mercy shown her,
are some of the very fiends in human shape who committed those dia-

bolical outrages. "Their sins have found them out," and I was constrained to give God the glory, for He has done a great work for our people.

I preached twice in Columbia in hearing of the old slave-pen. Colored and white came to hear me. They had all heard of Jarm's running away over thirty-two years ago, and had not a little curiosity to see and hear him. The Lord was with me and gave me great liberty on that occasion, as we Methodist preachers sometimes say. My old mother, though very feeble, rode ten miles that she might hear her long-lost son. On the old plantation all had changed.[3] The home of my childhood was like a strange land.

It is almost impossible for a person to realize the changes brought about by this war without visiting the South. In place of slave-pens, you will see churches and schoolrooms filled with happy souls. In place of auctioneers there are missionaries who preach a full, free Gospel to the eager listening ones. They are anxious to learn to read and write, and the privilege to do so makes them appear happier than any other people in that part of the country.

God in His goodness has opened wide the door for the schoolteacher and missionary. Hundreds are needed to labor for the freedmen in Tennessee as well as in other States. There are many noble men and women in the cities of Nashville and Knoxville who stand ready to assist all who may go to labor. As in those two places, so in many others throughout the State, there are noble specimens of gentlemen and ladies among the colored people, and those are they that stand ready to help in the great work of elevation.

I found some whites there from the free States who were very kind, others who were very mean. Many of the copperheads from the North, who are in military power, are meaner than the Southerners; yes, meaner than the rebels themselves. We must work while it is day. If the military is withdrawn ere the colored man has his God-given rights granted and guaranteed to him, it will be a dark day for the friends of freedom all over the land. The black man *must* have equal rights before the law, or I fear this is a ruined Nation after all that has been done. The country so far has been greatly aided by the black man, and it still needs, in fact, and must have his support, if it would survive. The loyal representatives in Tennessee, Alabama, and Kentucky, are the colored soldiers; God bless them! Wherever they are there is safety for the colored people. I never spoke to a more noble set of men in my life than the colored soldiers at Chattanooga.[4] Many of the white soldiers were drunken, and loafing about abusing colored people. The only trouble I had was with some of the white soldiers. Quite different with the black soldiers; they all *acted*, as well as *looked like men*. You can see in their every action that a great work is to be performed by them, and with dignity and manliness are they preparing themselves for the work.

> He is a hero, truly brave,
> That wars for freedom, not a throne.

It is necessary that we urge every strong man and woman, preacher and teacher, who can leave for a time their Northern laboring fields, to go and spend all the time they can in the South. Let them stay two, three, or more months, just as they can afford. The work must be done, and it is for us to do who have had the advantages of a free North and free schools. I am willing and ready to go again just as soon as I recover my health. Let us go and see our brethren and talk with them; they seem *glad* to see us. Why, my friend, I think you did more for God and humanity the months you spent in the South, than you could have done in so many years at the North.

We cannot all go South to live, but let all go who can and get acquainted with the freedmen. It does a Northern heart good to witness the meeting of husbands and wives, parents and children, brothers and sisters, and old friends long lost to each other. The whites are pressing in among them, some to do good, many to make money only; the latter class do more harm than good.

To show the patriotism and loyalty among the Southern people, I will say, that in Nashville, the capital of Tennessee, the colored people alone celebrated the Fourth of July. The celebration was a success, and it was with a feeling of pleasure that your humble servant delivered the oration.[5]

I have many things to tell you, when we meet, of the old plantation, my mother, and old mistress. Yours, for the work,

J. W. LOGUEN

Weekly Anglo-African (New York, N.Y.), 5 August 1865.

1. Syracuse was often called "the Salt City," because salt production was its dominant commercial activity until the 1860s. Roberta B. Miller, *City and Hinterland: A Case Study of Urban and Regional Development* (Westport, Conn., 1979), 97–99.

2. Because of Tennessee's geographical location, Memphis, Nashville, Columbia, and other cities in the state became convenient entrepôts for slaves sold to planters in the lower Mississippi Valley. Although the state banned the importation of slaves for sale between 1827 and 1853, many leading trading firms maintained offices and slave pens in these cities. Tadman, *Speculators and Slaves*, 65, 84n, 90.

3. Loguen refers to the plantation of Manasseth Logue on the Little Tombigbee River near Columbia, Tennessee. He escaped from this plantation in 1835, but his mother, Jane, remained. She had been born free in Ohio, but was kidnapped at the age of seven and sold to David, Carnes, and Manasseth Logue of central

Tennessee. They changed her name to Cherry and David Logue fathered her child. She eventually became the sole property of Manasseth Logue and was living on his old plantation at the time of Loguen's return. *DANB*, 404; Jermain W. Loguen, *The Rev. J. W. Loguen, As a Slave and as a Freeman* (Syracuse, N.Y., 1859), 12–18, 75–76, 93–94.

4. At the time of Loguen's visit to Chattanooga, the black regiments stationed there included the Fourteenth, Sixteenth, Eighteenth, Forty-second, and Forty-fourth U.S. Colored Troops. *WAA*, 29 April 1865; Berlin et al., *Freedom*, 2:773–74.

5. On 4 July 1865, Loguen addressed an interracial gathering of three to four thousand people in Nashville, Tennessee. His audience was primarily black, as most local whites found little to celebrate in the recent collapse of the Confederacy. Loguen's speech called for equal rights and asserted that "nothing short of the ballot would protect the people of his race at the south." *CR*, 12 August 1865.

73.
Editorial by Philip A. Bell
28 July 1865

Suddenly made president by an assassin's bullet, Andrew Johnson attempted to restore the Union on his own initiative. He consented to a brief and lenient Reconstruction—once the rebel states disavowed secession, repudiated the Confederate war debt, and ratified the Thirteenth Amendment abolishing slavery, they were welcomed back into the nation. Johnson permitted these new state governments to elect former Confederates to political office and to pass "black codes" abridging the rights of the emancipated slaves. Black abolitionists bore witness to the injustice of Johnson's restoration policy and pointed angrily to the reenslavement of the freedmen under a new guise. Philip Bell's 28 July 1865 editorial in the *Elevator* described the "fruits of failure" of Presidential Reconstruction. Bell dismissed the anxious ravings of those southern whites who feared barbarism and insurrection from the recently freed slaves, and he reprimanded Johnson for authorizing "liberal but injudicious pardoning" of former Confederates while ignoring calls for black suffrage. Stressing the injustice of a government policy that neglected loyal blacks while rewarding disloyal whites, Bell insisted that Reconstruction was a fraud unless the former rebels were disfranchised and blacks were given the vote. *WAA*, 13 May, 24 June, 1, 22 July, 5, 19 August, 11 November 1865 [16:0059, 0419, 0420–21]; *CR*, 14 October 1865 [16:0313]; *Lib*, 14 July 1865 [15:1032]; McPherson, *Struggle for Equality*, 320–40.

A BRIEF REVIEW

The telegraph works spasmodically. Considerable news has come over the wires lately, but not much of general import. We give a brief abstract under the proper head.

The war does not appear to us to be ended, nor rebellion suppressed. They have commenced reconstruction on disloyal principles. If rebel soldiers are allowed to mumble through oaths of allegiance, and vote Lee's officers into important offices, and if Legislatures, elected by such voters, are allowed to define the provisions of the Amnesty Proclamation,[1] then were our conquests vain, and we may soon expect the reestablishment of slavery in its most hideous forms, to be followed by the worst of all wars—a servile insurrection—preceded, perhaps, by another rebellion—but not of the South this time; the North will rise and demand their rights as conquerors—the right of submitting terms to the conquered. Instead of pursuing a system of "liberal, but judicious hanging," as recommended by General Scott,[2] the Government appears to have adopted a system of liberal but injudicious pardoning. Already we see the fruits of this failure on the part of Government to mete out full justice to the loyal blacks, and retribution to disloyal whites.

During the whole four long years of the war, we heard of no insurrection among the slaves; they escaped when they could to the Union ranks, often to be repulsed and driven back, but those anticipated horrors of slave rising, murdering, ravaging, pillaging, destroying plantations, and the "barbarities of St. Domingo," were never realized.[3] The slaves waited long and patiently; they believed in the mercy of God and the justice of "Massa Linkum." Ours is a race proverbial for their faith, and the day at last came when they supposed their faith was to receive its reward and its full fruition. What is now the result? They are declared free, but they are turned over to the tender mercies of their former oppressors, full of hatred and rebellion as ever, and burning for revenge on somebody. Can we wonder at the daily accounts received of "Troubles with the negroes," "Mutiny among the black soldiers," and the like?

Everywhere throughout the country, men of true Union principles declare in favor of granting blacks the elective franchise. Gen. Banks, who of late has not appeared to be overburdened with negro sympathy, but who has witnessed in his own State of Massachusetts the salutary effects of negro suffrage, in a Fourth of July oration in New Orleans, asserted "the justice, right and necessity of conferring the elective franchise on the colored people of the South."[4]

The rebels and traitors of the Southern States are doubtless willing negro suffrage should prevail at the North, but they wish to govern their own institutions. Just so here; doe-faced Northern political hybrids, semi-Union men, say there is no necessity of giving the blacks the elective franchise here, *we* (they) can do without their votes. The *Morning Call*[5] is playing this tune on its one-stringed fiddle, and it makes most abominable discord, which it mistakes for harmony. We tell them the Union wants Union voters everywhere. "Liberty and Union" can never become "one and inseparable"[6] until every Union vote is polled, and every traitor disfranchised. Then, and not till then, will the glorious old flag wave in triumph over a free land and a free people.

>   Where'er a wind is blowing,
>   Where'er a wave is flowing,

the banner of the Republic will be recognized as emblematic of Loyalty and Freedom.

Elevator (San Francisco, Calif.), 28 July 1865.

1. On 29 May 1865, President Andrew Johnson issued an Amnesty Proclamation offering amnesty, pardon, and restoration of property rights (except slave ownership) to all former Confederates willing to take an oath of loyalty to the United States. A related proclamation ordered provisional governors to call con-

ventions to revise their state constitutions. Those rebels pardoned under the first declaration were eligible to vote for convention delegates, but blacks were denied the franchise by antebellum state laws still in force. These proclamations were the first definitive statement of Johnson's Reconstruction policy. Foner, *Reconstruction*, 183–84.

2. In 1865 General Winfield Scott called for the hanging of Jefferson Davis and other Confederate leaders. Scott (1786–1866), a veteran of the War of 1812 and a hero of the Mexican War, was general-in-chief of the U.S. Army from 1841 to the beginning of the Civil War. A popular figure, he was chosen as the presidential candidate of the Whig party in 1852. Scott developed the overall military strategy used to defeat the Confederacy. C. Vann Woodward and Elisabeth Muhlenfeld, eds., *The Private Mary Chesnut: The Unpublished Civil War Diaries* (New York, N.Y., 1984), 260n; *DAB*, 16:505–11.

3. Bell alludes to the massacre of whites in Haiti—called St. Domingo by the Spanish—during the slave revolt and political revolution of the 1790s. Nearly sixty thousand whites were killed or forced to flee the island, arousing fears that a similar slave insurrection would occur in the South. Perusse, *Historical Dictionary of Haiti*, 27–28.

4. Speaking at a Fourth of July celebration at the U.S. Customs House in New Orleans in 1865, General Nathaniel P. Banks repudiated his former opposition to black suffrage. He proclaimed that the black vote was necessary to prevent a resurgence of rebel power and declared that blacks best understood their own situation and "what is necessary for their welfare." Lawanda Cox, *Lincoln and Black Freedom: A Study in Presidential Leadership* (Columbia, S.C., 1981), 120–21; McCrary, *Abraham Lincoln and Reconstruction*, 320–21.

5. The San Francisco *Morning Call*, an extremely conservative daily paper begun in 1856, was an outspoken opponent of Radical Reconstruction. William Randolph Hearst purchased the paper in 1928 and merged it into the *Call-Bulletin*. Mott, *American Journalism*, 474, 573.

6. Bell quotes from Daniel Webster's second reply to Senator Robert Y. Hayne on the floor of the U.S. Senate on 26 January 1830. Maurice G. Baxter, *One and Inseparable: Daniel Webster and the Union* (Cambridge, Mass., 1984), 181–88.

74.
Editorial by Robert Hamilton
3 September 1865

President Andrew Johnson's 1865 declaration that "white men alone must manage the South" predicted the future of Reconstruction. Johnson sought to preserve white rule by restoring the seceded states to the Union, reinstating former rebels to positions of authority, and returning the freedmen to the plantations. Involuntary servitude, whipping, or a worse fate awaited blacks who violated curfews, the pass system, or traditional racial etiquette. Thousands were beaten, shot, and lynched in the years after the Civil War; hundreds of black homes, churches, schools, and businesses were burned. Quickly discerning the full implications of Presidential Reconstruction, black leaders saw that slavery and inequality had survived the war and that the only black right the federal government wished to protect was the right to work. The black press sounded the alarm. In this 3 September 1865 editorial in the *Weekly Anglo-African*, Robert Hamilton explained that the nation was forsaking its obligations to blacks and denounced the reign of terror being waged against the freedmen. "The scheme is now, preparatory to another attempt to break up the Union," he declared, "to exterminate the negro." Foner, *Reconstruction*, 119–23, 180; WAA, 24 June, 22 July, 5, 19 August 1865.

THE EMANCIPATION PROCLAMATION
IGNORED, AND A NEW SCHEME OF
SOUTHERN DESPOTISM BOLDLY
INITIATED

The negroes, having rendered the most efficient aid to the National Government in suppressing the slaveholders' rebellion, and saving the Union from utter ruin, the scheme is now, preparatory to another attempt to break up the Union, to exterminate the negro. Some may smile at this idea; but no delusion is too great for those who are, on the one hand, smitten with the mania of eternal negro slavery, and on the other, with the virus of negro hate. That the rebels of the South should feel an intense dislike to the negro is the most natural thing in the world, in view of the depravity of man. The rebel hates the negro because he has thrown off *his* yoke and become free, and, likewise, because he defeated the object and aim of the rebellion; and, then, the vast numbers who, in all parts of the land, have been taught to hate the negro without a cause, find that feeling of hate intensified by the mean spirit of jealousy, because the colored soldiers have, on the battlefield, redeemed the name of their race from scorn.

Cruelty, jealousy, and meanness are among the lowest and most barbarous of human vices. They eat out and destroy all greatness of soul and nobleness of nature in man. They kill all kindly sympathy, and create within him a heart of stone. The late war grew out of a quarrel between the North and the South, which had been going on for many years. Session after session, the American Congress was like a debating club on the public lands, and Indian questions, tariff, United States Bank, etc., etc. Mental pitch-battles were fought every year between Northern and Southern champions of logic, eloquence, and learning. Not unfrequently the dirk-knife, the pistol, or club were also introduced, with terrible effect.[1] Thus, almost every year, somebody went home, North or South, whipped, either mentally or physically. Hence, from year to year, this bad feeling became more and more intense between the North and the South. The feeling culminated upon the negro question; and there are at this moment other questions underlying the subject of reconstruction, which the opposing parties are not frank enough to bring out to view—they are playing those points under disguise of the negro question. We put it to the American people, both North and South—is it wise, is it safe, is it fair and honest to continue playing this cruel sham game with the black man? The American people and Government have got their politics, religion, education, and civil affairs all in a muddle. The wisest man among us cannot tell where our ship of State will be twelve months hence. We warn the people and the Government against any attempt to make a sacrifice of the just rights of the black man, or to force him into a false position by any wholesale cruelty, or to violate or abrogate the Emancipation Proclamation. Let gambling politicians beware of trifling with blood-printed documents.

NORTHERN MOB SPIRIT

Many letters come to our office containing facts of the widespread and increasing spirit of violence against colored men in the North. A few weeks ago, one of the Bishops of the A. M. E. Church was seriously threatened with personal violence while preaching at a camp-meeting in Delaware, near Dover; and after discharging his duties on the campground, was followed to his lodgings in Dover, and would have been attacked there, but for a few friendly soldiers.[2]

A few days ago Rt. Rev. J. D. Brooks, of the Zion A. M. E. Church, with one of his elders, was assaulted in one of the cars at Scranton, Pa.[3]

These outrages are committed at the North, where the war has not suspended the functions of civil authorities. It may be said that others suffer as well as colored people, that the tide of wickedness is so strong, robberies, murders, and riot being so universal, that no one is safe; but that is no reason why the colored people as a class should be made the object of outrage and insult by all classes of white rowdies. The wonder is that the teaching class among the whites make so little impression upon their own masses on this subject. We believe that a few words from each of the religious teachers of the whites, reproving the public crime of breaking the peace of the streets and highways, would do good. The leading men of the ruling classes at the North will do well to take our advice and re-educate their people. Their masses must be reformed, or the country is gone. It will be no excuse to say that such outrages are committed because they do not like colored people. Bad morals and bad manners will have their bad effects upon the country and the Government.

ANARCHY AT THE SOUTH

The fearful state now existing and spreading over some parts of the South has a twofold source, hatred of the North and the insanity of slavery. There are many of those former slaveholders at the South, who will never be able to govern themselves or anyone else. Their jealousy of their former slaves is such that they would rather see every one of them blotted out of existence, than to see them free. This feeling is shared by thousands at the South who have not been slaveholders The shocking barbarities now suffered by the colored people at the South affords a solemn lesson for the Government. It is evident that the States in which such a state of things exists are not fit for civil government. The Government has a character at stake in this matter. The eyes of the civilized world are upon the authorities at Washington. We very much fear there is something wrong about some of our military commanders in charge of Southern posts. Read the following, as a specimen of the statistics that are taking place daily:

The Southern *Christian Intelligencer*[4] of Aug. 5th says:

> If one-tenth part of the reports are true which are coming from all points of the South thicker and faster, a most shocking state of things exists. From localities where there are no national troops, come reports that those unfortunate creatures are being hunted down like dogs, and despatched without ceremony. The newspapers in the South are filled with accounts of these brutal murders, which foot up to an aggregate of several hundred deaths per day, which is doubtless only a small portion of the number noticed.

> An Alabama paper says this business has become so extensive and common that some places even boast that they could manure their farms with the dead carcasses of negroes. If negroes can be shot down openly in garrison towns, where our authorities are unable to stop this course of things, it is reasonable to suppose that this state of things is carried on more extensively where the blacks have no protection. The wholesale murder of human beings is, we fear, the practical working of the conspiracy to exterminate the colored race, which is revolting to this Christian age.

15. Burning of a freedmen's school in Memphis, 1866
From *Harper's Weekly*, 26 May 1866

The Raleigh *Progress*,[5] of the 10th, learns from Col. Lawrence, Commandant of the Post at Goldsboro', that six negroes were killed at or near Warsaw, two weeks ago. Their former owner left on the approach of the Union army, the negroes remaining. They went to work and made a crop. The former owner returned recently, and ordered them to leave. The negroes refused, and the proprietor of the place, getting some neighbors together with arms, ordered them off again, and on their refusal attacked them, killing six. A company of soldiers was sent up from Wilmington, and an investigation will be made, if it is not done already.

What use, we may ask, is being made of our brave colored troops yet at the South, if they cannot have a chance to protect their brethren, who are thus suffering at the hands of their cruel foes? If the Government needs more colored soldiers, let us give them, but let them protect their brethren from such savage barbarities. We trust that Congress will ventilate this matter when it meets, and let the country and the world know if there is a conspiracy to institute a massacre, or to reestablish slavery at all hazards.

As a loyal race, and a part of this nation, which has richly earned a claim to the consideration of the Government of the United States, we ask and demand, as a first and indispensable consideration, PROTECTION. We ask the authorities at Washington, "don't tie our hands, and then leave us at the mercy of merciless men!" If Government needs one hundred thousand more black troops to put a stop to these proceedings, and to make life, liberty, and the pursuit of happiness a reality in the South, they can be had, but give us protection!! We would put the same case, in a little modified form, to the State authorities North. At present we rest the question, but we intend to show our Northern civil authorities their duties more plainly, in the matter of protecting the peace of black men for their own sakes.

Weekly Anglo-African (New York, N.Y.), 3 September 1865.

1. Violence was endemic to antebellum American politics, even in the halls of the U.S. Congress. Politicians traded threats and insults and occasionally challenged each other to duels. The most notable episode of political violence occurred in May 1856, when Congressman Preston Brooks of South Carolina brutally assaulted Charles Sumner with his cane in the Senate chambers. During the contentious 1859 Speaker's election in the House of Representatives, many congressmen came to the Capitol armed with guns and knives. Potter, *Impending Crisis*, 209–11, 221, 388–89.

2. Bishop Alexander A. Wayman of the African Methodist Episcopal church was repeatedly harassed and threatened with violence by Confederate sympathizers while he was conducting camp meetings between 27 July and 4 August 1865 near Dover, Delaware. *WAA*, 19 August 1865.

3. Hamilton refers to an August 1865 incident involving Bishop John D. Brooks and elder John Thomas of the African Methodist Episcopal Zion church. A Union soldier assaulted Thomas and threatened Brooks when they refused to give up their seats on a train traveling between Wilkes-Barre and Montrose, Pennsylvania. Brooks (1803–1874), who was born in Baltimore, joined the AMEZ's Philadelphia Conference in 1842 and served several congregations in Pennsylvania and the upper South. Although he was highly regarded for his dedication and irreproachable personal conduct, his "rigid and dogmatic" manner, both as a minister and an administrator, alienated many church members. Brooks was elected to an AMEZ bishopric in 1864. *WAA*, 1 April, 26 August 1865; Hood, *One Hundred Years*, 182–84; William J. Walls, *The African Methodist Episcopal Zion Church: Reality of the Black Church* (Charlotte, N.C., 1974), 572–73.

4. Hamilton apparently refers to the *Christian Intelligencer*, the only Disciples of Christ periodical published in the South during the Civil War. A biweekly paper, it began publication in 1840 as the *Union Christian Intelligencer* in Charlottesville, Virginia. John G. Parrish edited the paper in Richmond during the war. Lester J. Cappon, ed., *Virginia Newspapers, 1821–1935* (New York, N.Y., 1936), 66; Louis Cochran and Bess White Cochran, *Captives of the Word* (Garden City, N.Y., 1969), 158.

5. The Raleigh (N.C.) *Progress* appeared in daily and weekly editions from 1859 to 1867. It continued the New Bern (N.C.) *Progress* and was published by Union forces during the Civil War. Gregory, *American Newspapers*, 506; H. G. Jones and Julius H. Avant, eds., *Union List of North Carolina Newspapers, 1751–1900* (Raleigh, N.C., 1963), 87.

75.
Editorial by Robert Hamilton
9 September 1865

Northern blacks and former slaves viewed education as a tool for self-improvement and a weapon for assaulting white control and the remnants of slavery. As denominations, missionary societies, and government officials established freedmen's schools throughout the South, black leaders tried to protect the former slaves from what Robert Hamilton described as "a type of education which . . . will train our race in *mental subserviency* for fifty years to come." They acknowledged that some whites sympathized with the freedmen and could do a proper job as teachers, if they believed in racial equality, but they charged that "the great mass" of whites failed to meet that standard. Some blacks argued that freedmen's education required "good competent earnest devoted *colored persons*" who could impart racial pride and a sense of equality with whites. Hamilton's 9 September 1865 editorial in the *Weekly Anglo-African* anticipates the findings of several generations of social critics by concluding that southern race relations would suffer if racial equality was not part of black education in the South. Richardson, *Christian Reconstruction*, 13, 23–24, 27, 37–40, 114, 191–93, 196; Carter G. Woodson, *The Mis-education of the Negro* (Washington, D.C., 1933); Donald Spivey, *Schooling for the New Slavery: Black Industrial Education, 1868–1915* (Westport, Conn., 1978).

THE SOUTHERN FIELD AND THE
PROPER AGENTS

We notice an increasing solicitude among the whites as to the influence likely to be exerted upon their freed brethren by those talented colored men who are now going South. This is quite natural. The whites are conscious of the fact that, heretofore, they have had the field all to themselves; that for patronage and perquisites they have taught what and how they pleased. It is natural and proper that colored men should feel that it is their mission now to enter this field, and educate and elevate their freed brethren. The field is appropriately ours—it is the only fair scope we ever had for usefulness before. Moreover, the race to be educated and elevated is ours, therefore we are deeply interested in the kind of education it receives.

1. There is a type of education which, if introduced at the South, will train our race in *mental subserviency* for fifty years to come. This would be a disaster. It would be exchanging physical for intellectual bondage. We object to teaching from the pulpit, the schooldesk, or from the platform that which will train the freed people to regard themselves as an

inferior race. We claim no *superiority* over the whites, and we admit of no *inferiority*. We reject the patronizing style of some who would have us believe that the colored people are a race of Uncle Toms, or that they are calculated to be better Christians than whites. We do not need any such flattering. It will not stand the test of our Christian philosophy. We hold that nature has made all men alike, and that by means of the Gospel and civilization they can be educated and elevated alike. This is the true standard. Anything lower than this is degrading. So far from aiming to develop the whole man, it tends to suppress the man.

2. No teacher or preacher, be they white or colored, should be entrusted with the education of freed people or their children, who is not prepared to teach and vindicate this doctrine. Unfortunately for them and for us, the great mass of the whites do not believe in the equality of the races. The influence of slavery, selfish interests, and a long course of training have established the whites in this opinion. That opinion they are free to exercise among themselves; but have they a right to impose that opinion upon us? Is it fair that they should use their influence to infuse or insinuate it among us to our degradation? We think not; and upon this point we are solicitous. We are deeply concerned about the fact that there are many whites now teaching among the freed people, and occupying other positions where they can mould their minds, who do not accord with us upon the subject under consideration. They have kindness of heart enough to regard the freed people as "poor unfortunate creatures," for whom something must be done; but on the main question of the manhood of the black man, they are not sound. They hold to the opinion of the inferiority of our race. Such persons should not seek or desire to be teachers among us—they cannot do us good. There are, we are happy to say, noble exceptions. Some of the whites now engaged in the work of teaching among us are as true as steel. Their hearts are in the right place and in the right state. Such we welcome to the field, and to our fellowship in the great work in which we are engaged. They help us; they do not hinder us. They elevate us; they do not degrade us. We do not feel ill at ease with them as co-workers; we do not feel inferior to them, and we do not wish them to feel inferior to us; we are not jealous of their influence among our people, and we do not wish them to be jealous of ours.

We think this is the way to evince the consistency of our principles; we welcome the whites to a fair mental and moral competition on our own ground, provided they are sound on this point.

In reference to the question of education at the South, we cannot speak about "reconstruction," for the colored people never had any system of education, but we can speak of construction, or organization. The educational system must be constructed or organized upon our basis—the equality of the race. Those who have not faith enough to undertake to assist in educating the race up to this standard should not enter the field as educators, for they will do more harm than good. As to the old system of preaching submission to slavery to these people, that must be utterly and forever abolished; it must be buried in the same grave with slavery. We do not see how men who have preached such doctrines can presume to stand up before the freed people.

3. In what we have written, we are not to be suspected of aiming to create any jealousy, or as fostering a feeling of bitterness toward any class of our fellow citizens, however misguided they may be; but the sacred obligations of patriotism impel us to state these views. We love our country, and we love our race; we wish to make the latter more valuable to the former. This can only be done by bringing the race up to the standard we have set. We must be true to our position, but we shall cultivate a spirit of kindness to all. Those with whom we cannot agree, we shall differ from, with firmness mingled with kindness, hoping that they may yet be brought to a right state of mind, and see that ours is the true principle of political economy. If we can succeed in bringing up the millions of our race to an equal standard of manhood with the same number of whites—as we believe we can—will it not, in that proportion, add to the strength and vital manhood of the population of the Republic for any State emergency? Why should the Republic be deprived of half the manhood of those millions, as will be the fact if they are to be educated only up to the halfway standard, against which we are objecting? We suppose it to be a sound principle of political economy that a State increases the productiveness of its population by providing that the masses not only be educated, but that they be educated to the highest possible capacity. The emergency of the late war has brought from among the race hundreds of thousands of ablebodied men for military service. Why should it be doubted that the same race may produce equally able*minded* men? How shall we know unless we *aim* to educate up to a first-class standard? We take it that there is power in the *hearts* and *brains* of those sable sons of the South, as well as in their right arms, that will yet command the respect of the nation.

Weekly Anglo-African (New York, N.Y.), 9 September 1865.

76.
Editorial by Philip A. Bell
15 September 1865

Black abolitionists joined with Radical Republicans to challenge Presidential Reconstruction. They rejected Andrew Johnson's premise that secession was the act of individuals, rather than states, and they argued that reconstructing the Union demanded more severe measures than merely installing a loyal leadership in the South. Blacks and their white Republican allies viewed secession as "state suicide." They reasoned that by leaving the Union, southern states had reverted to the status of territories and were under the jurisdiction of Congress, where Radical Republicans had the votes to implement a Reconstruction plan that would limit the political role of former Confederates and provide equal rights to southern blacks. Philip Bell spoke for black advocates of Radical Reconstruction in the 15 September 1865 issue of the San Francisco *Elevator*. His editorial, simply entitled "Reconstruction," offered commentary on a process that he believed would determine "the destinies of a race but partially redeemed from bondage." Bell criticized Johnson's contradictory policies and invoked a basic tenet of Radical Reconstruction—having left the Union, "the rebel States have no rights which the Government is bound to respect." Foner, *Reconstruction*, 228–51; McPherson, *Struggle for Equality*, 238–39.

RECONSTRUCTION

This is the most important subject which now engages the attention of the American people, for on it depends the future welfare of the nation, and the destinies of a race but partially redeemed from bondage. It is a question which absorbs the minds of all reflecting men, and all energies, all thoughts are now directed to that point. Not only in America, but in Europe, also, does this subject attract marked attention,[1] as it involves other momentous subjects of civil, political, and philanthropic importance, as well as the theory of republican or representative government.

The whole subject seems to revolve itself into this: Have the rebel States ever lost or renounced their position as members of the Union? If they have not, as President Johnson avers,[2] why treat them as territories or subjugated provinces by appointing officers which it is the prerogative of the State to elect? Why prescribe rules and regulations for their government, when they have their own State Constitution? All that is required, according to this theory, is for them to resume their former functions, acknowledge the supremacy of the General Government, and take their position again as States of the Union. They can establish slavery, for until the Constitutional Amendments are confirmed, Congress cannot prohibit slavery by virtue of the Proclamation, for the necessity which called for that is passed, and the States return to the "Union as it was and the Constitution as it is."[3]

We must confess we were somewhat inclined to President Johnson's theory, but we cannot reconcile the idea of an appointing power for States which are members of the Union—integral portions thereof. We have seen the fallacy of that theory which the practice of the President contradicts, and are now convinced that the rebel States have no rights which the Government is bound to respect.

If the theory of the President is correct, he has overstepped the bounds of his authority by appointing Provisional Governors over sovereign States which had their fundamental laws intact, and had power to elect their own Governors. If he has that power, he should exercise it to its fullest extent—first, by appointing *all* the officers of State government, and, secondly, by appointing men of sound Union sentiments, not endeavor to coax and conciliate the rebels by appointing men of known secession proclivities, some of whom have taken an active part in the rebellion.[4]

Again—it must be obvious to all that by allowing the rebel States to return to the Union without purgation, is but sowing seed for future difficulties.

We now come to the most important point, and to which Government has paid no attention whatever—the suffrage question. In his various proclamations, the President has declared what classes are not entitled to citizenship, but he has apparently lost sight of the negro population, which will ever be a disturbing element as long as they are an oppressed race. They form a large proportion of the Southern States, and will become as necessary to the Government in the future as they have been in the past, if they are treated like men and have the rights of citizens. But in their present anomalous position as freedmen, not freemen, they can render the Government no aid political, and in case of another outbreak, they would not render military service to a government which has once broken faith with them.

Considerable speculation is raised on qualifications for voters. We were never very democratic in our political opinions; we care not for universal suffrage—what we want is equal suffrage; and in reconstructing the States we only desire "Equality before the Law." The difficulty on this point is to make the qualifications such as to take in the most worthy and intelligent, and exclude the vicious and ignorant. No human judgment, nor laws framed by fallible man, could do that—hence we must expect, under any qualification, some who are worthy and capable would be excluded, and others the reverse, admitted. Still we will be content with any law which bears equally on all.

Elevator (San Francisco, Calif.), 15 September 1865.

1. The Civil War generated a widespread European interest in American affairs, which continued into the postwar years. British and French newspapers carried reports from correspondents in the United States, reprinted articles from the American press, and published commentary on the political and social issues of Reconstruction. The most notable reports came from Georges Clemenceau, the future prime minister of France, whose pieces for the Paris-based *Le Temps* were eventually compiled and published as *American Reconstruction* (1928). *TL*, 3, 5, 10 July, 14 August, 4, 16 September 1865; Foner, *Reconstruction*, 32n, 229, 240, 315.

2. President Andrew Johnson refused to recognize the secession of the Confederate states, viewing it as a constitutional impossibility. He maintained that once the war had ended and order was brought to the southern states, no further legislation was required "to restore them to their relations with the Union." Hans L. Trefousse, *Andrew Johnson: A Biography* (New York, N.Y., 1989), 235.

3. Bell quotes the political slogan of Clement L. Vallandigham (1820–1871), an Ohio Peace Democrat and the leading critic of Lincoln's war policy in the North. Vallandigham was arrested, imprisoned, and banished to the Confederacy in 1864 for his public opposition to the Union war effort. *HTECW*, 775.

4. In June 1865, President Andrew Johnson appointed provisional governors for South Carolina, Georgia, Alabama, Mississippi, Florida, and Texas. All were conservative Unionists, although several had grudgingly accepted secession, and one—Benjamin F. Perry of South Carolina—held office under the Confederate government. These appointments, which outraged Radical Republicans, inaugurated the process known as Presidential Reconstruction. Trefousse, *Andrew Johnson*, 217–19, 230.

77.
George T. Downing to Robert Hamilton
20 October 1865

Prior to the Civil War, black abolitionists took their concerns about suffrage, segregation, and discriminatory laws to northern state legislatures. They attempted to influence state lawmakers through petition
campaigns, personal contacts, and testimony before legislative committees. The war raised many of these questions to the national level. The
final authority on many crucial Reconstruction issues, especially land
and the ballot, now rested with the federal government. Black leaders
altered their political strategies to meet postwar political realities. In
September 1865, the Pennsylvania State Equal Rights League called for
the appointment of a black agent to lobby Congress. In this 20 October
letter to the *Weekly Anglo-African*, George T. Downing recommended
that blacks support a lobbyist in Washington, D.C., to press for black
rights. Downing later moved to the nation's capital and acquired political influence through business contracts with the House of Representatives. Using his personal and professional associations with Radical Republicans, he promoted passage of the Fourteenth Amendment and the
repeal of Jim Crow restrictions in the district. Foner and Walker, *Black
National and State Conventions*, 65, 202; *DANB*, 187–88; Whyte,
Uncivil War, 36, 52, 251–52.

Newport, R[hode] I[sland]
Oct[ober] 20, 1865

MR. EDITOR:

Permit me through your columns to make the suggestion that the colored people send to Congress representatives to the third house, or, in
other words, "lobby members," to be known as such, with a representative character. To do so would attract such general notice, would evince
so much concern and interest, and, on the whole, command respect, and
strengthen our friends in Congress, that no time should be lost in carrying out the idea.

The representatives should have a good address, be marked for taste
and neatness in attire, and well-informed generally as to facts and arguments affecting the interest of the colored man, and the relative interests
of the nation.

Congress has been occupied heretofore almost exclusively with the colored man as a slave; it has now to deal and legislate with him as a freeman. In that legislation, so much is involved affecting our and our children's dearest interests for centuries that no ordinary considerations
should stand in the way of our having a special representation this winter
at Washington.

Let the south, as it assuredly would, send one or more of its most intelligent men, let the north, west and east do likewise; the east will. It will soon be in the field. Let the delegations have an office, with a clerk, if you please; let the office be the headquarters for the reception of facts and documents, where friends may come and find compiled facts to serve us, and obtain immediately any information relating to the colored people.

These representatives should lose no proper opportunity to engage the attention of every member of Congress, and endeavour, by argument and appeal, to interest as many as possible of them in the interest of the colored man, which is happily allied with the best interests of the nation.

Let the representatives which we should send be, within bounds, liberally compensated, and supplied with means; this would be as others do; and if we would succeed, we must hope to succeed by just such agencies as are used by others. Do this, and the move would be productive of much good, more than it would cost. The money can be raised. In a few days New England will be in the field.[1] It will invite cooperation.

GEORGE T. DOWNING

Weekly Anglo-African (New York, N.Y.), 11 November 1865.

1. Downing refers to the Convention of the Colored People of New England, which met on 1 December 1865 in Boston. Acting as chairman of the session's business committee, Downing asked the convention to send a black representative to Washington, D.C., "to endeavor to influence the legislation of Congress." The delegates approved his suggestion, appointed him to fill the post, and voted to raise $10,000 for his support. Foner and Walker, *Black National and State Conventions*, 202–4.

78.
Speech by John Mercer Langston
Delivered at the Masonic Hall
Indianapolis, Indiana
25 October 1865

As early as 1861, black abolitionists outlined their vision for the post-war South. They sought free labor, redistribution of rebel lands, education, and full civil rights. More than any other element of their Reconstruction program, the ballot represented Afro-American hopes for freedom and justice. "Let the slaves be counted each one as five-fifths of a citizen," declared one black editor. Restating themes developed in the 1830s, blacks maintained that the Constitution and the Declaration of Independence guaranteed their rights as American citizens. And they contended that their voluntary service in the nation's wars, especially the American Revolution and the Civil War, established their right to vote. But as 1865 progressed, blacks increasingly worried that whites intended to exclude them from the ballot. After completing his wartime recruitment work, John Mercer Langston—the president of the National Equal Rights League—presented the case for black suffrage in dozens of speeches across the nation, including this 25 October address before a state convention of Indiana blacks at Indianapolis's Masonic Hall. "Shall those who are natives to the soil, who fight the battles of this country, who pledge to its cause their property and their sacred honor be longer denied the exercise of the ballot?," he asked. "It ought not, it cannot be." *WAA*, 30 November 1861, 1 July, 9 December 1865; Cheek and Cheek, *John Mercer Langston*, 418–21.

CITIZENSHIP AND THE BALLOT

In the broad and far-reaching track of slavery across this country, we witness a grand desolation of civil and political rights. Every class in the American population can enter its complaint that it has been shorn of many rights and privileges, by reason of its existence. But none can utter that long, loud, lamentable complaint, making the ear to tingle and the heart to bleed, that can be uttered by the colored American, the immediate victim of its barbarous torture. As a slave he has been denied himself, his wife, his children, and his earnings. And when emancipated his freedom has been, in some sense, a mockery, because he has been deprived of those civil and political rights and powers which render enfranchised manhood valuable and its dignities a blessing.

The colored man is not content when given simple emancipation. That certainly is his due, at once and without condition; but he demands much more than that: he demands absolute legal equality. He claims the right

16. John Mercer Langston
Courtesy of Library of Congress

to bring a suit in any and all courts of the country, to be a witness of competent character therein, to make contracts, under seal or otherwise, to acquire, hold, and transmit property, to be liable to none other than the common and usual punishment for offences committed by him, to have the benefit of trial by a jury of his peers, to acquire and enjoy without hindrance education and its blessings, to enjoy the free exercise of religious worship, and to be subjected by law to no other restraints and qualifications, with regard to personal rights, than such as are imposed upon others. All this he claims. In some States all this is conceded to him. There is one thing more, however, he demands; he demands it at the hands of the nation and in all the States. It is the free and untrammelled use of the ballot. Shall he have it?

Never was there a more fitting time to consider, discuss, and decide this question. Since the outbreak of the terrible rebellion, the colored American has had another and better introduction to the American people. They are beginning to regard him with greater favor, and their old stubborn prejudices are beginning to soften. Indeed, in some States they have already entered upon the work of repealing those legislative malformations known as Black Laws.[1] Once in the path of justice and of duty, it is easy for us to pursue it till we reach the glorious goal.

It becomes our duty in this connection to consider and refute, if possible, the chief objections urged against Negro suffrage.

In the first place, it is urged, with an air of very great confidence, that none other than a white man can, or ought to be, an elector. Hence it is that in well nigh all the States in which persons of African descent are denied the elective franchise, you will find in their organic laws language like the following:

> Every *white* male citizen of the United States, of the age of twenty-one years, who shall have been a resident of the State one year next preceding the election, and of the county, township, or ward in which he resides such time as may be prescribed by law, shall have the qualifications of an elector and be entitled to vote at all elections.

What is meant by the word white as here used? The courts have not left us without an answer to this question. For the courts of Ohio, from whose constitution these words are quoted, both under the constitution of 1802 and the constitution of 1851,[2] have given a full consideration to the word "white" and settled its definition for all time in the light of what they please to call well-established legal principles. They furnish us in their definition this very unique and remarkable classification of the people, to wit, the black, the mulatto, and the white; and they hold "that all men nearer white than black, or of the grade between the mulatto and the white are white, and entitled to vote as white male citizens." This certainly gives breadth and comprehension to the word "white," and makes all persons except blacks and mulattoes "white." Let one more drop of Anglo-Saxon blood than Negro course your veins and you are at once endowed with the requisite qualifications of an elector.

On this point let full justice be done the court. Let it speak for itself. In the case of *Parker Jeffries* vs. *John Ankeny and others*,[3] at the December term of the court in banc, this doctrine was held, in the following words:

> In the constitution and laws on this subject there were enumerated three descriptions of persons, whites, blacks, and mulattoes, upon the last two of which disabilities rested; that the mulatto was the middle term between the extremes, or the offspring of a white and a black; that all the nearer white than black or of the grade between the mulattoes and the whites were entitled to enjoy every political and social privilege of the white citizen; that no other rule could be adopted so intelligible and so practicable as this, and that further refinements would lead to inconvenience and no good result.

This is the law of Ohio today.

In 1859, when the Legislature of Ohio was within Democratic control, "an act to prescribe the duties of judges of elections in certain cases and preserve the purity of elections," was passed, the first section of which reads as follows: "That the judge or judges of any election held under the authority of any of the laws of this State, shall reject the vote of any person offering to vote at such election and claiming to be a white male citizen of the United States whenever it shall appear to such judge or judges that the person so offering to vote has a distinct and visible admixture of African blood." This statute, however, has been pronounced unconstitutional by the Supreme Court, in the celebrated case of *Anderson* vs. *Millikin and others*, as reported in the eleventh of the *Ohio State Reports*, and the old doctrine on this subject reaffirmed.

Upon what principles of humanity, justice, and law is this doctrine founded? And upon what principles of logic or law are such complexional discriminations made? This color theory of the elective franchise finds no sanction in the affirmations of reason, or in the dictates of common sense. Nor is any sanction given it in the organic law of our nation. The Declaration of Independence announces the doctrine, "that all men are created equal," and the Constitution, in which no word "white" is found, provides "that Congress shall guarantee to each State a republican form of government," and "that the citizens of each State shall be entitled to all the privileges and immunities of the citizens of the several States."[4] Democracy, too, which is the soul of law, and but another name for justice itself, "conceding nothing but what it demands, and demanding nothing but what it concedes," guarding the rights of the humble as well as the exalted, and protecting the rights of the black man as well as the rights of the white man, scouts it as absurd and unjust, inconsistent and irrational.

It is true that the opinion obtains to a very great extent among all classes of our people that the Constitution of the United States, either by the direct use of the word "white," or by some phraseology equivalent thereto, does, and was intended to exclude colored men from every right and privilege of a legal and political character under it. Hence the gibberish jargon "that our government is a white man's government." This notion, however, is forever refuted by these masculine and truthful words of one of the justices of our national Supreme Court. He says:

> It has been often asserted that the Constitution was made exclusively by and for the white race. It has already been shown that in five of the thirteen original States colored persons then possessed the elective franchise, and were among those by whom the Constitution was ordained and established. If so, it is not true, in point of fact, that the Constitution was made exclusively *by* the white race. And that it was made exclusively *for* the white race is, in my opinion, not only an assumption not warranted by anything in the Constitution, but contradicted by its open declaration, that it was ordained and established by the people of the United States, for themselves and their posterity; and, as free colored persons were then citizens of at least five States, and so in every sense part of the people of the United States, they were among those for whom and whose posterity the Constitution was ordained and established.[5]

On what ground, then, does the white man claim to be a voter? And on what argument can he predicate his monopoly of the voting privilege? Does he claim it as an inherent and natural right, peculiar to himself? Does he claim it on the ground of peculiarity of origin? Does he demand it on the basis of peculiar conventional regulation? What are the peculiar legal or political characteristics that distinguish him to the exclusion of his black fellow-countryman as a citizen of the United States and a voter? Blind prejudice can make answer to these questions with great readiness. It would say, *he is white*. But what is the answer of wisdom, logic, and law? They would say, the color of a man's skin is no criterion or measure of his rights.

This fact will be fully recognized by our courts when they come to make that definition of citizenship, and the rights and powers of a citizen, which, while it excludes the elements of white and black, but contains all the essential qualities that distinguish the citizen, will challenge criticism and defy refutation. It is to be hoped that the Supreme Court of the nation will have occasion to give us this definition very soon. We certainly need it. It ought to be given, in justice to the colored American, and that the whole people of the country may learn from some authoritative source who constitute the citizens of the land, and upon what their rights and powers depend.

This objection to the black man's voting is wholly physical and external. He is *black*, and therefore he shall not vote.

It is as if all the men who have black hair and black beards, being in the majority and having the power, should decide that they alone are voters, and that no man having light hair and sandy beard shall vote; or, as if all the men of large noses in the land banding themselves together, should decide that they alone are voters, and that no man having a small nose shall vote. One might well ask, where is the justice of this procedure? Men of light hair and sandy beards might resist with propriety the decision of the black-hair and black-beard gentry. And who would say that the small-nose men had no right to utter powerful anathemas against the men of large nasal proportions, who had committed this unnatural outrage. These supposed cases sufficiently illustrate and refute this objection.

It is also urged, by way of objection to our use of the ballot, "that we are an ignorant and degraded class, and would not use the elective franchise in an intelligent and manly manner if we had it."

This objection, like all others of similar character, is to be met with firmness and candor. It is not to be forgotten in this connection, that we have served as slaves in this country for more than two hundred years, and that during these many years of our servitude few indeed have been the rays of light that have streaked the darkness of our existence. Nor is it to be forgotten that the nominally free among us have been haunted by a prejudice more terrible than that which pursued the Cagots of Spain and France.[6] This proslavery public sentiment has been well nigh omnipotent, as omnipresent. It has entered every cranny and crevice of American society. It has closed against us the school, the college, the law, and the theological seminary. It has hindered our progress in politics, religion, literature, and the arts.

Notwithstanding all this, we have made surprising advancement in all things that pertain to a well-ordered and dignified life. Though uttered frequently, it may be, in unclassic and inelegant English, we have always been able to give the reason for our political as well as our religious faith.

We have grown among us authors and orators, doctors and lawyers; we have established newspapers and periodicals; we have founded churches and erected schools; we have furnished our pulpits with ministers and our schoolrooms with teachers of our own complexion.

We have held large State and national conventions, conducting our business with accuracy and precision, according to the rules by which ordinary deliberative assemblies are governed. The leading men of these gatherings, in handling the great subjects of interest to the American people at large, as well as the topics pertaining more especially to our own welfare, have made exhibitions of a very correct and thorough understanding of our national history, the genius of our institutions and the philosophy of our politics. Indeed the newspapers and periodicals of this and foreign countries on such occasions have made handsome and flattering mention of their displays of learning, eloquence, and power.

It may not be inappropriate to offer here the opinion of Hon. Samuel Galloway[7] on this very point, given as long ago as 1849. In speaking of our condition and progress, he said:

> Now they (the colored people) have many and well-conducted schools; they have teachers of respectable intellectual and moral qualifications; there are many who command general respect and confidence for integrity and intelligence; questions of general and proper interest have become with them topics of discussion and conversation; in a few words, the intellectual and moral tone of their being is ameliorated.

But it may be said that such words, if true, can only have application to the colored men of the North. This, however, cannot be so, for it must be well understood by all conversant with the history and character of the colored people of this country, North and South, that very many of our most sober, industrious, and thrifty men come from the South; indeed it will not be denied that seven-eighths of our mechanics, gunsmiths, blacksmiths, brick and stone masons, carpenters, cabinetmakers, plasterers, and painters come from the Southern section of the land. This is said not in praise of slavery and slaveholding institutions, but in spite of them. This statement only testifies to the energy, the enterprise, the purpose and genius of the colored American.

On this point the history of our country will furnish us no inconsiderable evidence, for if it can be shown that in the past, when opportunity was given us, we wielded the ballot with intelligence and conscientiousness, who can say, after many years of progress in all substantial and valuable attainments, that we are not now able to vote in a skillful and conscientious manner.

It will be remembered that persons of African descent, under our old confederation, were voting citizens of the United States, and voted in at least five States of the Union at the time of the adoption of our national Constitution. With regard to this matter, Justice Curtis, formerly of the United States Supreme Court, in his dissenting opinion in the famous Dred Scott case, uses these words: "Of this there can be no doubt. At the time of the ratification of the articles of confederation all free native-born inhabitants of the States of New Hampshire, Massachusetts, New York, New Jersey, and North Carolina, though descended from African slaves, were not only citizens of those States, but such of them as had the necessary qualifications possessed the franchise of electors on equal terms with other citizens."[8] And he might have added that when the United States Constitution was framed colored men voted also in Pennsylvania, Connecticut, Rhode Island, Delaware, and Tennessee. Indeed they voted in a majority of the States, and in very many of the Northern States they have continued to vote to this day.

In this connection the manly and vigorous words of North Carolina's ablest and most distinguished jurist are of special value. The Hon. William Gaston, of the supreme court of North Carolina, in pronouncing the opinion of that court in the case of the *State* vs. *Manuel*,[9] makes use of these brave utterances:

> According to the laws of this State (North Carolina) all the human beings within it, who are not slaves, fall within one of two classes. Whatever distinctions may have existed in the Roman laws between citizens and free inhabitants, they are unknown to our institutions. Before our Revolution, all free persons born within the dominions of the King of Great Britain, whatever their color or complexion, were native-born British subjects—those born out of his allegiance were aliens. Slavery did not exist in England, but it did in the British Colonies. Slaves were not, in legal parlance, persons, but property. The moment the incapacity, the disqualification of slavery was removed, they became persons, and were then either British subjects or not British subjects, according as they were or were not born within the allegiance of the British King. Upon the Revolution no other change took place in the laws of North Carolina than was consequent on the transition from a colony dependent on a European King to a free and sovereign State—slaves remained slaves, British subjects in North Carolina became North Carolina freemen, foreigners, until made members of the State, remained aliens, slaves manumitted here became freemen; and, therefore, if born within North Carolina are citizens of North Carolina, and all free persons born within the State are born citizens of the State. The Constitution extended the elective franchise to every freeman who had arrived at the age of twenty-one, and paid a public tax, and it is a matter of universal notoriety that, under it, free persons, without regard to color, claimed and exercised the franchise until it was taken from freemen of color a few years since by our amended Constitution.

In none of these States, in which we have been allowed the use of the ballot, have we betrayed the confidence or the trust reposed in us. No flattering promises, no false statements of designing politicians, no offers of money or strong potations of liquor have been used by partisans with any degree of success in our case. We have constantly sought out the party and the candidates that would conserve and perpetuate American liberty and free institutions. No mere party shibboleth has ever had weight with us. Our training, secured in a life of oppression; our experience, gathered from contact with the instruments of torture and despotism, wed us to the party of freedom and free principles.

Touching the capability and sincerity with which the right of suffrage is exercised by the colored men of New York, the Hon. Wm. H. Seward, now occupying the first position in the Cabinet of President Johnson, holds the views presented in the following letter: [10]

> WASHINGTON, [D.C.]
> *May 16th*, 1850
> DEAR SIR:
>
> Your letter of the 6th inst. has been received. I reply to it cheerfully and with pleasure.
>
> It is my deliberate opinion, founded upon careful observation, that the right of suffrage is exercised by no citizen of New York more conscientiously, or more sincerely, or with more beneficial results to society, than it is by the electors of African descent. I sincerely hope that the franchise will before long be extended, as it justly ought, to this race who of all others need it most.
>
> I am, very respectfully, your obedient servant,
>
> WM. H. SEWARD

This objection, however, if it possesses any real significance, and if urged with any degree of sincerity and candor, covers entirely too much ground. For under it, what becomes of the ignorant and degraded white American, and what of the newly-naturalized foreigner, whose untutored mind fails to read and understand the meaning of American politics?

Leaving these objections, then, we come with sobriety and earnestness to the question: Upon what ground does the colored American plant his claims to the elective franchise?

As far as the native-born inhabitants of the country are concerned, we have no faith in the opinion that the right of suffrage is, in any sense to be regarded simply as conventional. We hold that it is an inseparable and essential element of self-government; and none, certainly, on reflection, will question this position. Without the privilege of saying who shall make our laws, what they shall be, and who shall execute them, there can be no self-government. This was the sentiment of the Fathers of the Republic; and upon this foundation-principle, as upon enduring granite, they established the free institutions of the land. This right is not created by constitutions simply, nor is it uncreated by them. Its existence does not depend upon the texture of a man's hair, the conformation of his countenance, or the color of his skin. It is a constituent element of manhood; and it stands prominent among the chief duties of civil society to sustain and guard it.

But are we men, and are we so related to the American Government that it owes us any obligation of protection in the exercise of this right? The declaration that we are men requires no amplification or illustration. The antislavery movement of this country has progressed too far, and the character and achievements of the colored American stand now too prominently before the world for his manhood to be doubted. Nor is it any denial of his manhood that his fellows, overcoming him by brute force, have enslaved and outraged him; for this notion was forever blasted when Terence, clad in chains, rushed out upon the Amphitheater of Rome, thrilling the vast concourse there assembled, by the announcement of the masculine and nervous sentiment: *"Homo sum: atque nihil humani a me alienum puto."* [11]

Our relation to the Government will be seen at once, when it is remembered, in the first place, that we are native-born inhabitants and therefore citizens. That nativity gives citizenship is a doctrine fully recognized by American law and American usage. Its existence, as far as our country is concerned, dates back to the very beginning of the Government. Chancellor Kent [12] gives it full indorsement in these terms: "Citizens, under our Constitution and laws, mean free inhabitants, born within the United States or naturalized by the laws of Congress. If a slave born in the United States be manumitted or otherwise legally discharged from bondage, or if a black man be born within the United States, and born free, he becomes thenceforward a citizen."

But when we urge our citizenship as a reason why we should be allowed to vote, we are very gravely informed that voting and holding office are not essential to citizenship. It is said, women are citizens, and so are minors, but they are neither allowed to vote nor hold office. Why put us in the category and condition of women and minors? Qualified by age, residence, and general attainments, our position is now one of men, and we demand this right *prima facie* as such. There may be ingenuity in this ambidexterity, but certainly no reason. It is but a crude and inconsistent dogma, injected into American law and American politics by slavery. Its true character, however, becomes more apparent as we progress.

Our relation to the Government and its duty toward us will be more fully apprehended when we call to mind the fact that we are, and always have been, taxpayers. Nor is the amount of tax we pay to be regarded as trivial and of small account. In proportion to our number, we pay a very handsome and considerable sum. In the State of Ohio, in which, according to the census of 1860, the colored men number only 36,673, over ten millions of dollars are held by them, subject to taxation. In the city of Cincinnati alone, they are owners of nearly two million of dollars' worth of personal property and real estate. In the farming districts of the State—in Gallia, Jackson, Pike, Ross, Highland, Franklin, Clark, Shelby, and Mercer counties—the colored men are owners of large farms, which, in many instances, are well stocked and cultivated according to the most approved methods of agriculture. But the taxes paid by the colored men of Ohio are small, compared with those paid by the same class in the larger and more densely populated States. The taxes of the colored men of the States of New York, Pennsylvania, and Louisiana swell to large, indeed, enormous proportions.

These tax burdens, too, we have met most cheerfully. Never have we excused ourselves, and never have we been excused from them on account of our color or our race. Even when, after payment of them, denial has been made us of any advantage accruing therefrom, on account of our color, they have been levied and paid to the entire satisfaction of the Government.

It will not be denied that taxation and protection are correlative terms. If the Government taxes a man, it owes him protection. Nor can it be justly denied that he who meets the burden imposed by the Government, who pays its taxes, who supplies it with the materials of life and development, should have a voice in the enactment and execution of the laws according to which its taxes are imposed, collected, and expended. Taxation, protection, and representation we hold, therefore, to be inseparable, constituting at once the bond of union and the bond of obligation between the Government and the citizen.

It is to be borne in mind, also, that we have not only promptly met our obligations as taxpayers, but we have behaved ourselves, at all times and under all circumstances, as earnest and devoted patriots.

Indeed, we love this country. We love it as our native country, although it has been the land of our sore oppression. Its Constitution and the free institutions, which are its natural outgrowth, are objects of our fondest affection. The evidences of this affection are found scattered through the history of the country, as it records the heroic deeds of the colored American in our revolutionary struggles, the war of 1812, and the bloody battles of our late stupendous rebellion.

Always on the side of Government, always struggling for the maintenance of law and order, we have rallied at the call of the country, bringing her our strong arms, our indomitable courage, and our unswerving loyalty.

To our own conduct, in this respect, our statesmen, orators, and generals have borne their testimony in the most eulogistic terms. Over the gallant conduct of the colored soldiers of the Revolution, the glowing periods of Eustis and Pinckney cast a halo of immortal beauty, while their brilliant achievements on Lake Erie and at New Orleans are immortalized in the eloquent sentences of Drake and Jackson.[13]

Says Governor Eustis, of Massachusetts, in a speech delivered in Congress, December 12, 1820:

> At the commencement of the Revolutionary War, there were found in the Middle and Northern States many blacks and other people of color capable of bearing arms, a part of them free, the greater part slaves. The freemen entered our ranks with the whites. The time of those who were slaves was purchased by the States, and they were induced to enter the service in consequence of a law, by which, on condition of their serving in the ranks during the war, they were made freemen. In Rhode Island, where their numbers were more considerable, they were formed, under the same considerations, into a regiment commanded by white officers, and it is required in justice to them to add that they discharged their duty with zeal and fidelity. The gallant defence of Red Bank, in which this black regiment bore a part, is among the proofs of their valor.
>
> Among the traits that distinguish this regiment was their devotion to their officers; when their brave Colonel Greene was afterwards cut down and mortally wounded, the sabres of the enemy reached his body only through the limbs of his faithful guard of blacks, who hovered over him, and protected him, every one of whom was killed, and whom he was not ashamed to call his children. The services of this description of men in the navy is also well known.

The Hon. Charles Pinckney, of South Carolina, when addressing the House of Representatives of the United States on the same occasion, also said:

> It is a most remarkable fact that, notwithstanding, in the course of the Revolution, the Southern States were completely overrun by the British, and that every negro in them had an opportunity of leaving his owner, few did. They were then, and still are, as valuable a part of our population to the Union as any other equal number of inhabitants. They were in numerous instances the pioneers, and, in all, the laborers of your armies. To their hands were owing the erection of the greatest part of the fortifications raised for the protection of our country some of which, particularly Fort Moultrie, gave at that early period of the inexperiences and untried valor of our citizens, immortality to American arms, and in the Northern States numerous bodies of them were enrolled into and fought, by the side of the whites, the battles of the Revolution.

In the constitutional convention of New York held in 1821, Dr. Drake, the delegate from Delaware County, said:

In your late war they (the colored people of New York) contributed largely to some of your most splendid victories. On Lakes Erie and Champlain, when your fleets triumphed over a foe superior in numbers and engines of death, they were manned in a large proportion with men of color. And in this very house, in the fall of 1814, a bill passed, receiving the approbation of all branches of your Government, authorizing the Government to accept the services of a corps of 2,000 free people of color. Sir, these were times which tried men's souls. In these times it was no sporting matter to bear arms. These were times when a man shouldered his musket he did not know but he bared his bosom to receive a death wound ere he laid it aside; in these times these people were found as ready and as willing to volunteer in your service as any other. They were not compelled to go. They were not drafted. No! Your pride had placed them beyond your compulsory power. But there was no necessity for its exercise; they were volunteers; yes, they were volunteers to defend that country from the inroads and ravages of a ruthless and vindictive foe, which had treated them with insult, degradation, and slavery.

The hero of New Orleans, Gen. Andrew Jackson, addressed his colored troops in these complimentary and matchless words:

Soldiers! When on the banks of the Mobile I called you to take up arms, inviting you to partake the perils and glory of your *white fellow citizens*, I expected much from you; for I was not ignorant that you possessed qualities most formidable to an invading enemy. I knew with what fortitude you could endure hunger and thirst, and all the fatigues of a campaign. I knew well how *you loved your native country*, and that you as well as ourselves had to defend what *man* holds most dear—his parents, wife, children, and property. *You have done more than I expected*. In addition to the previous qualities I before knew you to possess, I found among you a noble enthusiasm which leads to the performance of great things.

Soldiers! The President of the United States shall hear how praiseworthy was your conduct in the hour of danger, and the representatives of the American people will give you the praise your exploits entitle you to. Your general anticipates them in applauding your noble ardor.

The enemy approaches, his vessels cover our lakes, our brave citizens are united and all contention has ceased among them. Their only dispute is, who shall win the prize of valor, or who the most glory, its noblest reward.

That the blood of loyal fathers courses the veins of loyal sons is manifest from the fact that the only loyal class in our population is that fur-

nished by the colored American. He has conceded to others the monopoly of treason. No traitor encased in *ebony* has been found in all the
land. Those who boast of *ivory* encasings furnish the traitors. Davis and
Stephens, Vallandigham and Pendleton,[14] together with all the lesser bodies that reflect their treason, claim any other than a Negro origin. We are
glad of it. We lay no claim to these men. They may be learned, able, and
eloquent, but with hearts surcharged with treason their learning, ability
and eloquence are not to be prized as the common sense and sound judgment of a loyal man, however black, whose soul is obedient to the commands of liberty and patriotism. When, at the commencement of the
present rebellion, we proffered the Government our services, and the
President, the governors of the various States, and the chief commanders
of our army rejected them, informing us that this was a "white man's
war," our ardor and enthusiasm abated not a single tittle. We were patient. We did not run to the enemy. We gave him no aid. With us he found
no comfort. At length the time came when our learned statesmen, our
sagacious politicians, and our earnest generals discovered that the rebellion was of such proportions, its spirit so malignant and obstinate, that
"military necessity," if not justice, demanded that the colored American
have a place as a soldier in the mighty contest which has been waged for
the maintenance of liberty, free principles, and democratic institutions.
We were then called to the service; and that our response has been manful
is proved by the fact that notwithstanding we were at first denied equal
pay, the usual allowance for clothing, and every opportunity for promotion beyond the rank of a non-commissioned officer, we have already
given to the service over two hundred thousand stalwart, brave, and gallant men. And since entering the service, the colored soldier has been
truly heroic. You will seek in vain among the soldiers of any land, ancient
or modern, for exhibitions of greater endurance, more undaunted courage, and more enthusiastic devotion than he has displayed. His behavior
at Port Hudson, at Milliken's Bend, at Nashville, at Petersburg, at Suffolk, at New Market Heights,[15] at Fort Wagner and Olustee, not to mention many other places at which the colored soldier played a conspicuous
part, covers him with imperishable glory. It has been especially fortunate,
too, for this country that the colored American has been so earnestly
patriotic and loyal. For divided as the country has been, the South arrayed against the Government, and thousands of disaffected persons in
the North indirectly giving sympathy and aid to the rebellion, the colored
American has been, by reason of his numbers and Spartan qualities as a
soldier, a power aiding greatly in bringing victory to the arms of the
Government.

With regard to our numbers, our strength, and the value of our loyalty
to the Government, the judicious and truthful statements of Robert Dale
Owen in a letter addressed to the Hon. Salmon P. Chase, on the condi-

tions of lasting peace,[16] and founded upon the facts and figures of 1860, are comprehensive and clear. He says:

By the census of 1860 the number of white males between the ages of 18 and 45 is, in the loyal States, about four millions, and in the disloyal States about one million three hundred thousand; a little upwards of three to one. The disproportion seems overwhelmingly great. But this calculation, as a basis of military strength, is wholly fallacious, for it includes persons of one color only. Out of the above four millions the North has to provide soldiers and (with inconsiderable exceptions, not usually extending to field labor) laborers also. But of the three millions and a half of slaves owned in the rebel States, about two millions may be estimated as laborers. Allow three hundred thousand of these as employed in domestic services and other occupations followed by women among us, and we have seventeen hundred thousand plantation hands, male and female, each one of which counts against a Northern laborer on farm or in workshop. Then of that portion of population whence soldiers and out-door laborers and mechanics must chiefly be taken, the Northern States have four millions and the Southern States three millions. Supposing the Negroes all loyal to their masters, it follows that the true proportions of strength available in this war—that is, of all soldiers to fight and laborers to support the nation while fighting—may fairly enough be taken at three in the South to four in the North. Under the supposition of a South united, without regard to color, in an effort for recognition, shall we obtain peace by subduing her? If history teach truth we shall not. Never, since the world began, did nine millions of people band together, resolutely inspired by the one idea of achieving their independence, yet fail to obtain it. It is not a century since one-third of the number successfully defied Great Britain. But let us suppose the Negroes of the South loyal to the Union instead of to their masters, how stands the matter then? In that case, it is not to a united people, but to a Confederacy divided against itself, that we are opposed; the masters on one side, the laborers, exceeding them in number, on the other. Suppose the services of these laborers transferred to us, what will then be the proportion on either side of forces available, directly and indirectly, for military purposes? As about five and three-fourths to one and one-third; in other words, nearly as nine to two. Such a wholesale transfer is, of course, impossible in practice. But in so far as the transfer is possible, and shall occur, we approach the above results.

But, indeed, our transfer has been, as a class, a wholesale one. It has been so all along the past. It is so today; if not in bodily presence, certainly in spirit and aspiration. And it is a source of special pride and pleasure that we are able to announce the fact that this has been so from the very beginning of the American Government. For if history be true, he who on the second day of October 1750 was advertised in the Boston *Gazette* or *Weekly Journal* as a runaway slave, fell twenty years afterwards in the Boston massacre, March 5th, 1770, in "the first act of the drama of the American Revolution," a hero and a martyr. Crispus Attucks, a mulatto slave, was the first American that fell giving his life and blood in defense of his country. His bold and daring conduct stirred the hearts and nerved the arms of his comrades, whom John Adams describes in his plea in defense of the soldiers who shot him, as a "motley rabble of saucy boys, Negroes and mulattoes, Irish Teagues and outlandish jack tars." Be it so. God takes the weak things of the world to confound the mighty. And Attucks and Gray, Caldwell, Maverick and Carr, were the first offerings of the country deemed worthy to be made against "the encroachments of arbitrary power."[17]

As the first hero of the Revolutionary War was a black man, may we not indulge the hope and prayer that the last hero of our present struggle may be one of the dark-hued sons of American toil. And when we rear that monument in the midst of the Mississippi Valley, which shall perpetuate the glory of our present victorious achievements, a monument of grander and loftier proportions than Bunker Hill monument,[18] may we not inscribe his name upon its granite sides in golden characters.

We claim the elective franchise in the name of our manhood, our nativity, and our citizenship; in the name of the doctrine that taxation, protection, and representation are naturally inseparable; and in the name of that loyalty under the promptings of which we have performed for the country and the Government, in the army and the navy, such brave and manly deeds. We claim it, too, because we are intelligent men, men of sufficient intelligence to wield it conscientiously and with good results to the State.

In making our claim in the light of these considerations we come with no new and unusual theories, in the name of no false and fanatical conceptions of right and law. Our claim is based upon principles which, when applied to any and all other classes of the people, are recognized as just and democratic.

In addition to these all-sufficient reasons in favor of our claim we cannot fail to mention a consideration that must sooner or later result favorably to us from political necessity. Our arms are victorious; the revolted States are now to be reconstructed in accordance with the fundamental principles of the Constitution and the antislavery policy of the Government. As the Government has, for the last four years, needed loyal and earnest men to handle the musket in war, so it today needs men of the same character to wield the ballot in sustaining its principles. The ballot is no less potent than has been the musket. From what source can these loyal and earnest voters be had? The white men of the seceding States have almost all shown themselves unfaithful to the Government; not more than one-fourth of them have remained heartily true to the Union.[19] This faithful and honorable minority will not be able by its votes to sustain the policy of the Government. The other part of the white population has been conquered, it is true, but not converted. Their submission is only that of restive and malignant rebels—sullen acquiescence, while they are actuated by no other purpose than to hinder and, if possible, prevent the establishment of the great principles that underlie our governmental policy. What more could be expected of men whose souls have been embittered by their sad experiences in the effort to establish their independence, and who have been educated by the teachings of slavery and the false social influence it engenders to hate the Government and despise the free principles it seeks to establish in the subjugated States. But one course will be left the Government. It cannot import voters. They must certainly be residents of the States in which they vote. Its only course will be to put the ballot in the hands of the Negro, who, in all the history of the past, has given incontestable evidence of his devotion to the Union of the States founded on the Constitution and freedom. Thus, as military necessity brought us emancipation and arms, political necessity may yet bring us enfranchisement and the ballot. Touching this point, one of the ablest and most profound thinkers of our country utters the following pregnant words on the question:

> Do we need the aid of the Negro as a loyal citizen? They (all thoughtful men) will admit it to be one of the great questions of the day, whether (leaving the abstract right or wrong of the case untouched) we can prudently or safely for our own sakes withhold from the freedman his political rights, and thus leave disfranchised, at a critical juncture in our history, a loyal half of a disaffected population. They will ask themselves whether, as we have found need of the Negro as a soldier to aid in quelling the rebellion, we do not require his assistance as pressingly in the character of a loyal citizen in reconstructing on a permanently peaceful and orderly basis the insurrectionary States.

This is a fit theme for the consideration and reflection of our wise men. Upon it we need not dwell at length in this connection. The future will bring us its golden promise.

The path of duty with regard to us is plain to the American people. Justice and magnanimity, expediency and self-interest indicate but one course. Shall those who are natives to the soil, who fight the battles of the country, who pledge to its cause their property and their sacred honor be longer denied the exercise of the ballot? It ought not, it cannot be. The great events that are coming to pass in this nation, the crumbling of slavery and the dissipation of prejudice, give prophecy of a different result. God and destiny are on our side, and it becomes the colored American to prepare himself at once for the complete investure of legal equality.

John Mercer Langston, *Freedom and Citizenship: Selected Lectures and Addresses* (Washington, D.C., 1883), 99–122.

1. Northern state legislatures struck down many of the black laws during the Civil War. By the end of the war, Indiana was the only northern state that retained its black exclusion and testimony laws, and these were repealed within a year. Foner, *History of Black Americans*, 3:402–3.

2. Langston refers to article 4, section 1, of the 1802 Ohio state constitution, which limited the franchise to "all white male inhabitants above the age of twenty-one." This section was retained in the 1851 Ohio state constitution.

3. The Ohio Supreme Court made several rulings in the 1840s and 1850s that permitted adult males of more than one-half white ancestry to vote. Key decisions occurred in the cases of *Parker Jeffries* v. *John Ankeny et al.* (1842) and *Alfred J. Anderson* v. *Thomas Millikin et al.* (1859). *Ohio Reports* (Columbus, Ohio, 1843), 11:372–76; Cheek and Cheek, *John Mercer Langston*, 322–23, 344n.

4. Langston quotes from article 4 section 4, of the U.S. Constitution and article 4 of the Articles of Confederation.

5. Langston quotes from a dissenting brief by Justice Benjamin R. Curtis in the case of *Dred Scott* v. *Sanford* (1857). Curtis (1809–1874), a Massachusetts Whig politician, was appointed to the Supreme Court in 1851 and resigned shortly after casting one of the two dissenting votes in the Dred Scott decision. Don E. Fehrenbacher, *The Dred Scott Case: Its Significance in Law and Politics* (New York, N.Y., 1978), 403–13; *DAB*, 4:609–11.

6. The Cagots, a distinct ethnic group in the Pyrenees Mountains between Spain and France, were isolated and persecuted for several centuries before the French Revolution due to ethnic and religious prejudice.

7. Samuel Galloway (1811–1872), an educator and Whig politician, served as Ohio's secretary of state (1844–50) and represented the state in the U.S. Congress (1854–56). He supported a variety of social reforms, including antislavery and the reorganization of the public schools. *DAB*, 7:117–18.

8. Langston quotes from a section of Justice Benjamin R. Curtis's dissenting brief in *Dred Scott* v. *Sanford*. Curtis argued that American citizenship was originally derived from state citizenship, therefore all those accorded citizenship by their state—including blacks—were also American citizens. Fehrenbacher, *Dred Scott Case*, 403–13.

9. In *State of North Carolina* v. *William Manuel* (1838), the North Carolina Supreme Court overturned an 1831 law that permitted authorities to hire out blacks unable to pay court fines. Justice William Gaston ruled that the insolvency laws that protected whites also applied to free blacks. Gaston (1778–1844), a Federalist, served in the state legislature and the U.S. Congress (1813–17) prior to his 1834 appointment to the court. He became nationally recognized for his liberal rulings on civil rights questions during his ten years on the court. Justice Benjamin R. Curtis cited Gaston's legal opinions in his dissenting brief on the

Dred Scott decision. *North Carolina Reports* (Raleigh, N.C., 1901), 20:144–66; *DAB*, 7:180–81.

10. Seward wrote this letter to black abolitionist William Howard Day of Cleveland. William H. Seward to William Howard Day, 16 May 1850, William H. Seward Papers, NRU [6:0505].

11. Langston quotes from *Heauton Timorumenos*, a work by the Roman dramatist Terence (ca. 190–159 B.C.). This Latin phrase means "I am a man, I count nothing human indifferent to me."

12. Langston refers to James Kent (1763–1847), a Federalist jurist and legal authority. Kent served as a justice of the New York Supreme Court (1798–1814), chancellor of the New York court of chancery (1814–23), and lectured on law at Columbia College. His four-volume *Commentaries on American Law* (1826) is considered a landmark in American jurisprudence. Kent argued against the arbitrary restriction of black rights on several occasions. *DAB*, 10:344–47.

13. Langston quotes the following excerpts from political leaders who praised black military service. These extracts were undoubtedly drawn from William C. Nell's *Colored Patriots of the American Revolution* (1855). William Eustis (1753–1825), a Continental army surgeon, held several cabinet positions after the war and served as governor of Massachusetts. Charles C. Pinckney (1757–1824), a South Carolina statesman, fought in the American Revolution and had a distinguished political career that included service in Congress and as governor of South Carolina. They made these remarks during congressional debate over Missouri statehood. Robert Clark (1771–1835), whom Langston mistakenly identified as a Dr. Drake, was a physician and member of Congress. His comments about black military service were made as part of a debate over black suffrage at the 1821 New York state constitutional convention. Andrew Jackson's declaration, issued in French on 18 December 1814, was intended to rally black volunteers on the eve of the battle of New Orleans. Nell, *Colored Patriots*, 126–27, 148–50, 236–37, 288; *DAB*, 6:193–95, 14:614–16; Charles Lanman, *Biographical Annals of the Civil Government of the United States* (Washington, D.C., 1876; reprint, Detroit, Mich., 1976), 81.

14. Langston names four political figures known for their secessionist or Copperhead sentiment. Jefferson Davis and Alexander H. Stephens (1812–1883) were the leaders of the Confederate government. Stephens, a Democrat, represented Georgia in the U.S. Congress before the Civil War. He was elected vice-president of the Confederacy. Clement L. Vallandigham and George H. Pendleton (1825–1889) were leading Peace Democrats in the North. Pendleton, an Ohio congressman, campaigned as George B. McClellan's running mate in the 1864 presidential election. He later served a term in the U.S. Senate (1879–85). *DAB*, 14:419–20; *HTECW*, 717–18.

15. Langston refers to a number of Civil War battles in which black troops demonstrated their ability as soldiers. In late 1864, Confederate forces under General John B. Hood invaded Tennessee. On 15–16 December, at the battle of Nashville, nine black regiments employed a diversionary tactic that exposed Hood's troops to a crippling strike. By 27 December, Hood was forced to withdraw his Army of Tennessee from the field. During this time, black regiments were serving in the Petersburg, Virginia, campaign. The Second U.S. Colored Cavalry fought at the battle of Suffolk on 9–10 March 1864. Some twenty-two

black regiments participated in the siege of Petersburg, which lasted from June 1864 to April 1865—the longest sustained military operation of the Civil War. The battle of New Market Heights, which was fought on 29–30 September 1864, was a flanking action associated with the Petersburg campaign in which twelve black artillery regiments, twelve infantry regiments, and one cavalry unit distinguished themselves in some of the most vicious fighting of the war. In a bayonet charge against Confederate positions on high ground, several regiments of U.S. Colored Troops were caught in the open and overwhelmed; many were captured and some were executed by their captors. Despite horrific losses, black troops renewed the attack, following the same bloody line of advance, seized the summit, and forced the enemy to withdraw. *HTECW*, 285–86, 528, 577–79; Cornish, *Sable Arm*, 266, 279–80, 283–85; Dyer, *Compendium*, 2:876, 954.

16. Robert Dale Owen wrote this letter to Secretary of the Treasury Salmon P. Chase on 10 November 1862, outlining the conditions necessary for a lasting peace. It was reprinted in the 6 December issue of the *National Anti-Slavery Standard*. Owen (1800–1877), a social reformer and journalist, was born in Glasgow, Scotland. He immigrated to the United States in 1825 and helped his father, Robert Owen, establish a communitarian settlement at New Harmony, Indiana. He later edited the New York *Free Enquirer*, served in Congress (1835–38, 1843–47) and the Indiana legislature, and chaired the American Freedmen's Inquiry Commission. *BDAC*, 1500–1501.

17. Ropemaker Samuel Gray, seaman James Caldwell, apprentice joiner Samuel Maverick, and Irish leather worker Patrick Carr fell beside Crispus Attucks in the "Boston Massacre" of 5 March 1770. John Adams defended the British soldiers who fired upon them in the trial that followed. Kaplan and Kaplan, *Black Presence in the Era of the American Revolution*, 6–11.

18. Langston refers to the monument erected on Breed's Hill in 1843 to commemorate the Revolutionary War engagement popularly known as the battle of Bunker Hill, which occurred there on 17 June 1775.

19. A majority of whites in the Confederacy approved of secession, but a substantial minority opposed leaving the Union. In some states, Unionist sentiment ranged from 20 to 30 percent or more. It was typically concentrated in upcountry districts and mountainous regions of the South where few slaves lived, but it also appeared in slaveholding areas where the Whig party was traditionally dominant. Daniel W. Crofts, *Reluctant Confederates: Upper South Unionists in the Secession Crisis* (Chapel Hill, N.C., 1989), 130–94; McPherson, *Battle Cry of Freedom*, 235–39, 242.

79.
Essay by J. W. C. Pennington
29 November 1865

By the early days of Reconstruction, black abolitionists had labored for more than three decades to end slavery and reshape American race relations. With the promise of freedom and equality still unfulfilled, many carried the struggle to the South. Their firsthand accounts of Reconstruction reveal a mixture of hopefulness and foreboding about the future of Afro-Americans. J. W. C. Pennington, who had recently been assigned to an African Methodist Episcopal congregation in Natchez, reported on Reconstruction in Mississippi in a 29 November 1865 letter to the *Weekly Anglo-African*. Pennington voiced concern over unfair labor contracts, the failure of land confiscation, the consequences of a possible withdrawal of Union troops, and the obstinance of planters, who he predicted would "worry the black man badly." Reflecting black abolitionists' continuing concern for racial progress and their abiding commitment to a just and equitable society, he announced plans to give a series of lectures advising the local freedmen's community on land and labor issues. Pennington echoed the view of fellow black abolitionist Henry Highland Garnet that "the battle has just begun." Blackett, *Beating against the Barriers*, 80–81; *WAA*, 26 August 1865 [16:0124].

Natchez, Miss[issippi]
Nov[ember] 29*th*, 1865

At the time I left New York, on the 7th of October last, for New Orleans,[1] I had a desire to penetrate as far into the southwest as possible; but I did not indicate to my friends this fact, because I did not know, of course, how far my wish would be gratified; but after spending some weeks at New Orleans, looking over the field from that standpoint, I have secured the place I consider the most important, Natchez, Mississippi. The legislature of this State, now in session, has memorialized the President in a somewhat lecturing tone for the pardon of Jeff. Davis. They say, "The people who know Jefferson Davis so well, know that if there is a moral impossibility, it is morally impossible that his name can be justly chargeable with assassination, with cruelty, or with crime."[2] How differently white men reason about each other from what they do about colored men. If Jeff. Davis was a colored man these same men would, without any investigation, presume just the reverse.

RECONSTRUCTION
I find my apprehensions correct, that the work of reconstruction will be most difficult in this State. I am not yet in possession of all the causes

that will hinder the work, and, therefore, will not risk a judgment. I have, however, no hesitation in saying that the greatest hindrance will come from the old planters. For the welfare of all parties, it is to be hoped that the military forces will not be withdrawn from this State, and especially the colored forces.[3] We have a colored regiment here, and all things are quiet, which, I think, would not be the case in the absence of one; and what I hear from the interior, by those who come from there, efforts are being made to deceive the people, and to mislead them in reference to their rights and duties. I will give you an instance: The other day I had just been into a paper store and bought a copy of the *New York Tribune*, for which I paid fifteen cents, when a man from the opposite side of the street made towards me and said, "Uncle, what is the news?" "Well," said I, "what kind of news do you wish to hear?" Said he, "I come a good ways from here, away from the swamp, and I would give half a dollar to know the news about dis here hiring business. Now, de way day tell us out dere, it seems, when my year is out, next Christmas, I can't hire for another year without being bound five years." I said, "You are willing then to hire for another year—are you?" "O, yes; but then I don't want to bind myself for five years." I asked him a few other questions, and learned from him that he was one of four or five who came some forty miles, principally for the purpose of obtaining information on the subject, and that they expected to go out that same evening. I gave them such advice as they needed, and they went away relieved. The cheat attempted to be palmed off upon these men was that the law required them to hire themselves for five years, and on refusing to do so, they are then charged with laziness, &c., &c.[4]

Gen. Howard, who is on a tour in this State,[5] has issued the following

CIRCULAR LETTER

Bureau R., F. and Abandoned Lands,
Jackson, Miss[issippi]
Nov[ember] 11, 1865

It is constantly reported to the Commissioner and agents that the freedmen have been deceived as to the intention of the Government.

It is said that lands will be taken from the present holders and divided among them on next Christmas or New Year. This impression, wherever it exists, is wrong.

All officers and agents of this bureau are hereby directed to take every possible means to remove so erroneous and injurious an impression. They will further endeavour to overcome other false reports that have been industriously circulated abroad with a purpose to unsettle labor and give rise to disorder and suffering. Every proper means should be taken to secure fair written agreements or contracts for the coming year, and the freedmen instructed that it is to their best interest to look to the property holders for employment.

The Commissioner deprecates hostile action, and wishes every possible exertion made to produce kind feeling and mutual confidence between the blacks and whites.

O. O. HOWARD
Major-Gen. Commissioner
Official:
E. BAMBERGER, Lt. A. A. A. G.

I have made and am still making inquiries about these reports, and I am satisfied that the whole thing rests upon the question of the Confiscation Act. Colored freedmen do not expect to have the land of their masters without buying or leasing from the Government. They think that if Government intends to hold and lease or sell these lands, they should have a chance in the market, that's all. The parties who circulate the reports referred to above are friends neither to the freedmen, the planters, nor the cause of freedom, but of mischief and disorder. Let Congress settle the validity of the Confiscation Act,[6] and determine what lands are to be sold at a Government rate in the rebel States, and the people will buy them. I intend to see to it, God being my helper, that right and truth shall go from this point throughout this State on the whole question of land, labor, and wages. To this end I have notified my people of a course of lectures from my pulpit. The people do not need anything more than a fair chance in the market to buy or lease lands upon just terms and good titles. If the Government or individuals have lands to sell or lease, the people can purchase and lease, and cultivate, and will do, if they are protected, and not cheated and abused.

WHO WILL ADVISE THE WHITES?

The Southern whites need advice very badly. The whites here comment on Gen. Howard's order and his addresses to the freedmen as good advice to the blacks, while they themselves need just as much advice. 1. There are hopeful signs of the returning vigor of business. On the Levee at New Orleans, in many of her public streets, and all along up the Mississippi river to this place, the cotton trade is being brisk; and where you see one white man handling cotton, you shall see five blacks. Now, the whites should be advised by such papers as the *Herald*, the *World* and others, who claim to be their best friends,[7] to let things work on peaceably. They should be cautioned against the folly of again breaking up the course of law and order of business; for they should be aware that if they again break the peace, there will be no hope for them in the future. Their great hope lies now in reconciliation to the new order of things, and to the fact that the freedmen are not only the best friends of the country and the

Government, but also of their former owners. 2d. Slavery has made and *left its direful mark upon this whole region of country, upon the ground, upon the houses, and upon every aspect of beauty. You may see the impress of the hand of slavery—slavery under the rule of Jeff. Davis & Co.* Now, the whites should be advised not to attribute all this to emancipation. I stepped into a paper store the other day and bought a copy of the *Herald*, from the editorial of which I clip the following:

The idea of making another St. Domingo or Jamaica of the magnificent territory of the South—of giving the negro possession of and control over the fairest portion of the American continent, as our Jacobin republicans[8] would, is the most insane and impossible one that ever entered into the mind of man. The negro, however, will become a useful element, though a subordinate one, in this great work of development and progress. His labor will be made available and be rewarded throughout the whole South where the race is now scattered. But in the course of time, as the States become settled more with white people, he will find his home on the rice and cotton lands of the Atlantic coast and South Georgia, on the shores of the Gulf of Mexico, and over the deep alluvial lands of the Lower Mississippi. These regions are adapted to his constitution. He can thrive in all the vigor of manhood, and luxuriate under a tropical sun in canebrakes and rice swamps, where the white man cannot. This must be the ultimate home of the mass of the negro race. Those Southern States that border the North, the uplands, hilly and mountain country of the Carolinas, Georgia, Alabama, Mississippi, Arkansas and Texas, will be settled by a numerous working population.

The Republicans can defend themselves; but when the *Herald* says that "The idea of making another St. Domingo or Jamaica of the magnificent territory of the South—of giving the negro possession of and control over that fairest portion of the American continent," &c., I can tell that sheet that it is sowing the seed of discord to the injury of the cause—its own client. What has St. Domingo or Jamaica to do with the magnificent territory of the South? Why go back a half or three quarters of a century to rake up old buried bones to make a living body of political economy for an emergency? I trust that neither the Government at Washington, the State Governments, nor the planters, will be at all influenced by such insinuations, as I am sure that no sensible freedman is. There is an abundance of unoccupied land in this splendid Republic, and we do not believe it will be as the *Herald* says, where the black man shall live and thrive. I think that men who claim to be the best friends of the Southern whites should avoid all such hypothetical matter as is calculated to lead them astray, or to hold out false inducements to them. They should be taught and advised that they, as well as the blacks, are in duty bound to conform to the present dispensation of Providence, which calls party to RECONSTRUCT, FORM and REFORM. 3. Just now I see that a great deal of ink and paper is being expended on the subject of AMALGAMATION. I see copied into the *Courier* of this city a long and wishy-washy article from the *New York Day-Book*, which, by the bye, is advertized here as the white man's paper,[9] under the caption, "Can we amalgamate with the negroes?" Why, this is fifty years behind the age.

Slavery has dug its canals, connecting the waves of the Black Sea, the Red Sea, the Yellow Sea and the White Sea together, so to speak, all in these regions; nor has the late war done anything less, as may be seen by a glance over the surface of the present generation of children in many places. A few flysheets might be written upon this subject which would make some of the proudest and bravest of your Northern soldiers and officers blush to their temples, and their friends and families hang their heads in shame. But no practical result can be realized from the agitation of this subject in its vulgar style. The true policy of every friend of human progress should be to educate and protect the colored race in the full enjoyment of all their civil, religious and political rights.

The population of the South is not only of every possible mixture, but as she has been subjected to such a fearful waste of population in the war, it is obviously her wisdom to measure her population by manhood and vitality, and not by the mere color of the skin. Thousands of the blacks left the South during the war, and many thousands of whites also left, to say nothing about those who have been killed. Those who seek the best good of the whites of the South, these do well to regard them as subjects of advice. It is a false delicacy to suppose that because they are proud-spirited that they need no advice, and improvement in their spirit and manners.

THE REAL STATE OF THINGS AMONG THE FREEDMEN

From all that I have observed, I conclude that they need much instruction. Therefore, they having been instructed and governed wrong, makes them cautious, while at the same time they are very anxious to receive instruction. As to the handicraft arts and the cultivation of the staples of the country, they can compete with any incoming population. They have cabinetmakers, builders, bricklayers, blacksmiths, painters, and trades of various classes in various numbers. What they need to learn is the practical principles of domestic economy, the saving of time and money, the laws of health, and the training of children, &c. To secure these objects, they must be treated just as other classes of the human family. Those who would teach them successfully must have their confidence, and aim to convince them that they can be elevated, and that they are bound to make every endeavour to elevate themselves by the use of the same means that other people use to that end. The plain but full standard of Christian civilization must be set before their minds, and every effort made to impel them up to it. But the difficulties which lie in the way are obstinate. A people who have been so long sunk down and brutified by custom and legislation cannot be brought up to the right by public discourse or lesson in the schoolroom alone.

THE SOCIAL WANTS OF THE FREEDMEN

The freed people are pre-eminently sociable beings. There is an overflow of cordial, genial feeling, mingled with a childlike simplicity. In some respects, this feeling needs to be judiciously remoulded and properly trained. It requires no common class of agencies to do this; it requires a class of minds who can at once fathom the working of human nature in the minds of those adult children. Kindness must be mingled with firmness, decision with forbearance, frankness without domineering; lead them without driving, encourage them without catering, go down *to* them with a view to *bring them up*. The converse must be plain and colloquial, but every word must be full of light and knowledge, for the people hunger and thirst for knowledge; and above all, one must be thoroughly posted on the great subject of the day.

THE LEGAL PROTECTION OF THE FREEDMEN

Not only in person and property, but in the persons of his wife, and each and every one of his children, in his conscience and private judgment, to write, speak and publish his own thoughts, views, reviews, assents, dissents, beliefs and disbeliefs, subject only to constitutional liabilities under due process of law. The enemies of the enlightenment of the freedmen know well enough that the education of those people would uncover a frightful dark spot in the social history of the dominant race. They know that the worst that has been written about slavery is scarcely a key to the history of the devilishness which has been perpetrated upon the colored race; and they know that educated freedmen and freedwomen could speak burning words, and write with biting pens. Instead, therefore, of troubling the blacks of the South about ignorance, laziness, vice and immorality, the whites have every reason to congratulate themselves that they escaped with so little exposure. But the disaffected exslaveholders, and their professed pro-slavery friends at the North, seem to be bent upon *uncovering their weak points: their dependence upon the negroes.* Every story they put in circulation about the unwillingness of the freed people to work (and many of these are gross fabrications), go to prove their dependence, and yet many of them are unwilling to let the people have fair wages, and lawful protection. If the whites of the South, both rich and poor, would make up their minds to let bygones be bygones, accept of the state of facts which their own gotten up war has created for both themselves and the freed people, would stop their croaking about amalgamation and the inferiority of the negroes, things will go on well. But let me not be misunderstood.

Two things are certain; the South will not attempt to re-enslave us again, nor will she attempt again to overthrow this Government. On these two points she is whipped, and will stay whipped for the present generation. *She will not rebel again*, of this, be assured; *but she will worry the black man badly.* The *mob* spirit will pursue him, and try to vex him, to do, to say, or write something rebellious; I pray God that he may continue loyal and quiet. The present state of things in Jamaica, St. Thomas in the East, is painful in the extreme.[10] When I visited that glorious country in 1846, I warned the people against this mischief, and now I find it important to warn our people—our freed people—against the same delusion of the whites. But let that pass, I only remark that it is the result of the foolish prejudice between whites, blacks and browns, or mulattoes. God deliver us from this devilish principle.

MISSISSIPPI

I have delayed writing you, because I wished to see how the reconstruction legislature of this great Cotton State would come out. I think we have got her right. At all events, I give the following as the last act, which we mean to follow up with a sharp stick. In the majority vote, you will see name of "HILLYER." He is the editor of the leading paper in this city.[11]

THE NATCHEZ DAILY COURIER

Jackson, Nov. 21, 1865—The struggle is over, on the negro testimony question, as far as the House is concerned. The Committee on Freedmen reported today a substitute for the fourth section, as follows:

"Be it further enacted, that in addition to cases in which freedmen, free negroes and mulattoes are now by law competent witnesses, freedmen, free negroes and mulattoes shall be competent in civil cases when a party or parties to the suit, either plaintiff or plaintiffs, defendant or defendants, also in cases where freedmen, free negroes and mulattoes is or are either plaintiff or plaintiffs, defendant or defendants, and a white person or white persons is or are the opposing party or parties, plaintiff or plaintiffs, defendant or defendants.

"They shall also be competent witnesses in all criminal prosecutions where the crime charged is alleged to have been committed by a white person upon or against the person and property of a freedman, free negro or mulatto. Provided in all cases said witnesses shall be examined in open court on the stand, except however they may be examined before the Grand Jury, and shall in all cases be subject to the rules and tests of the common law, as to competency and credibility."

The substitute gives the right to testify in all civil cases, except *between* white *parties* and in all criminal cases where the charge is against a *white person* for a violation of the rights of person and property of a *negro*; and this, in addition to all cases where the negro is now competent by law. Four test votes were taken by yeas and nays; the first, on a motion to lay the substitute on the table, which was lost, 25 to 63; the second, on a motion to lay on the table a substitute offered by Mr. Martin, of Itawamba, which was carried, 58 to 27; a third, on the substitute reported by the committee, which was adopted, 56 to 30; and the fourth and last, on the passage of the bill, which was passed on the same vote. I send a list of the yeas and nays.

Yeas—Messrs. Acker, Arnold, Barry, Beauchamp, Blanchard, Boddie, Boone, Brown of Issaquena, Brown of Kemper, Bridges of Choctaw, Bridgers of Tallahatchie, Burress, Burton, Cameron, Ellis, Gillstrap, Grace, Graham, Griffin, Hamilton, Hanson, Hillyer, Huffman, Irby, Lewis, Lewers, Liddell, Luse, Mabry, Manning, Marable, Meares, Merrill, Medearis, Milton, Morphis, McInnis, McLaurin, McNiel, McRaney, McRae, McWhorter, Murdock, Murray, Nye, Owen, Peace, Philips, Read, Simrall, Tankersley, Thompson, Walker, Webb of Amite, Webb of Franklin, and Williams.—56.

Nays—Mr. Speaker, Messrs. Bowen, Brown of Yalobusha, Brooks, Caperton, Carter, Cromwell, Daniel, Dotson, Duff, Easterling, Foxworth, Gresham, Henly, Kennedy, Labauve, Lyles, Martin, Mayson, Morris, Pennybacker, Phipps, Pound, Powers, Robertson, Seal, Shannon, Suratt, Wall, and Webber—30.[12]

J. W. C. PENNINGTON

Weekly Anglo-African (New York, N.Y.), 23 December 1865.

1. Pennington traveled to New Orleans in October 1865 to attend the Missouri Conference of the African Methodist Episcopal church. At this meeting, he was made an itinerant minister and appointed to an AME mission station in Natchez, Mississippi. Blackett, *Beating against the Barriers*, 81.

2. Several southern state legislatures and private individuals sent appeals to President Andrew Johnson requesting clemency for Jefferson Davis, then in a federal prison awaiting trial for treason. In October 1865, the Mississippi legislature submitted a memorial written by state representative Giles M. Hillyer of Natchez, which recognized Davis as one of the state's most distinguished citizens and called for a presidential pardon. *MDC*, 11, 13, 25, 26 October, 4 November 1865.

3. By late August 1865, 8,784 of the 10,193 Union soldiers stationed in Mississippi were black, and relations between local whites and the occupying forces were tense. Whites grew restive as the freedmen associated with black troops

who, they asserted, threatened white control of blacks and offered poor examples for local blacks. Skirmishes broke out between white militia and black soldiers in many garrison towns. William C. Harris, *Presidential Reconstruction in Mississippi* (Baton Rouge, La., 1967), 63, 70–71.

4. Southern state legislatures attempted to preserve the plantation system and limit black economic freedom through mandatory labor contracts. Mississippi enacted some of the earliest and most stringent regulations in late 1865. Blacks in the state without annual labor contracts were subject to arrest. The freedom of black workers was further restricted by broadly defined laws against vagrancy and disorderly conduct, the penalties for which included forced plantation labor. Foner, *Reconstruction*, 198–200.

5. Brigadier General Oliver Otis Howard (1830–1909), a Maine native and Civil War veteran, served as the commissioner of the Freedmen's Bureau from 1865 to 1874. Although he sympathized with the plight of the former slaves, he bowed to political pressures and failed to make the agency into an effective voice for the freedmen. In the fall of 1865, President Andrew Johnson sent Howard on a tour of the South, hoping to convince southern whites to accept Presidential Reconstruction and to assure them that their domination over black workers would continue. By sending an abolitionist like Howard, the president hoped to maintain an appearance of concern for the freedmen. Howard made several speeches in Mississippi. On 11 November, he informed blacks at Jackson that the federal government would not grant them the lands of their former masters. Assuring them that slavery had been permanently abolished, he admonished "that freedom means work" and issued stern warnings against dishonesty and idleness. During the late 1870s and 1880s, Howard fought in the Indian Wars in the West and served as superintendent of the U.S. Military Academy at West Point. William S. McFeely, *Yankee Stepfather: General O. O. Howard and the Freedmen* (New York, N.Y., 1968); *JDC*, 12 November 1865.

6. Pennington refers to the Second Confiscation Act.

7. Pennington refers to the *New York Herald* and the *New York World*. The *World* was founded in 1860 and began as a Republican paper, but it became an organ of the Peace Democrats after being taken over by Manton Marble during the Civil War. The journal condemned the Emancipation Proclamation, denounced calls for black suffrage, and bitterly opposed the Radical Republicans. Mott, *American Journalism*, 350–51; David Black, *The King of Fifth Avenue: The Fortunes of August Belmont* (New York, N.Y., 1981), 301–3.

8. The *New York Herald* characterizes Radical Republicans here as "Jacobins," likening their actions to the political extremism of the Jacobin leaders of the French Revolution.

9. The New York *Day-Book* was founded in 1848 to promote the proslavery cause among New York City's commercial interests. The weekly journal changed its name to the *Caucasian* in 1861, but was forced to suspend publication because of allegedly treasonous remarks. It resumed operations under its original name two years later and continued until 1868. Alfred McClung Lee, *The Daily Newspaper in America: The Evolution of a Social Instrument* (New York, N.Y., 1937), 305; Mott, *American Journalism*, 354.

10. Pennington refers to the black rebellion at Morant Bay, Jamaica, in October 1865. When blacks protested a decision of the local magistrates, the militia

intervened and black rioting ensued; fifteen magistrates were killed. Fearing full-scale revolt, Governor Edward John Eyre reacted severely, declaring martial law and initiating thirty days of reprisals; 439 blacks were executed, 600 were flogged, and more than 100,000 homes belonging to suspected rebels were burned. The black violence at Morant Bay reinforced racial stereotypes in Britain and the American South. Green, *British Slave Emancipation*, 381–405.

11. Giles M. Hillyer edited the weekly *Natchez Courier* from 1850 through Reconstruction. He represented Adams County in the Mississippi legislature over the same period, successively serving as a member of the Whig, Know Nothing, Republican, and Democratic parties. Hillyer was one of the state's most vocal Unionists before the Civil War. But as Reconstruction progressed and blacks demanded equal rights, Hillyer pledged to prevent the creation of "nests of Negro colonies" in the state. By 1869 he had repudiated the Republican party and urged all former Whigs to join the Democrats in preserving a "white man's government." Harris, *Presidential Reconstruction in Mississippi*, 62, 130–31, 230, 242; William C. Harris, *The Day of the Carpetbagger: Republican Reconstruction in Mississippi* (Baton Rouge, La., 1979), 35, 131, 165; James B. Ranck, *Albert Gallatin Brown: Radical Southern Nationalist* (New York, N.Y., 1937), 95, 140, 300.

12. The question of black testimony in the courts was the first civil rights issue considered by the Mississippi legislature during Reconstruction. In November 1865, proponents of unqualified black testimony introduced a bill to that effect, but were unable to muster a majority. H. J. Simrall of Wilkinson County and George Webb of Amite County led the fight against section 4, which most viewed as the offensive portion of the bill. On 20 November, the legislature approved an amended Negro Testimony Act, which permitted blacks to testify only in cases involving members of their race. A more lenient substitute amendment by H. K. Martin of Itawamba County was overwhelmingly rejected. Support for the new act came from throughout the state, but was strongest in upcountry districts. A federal judge overturned the law one year later and in 1867 the legislature removed all restrictions on black witnesses, placing them on the same basis with whites. Vernon L. Wharton, *The Negro in Mississippi, 1865–1890* (Chapel Hill, N.C., 1947), 134–36; *JDC*, 16, 17 October, 16, 22, 26 November 1865.

80.
Samuel Childress to Robert Hamilton
29 November 1865

No one better understood the injustice of Presidential Reconstruction than the freedmen themselves. Their postwar experiences offered a disturbing preview of the course of Reconstruction. Apprehension grew in the summer and fall of 1865 as southern white resistance and northern indifference threatened to deny blacks the "fruits of impartial freedom." In a 29 November letter to the *Weekly Anglo-African*, Samuel Childress, a former slave in Nashville, Tennessee, provided a discouraging assessment of Reconstruction, which had once promised freedom, equality, and a fair opportunity to four million freedmen. He expressed the pessimism and anxiety of the homeless freedmen, abandoned by the government, exploited by their former masters, and terrorized by racist violence. In attacking Andrew Johnson's policies—which made it "a greater crime to be black than to be a rebel"—Childress voiced the lingering bitterness of a people betrayed. *CR*, 14 July 1865; Foner, *Reconstruction*, 185–91, 198–210; McPherson, *Struggle for Equality*, 408–9; *WAA*, 3 September 1865.

Nashville, Tenn[essee]
Nov[ember] 29, 1865

MR. EDITOR:

You desire to know our opinions respecting the policy of the President concerning the colored race.[1] We are not acquainted with the whole of it—we do not feel confident to advise the President, nevertheless we cannot avoid having impressions of some sort respecting some things which have been done, and some things which have been left undone. To us the prospect seems gloomy. We have no permanent homes, and we see no prospect of getting any.

Most of us are accustomed to farm labor, and whatever skill we possess is chiefly in that direction. Land is dear, and few of us are able to buy it. We can hire out to our former masters, it may be said. It is true that we can do so to a considerable extent; but it is well known that the temper of our former masters has not greatly improved toward us.

Is it the intention of the Government to drive us to our worst enemies to ask for work, and that too upon the very soil which has been forfeited by the treason of the pretended owner? Our race has tilled this land for ages; whatever wealth has been accumulated South has been acquired mainly by our labor. The profits of it have gone to increase the pride and wickedness of our old masters, while we have been left in ignorance and degradation; all this oppression and wrong were committed under the United States Government, which stood ready with loaded guns and fixed bayonets to strike us down if we resisted our masters.

The small oppressor was the State; the great oppressor was the United States. When the nation conquered the rebels, the property of the latter was forfeited to the Government. Accordingly Gen. Sherman says! "Soldiers, when we marched through, and conquered the country of these rebels we became owners of all they had, and I don't want you to be troubled in your consciences for taking, while on our great march, the property of conquered rebels. They forfeited their right to it, and I being agent for the Government to which it belonged, gave you authority to keep all the Quarter-masters couldn't take possession of, or didn't want."[2]

It cannot be denied that the colored race earned nearly all this property. The United States, as High Sheriff of the Court of Heaven, held it in its hand, and could do with it what it pleased. Justice required that it should be paid over to the colored race who had been robbed of it. But what did it do with it? Let the Proclamations and pardons of the Government answer. It has gone back again to the very men whose hands are dripping with the blood of murdered prisoners, and whose cruelties cry to heaven for vengeance.

It would seem that it was regarded as a greater crime to be black than to be a rebel. If this is the ethics which is to prevail, then we have more judgments in store for the nation.

We think the Government ought in justice to the race to provide for their obtaining farms at such prices, and on such terms as would enable our people in a reasonable time to have a home of their own, on which they might hope to earn a living, and educate their children. Yours truly,

SAMUEL CHILDRESS[3]

Weekly Anglo-African (New York, N.Y.), 16 December 1865.

1. Andrew Johnson believed that blacks were racially inferior and declared that "this is a country for white men, . . . as long as I am President, it shall be a government for white men." He once advised southern governors to permit limited black suffrage to defuse a potentially potent issue for the Radical Republicans, but he generally opposed black enfranchisement and other civil rights legislation. Trefousse, *Andrew Johnson*, 190, 223–25, 236, 242, 246, 268–69, 299, 341.

2. William Tecumseh Sherman (1820–1891) of Ohio was one of the Union army's most daring and effective generals during the Civil War. Placed in command of all troops in the conflict's western theater in March 1864, he undertook a devastating campaign designed to destroy the Confederacy's ability to wage war. Sherman's army marched through Georgia and the Carolinas, acting independently of its supply base, living off the land, wrecking communications and

supply lines, and seizing rebel property at will. After the war, Sherman replaced Ulysses S. Grant as the U.S Army's general-in-chief until his retirement in 1884. *WWWCW*, 590–91.

3. Samuel Childress (sometimes spelled Childers), a former slave, made Robert Hamilton's acquaintance during the editor's April 1865 visit to Nashville. Hamilton described him as "an old gentleman" and a lay leader in the city's Calvary Baptist Church. *WAA*, 13 May, 5 August, 3 September 1865.

Index

Page numbers in boldface indicate the main discussion of the subject. Boldface numbers broken by a colon indicate notes in a previous volume in the series.